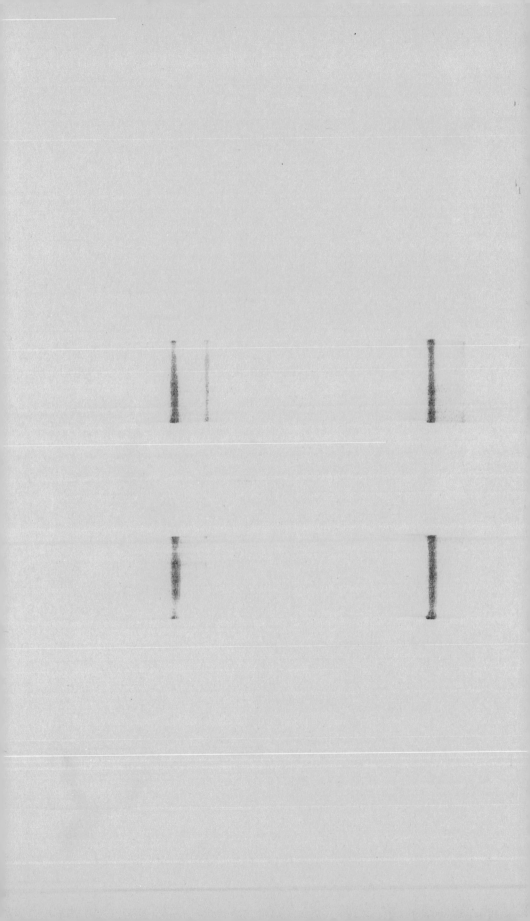

JOHN CONSTABLE'S
CORRESPONDENCE
VI

ARCHDEACON JOHN FISHER

c. 1816, by John Constable

JOHN CONSTABLE'S CORRESPONDENCE

VI

THE FISHERS

Edited, with Introduction and Notes, by

R. B. BECKETT

With a Preface by Geoffrey Grigson

1968
SUFFOLK RECORDS SOCIETY
VOLUME XII

The Suffolk Records Society was founded in 1958. The titles of its eleven previous volumes of records are:

1. *Suffolk Farming in the Nineteenth Century*, edited by Joan Thirsk, B.A., Ph.D., and Jean Imray, B.A.

2. *The Sibton Abbey Estates: Select Documents, 1325–1509*, edited by A. H. Denney, B.A.

3. *Suffolk and the Great Rebellion, 1640–1660*, edited by Alan Everitt, M.A., Ph.D.

4. *John Constable's Correspondence: I. The Family at East Bergholt, 1807–1837*, edited by R. B. Beckett, and published jointly with Her Majesty's Stationery Office.

5. *The Letter-book of William de Hoo, Sacrist of Bury St. Edmunds, 1280–1294*, edited by Antonia Gransden.

6. *John Constable's Correspondence: II. Early Friends and Maria Bicknell (Mrs. Constable)*, edited by R. B. Beckett.

7. *A Dictionary of Suffolk Arms*, compiled by Joan Corder, and with a Foreword by Sir Anthony Wagner, K.C.V.O., D.Litt., Garter King of Arms.

8. *John Constable's Correspondence: III. The Correspondence with C. R. Leslie, R.A.*, edited by R. B. Beckett.

9. *Poor Relief in Elizabethan Ipswich*, edited by John Webb, M.A., F.R.Hist.S.

10. *John Constable's Correspondence: IV. Patrons, Dealers and Fellow Artists*, edited by R. B. Beckett.

11. *John Constable's Correspondence: V. Various Friends, with Charles Boner and the Artist's Children*, edited by R. B. Beckett.

The Society has produced one additional publication, *Great Tooley of Ipswich*, a biography of a sixteenth-century merchant by John Webb.

*Published by the Suffolk Records Society,
The Record Office, County Hall, Ipswich,
and printed by W. S. Cowell Ltd,
Butter Market, Ipswich, Suffolk*

Preface

To talk of the sixth and final volume of *John Constable's Correspondence* as an introduction to Constable may seem peculiar. Yet in a sense it is true, because in this classic interchange of letters, we come nearest of all to the painter and to the springs of his life and his art. Other volumes—to me the most warming and revealing was the first, the correspondence with the family at East Bergholt, which stripped away certain social misconceptions we may have entertained about Constable—have shown the great artist in his environment. Here, at last, we are with him in the company of his most intimate friend. In fact, this volume is an introduction twice over; and to be doubly introduced in this way to a pair of such admirable men—for there are features in which John Fisher was scarcely less remarkable than John Constable—to be enabled to understand them in their friendship, through their own letters, to be given this taste of their minds and their hearts, is a privilege both exhilarating and uncommon. The letters, or most of them, were used in the famous life of Constable compiled by C. R. Leslie. But Leslie, as we now realize, smoothed away the grain of his character, corrected his English, omitted his asperities, and much of his boldness, and made him the counterpart of a too sentimental interpretation of his painting. This was pointed out many years ago by the Redgraves in their *Century of British Painters*. Leslie, they wrote, 'painted him *couleur de rose*, and transfused his own kindly and simple spirit into the biography. The landscape painter, though of a manly nature, was eminently sarcastic and was very clever at saying the bitterest things in a witty manner.' The Redgraves, though, admitted that this trait 'had no doubt been increased by the neglect with which the would-be connoisseurs had treated his art, and by the sneers of the commonplace critics'. Here is the truer Constable, manly, independent, sane, needing no Redgravian excuse, in letters unexpurgated and unsandpapered; here we discover how this friend, so important in the penetralia of Constable's life, this astonishingly clear-eyed and forthright clergyman supported him and encouraged him through a vexed career. Of course this correspondence illuminates Constable as a painter. It does more, it deserves readers to whom painting is of less concern than life. Revealing the full personality of two such men, it is an English classic of universal human relevance.

Consider first a single point about Constable. No account of him has made clear until now the *milieu* of Bishop Fisher, his brothers and his nephew the Archdeacon, into which they welcomed this raw young painter from Suffolk. The Bishop was secure in the best society of the age, enjoying royal favour and esteem. He was charged with the education of Queen Victoria's father and of the Princess Charlotte. This was the man whom Constable described as his 'kindly monitor for twenty-five years', who would invite the young artist to dine with

v

him at the Chaplain's Table in St. James's Palace or to stay in the Palace at Salisbury. The Fishers were not unskilled in drawing or without interest in the arts; they were a civilized, virtuous, untoadying family who accepted rewards, advancement and emoluments as they came. If this suave and cultured bishop made a friend of the painter, the first cause may have been that he painted, but the enduring cause was the painter's character and the bishop's recognition of its quality. The *kind* of painting this ecclesiastic of an older generation did not like so much. It was blue skies of a clear serenity he preferred in landscape, not the troubled cloudage which hung or drove across so many of Constable's pictures. Yet such was the force of Constable's being and convictions that without bending to the Bishop's view of art or that of such powerful men as he would have met in the Bishop's company, he stuck to his own vision. Of how few English artists could this be said! How many have been seduced, from Constable's day to our own, by country house lackeyism and by weak compliance! 'The enquiry in England', Blake once wrote, 'is not whether a man has talents and genius, but whether he is passive and polite and a virtuous ass and obedient to noblemen's opinions in art and science. If he is, he is a good man. If not he must be starved.' Constable took the risk of starvation; and in this how much he was helped by the constant friendship and the wise perception of John Fisher (whose views were broader and deeper than those of his uncle)! 'I now fear (for my family's sake)', Constable wrote to John Fisher in 1821, 'I shall never be a popular artist—a Gentlemen and Ladies painter—but I am spared making a fool of myself—and your hand stretched forth teaches me to value my own natural dignity of mind (if I may say so) above all things. This is of more consequence than Gentlemen and Ladies can well imagine as its influence is very apparent in a painter's work— sometimes the "*Eclats*" of other artists occasionally cross my mind—but I look to what I possess and find ample consolation.' Compare the straight and uncompromising expression of such letters from Constable (this passage, by the way, was emasculated and contracted by Leslie, who as an R.A. of the weaker kind felt Constable's speech, as so often, to be too plain) with the glossy and impersonal letters of Sir Thomas Lawrence. One is the language of the artist, the other of the nobleman's tailor; and Constable had occasion to describe Lawrence as cold and sly. Like man, like picture. It is a safe enough rule to say like letter, like man. Constable's letters, no less than his pictures, remind us of Coleridge's conviction that good art proceeds only from good men. Whatever his limitations, the goodness and the honesty of Constable are never in doubt.

Still, the eminence of Constable must not obscure the eminent goodness of John Fisher. Constable wrote to him in 1822: 'I have no patron but yourself— and you are not the Duke of Devonshire—or any other great ass. You are only a gentleman and a scholar and a real lover of the art, whose only wish is to see it advance.' Fisher had an insight into Constable's purpose which was not far from unique. He may have come to it first of all by his appreciation of Constable as a man. For example, the business over the miserable artist Read with the flowing locks may suggest the restrictions of an amateur approach, since Fisher was ready to approve the man's paintings when he thought them approved by Constable. But Fisher was in no hesitation, doubt, or perplexity about his friend's art; and he felt, as he wrote when agreeing to be godfather to one of Constable's children, that he would go down to posterity on the score of his association with Constable.

He has done so, and he deserved to. Like appealing to like, Fisher knew where Constable was strong and weak, how to advise, when to push, when to soothe, how with delightful tact to be patron as well as friend. Both were undeluded men. 'There has been sad work in the Academy', Constable could tell Fisher with his customary baldness, 'but it is too contemptible to talk about, as usual in bodies corporate—the lowest bred and the greatest fools, are the leaders'. Fisher, equally, could tell Constable of the shams and the follies of ecclesiastical life in Salisbury Close—'What a mistake our Oxford and Cambridge Apostolic Missionaries fall into, when they make Christianity a stern haughty thing. Think of St. Paul with a full blown wig, deep shovel hat, apron, round belly, double chin, stern eye, rough voice, and imperious manner, drinking port wine, and laying down the law of the best way for escaping the operation of the Curates Residence Act.' Fisher writes his letters, as he said when he advised Constable to marry his lady and have done with it, in no roundabout phrases. Even the shortest of his notes is alive with the kind of man he was. Like Constable in painting, at times all of something felt he gives unpretentiously and sharply in the briefest of sentences or descriptions—as when he writes of the ferry house on the Isle of Portland in its 'sea bleached desolation' or when he looks from the heights at Osmington and achieves this record: 'A large black misty cloud hung to day over the sea and Portland. The Island could be but just discerned. The smoke of Weymouth was blown off towards Portland and was illuminated by the Western sun and relieved by the dark cloud. As I rode home a complete arch of a rainbow came down to my very feet: I saw my dog running through it.' Or turn to his remarks (p. 70) on 'the crowded copal atmosphere' of an Academy exhibition or to his sketch (p. 126) of the old Dean of Winchester and the Bishop, the Bishop skipping and showing off the improvements in the Palace garden about which the Dean cared nothing, and the Dean 'hobbling along, spouting Greek and spittle, both which the Bishop holds in equal detestation'.

Humble about his own powers in relation to those of his friend, Fisher is nevertheless always on his own feet, always himself, always, if need be, ready either to prop Constable or to tease him in good humour. 'Where *real* business is to be done you are the most energetic and punctual of men: in smaller matters, such as putting on your breeches, you are apt to lose time in deciding which leg shall go in first.' Throughout, these two, the painter and the parson, are mutual respecters and stimulators of each other's natural dignity of mind; on the basis of which, by the way, neither one is above telling the other some bawdy incident of the comedy of men.

Of these essentially good creatures, neither was a prig; in Constable there was more asperity mixed into the goodness and the self-knowledge, in Fisher more gentleness with which he could allay Constable's feelings of misuse or of a disdain which is nearly always justified. All such true beings as Constable (or Fisher) are lonely, all of them are assailed by the rest of us. 'To succeed in art', said another of the painters of Constable's time, 'a man must avoid all appearances of keenness and especially of wit. It is very necessary for any painter to get connections by every possible means as no one, not even the finest painter, can succeed without them.' He was saying what Blake had written more explosively or what with a more elegant precision Ruskin was also to pronounce—that 'society always has a destructive influence on the artist: first by its sympathy with his meanest powers; secondly, by its chilling want of understanding of his greatest; and thirdly, by its vain occupation of his time and thoughts.' In this loneliness Constable showed considerable strength, independence, pertinacity and balance, but if he had been unfortified by Archdeacon Fisher might he not, after all, have wavered, and failed? 'We loved each other', he told Leslie, 'and confided in each other entirely . . . I cannot tell how singularly his death has affected me.' Is it fanciful to suggest that without the Archdeacon's friendship the painter's achievement would never have been so thorough? If that is so, then the Archdeacon in his Dorset parsonage or in Salisbury Close had his moiety of influence upon a hundred years of European painting.

GEOFFREY GRIGSON

Editor's Foreword

When *John Constable and the Fishers* was compiled some years ago, a number of original letters were not available for inclusion. These are now given, by way of completing the present series of Constable's collected correspondence; and the opportunity has been taken of correcting mistakes and supplementing omissions in the book as published in 1952.

My thanks are due to Colonel John Constable and Mr. H. F. J. Leggatt for allowing me to copy the new letters, and to Messrs. J. M. Sinclair and J. Woodward for information supplied. I need not repeat here my prefatory note to that 1952 edition, except to recall that I have drawn freely on *The Farington Diary*, and I must express my gratitude to his late Majesty King George VI for his gracious permission to incorporate unpublished passages from the manuscript at Windsor. William T. Whitley's books on art in England in Constable's time have provided another source of relevant information. Specific references to these works have not been given because any facts taken therefrom can be easily found under their appropriate dates. Biographical details have been culled from *The Gentleman's Magazine*, *The Dictionary of National Biography* or other standard works of reference, while that excellent book *Fasti Ecclesiae Sarisberiensis*, by Canon W. H. Jones, has provided ecclesiastical data.

The history of the letters themselves, after they had passed through Leslie's hands, is obscure. One would have expected that he would have returned the documents to their owners, the children of the recipients, but he seems to have done the opposite. Most of the letters written by Fisher descended to the late Mr. Edward Fisher. Only one letter from Constable is included in this bundle. The rest of Constable's letters were most probably handed over to his own children. All that is definitely known is that a large number of these and other letters came into the hands of the 1st earl of Plymouth before the publication of his book on Constable in 1903. Some of the letters on either side have passed to museums or other private owners, while some seem to be irretrievably lost. It may be taken that all the Fisher letters here printed are from the Fisher Collection, and that all those written by Constable are in the Plymouth Collection, unless otherwise indicated in the text. I need hardly say how grateful I am to the present Lord Plymouth and to the late Mr. Edward Fisher for allowing me to make transcripts of the documents in their possession.

In this new edition, the grouping into chapters has been abandoned in favour of a continuous narrative form, with the number of the year taking the place of the running chapter-titles at the head of each right-hand page.

R. B. BECKETT

General Editor's Note

The Society is glad to announce its decision to publish *John Constable's Discourses*, compiled and introduced by Mr. Beckett. This small volume will contain all Constable's public utterances on art, whether in his own publications or during his lectures. Mr. Beckett has for the first time collated Constable's own lecture-notes with the surviving transcripts of those who heard him speak.

John Constable's Discourses will complete the Society's publication of Mr. Beckett's monumental work on Constable. Please notice that it will contain in an Appendix any significant correspondence of Constable's that was not available to Mr. Beckett during his work of transcription and edition. May we renew our appeal to owners and students of Constable's letters to inform us as quickly as possible of any that have been omitted from these six volumes?

All rights in the illustrations of the present volume are reserved to the owners by whose courtesy they have been reproduced. The Society wishes once more to record its thanks to its own printers, Messrs. W. S. Cowell, for their continuous care and skill, and to Mr. C. Glasgow, of the East Suffolk County Library, for undergoing the burden of another index. We are very grateful to Mr. Geoffrey Grigson for contributing his admirable Preface.

Finally, the Society has to express again its high obligation to the generosity of the Paul Mellon Foundation for British Art, who have borne the whole cost of producing this volume, and made possible the undertaking of *John Constable's Discourses*.

Norman Scarfe

CONTENTS

ILLUSTRATIONS

Introduction

Bishop John Fisher

Though Constable spent his youth at East Bergholt, a sequestered village in Suffolk, he was within walking distance of Dedham, a fashionable resort in the summer for visitors of rank and fashion from London. One of these was Sir George Beaumont who came regularly to pay his respects to his widowed mother. Another was Dr. John Fisher, titular rector of Langham in Essex.

Since Langham lies only just across the valley from Bergholt, it may seem strange that Dr. Fisher should be numbered among the summer migrants; but it was not to be expected that so great a man, known to be a personal friend of the sovereign, should attend in person to the duties of a country parish. These were performed for him by his curate, the Rev. Brooke Hurlock, with whom Constable was already acquainted; and it was through the Hurlocks that the two presently met, to become friends for life. This volume will be concerned mainly with another friendship, that between Constable and Dr. Fisher's nephew, the younger John Fisher; but young Fisher came into Constable's life with a share of the prestige and feelings of strong affection which had previously attached themselves to his family in Constable's mind. To explain what comes later, it may be best to begin at the beginning, with some account of the Fisher family. This will have the further advantage of making it possible to trace certain recurrent characteristics of its members. Among these may be included great charm of manner, an aptitude for pedagogy, the love of art, fondness for the banks of the Thames, and a habit of prudent marriage.

The earliest of the line to be recorded is Tristram Fisher, of Stowey in Somerset. His son, the first of the John Fishers, was baptized at Stowey in 1696, and in due course passed from Cambridge into the Church. He had the good fortune to become chaplain to Bishop Thomas, the preceptor of George III, and was rewarded for his services with the incumbency of Peterborough, which he later exchanged for a living in the Isle of Wight, as well as with the prebendal stall of Preston in the Cathedral of Salisbury, where one of his sons was to become bishop in the next century. He married Elizabeth Laurens, a Huguenot heiress; and it is possibly to this lady that the Fishers owed their artistic leanings, as well as their love of the Thames: for we are told that she possessed the pretty accomplishment of cutting out landscapes with her scissors, one of her views being of the Thames at Hampton under ice.

There were nine sons of the marriage. The eldest was the Dr. Fisher whom we have already met as Rector of Langham. He was born at Hampton in 1748, with Windsor Castle beckoning to him, as it were, from not very far away. His father sent him to be educated in London, at St. Paul's School, from which he proceeded to Peterhouse College in Cambridge. His university career was

1

brilliant, combining classics with mathematics, in which he graduated as Tenth Wrangler. He then became Fellow and Tutor of his father's old college, St. John's. In this capacity it is said that he distinguished himself not only by the diversity of his talents but also by 'the suavity of his manners and the peculiarly felicitous manner with which he conveyed instruction'. He also distinguished himself in another way. While he was still a junior fellow the Mastership of the college fell vacant, and it looked as though young Fisher's vote might determine the election of a new Master; but he had already promised his vote to a bene-factor, and he refused to change sides even when some of the most powerful influences in the land were brought to bear upon him. This disinterested piece of behaviour—which must have seemed merely eccentric and irrational in the eyes of his contemporaries—threatened at the time to spell ruin to his hopes of further advancement: and yet it was to this very act that he was afterwards accustomed to attribute the good fortune which befell him. It brought him to the notice of Bishop Hurd, on whose recommendation he was summoned to Windsor to take charge of the education of H.R.H. Prince Edward, later Duke of Kent, and father of Queen Victoria.

In the summer of 1780 we catch a glimpse of Mr. Fisher at Eastbourne, where certain of the junior members of the Royal Family were taking the sea air, our informant being one of Queen Charlotte's Maids of Honour. At three o'clock Prince Edward and his Governor would come to dinner in the house where the princesses were staying. Sometimes Mr. Fisher would be obliging enough to instruct the Princess Elizabeth in drawing.[1] At nine o'clock Their Royal High-nesses would be packed off to bed, after which the older members of the party would sit down to supper and spend an hour or more in 'agreeable conversation'.

Whether the tutor's peculiarly felicitous manner of imparting instruction left any strong trace on Queen Victoria's father would be difficult to determine; but apparently it worked as well as could be reasonably expected. It was of more importance for Mr. Fisher that his suavity of manner won him the confidence of King George III, who made him a Royal Chaplain and Deputy Clerk of the Closet. It soon became known that the monarch chose to treat him rather as a personal friend than as a subject. In any other man this might have been an invidious distinction; but Fisher's unassuming ways, and perhaps still more the total absence of that dreaded quality 'enthusiasm', admitted no jealousies. As Dr. Parr put it in pedestrian numbers:

> Unsoiled by courts and unseduced by zeal
> Fisher endangers not the common weal.

The preceptorship came to an end in 1785, when the royal pupil was considered to be sufficiently advanced to be sent to a German university. It is now that we first hear of the constitutional weakness which pursued Fisher throughout his life. This led him to indulge himself in a well-earned holiday abroad. We are told that he travelled all through Italy and Switzerland with a pencil in his hand, taking landscapes in a most pleasing manner, the views being from well-chosen prospects. In Italy he met Mrs. Piozzi; and though she and her friends might laughingly dub him 'the King's Fisher', she too fell under his charm. So did Fanny Burney when he was recalled to Windsor Castle, to be installed as one of

---

[1] Some of Dr. Fisher's drawings are still to be seen at Windsor.

the Canons of Windsor in 1786. This brought with it an official residence in the castle; but while it was being got ready for him he was granted the use of the same apartment that he had occupied before. It seems that the personable and eligible young Canon was a welcome entrant to the tearoom where the ladies congregated and could make a small dinner-party pass off happily while his drawings were being handed round for their admiration.

It was thus perhaps with a slight *moue* of disappointment that Fanny recorded in her diary for October 1787: 'Mr. Fisher returned, *married*, to Windsor.' On New Year's Day the bride was brought round for closer inspection by Miss Burney, who noted: 'Mrs. Fisher seems good-natured, cheerful, and obliging, neither well nor ill in her appearance, and I fancy, not strongly marked in any way. But she adores Mr. Fisher, and has brought him a large fortune.' Indeed, John Fisher had exercised all the family prudence in choosing his future help-meet. She was Dorothea Scrivener, from Sibton Park in Suffolk: the family was in some way connected with Lord Nelson,[1] and she brought with her a settled income of between sixteen and seventeen hundred pounds a year. There were three children of the marriage: Edward, Dorothea, and Elizabeth.

It was about this time that King George embarked upon the restoration of the choir in St. George's Chapel, locally known as 'the Cathedral', while the Dean and Chapter undertook to improve the rest of the edifice, contributing to the heavy cost from their own stipends. Fisher was treasurer at the time, a part of his duty being that of attending to the fabric of the building; and the king gave further proof of his confidence by directing that he should be appointed to superintend the whole of the work. This was carried out during the king's 'illness'; and when George III emerged from his retirement he was able to express his satisfaction with the new state of the Chapel. The work, incidentally, must have brought Dr. Fisher in touch with Benjamin West, who had unfortunately persuaded the king to allow him to fill the great east window with painted glass of his own design. Other marks of the royal favour came Fisher's way, each bringing with it a useful addition to his income. In 1790 he was made Rector of Langham in Essex, this being in the gift of the Duchy of Lancaster. He further enjoyed the chapter living of his grandfather's parish of Stowey in Somerset, and also that of Hartley Westpall in Hampshire.

As already explained, a Canon of Windsor was not required to live in any of the parishes which might be committed to his charge. Dr. Fisher officiated at a marriage in Langham Church in the year of his institution, but after this his presence is not recorded till 1794, when he once called the banns, and then not till 1798, when our story begins. For most of the time he continued to live with his family at his house in Windsor, slipping up to town as occasion required to stay in lodgings near St. James's Palace, where he could entertain his friends. Joseph Farington, the Royal Academician, has left us an account of how he dined there as Dr. Fisher's guest in 1793. It seems to have been a somewhat melancholy occasion, for the war was making the rigours of austerity felt for the first time in England. The 'distracted state of the country' had made it difficult to be certain of supplies of wine from France, so that champagne and burgundy

---

[1] M. Eyre Matcham, *The Nelsons of Burnham Thorpe*, 1911, pp. 26–7, where in 1787 Nelson's sister Kate had gone to stay in Bath with Dorothea Scrivener, apparently her cousin.

B

were now reserved for His Majesty's table. The unfortunate chaplains and their guests were left to console themselves for the sad state of affairs with 'Claret, Hock, Madeira, and Port'—and it was rumoured that even claret might soon be withdrawn from them.

This description of Dr. Fisher's antecedents has been given for the purpose of showing how very different was the life he had been leading while Constable was growing up from anything that Constable could have known in the quietude of East Bergholt. A briefer account may now be given of the rest of the brothers, so far as they play a part in this history. The second of the nine was Dr. Philip Fisher. Like his elder brother he had been educated in London, becoming an exhibitioner of Charterhouse. He went on to University College, Oxford, where he was elected to a fellowship and succeeded Sir William Scott as Tutor. In 1780, and again in 1787, he was instituted to college livings, in each instance being given a year's grace in which to make up his mind whether he preferred the fellowship or the living. On the former occasion he chose to return to college life; but when the offer was made again he had already decided to marry Mary Roberts, and resigned his fellowship to do so. Three rectories had made it possible for him to bring up a family in decent comfort, and one of his sons was the younger John Fisher already mentioned, who was to become Constable's greatest friend. He was now living in the country; but he was to return to London in 1801 as Master of his old school, and Constable met him presently at Dr. John Fisher's table. He had enough of the family taste in art to appreciate Constable's work, though with donnish humour he would make a pretence of not being able to remember the name of his son's young friend, a mannerism which may go back to the time when he was Proctor in 1779. His wife was the worthiest of women, for whom Constable had the greatest respect.

The third of the brothers was Benjamin, who entered the army as a Royal Engineer. He was an amiable person, much like his eldest brother in character and greatly beloved of his family, to whom he was known as 'the General', by way of distinguishing him from his younger brother George, who was known as 'the Colonel'. It would appear from his name that Benjamin had been intended to be the last of the family; but it was not always possible for country parsons in those days to limit their families, nor were they under any pressing necessity to do so. George born at Peterborough in 1764, was in fact the youngest son. He entered the regiment of Royal Artillery, and managed to combine service abroad with the exercise of artistic talents. As General Sir George Bulteel Fisher, K.C.H., he is still known as a landscape-painter of repute, who worked in oils as well as water-colours, and several of his views were engraved, including works which he had done in North America.[1] He too took an interest in young Constable, whom he sought to advise; but unfortunately his pedagogic manner proved tiresome to the younger man, who held a poor opinion of the Colonel's own work.

Another of the brothers was Dr. Samuel Fisher, who had a medical practice in fashionable Bath; but it is unnecessary to go further. Taken together, they were an extremely distinguished family, the Fishers. They formed a circle with which old Mrs. Constable, the most respectable of women, might well be proud that her son was found worthy to associate.

---

[1] Some of Sir George's works can be seen at the Victoria and Albert Museum.

The Correspondence

It must have been in the summer of 1798 that Constable first met Canon Fisher, who was then on one of his visits to Dedham. In 1824 Constable was able to remind the Bishop (as he had then become) that his Lordship had been his 'kind monitor for twenty-five years'. In 1799 Dr. Fisher's presence at Dedham is not recorded; and by 1800 it appears that he and Constable were already acquainted with each other. Nothing is known of this meeting, beyond the fact that it was a memorable occasion, which created a permanent impression on the younger man's mind. It may be noted, however, that the best views of Dedham Vale are to be had from a spur of land jutting out just below Langham Church, and that Dr. Fisher once made a drawing of the valley from the rectory lawn: so it may be presumed that the beauties of the Vale formed one of the topics of conversation that created an instant bond of sympathy between them.

Some six months later Constable at last won his father's consent that he should be allowed to try his fortune in London. Early in 1799 he set out on the Ipswich coach for Charing Cross, carrying with him a letter of introduction to Canon Fisher's old friend Joseph Farington, an 'elegant and dignified figure', to use Constable's own words. Farington, learning that the young man from the country was also acquainted with another of his old friends, Sir George Beaumont, gave him a cordial reception and arranged that he should realize his immediate ambition, which was that of being admitted to the Royal Academy school, where Constable was soon hard at work as a probationer.

The impression that one gets of Constable during these early years in London is that of a very lonely young man, with a large circle of acquaintances. An experiment in friendship with the younger Reinagle dissolved into nothing as soon as he discovered that Reinagle was simply a very sharp young man, with a not too scrupulous eye on the main chance. The other students, he complained to Farington, thought only of 'execution', and had no regard for 'sentiment', which was Constable's word for that indefinable element without which art could hardly amount to more than another form of commerce.[1] In these circumstances he came to cling more and more to his trio of elderly monitors, Sir George Beaumont, Dr. Fisher, and Mr. Farington, in whom he could at least respect their sincere belief in the values of a great tradition, even though it might be a tradition from which he was already seeking to break away.

As often as he could he returned to East Bergholt, to shake off the depressing gloom of London and lay in a store of fresh countryside memories for the winter. It was apparently on one of these visits, soon after his first meeting with Dr.

---

[1] See S.R. IV, p. 216.

Fisher, that Constable laid the foundations of what was to prove something more than a lifelong friendship. The rectory in his own village was occupied by another of His Majesty's chaplains; and this was not so very surprising, since the living, like that of Langham, was in the gift of the Duchy of Lancaster. Unlike Dr. Fisher, Dr. Rhudde lived in his own rectory, with a team of popular young curates to help him with the combined charge of the neighbouring parishes of Brantham and Wenham. His daughter was married to Mr. Charles Bicknell, solicitor to the Prince Regent; and Mr. Bicknell's daughter Maria, then thirteen or fourteen years old, came down to stay with her grandfather at East Bergholt. Dr. Rhudde had a high opinion of his own social importance; but Maria's age may have put him off his guard, or it may be that he failed to foresee that a young lady from London would take more than a passing interest in the local miller's son. Be that as it may, it seems that she and Constable were allowed to wander about together on the rectory lawn or in the country round; and on his return to London Constable became a regular caller at the house in Spring Gardens where Mr. Bicknell lived with an invalid wife, conveniently close to his work.[1]

After this necessary interruption, we may return to Dr. Fisher, who was still living at Windsor. The next news we have of him is in a letter written to Constable on the 9th April, 1800, by Miss Lucy Hurlock, who shared the interest in John Constable's art which had recently become endemic among the young ladies of Dedham Vale. 'Dr. Fisher', she wrote, 'was to have been with us for two Sundays last month but was prevented by a bad cough; I believe you will meet with him any day this week at No. 3 King Street St. James; whether he will be in Town on the Easter Sunday I cannot tell.'[2] We know that Dr. Fisher's visit to Dedham was only postponed to October, when it is likely that he and Constable met again.

For the next year there is nothing to record; but it is evident that Dr. Fisher continued to take a lively interest in his young friend. On the 12th May, 1802, Constable went round to tell Farington that he was to go down to Windsor with Dr. Fisher to be introduced to General Harcourt, who wanted someone to teach drawing at a military school. The Royal Military College had only recently been founded at High Wycombe, and General Harcourt was its first Governor, while residing himself at St. Leonards in Windsor. A junior department was opened at Great Marlow in 1802, and this led to the need for an extension of staff. Constable must have spent the night with the Fishers in their official residence, for he was up at seven o'clock on the morning of the 17th May to make drawings of Windsor Castle from the other side of the river,[3] presumably with a view to satisfying the General of his suitability for the post of drawing-master; and presumably also the test was satisfactory, since Constable went round again to Farington on the 20th to say that he had seen General and Mrs. Harcourt at Windsor, and to take his advice as to whether he should accept the post.

Farington told Constable that, since he stood in no need of it, he should not accept a situation which would interfere with his professional pursuits. Sir George Beaumont came in soon after, and it was probably Constable to whom

---

[1] See S.R. II, pp. 45–6.
[2] The letter is given in S.R. II, pp. 19–20.
[3] Victoria and Albert Museum, Nos. 33–35.

he referred when he made the remark: 'The young man wants application'. Still in some doubt, Constable sought further counsel from the kindly American President of the Academy, Benjamin West, who had already shown an interest in his work. West advised strongly against acceptance of the post, saying that if Constable took it he would have to give up all hope of future distinction. Advice which accords with the inner feelings of the donee is usually taken; and Constable had just had his first picture accepted for exhibition at the Royal Academy, which encouraged the hope that he might some day become famous. The difficulty still remained of how the offer might be declined without giving offence to Dr. Fisher. West kindly undertook to convey the refusal, and did so successfully. This may have been made easier by the fact that Fisher was a great admirer of West's work. 'Had I accepted the situation offered,' Constable wrote to his friend Dunthorne on the 29th, 'it would have been a death-blow to all my prospects of perfection in the art I love.'

That Dr. Fisher bore no malice is shown by an invitation which he sent to Constable later in the same year, the first of the Fisher letters to survive.[1]

> 34 Duke Street, St. James's
>
> Sat: Nov. 27.

Dear Sr.

I write this at a venture not knowing whether you are in town or not, & not having time to call upon you at present. I came to London last night upon particular business, & can stay but three or four days.

Will you have the goodness to dine with me at the Chaplain's Table in St. James's Palace on Monday at 4 o Cl. If you can call upon me at my Lodgings about half past 3 I will conduct you, & we can have a little previous conversation.

> I am Dear Sr.
>
> yours most faithfully
>
> J Fisher

Whether Constable had returned from the country soon enough to accept this invitation or not, we do not know: but if he did, it is to be hoped that the threatened ban had not extended to claret after all; for claret happened to be Constable's favourite dinner wine.

In the following year Dr. Fisher was elevated to the bench of Bishops. His diocese was that of Exeter, which was not one of the wealthier sees, being worth only about £2,000 a year; but there were added to it the treasurership of the cathedral, a prebend, an archdeaconry, and a rectory, while he was allowed to retain for the time being his other livings. It also gave him an opportunity to make some provision for members of his family less fortunate than himself. The Bishop, ever the most charitable of men, shared in the prevalent belief that charity begins at home; and he was now enabled to put in his brother Jonathan as a Canon of the Cathedral, besides presenting him with two livings, while

---

[1] In the Plymouth Collection.

Philip became Prebendary of Exeter in 1805. In his new situation, Dr. Hughes reported, the Bishop of Exeter 'preserved his natural manner and was just the same as before'. This was not apparently usual among bishops of that age: for Farington's brother, when visiting the Bishop at a later date, remarked that 'he had not before seen a man of his rank in the Church who could be compared with him for gentlemanly, easy, and unassuming manners'. (Was it not Horace Walpole who expressed his surprise at meeting an archbishop with the manners of a gentleman?)

It may have been a greater drawback in the Bishop's eyes that Exeter was so far removed from London. He had not been allowed to keep on his canonry at Windsor, a fact that greatly grieved him; and it is probable that London saw less of him than usual for the next year or two. The period of his exile, however, did not last long. In March 1805 the Bishop was summoned to the capital for the purpose of taking over a more responsible task than any that had been given to him before: nothing less than that of forming the mind of the nine-year-old princess who was expected to succeed some day to the British throne. This meant spending a large part of the year in London or Windsor, and it was probably now that the Fishers set up their establishment in Seymour Street, at which Constable soon became a regular visitor.

The Lord Chancellor was instructed to convey the king's intentions to the Prince of Wales. After remarking on the magnitude of the object which His Majesty had at heart, and the great assiduity with which Dr. Fisher had attended to the Duke of Kent, he went on to say that the Bishop of Exeter had the particular advantage of being of a very mild disposition, and possessing a most engaging manner, likely to gain the esteem of any young person he was required to converse with. His Majesty thought that under the care of Dr. Fisher the Princess Charlotte would be rendered an honour and comfort to her relations, and a blessing to the Dominions over which she might thereafter preside.

Lady Elgin on resigning charge declared that she was handing over the princess 'free from all fault whatever, both in character and disposition'; but this statement can only throw doubt on Lady Elgin's veracity. Charlotte suffered from all the defects natural to an impulsive and affectionate child, described as 'bright and intelligent, very merry, but pepper-hot, too'. Her character was further complicated by the separation of her parents soon after her birth.

One of the first things the Bishop did was to attend to her artistic education: he was desirous 'to create in her mind an inclination for the arts', to which she had at present no disposition. For this purpose he arranged that she should be taken privately to see the pictures at Somerset House, where the exhibitions of the Royal Academy were then held. It is possible that they paused to examine a landscape by the Bishop's young friend John Constable, entitled *Moonlight*: but if so they must have been among the few to notice it, and it has long since passed out of human ken.

The Bishop of Exeter was becoming a person of consequence in the art circles of London: that small gossipy world of collectors, connoisseurs and academicians, which Constable was finding to be not so much larger after all than the world he thought he had left behind him at East Bergholt. There was at this time 'a proposal to do something for the arts of this country'; and those concerned turned to Dr. Fisher as an intimate friend of the king for advice on the best way to bring the project to His Majesty's favourable notice. His advice led to the foundation in 1806 of the British Institution, of which frequent mention will be found in these pages; and this in turn may have led to his election as Chaplain to the Royal Academy in 1807. On that occasion a curious tribute was paid to his social prestige. It was suggested that lecture tickets should be sent to the Bishop for himself 'and others', since this would 'probably bring an addition of respectable company on those occasions'.

In the meantime Dr. Fisher was having an uphill task with the education of the princess. However felicitous his manner of imparting instruction may have seemed to the young gentlemen with whom he had previously had to deal, it failed to appeal to Charlotte at eleven years old when the instruction was conveyed through the medium of the *Posthumous Works* of Mrs. Chapone, even though her aunt the Princess Royal had been brought up on that lady's *Letters on the Improvement of the Mind*; nor did she find the hours any less long when at a later age the Bishop read to her from Miss Hannah More's *Hints for Forming the Education of a Princess*—'*I am not quite good enough* for that yet', she wrote. At the same time, she must have had a certain amount of esteem for her preceptor. When Charlotte made her will in 1807, and left nothing to one of her governesses, 'for reasons', she bequeathed to the Bishop the bible and the prayer-book she had been given by Lady Elgin, and directed that all her playthings should be made over to the Miss Fishers.

The trouble did not, however, end here. While the Bishop had charge of Charlotte's mind, the care of her person was committed to women appointed by the Prince of Wales, who does not seem to have shared his father's high opinion of the Bishop; and the charm which had won the hearts of the ladies of Windsor when he was an unmarried young Canon no longer proved so irresistible to their successors now that he was an elderly married Bishop. The manners of the princess, he complained to Farington, were not being attended to. As an instance, he said that he had noticed that 'her nose requiring to be *wiped*, she did not apply her handkerchief, but wiped her nose with *her sleeve*, as vulgar people do'. It was all very distressing; and when the sovereign, now growing old and blind, showed his inability to grasp the gravity of the situation, Dr. Fisher seriously thought of throwing up his post and retiring to the less disturbing atmosphere of Exeter.

His labours did not go without their reward. It had become a regular habit with George III to appoint the Bishops of Salisbury from among the men he had known and approved at Windsor; and when the see fell vacant in 1807 after the death of Bishop Douglas, Dr. Fisher was chosen to succeed him. Salisbury was a wealthier see, worth twice as much as Exeter, and the Bishop had to surrender his country livings. As against this, there were compensations. By ancient custom the Bishop of Salisbury is Precentor of the Province of Canterbury; and at a chapter of the order held on the 18th July the new Bishop was sworn in as Chancellor of the Most Noble Order of the Garter. An appanage of the bishopric was an official residence in Windsor Castle, still known as Salisbury Tower, for use as a stopping stage when his Lordship drove up to London. It ceased to be so used when communications grew easier; but this was not until after Bishop Fisher's day, and for the time being he now had a home again in his beloved Windsor.

If little has been said of Constable during this time, it is because there has not been much to say. The following note bears the postmark of the 10th February 1809.

The Bishop of Salisbury begs the favour of Mr Constable's Company at dinner on Sunday next at half past four.

60 Seymour Street.   Feb. 9.

As already mentioned, Constable was a regular visitor in Seymour Street during the Bishop's periods of residence; and he was evidently a great favourite with Mrs. Fisher. Speaking to Farington about him in the following year she said that his countenance was like one of the young figures in the works of Raphael, and that his appearance was that of one *guileless*.

Col. George Fisher was at this time in the Peninsula, commanding the forts on the Tagus, where he gave 'proofs of vigour and arrangement in conducting his department'; but Constable may have met him in Seymour Street when he returned in 1810, after an unfortunate misunderstanding with the Duke of Wellington. While in Portugal the Colonel had visited Cintra in the company of the painter Robert Barker, and they had made many drawings of the scenery round, which Barker intended to use for his Panorama in Leicester Fields. This was made known at a dinner-party in Seymour Street attended by Farington and Constable on the 10th April, when Constable was placed next to the Master of Charterhouse. The party included no less than three Miss Fishers in a row, to which the Charterhouse had presumably contributed its quota.

Constable himself was not very happy at this time. His father continued to think that in following art his son was 'pursuing a shadow'.[1] He had put his name down for election as an Associate of the Royal Academy, which he thought might influence his father's opinion, but without success.

As usual, the good Bishop did not keep the favours of fortune entirely to himself. In the year following his translation, Dr. Philip Fisher was installed in Salisbury Cathedral as Prebendary of Stratton in Dorset, a dignity which he ceded in 1810 in return for the more valuable prebend of Ilfracombe in Devon, also attached to the Cathedral.

On the 3rd May, 1810 Constable's uncle David Pike Watts called on the Bishop, whom he found indisposed. 'Mrs. Fisher received our visit very kindly and enquired after you,' he wrote to his nephew. 'She said "She had not seen you for some time." A visit from you will be acceptable in Seymour Street.'[2]

Towards the end of the year it appears that Constable received an invitation to stay at the Palace in Salisbury, since his mother wrote to him on the 29th November, 'I hope nothing will prevent the favor & pleasure of a visit to the Bishop at Salisbury—but you must I doubt work hard to defray travelling expenses'. This visit was postponed till the following year.

[1] S.R. I, pp. 14, 73.
[2] S.R. IV, p. 18.

1811

From a letter written to his mother on 27th August 1811 it seems that Constable was then preparing for his visit to Salisbury. He then went down to spend the next three weeks at the Bishop's Palace, which Dr. Fisher had been refurbishing after its long tenure by Bishop Douglas, who had done nothing to it: cutting down trees, opening up views, and altogether making the grounds as picturesque as they could be made. Thus Constable was introduced to another of his small worlds, that of Salisbury Close, where he could be certain of a warm welcome whenever he chose to return.

Dr. and Mrs. Fisher proved themselves good hosts. 'The great kindness (I may almost say affection) that the good Bishop and Mrs. Fisher have so long shown me,' Constable wrote to Miss Bicknell when the visit was over, 'was never more exerted in an unusual degree to make every thing agreable to me.' At the beginning of October they took their guest with them to spend a few days at Stourhead with the banker and antiquary Sir Richard Colt Hoare, whom the Bishop had met in Italy. 'We were not fortunate in the weather,' said Constable, 'but the inside of the house made ample recompense. Sir Richard is no inconsiderable artist himself.'[1]

In spite of the weather Constable made a pencil sketch of the famous gardens[2] which had been laid out so as to resemble the landscapes of Claude. He also met a well-known Salisbury character, Archdeacon William Coxe, brother of the poet Peter Coxe, and himself author of several books of travel, one of which the Bishop had long ago commended to Fanny Burney. Coxe was the local rector (thanks to a meeting with Sir Richard on the Continent); but he also held a prebend in Salisbury where he spent much of his time, 'carrying himself high among the clergy, who looked up to him as a superior man'. Constable did not form a very favourable opinion of the Archdeacon on this occasion, considering that he paid very little attention to others in his manners; and he was chiefly struck by the rector's love of good eating, which was remarkable even in Salisbury where great dinners were the order of the day. As Coxe took his departure for Sarum Sir Richard remarked sardonically: 'He is gone away well filled,—as I have given him venison every day'.

It seems that visits were also arranged to other places of interest, such as Longford Castle which housed the Earl of Radnor's famous collection of pictures. 'Salisbury has offered some sketches,' Constable wrote in another letter to Miss Bicknell. 'Mr. Stothard[3] admired them and one in particular (a general view of Sarum) he recommended me to paint, & of a respectable size. I did not however do so much as I might while I was there. I was not in the humour, to avail myself of the many interesting plans which the Bishop and Mrs. Fisher proposed to me.' The drawings to which Constable refers were done in a small pocket sketch-book[4] from which several pages have survived, but not the one with the view of Salisbury, of which more will be said later.

---

[1] S.R. II, p. 50.
[2] Now in the Fogg Museum, Harvard University.
[3] Thomas Stothard, R.A., Constable's companion on long walks. See S.R. IV, pp. 241–3.
[4] Measuring about 3½ × 5¼ inches: the contents have been scattered.

A final proof of the Bishop's kindness lay in the fact that before Constable left he had been given a commission to paint the Bishop's portrait. The news of this evoked a typical response from his uncle David Pike Watts, who had the habit of giving his nephew advice couched in terms of incredible pomposity. While he would speak decorously of those eminent artists who had already painted the portrait (this could only refer to the portrait by Northcote, since the Bishop had sat to no one else), and could take no objection to the execution, dress, or ornamental parts of the pictures, yet the similitude, that chief point, had not satisfied Mr. Watts's share of discrimination. He went on: 'I do not look for more likeness in the Portrait of a Prelate, but the combined traits of Religion, Learning, Manner and especially in the Bishop of Salisbury, Goodness so congenial to his Nature. You have attempted a great task and I wish you may acquire the general Vote of *Probatum est*.'[1] No doubt Constable did his best to comply with his uncle's requirements.

The time has now come to introduce the Bishop's nephew, who had recently left Cambridge and had come down to stay at Salisbury for his ordination as deacon in the previous July. It is, of course, possible that Constable may have met him already either in Seymour Street or at the Charterhouse, though there is no evidence of any earlier intimacy between them. In a letter written many years later, Constable speaks to Fisher of his desire of revisiting Salisbury 'to renew our friendship in those walks where it first took so deep a root'.[2] Since this was Constable's first visit to Salisbury and the friendship had evidently ripened by the following year, it may be taken as reasonably certain that it was during the autumn of 1811 that they first came to know each other so well.

This John Fisher was the eldest of the six children of the Master of Charterhouse. Like the Bishop, he had been born by the side of the Thames. This event had taken place at Brentford in 1788, so that he was now twenty-three, and twelve years younger than Constable, who was no longer quite such a young man. He too had been to school in London, being admitted a scholar upon the foundation of the Charterhouse at the nomination of the King in 1802, becoming Orator in 1805 and Exhibitioner in 1806. He was then admitted a pensioner of Christ's College, Cambridge, of which he was made a scholar in 1807. His university career, however, had not been quite so brilliant as those of his father and uncle, for he ranked only as a twelfth Junior Optime when he took his degree in 1810.

One of the tragedies of the good Bishop's life may now be revealed. His only son Edward, in whom his hopes would naturally have centred, had turned out to be mentally deficient, and had presently to be committed to the care of a clergyman in the country. It would seem that his nephew of the same name as his own now took the part of a son in the Bishop's affections and was living with him as if he had been an even closer member of the family. It is not altogether impossible that the Bishop may have invited Constable for the purpose of providing his nephew with company.

Enough has perhaps been said already to explain why Constable and young John Fisher should at once have become fast friends, in spite of the considerable

---

[1] S.R. IV, pp. 29–30.
[2] See below.

disparity between their ages. However strongly Constable might be attached to his older friends, the fact remains that their tastes were firmly rooted in the eighteenth century, while Constable belonged, in all essential respects, to the nineteenth; and they could hardly be expected to display any great enthusiasm for the revolutionary doctrines which he was already anxious to preach in the matter of art. Fisher represented the new generation—he was in fact in some ways ahead of his times—and Constable found in him an eager young proselyte, who would be sure to listen to anything he might say with interest. The difference in age was balanced by the fact that the Cambridge graduate was already an older man in the ways of the world than Constable, who still retained much of the simplicity of his rural youth; it will be found that Fisher had an altogether more objective outlook, and the buoyancy of his temperament could do much to counteract Constable's continual fits of depression.

To this we may add that Fisher had probably spent much of his childhood at one of his father's country rectories, and shared Constable's deep love for the countryside and the life it enshrined. They also had in common a deep strain of unaffected piety, in which the enjoyment of landscape was inextricably mingled with gratitude towards its creator, and which was not found to be inconsistent with a fund of healthy ribald humour.

Curiously enough, it was soon after his return from this visit to Salisbury that Constable drew closer the bond of union which already linked with another young friend of about Fisher's age. During the years which had elapsed since their first meeting, Maria Bicknell had been growing up from a gawky little girl into a pretty but hard-headed young woman with a strong sense of humour. In November they decided to make their attachment known, though Constable had little money beyond what his father allowed him, and little in the way of prospects except his unquenchable hopes. Naturally they thereby called down a storm of opposition on their devoted heads. Dr. Rhudde, old and crotchety, was furious over an affair for which he may have felt that he was himself largely to blame; and since he was possessed of a considerable fortune which might be expected to descend on the Bicknell family in the absence of any children of his own, his lead was followed by the parents of Maria, who could not help feeling that there was much to be said for prudence.

The year of the following note from young John Fisher is not given, but may be 1811.

Seymour Street. Dec. 2nd.

Dear Constable,

The Bishop of Salisbury requests the favour of your company tomorrow to meet

Your very sincere

John Fisher

dinner – 5 o'clock.

In whatever year this note may have been written, it appears from one of the letters to Miss Bicknell that the Bishop invited Constable to dine with him in Seymour Street on the 22nd December 1811. Constable, however, had made a

sudden dash down to Worcestershire in order to speak to Maria and only received the invitation when he returned to London late on the day named therein.
In spite or because of his hurried meeting with Maria at the end of 1811 Constable returned to London feeling more depressed than ever; and his mother,
who had been pressing him to come down to Bergholt for a chat over the
Salisbury tour, diagnosed his despondency as due to the need for a little female
companionship. So his favourite sister Mary was sent up to keep him company
in the lodgings he had taken near Farington in Charlotte Street. Since Mary is said
to be the only one of her family who had actually met the younger Fisher it
seems probable that she was introduced to him on his next visit to London.

The following note addressed to Constable bears the postmark of 1812:

Dear Sir

Will you & your Sister have the goodness to favour us with your
Company at dinner on Thursday next at 5 o'clock.

I am Dear Sir yours faithfully

J. Sarum

Seymour St.   Jan. 28.

The next note is also shown by the collocation of dates to have been written in
this year.

Dear Sir

I wish you could dine here tomorrow at 5 o'clock to meet my
Nephew from Salisbury.

Yours truly

J. Sarum

Seymour St. March 6, Friday.

Stothard's advice was taken, and the general view of Sarum was nearly ready to
be sent to Somerset House by the end of March, when Farington called to in-
spect it and recommended a lightening and clearing of the picture to improve
the effect. This was duly done before the painting was sent to its destination.
Among others who called at 63 Charlotte Street to see the painting before the
exhibition, so Constable told Maria, were his good friends the Bishop of Sarum
and Mrs. Fisher. The picture was accepted, and *A View of Salisbury* appeared
in the Royal Academy exhibition of 1812 as Constable's principal offering for
the year.[1] It received a good place on the walls, but does not seem to have
excited any particular comment. Soon after the opening of the exhibition in May
Constable received another letter from Fisher, from which it appears that the
view now exhibited had been taken from the eminence of Harnham Hill, whence
the spire of the cathedral could be seen 'darting up into the sky like a needle'
from across the river, to use a phrase of Constable's making.

---

[1] Now in the Louvre, to which it was presented by the late P. M. Turner: it measures
$12\frac{1}{2} \times 19\frac{1}{2}$ inches.

Dear Constable

　　As I see the Exhibition (my pen is the better for mending; is it not?) is advertized I conclude your labours are over for the present; so I put you in mind of your promise to come & visit me here at Salisbury. I shall be in town on the twentieth of May shall be ordd. priest on the first Sunday: in June & immediately after that return into Wiltshire. You must prepare to accompany me. You know I take no refusals. All obstacles be they of whatsoever nature they may must be overcome by my impetuosity.—

　　But as some kind of animals lead better than they drive & as perhaps you belong to that class, I will try & coax you here by an account of the life we will lead. We will rise with the sun, breakfast & then out for the rest of the day—if we tire of drawing we can read or bathe & then home at nightfall to a *short* dinner—we'll drink tea at the Bensons[1] or walk the great aisle of the Cathedral—or if the maggot so bites puzzle out a passage or two in Horace together.—I think this life of Arcadian or Utopian felicity will tempt you, so come & try it. I would have painted in more glowing colours, but I eat a great lump of cheese just now & it has got into my head and muddied it.—Do not mention this scheme to anyone: I have my reasons.

　　I often walk up Harnham Hill to look at your view—I was right about St Martins—it is *connected* to the town by a street & is not a *detached* building. How have you finished—when I left, you was in jeopardy?—By the bye we will get leave before we leave town for you to copy that Rubens.[2] I hear that Ld Radnor is not likely to object.

　　Hugh Stevens, whose collection of pictures you went to see, has a very mean opinion of your judgments. You may be a very fair artist among the moderns but you know nothing of old pictures.

　　I am delighted with myself, which as you know is a very delightful feeling when it is an *honest* one.—Many people are delighted with themselves without reason—now my vanity is such that I do declare that I am delighted with myself with reason—I took out a few colours the other evening & drew & coloured a landscape on the spot & am really pleased with it. It is rough of course—but it satisfies in some measure my eye. But tho I am paying myself the compliment—I owe this pleasure to you—you fairly coached me & taught me to look at nature with clearer eyes than before I possessed.

　　I sat down to write this letter with an intention of being harum scarumly amusing—but the said bread & cheese has so sobered or stupified my

---

[1] The Rev. Edmund Benson was priest-vicar of Salisbury Cathedral: his youngest son Robert was later Recorder of Salisbury.
[2] A large view of the Escorial, given in the Longford Castle catalogue of 1909 under the names of Rubens and Peter Verhulst. The owner was Jacob Pleydell-Bouverie, 2nd Earl of Radnor.

spirits that I lay down my pen in despair; & dare not venture to read what I have written lest I should burn it.—

Mem: I shall be in town Monday week—Yours very truly

John Fisher

Sarum. May 8. 1812.

In view of the hints about secrecy, it is possible that the following letter, without address or date, was written during the promised visit to London.

Dear Constable

I will call on you again at three. If *I* do not then find *you* at home *you* may find *me* at the Tavistock Hotel Covent Garden at 5 or thereabouts.

Yours in a hurry as usual

J. Fisher.

Wednesday. 1 oclock.

After taking his sisters to the Royal Academy on one of the days of this visit Constable met Fisher and spent the rest of the day with him.

Young Fisher was duly ordained priest in May, and the time has come to say something about the cathedral body of which he was soon to find himself a member at Salisbury. The constitution of this body, going back as it did to the time when Osmund set up his bishop's stool at Old Sarum, differed in several respects from that of later foundations, and not least in the matter of prebends. Long ago the canons (or men on the roll) had lived together with their bishop, meeting their expenses out of a common fund; but there had grown up a practice of allotting to each a prebend or allowance for his individual needs. The prebend —a word cognate to 'provender'—might comprise a part of the altar offerings, but most often it consisted of one or more of the estates which had come to the cathedral by royal order or pious benefaction. Presently, as the bonds of residence were loosened, and the canons were expected to devote more time to looking after the welfare of their estates, the prebendaries became distinguished by the names of the localities from which their incomes were derived, and stalls were allotted to them in the choir of the cathedral by these names.

By Fisher's time the prebends had lost much of their original significance, even if many of the forms remained. Though they still gave a voice in the Chapter on special occasions, they were regarded chiefly as useful additions to church emoluments. They might be used to encourage promising entrants into the Church, and that no doubt was the justification; but in fact they had become marks of personal favour, and a high proportion of the dignities at Salisbury were reserved for the sons or connexions of the bishops, being combined with livings where the incumbent might or might not choose to live. No one among those immediately concerned saw anything wrong in such a system; but it was beginning to shock the consciences of some reformers, who knew the conditions of the poorer clergy, as a system entrenched in privilege.

For the time being, however, there was no questioning voice; and on the 20th June John Fisher was installed as prebendary of Hurstbourn and Burbage with all due ceremony. It was but a modest deacon-prebend, entered in 1536 as worth the net sum of £11 2s. 2d.; but Fisher had been preceded in this dignity by two bishops, and was succeeded by a third, so it might well be regarded as a stepping-stone to better things. In the same year he was made Rector of Idmiston in Wiltshire, worth about £250 a year. From this there would presumably have to be deducted the cost of maintaining a curate, since Fisher preferred to stay on with his uncle at the Palace, performing the duties of a domestic chaplain; but even so it gave him an income which should have been sufficient to meet the personal expenses of a bachelor canon living under the same roof as his bishop, thus carrying out the intentions of Bishop Osmund's charter.

Before these events had taken place, Constable had informed Maria of his second invitation to Salisbury. 'My friend John Fisher', he wrote on the 24th May, 'is half angry with me because I will not spend a little time with him at Salisbury, but I am determined not to fritter away the summer if I can help it. I will quote part of his letter (which he has followed to town), that you may see what an enthusiast he is.' This determination meant that, if Constable was ever to make a living on which he could afford to marry, he felt it to be a duty to Maria as well as to himself that he should spend the summer in Suffolk as usual, collecting material for his work.

Before he could devote himself to landscape, however, Constable had to stay on in London to complete one of those commissions for portraits whereby he was still forced to supplement the small allowance which he received from his father. Writing again to Maria on the 10th June he said: 'You will see by the cover that the good Bishop is as kind to me as ever. He and Mrs. Fisher were here yesterday for an hour or two, and I have completed the portrait quite to their satisfaction. I am to make a duplicate of it for the palace at Exeter. During their stay, Mrs. Fisher wrote to the Marchioness of Thomond to introduce me to a sight of Sir Joshua Reynolds's pictures.' Lady Thomond was a favourite niece of Sir Joshua, who had inherited many of her uncle's pictures, and Constable had formed a great admiration for the work of Reynolds while copying family portraits for the Earl of Dysart a few years before. Such private collections were not easy to see in those days except on personal introduction. The reference to the cover meant that the Bishop had exercised his privilege of franking the letter with his signature, as he often did for his nephew; and the heavy rates of postage would be a matter of some consideration when the letter was going to a young lady, who could not be asked to pay the cost on delivery.

On the 19th June Constable went down to East Bergholt where he stayed till the 3rd November, except for a brief visit to London to meet Maria and a short outing to Essex. On the 6th November he wrote to Maria: 'I have called on my dear old Stodthard . . . I had an opportunity of serving his son, when he went to Salisbury to draw the monuments in the Cathedral—he was quite unknown there, and I gave him two letters, one to the Palace, and the Bishop & John Fisher were very kind to him—and another to the Benson's, a very agreable family who are fond of drawing, and very musical, and as Charles fiddles remarkably well he was a welcome guest.' Fisher refers to Charles Stothard's visit in the following letter, which also seems to show that Constable had not been able to visit Salisbury this summer.[1]

---

[1] In the Victoria and Albert Museum, however, there is a drawing which seems to be inscribed 'Salisbury' and to be dated 2nd August 1812.

That Constable adhered to his determination not to visit Salisbury this year seems to be shown by the next letter which he received from Fisher, written after Constable's return to London in November. It would seem from this letter that Constable had sent Stothard to the Palace as a substitute for himself.

My dear Constable

You must think me a compound of every thing that is ungrateful in not having acknowledge months & months ago the receipt of your Letter and Picture.[1] But [it] was not ingratitude but Indolence. And let it be a warning to you how you venture to admit that Syren to have the least influence over you, when you see she can carry her powers so far as to render null & void all the good feelings & inclinations of a mans heart & make him appear guilty of vices the most foreign to his nature. She has made me appear ungrateful for a munificent present, she has given me the character of being insensible to the most marked & delicate attention to my opinion & wishes—For believe me I was more gratified with the proof of your good will in recollecting my casual admiration of the painting than I was by being put in possession of the thing itself. The one was a proof of the Painter's art the other of his esteem—

Having thus disarmed you by my confession of my errors; I'll next try to conciliate you by a little flattery—Not flattery either for flattery does not mean Truth which I do—Your painting has been much criticized—disliked by *bad* judges gaped at by *no* judges & admired (which is all that is valuable) by good ones. Among these Coxe the historian[2] who has seen it much was particularly pleased with it. It put him in mind he said of the good old Dutch forest painting school. He looks at it whenever he comes into my room which is most days. What it wants he says is, that what appears *depth* near, should not be *gloom* at a distance.—By the words far & near I mean as the spectator recedes from or approaches the Picture.— This is I think a just observation. I am now looking at it—It is most pleasing when you are directed to look at it—but you must be *taken* to it. It does not *sollicit attention*—And this I think true of all your pictures & the real cause of your want of popularity. I have heard it remarked of Rubens that one of his Pictures *illuminates* a room. It gives a cheerfulness to everything about it. It pleases before you examine it or even know the subject. How he obtained this, or how it is to be obtained—hic labor, hoc opus est. Don't laugh at my feeble criticisms Constable I *mean* your service & all men are allowed to talk *goodnatured* nonsense.—

You shall have something of mine to put you in mind of the great Escurial at Ld Radnors. I have to thank you for the ability of viewing that work as it ought to be viewed—You gave me another sense—I lay in

---

[1] Leslie says the picture was a small landscape: the letter has been lost.
[2] Archdeacon William Coxe, already mentioned.

PLATE 2

BISHOP JOHN FISHER

c. 1812, by John Constable

facing p. 19

darkness & shadow till the Sun of good sense arose & shewed me what beautiful scenes I was surrounded with but could not see—

I passed three most delicious days at Bradley in this county with Dr Callcott & his brother the artist.[1] We recognized each other, & had much chat about the art—He was good enough to give me all the information in his power.

I have a world of things to say to you, & do not know how to get them out—I keep scribbling away, but cannot write fast enough for my thoughts —I wish I could have been of more service to Stothard, but the Bishop was here, & I had my hands so full of other visitors & employments that I could find little time to be either useful or civil to him. The good Bensons however most amply supplied my defficiencies. I think they would take it kind to hear from you—Gilpins sketch book is valuable but he is as mathematicians say 'idem aliter'. The *same thing* in a *different manner*.—

How is your mind? at rest? Set it so if you can for your success much as you know depends upon it.—I shall see you soon in town till when adieu— adieu adieu remember me though I am no ghost—& believe me

my dear fellow

yours very faithfully

John Fisher

Palace Sarum

Novr. 13. 1812.

The Rev. William Gilpin, vicar of Boldre in the New Forest and a former prebendary of Salisbury, was a brother of Sawrey Gilpin the animal painter: his illustrated books on the picturesque in English landscape had achieved immense popularity while Constable was a young man, but represented a conventional view of the picturesque very different from that which Constable was now seeking to introduce to the world.

After this there is no more news of young John Fisher till the following spring, but another of Constable's letters to Maria, which seems to have been written about the 2nd December, gives further news of the Bishop and his wife. 'My good friends in Seymour Street,' he wrote, 'continue their great kindness to me; I have just completed another portrait for them, for the Palace at Exeter.[2] I told Mrs. Fisher yesterday how much I thought his Lordship had of the Archbishop of Cambray. She was pleased to hear me say so, and said that, although it had never been observed to her before, she had always called him her Fenelon.'

On the 13th December Constable wrote to Maria, 'I have tyed up two or three letters which perhaps may amuse you . . .—You will see how friendly John Fisher is.'

---

[1] Sir Augustus Wall Callcott, R.A.
[2] This is still at the Palace in Exeter, and is here reproduced by the kindness of the present Bishop. The original portrait has disappeared.

1813

It would seem that Constable and Fisher had another meeting in London during the following winter. The next letter, though undated, can be placed early in 1813. It is addressed to Upper Marybone Street, off the Tottenham Court Road, where Constable stayed for a few months after a fire at his house in Charlotte Street towards the end of 1812 had rendered him homeless for the time being. The exhibitions of the British Institution—which the Bishop had played a part in founding—were held at their galleries in Pall Mall at the beginning of each year: more effort was made to sell the pictures there than at Somerset House, so that exhibitors always had a hope of finding a purchaser for paintings which had remained over from the Royal Academy shows of the previous year, and Constable himself had a landscape in the current exhibition.

Dear Constable

The bearer of this is a cousin of mine—Mr. Haverfeild—He is fond of pictures & no bad tyro in the art. He leaves town tomorrow, & wishes to see the British Gallery before he goes—can you assist him: if you cannot Calcott may: I have written another note to him.—

Pray dine here tomorrow: come if you can earlier. I am laid up with a bad cold.

Yours very truly

J. Fisher

We dine quiet—& have no party & do not sit long after dinner Charterhouse. Saty morng.

Meanwhile the war continued to drag its weary length along, though with a quickening tempo now that news had come in of Napoleon's disastrous retreat from Russia. Perhaps everyone's nerves were strained. The news of the good Bishop, who had been down at Windsor with his royal pupil, was far from satisfactory. Mrs. Constable, who took a vicarious interest in his Lordship's health, wrote to her son in February to convey her hopes for his recovery; but a week or so later Constable reported to Farington that Dr. Fisher had been much out of order and was much altered in his looks. Constable thought that the Bishop might have suffered in his mind from what had passed with the Princess Charlotte, who had just celebrated her seventeenth birthday: and since that young lady had earlier on reduced one of her sub-preceptors to the point of a nervous breakdown, the conjecture seems by no means impossible. Farington notes later that there were many reports of her violent temper at this time.

His other worries, however, did not prevent the Bishop from attending the great dinner attended by the Prince Regent at Willis's Rooms on the 8th May in honour of Sir Joshua Reynolds, of whose works there was a special display in Pall Mall. Constable had been enabled to attend by the kindness of his uncle Mr. Pike Watts, and had the privilege of having Lord Byron (whose poetry he considered to be of the most melancholy kind, though it showed great ability) pointed out to him.[1] It was a month crowded with events for Constable, for the

---

[1] S.R. II, p. 106.

annual exhibition at Somerset House was also on, and he had some success with his large picture *Landscape, Boys Fishing*, afterwards engraved by Lucas as *A Lock on the Stour*.

Young John Fisher came up for the Academy exhibition; but since he did not find his friend at home on the visit mentioned in the next letter it may have been on a previous visit that he told Constable the story which his friend repeated to Farington at the Reynolds banquet. Carlisle, Professor of Anatomy to the Royal Academy, had been at Salisbury to perform an operation, and was tactless enough to choose Fisher as his audience for an attack on the Christian religion. Fisher, according to his own account, prevented Carlisle from proceeding, saying that 'in his opinion he was content to follow such authorities as Sir Isaac Newton and Sir William Jones, full and avowed believers in it'.

Such staunch adherence to the principles of his profession deserved its reward; and his many cares did not prevent the Bishop from remembering his nephew in a befitting manner. On the 29th May John Fisher was granted licence to hold the vicarage of Osmington in Dorset, with Ringstead Chapel in the same county, together worth £170 a year. It is perhaps hardly necessary to add that this was a living in the Bishop's gift. Ringstead was then a very lonely place, and the chapel in the little wood by the beach has long since been converted into a cottage; but Osmington was situated near to Weymouth, which George III had made fashionable as a watering-place. Fisher, however, did not go to live there till three years later; and in the meantime his work was done by a curate while he himself showed his gratitude by continuing to look after his uncle, when the latter found time to visit Salisbury.

It was from there that Fisher wrote presently to Constable to congratulate him upon the success of his Academy picture. The Smith mentioned in the beginning of the letter must have been one of those lame ducks whom Constable was always assisting out of his own slender means: possibly the 'Antiquity' Smith who had once been his host at Edmonton, and who got into financial difficulties later on.[1]

Dear Constable

This moment myself enjoying a good dinner & a glass of wine it struck me how wretchedly off I left poor Smith when I was in London & remembered with a qualm of conscience the promise I made you to assist him.—Not knowing however whether you was still in London I was afraid of remitting the money: but if you will acknowledge the receipt of this I will in a post or so send you two Pounds for him—

I have just heard your great picture spoken of here by no inferior judge as one of the best in the exhibition. It is a great thing for *one* man to say this. It is by units that popularity is gained—I only like one better & that is a picture of pictures— the Frost of Turner.[2] But then you need not repine at this decision of mine; you are a great man like Bounaparte & are only beat by a frost—

---

[1] S.R. II, p. 17 and V, pp. 104–7.
[2] *Frosty Morning*, now in the National Gallery.

I despair ever seeing you again down here. What a reflexion is it in this life that whenever we have a pleasant scene there is little hope of repeating the view. How many delightful hours of pleasantry have I passed in a society that will never meet together again except under the sod—It is an argument for living while you can live. Dum vivimus vivamus—

The same argument will by the bye hold good of reading—Read a book while it lies before you & do not shut it till you have finished it if possible. Ten to one if you read it or finish it another time. I only know the little knowledge I have, has been picked up by odds and ends, in a booksellers shop, late at night, at breakfast, or while waiting for a friend who was late at dinner. Humour, the Book & Opportunity are friends that never meet but once. Mind I am speaking of desultory genii like myself—

The poor Bensons have lost their eldest son. An officer in the army. They are much afflicted; but I think it will in the end turn out well as he was a sad drain up on the old gentleman's pocket—

I called on you in town but you were not at home—How goes on your St. Michaels Mount friends. Pray as you regard your interest call on the Bishop & his Lady as he attributes it to neglect & not to humility. Every body does not know as well as myself that there is an Exhibitioner & a Painter for fame, who is possessed of modesty & merit; & is too honest & high minded to push himself by other means than his pencil & his pallet.—

Believe me Dear Constable

Yours very faithfully

John Fisher

Palace Sarum
June 14. 1813

There are some prints of N. Poussin to be sold at Philips Warwick St. Golden Sq. on Monday 21, T. 22 & Wy. 23 12 oclock. If you can get me the celebrated Flood you will oblige me.

At the end of June Constable went down to spend the summer as usual with his family at East Bergholt and on his arrival found that Dr. Fisher was once more in the part of the world where they had first become acquainted. On the 3rd July his uncle David Pike Watts wrote to him: 'I have a letter by this day's post from the Bishop of Salisbury as amanuensis for Mrs. Fisher who is at present an invalid, dated Dedham July 2nd. They will be in town again on Monday sennight.'

Whether Constable took John Fisher's friendly hint about calling more often in Seymour Street after his return to town we do not know, but he had some excuse for his negligence in this respect, for continuous brooding on the apparent hopelessness of his prospects of marriage was making him morose and unwilling to seek the company of even his closest friends.

He was in the nethermost depths of depression when he wrote to Miss Bicknell on the 23rd December; but he concluded his letter by saying, 'My friend John Fisher is just come in, & I am comforted by his conversation.'

1814

Constable may have presently taken his friend's advice about calling more often in Seymour Street.

On the 9th February 1814 he wrote to Miss Bicknell to say that he had spent a very pleasant day on Thursday the 3rd in Seymour Street. 'I was invited,' he said, 'to meet a brother of the Bishop's, Colonel Fisher, who is an excellent artist. Many years ago he made some beautiful drawings in America, which are engraved.[1] The Colonel is just returned from Spain and was very interesting in his accounts of it—which part of his conversation I preferred to his telling me how Rubens made his pictures, for that I thought loss of time.'

Constable, it may be noted, was later to revise his opinion as to the merits of the Colonel's work. In the same letter he expressed his regret that Maria had not been with him to see the exhibition at the British Institution when it had opened on the 7th February, for there she would have met so many of his friends, including 'the good Bishop and Mrs. Fisher and family'.

On the 19th February he wrote to Maria again to urge an early marriage on the ground that he had many valuable friends whose patronage might be expected to supplement his present means. 'I expect my good friends the Fishers will be kind,' he said. 'Mrs. F the Bishop's Lady called here with all her family the other day—but she is now quite sensible there must be some great weight on my mind.'

On the 5th April we hear of Constable as dining again in Seymour Street. There he learnt that on the previous night Dr. Fisher and his family had been to a party where the Bishop's old friend Lord Ellenborough arrived in high spirits, and said: 'The negotiations for peace are at an end, I have the despatches in my pocket'.

For the good Bishop, however, there was no peace. Miss Bicknell was not the only young lady to fall in love, a malady for which the highest birth provides no exception. The Princess Charlotte seems to have been fully aware of her responsibilities as presumptive heir to the throne and knew that the country expected her to marry as soon as a suitable match could be arranged. She allowed it to become known that she was engaged to the Prince of Orange, and then sent him a letter breaking off the engagement. The excuse that she did not wish to run the risk of having to leave her own country may have had something in it, and made her popular with the people; but a safeguard against this had been inserted in the marriage-contract, and to many her conduct seemed to be yet another instance of her frivolity. The Bishop was greatly distressed, so much so that he was again reported to be looking ill, with 'a broken look'. He was not to know that 'our jilt', as he called her, had another reason, which must have seemed to her anything but frivolous. At the age of sixteen she had already fallen in love with a handsome young cavalry officer, a cousin it is true, but one born on the wrong side of the blanket; and now she had fallen even more deeply in love with Prince Frederick of Prussia, who had come over during the visit of the allied sovereigns.

---

[1] See for example the aquatint, *View of St. Anthony's Nose, on the North River, Province of New York*, engraved in 1795 by J. W. Edy after G. B. Fisher. A drawing by the same artist in the Victoria and Albert Museum, no. P. 3 - 1913, *The Montmorency Falls, near Quebec*, is dated 1792.

The Prince Regent now seems to have placed more trust in Dr. Fisher, as one of the few who might possibly have some influence over the unreasonable girl; for the Bishop was present at that stormy interview with her father as the result of which Charlotte fled for refuge to the side of her far more irresponsible mother. This was in July; and in August the Bishop wrote to the princess to assure her that whatever concerned her happiness, welfare and character occupied his most serious consideration, and that she engaged his thoughts both sleeping and waking. Next month he took lodgings with his family for a month at Weymouth so as to be beside her there: a token of sympathy for which it must be admitted that Charlotte does not seem to have been particularly grateful.

A more personal grief was soon to follow, for his brother Benjamin died at Portsmouth on the 19th September. His nephew wrote to give the news to Constable.

Portsmouth. Octr. 7. 1814.

My dear Constable

The papers will have informed you before you receive this, of the death of a brother of the Bishops, Gen. Fisher. I am down here with his family acting the part of a comforter where no comfort can be administered. Of all the scenes of distress I ever witnessed nothing has equalled what I have seen. His Son in Law Capt. Conroy a fine manly soldier weeping like an infant. His only daughter I tore from the coffin as they were conveying the remains from the house. The widow is little short of a state of distraction.

In this moment of distress one way in which I can gratify them has struck me. They have no picture of the poor General, nor does one exist, except a bad drawing made when he was about four & twenty: but which had the merit of being then extremely like him & of preserving its likeness to him to the day of his death. This is now at the Charterhouse, & if you will have the goodness to call & ask for my brother William he will give it you.—

Having done this, write & tell me whether you have time & inclination to paint a portrait: and whether with the *assistance of the family* you think a portrait could be taken from it. Of the size price &c we will talk when this is settled, I think it should be full length with the background containing the falls of Niagara he having been one of the earliest engineer officers that surveyed the great lakes of America.—

The question is can you give the appearance of age & preserve the likeness.—Part of his hair I send you lest I loose or forget it. Pray preserve it carefully.[1] He was remarkably like the Bishop both in mind & manner & had always the calm sickly patient appearance he has when labouring under indisposition—The Bishop with out his wig is one of the best

---

[1] The lock of hair is still preserved in a slip of paper on which Constable has written, 'Letter from Revd J. Fisher enclosing General Fisher's hair &c &c Rec'd at Bergholt.'

representations of him that I know.—Do you think with these assistances you could make a picture? Let me know what you think when you have been at the Charterhouse & got the portrait.

I wish you would exert yourself, as plates would be struck & the whole corps of engineers would *eagerly* & gladly take each a copy.—He was a man with every one his friend & no one his enemy.—Direct under cover to me Bishops Palace Salisbury—

My dear Constable

yours sincerely

John Fisher.

The following note, addressed to John Fisher's youngest brother William at the Charterhouse 'to be delivered by Mr. Constable' was enclosed with the above letter.

My dear William

Mr. Constable brings this from me to desire that you will give him the portrait of your late poor uncle the General. It hangs over the chimney piece in the school room. Do not mistake & give the Colonels picture instead. The Generals is very pale . . .

—Dear Peter

yours affectionately

John Fisher

Portsmouth. Octr. 7. 1814.

The General's son-in-law was Captain John Conroy, an adventurer of Anglo-Irish descent, with a small estate in Ireland worth £100 a year. Much will be found about him in *Victoria R.I.*, by Lady Longford (1964), who describes him as 'a man of extravagant ambition, an intriguer, a vulgarian and a scamp'.[1] Having married into the Fisher family, known as 'the loaves and Fishers', he made it his object, she says, to increase the loaves. Having been named Equerry to Edward, Duke of Kent, he then became Comptroller of the Duchess of Kent's Household, in which position he used his great influence over her to improve his own position, being made a baronet in 1827. He died in 1854.

Constable took great pains over composing his reply to Fisher, of which the following is a rough draft in his own hand.

East Bergholt. Octr 9th 1814.

My dear Fisher,

The great pleasure your correspondence never fails to impart to me was much obscured by the melancholy event you have given me of the death of General Fisher—and of the severe distress which it must have occasioned to every branch of the family.

---

[1] See pp. 35–36. Conroy's portrait by Fowler will be found on p. 96.

In reply to your wishes respecting the portrait be assured I shall make every exertion in my power to execute as satisfactory a resemblance of the valuable original as circumstances will admit—it was not my intention to have been in London before the end of this month and [I] could wish that would not intrude upon your patience—but if it is your intention to be in town before that time I will make it a point to meet you as you are well aware how much I shall need your help. You may rely upon my taking care of the precious enclosure of the hair.

Beleive me

my dear Fisher

to be yours most sincerely
J.C.

My dear Constable

I thank you for your ready zeal in offering to leave the country earlier than had been your intention for my accomodation.—However there is no manner of necessity for the measure. You may put yourself in possession of the portrait & set the features familiar to you as soon as you return to town at your own time: I myself shall not be in London till Decr. 10 when *we* will set to work on it.—I write this one of twenty letters. Excuse therefore my necessary brevity—Believe me

Yours very truly

John Fisher.

Palace Sarum
   Oct. 11. 1814.

There is nothing to indicate that the posthumous portrait was ever painted.

1815–1816

The peace so dramatically announced by Lord Ellenborough had proved of short duration. The June of 1815, however, brought news of the battle of Waterloo, in which Constable had three cousins engaged, one of whom was killed— he had already lost another cousin in Spain—and the glorious victory was celebrated by a jubilee at East Bergholt, where Constable had gone for the summer.[1] People then settled down once more to the blessings and inconveniences of peace.

There are again no letters from Fisher to Constable written during this year; and it is possible that both men had their time fully occupied with more important business than letter-writing. Maria's mother had died in May, at about the same time as Mrs. Constable. She had for a long time past been in 'a state of health tending to a decline', which had rendered her incapable of exertion in

---

[1] S.R. I, p. 28.

her domestic capacity; and easy-going Mr. Bicknell allowed Constable to become a regular visitor at Spring Gardens again, though the visits had to be concealed from Dr. Rhudde. Fisher too may have been courting, with business at Windsor for a pretext, if he needed one; but it is unlikely that any obstacles would be raised in the way of a promising young prebendary with matrimonial inclinations.

The lady of Fisher's choice was Mary Cookson. As might be expected, the match was in every way suitable. Mary was the eldest daughter of Dr. William Cookson, an old friend of both the Bishop and Joseph Farington. Like the Bishop he was a Canon of Windsor, and like the Bishop he was in high favour with George III, having had no less than three royal dukes for his pupils. His only weakness was an anxious desire to become 'a Dignitary of the Church': a bishopric, or even a good deanery, would have satisfied him. Dr. Fisher, talking the matter over with Farington, expressed the opinion that this was a highly improvident wish on their friend's part. He knew from his own experience that such preferment must add greatly to Dr. Cookson's expenses, and the Canon was a man with a family for which to provide. It would seem that Dr. Cookson had not married quite so prudently as Dr. Fisher had done.

There had been what some might consider a slight blot on the family scutcheon. Dr. Cookson's sister Ann had married a man named Wordsworth, and they had a son called William. William had not only turned out a poet, which might not have been such a very great disgrace in itself, but he had let himself become known as a supporter of 'French principles'. This had naturally led to a 'coolness' between Dr. Cookson and Mary's cousin. The poet had long since reformed himself in this respect, but the coolness between the two branches of the family seems to have remained, for it will be seen that Wordsworth's name is never mentioned in Fisher's letters. Constable, it may be noted, had met Wordsworth during his visit to the Lake District in 1806, when he had been chiefly struck with the high opinion the poet entertained of himself; but this did not prevent him from admiring Wordsworth's poetry.[1] There was now a double connexion between Mary Cookson and William Wordsworth, for his wife Mary Hutchinson was in some way connected with Mary's mother.

Constable's own affair had seemed for a time to be going well. He had gone so far as to hold Maria's hand in the presence of her father as 'the most approved of lovers'; but news of the meetings came to the ears of Dr. Rhudde, and he exploded in wrath. 'The doctor', wrote Maria in February 1816, 'has sent *such* a letter that I tremble with having heard only a part of it read. Poor dear papa, to have such a letter written to him! he has a great share of feeling, and it has sadly hurt him.' Maria was reluctant to do anything which might add yet further to her father's troubles; but Constable's own father died in May, and though his property had to be divided between six children, Constable was encouraged to hope that he might now at long last be possessed of sufficient means to make marriage possible. His professional income was at this time so small that the Commissioners of Income Tax regarded it as negligible.

Marriage was much in the air at this time. Princess Charlotte, when her Prince Frederick proved unfaithful, had managed to bring the inclinations of her heart

---

[1] S.R. V, pp. 74, 76–7.

into accordance with those of her advisers. On the 2nd May she was safely married to Prince Leopold of Saxe-Coburg, thereby relieving the Bishop of a great load of responsibility. John Fisher's marriage was to follow before long, and Constable was beginning to feel rebellious. It was true that his friend would have about £800 a year on which to live in a vicarage in the country, while Constable would have half that amount at most on which to support a wife in London—a figure on which Maria had assured him that people could not live nowadays. Nevertheless he called on Farington on the 2nd July to say that in all circumstances he had made up his mind to marry Miss Bicknell without further delay and take the chance of what further might arise.

On the morning before this conversation took place, John Fisher was married to Mary Cookson. The marriage must have taken place in London, since Constable was able to give Farington an account of it on the same day, the ceremony being conducted by the Bishop of Salisbury. Next day Constable went round to Farington again, to reaffirm his view that it would be 'most proper' for him to get married himself, taking the chance of what might eventually be the disposition of Dr. Rhudde. On the 13th July he told Farington that he was to be married in September.

It was decided that the ceremony should if possible be conducted by John Fisher, for Constable wrote to Maria on the 28th July to say that, if Fisher should not be able to marry them in September, he had another friend who would be prepared to do so. Fisher, he told Maria on the 1st August, said that he was perfectly happy and had written:

My *wife* has the sense of a man to talk with, the mildness of a woman to live with & the beauty of an angel to look at.

At the end of the month Constable was still waiting to hear whether Fisher would be able to comply with his wishes, and on the 30th August he wrote to Maria: 'I shall write to John Fisher soon. Have you heard of the Bishop's fall from his horse, in Salisbury—but I hope he is recovered.' By this time Fisher had already written to announce his plans, but Constable did not receive the letter till later as it had to be forwarded from East Bergholt to Wivenhoe Park in Essex, where he was seeking to earn some money in preparation for his marriage by executing a commission.

Fisher meanwhile had left his uncle to attend to his duties at Osmington, from where he now wrote.

> Osmington. Augst. 27. 1816
> near Dorchester

My dear Constable,

I am not a great letter writer: and when I take the pen in hand I generally come to the point at once. I therefore write to tell you that I shall preach at Salisbury on Sunday Sep: 22 on the occasion of an ordination: and that I intend to be in London on Tuesday Eveng. September 24. I shall go directly to my friend W. Ellis's no 39. Devonsh: St. Port: Place. And on Wednesday shall hold myself ready & happy to marry you. There

PLATE 3

Collection, the late Edward Fisher

MRS. MARY FISHER

c. 1816, by John Constable

you see I have used no roundabout phrases; but said the thing at once in good plain English. So do you follow my example, & get you to your lady, & instead of blundering out long sentences about the 'hymeneal altar' &c; say that on Wednesday September 25 you are ready to marry her. If she replies, like a sensible woman as I suspect she is, well, John, here is my hand I am ready, all well & good. If she says; yes: but another day will be more convenient, let her name it; & I am at her service. Reply to this letter under cover to the Bishop, and I shall receive your answer—

And now my dear fellow I have another point to settle. And that I may gain it, I shall put it in the shape of a request. It is that if you find upon your marriage that your purse is strong enough, to make a bit of a detour, I shall reckon it a great pleasure if you & your bride will come & stay some time with me & my wife. That Lady joins with me in my request. The country here is wonderfully wild & sublime & well worth a painters visit. My house commands a singularly beautiful view: & you may study from my very windows. You shall [have] a plate of meat set by the side of your easel without your sitting down to dinner: we never see company: & I have brushes paints & canvass in abundance. My wife is quiet & silent & sits & reads without disturbing a soul & Mrs. Constable may follow her example. Of an evening we will sit over an autumnal fireside read a sensible book perhaps a Sermon, & after prayers get us to bed at peace with ourselves & all the world.

Since I have been quiet down here out of the way of turmoil bustle & Douglas's[1] great dinners I have taken much to my easel & have improved much—Your visit will be a wonderful advantage to me—The inside of the Mail is both a rapid & a respectable conveyance & would bring you hither in 16 hours.

Tell your Lady that I long to be better acquainted with her as does Mrs. Fisher & beg her to use her influence with you to see yours with real sincerity

John Fisher.

Constable at once forwarded the letter to Maria, with the following comment: 'My dearest Love, I hasten to send you the enclosed letter from our friend Fisher. I can only say that I am ready to adopt any plan that may meet your feelings on this occasion, and, I repeat Fisher's words, that "I shall be happy and ready to marry you" at the time he mentions. I am much advised by my good friends here to try one more effort with the doctor; but I shall do entirely in this as you direct.'

Maria too was delayed by the presence of some friends and it was not till the 9th September that she was able to reply. 'How particularly kind, friendly and considerate is Mr. Fisher. He has answered for me, I cannot you know let him

---

[1] Canon William Douglas, son of Bishop Douglas. His hobby was that of collecting portraits of the Bishops of Salisbury.

suppose that I am not a sensible woman. . . . I shall be happy to give my hand, but I must go on, the day must be named, how long I wonder does Mr. Fisher stay in town, Saturday 28 or the Monday?' She had shown Fisher's letters to Papa, she said, but without making any impression on him. She was delighted with the description he gave of the way the time would be spent at Osmington, could have no reasonable objection to the mail (there had been some talk of indulging in the extravagance of a post-chaise for their honeymoon), and would feel happy that John should have so much pleasure as she thought the visit to Osmington would give him.

Constable's brothers and sisters were all agreed that Fisher's proposal was the most respectable that had yet been suggested and that such a chance should not be allowed to go by: so he wrote back to say that the invitation was gratefully accepted, asking at the same time how long his friend's stay in town was likely to be, and whether he would be bringing Mrs. Fisher with him.

When Maria wrote again on the 16th September she was inclined to have doubts over the haste they were now in, which would mean the sacrifice of one of John's commissions.

On the morning of the 20th September Constable received a letter from Fisher mentioning Tuesday the 1st October as a suitable date for the wedding. 'I have no doubt', he said when passing the news on to Maria, 'but Fisher & all of us when we meet may think of some very nice plans to start upon—good fellow— he says he "hopes the Bishop will sit to me for his picture in consequence of mine. It will do you a world of credit." ' On the 28th September he went up to London, having heard from Maria that she expected soon to recover her spirits at Osmington, which she hoped was still included in the programme. On the same day he showed Farington the ultimatum he had sent to Dr. Rhudde 'expressed in very respectful and proper terms'.

Maria Elizabeth Bicknell and John Constable were married by special licence on the 2nd October at the church of St. Martin-in-the-Fields, of which the bride was a parishioner. This is the church which Hogarth is said to have used for his picture of another wedding, and it may have recalled Hogarth's own runaway match with Jane Thornhill. The knot, as they say, was tied by the Rev. John Fisher, Prebendary of Sarum; and the witnesses were William Munning and Sarah Manning. From this it may be concluded that none of the Bicknell family lent countenance to such an imprudent proceeding. Constable's own family seem to have been kept aware of where he was going; but it was not till a fortnight later that he remembered to give them the address of where he was going.

After their marriage John and Maria Constable set off for their honeymoon in the south of England, but instead of taking the mail direct to Weymouth, as Fisher had suggested, it seems more likely that they began with a less tiring journey to Southampton,[1] and did not join the Fishers at Osmington till later. This may perhaps be deduced from their presence at Netley Abbey on the 11th October, since the distance would have made it a difficult place for an excursion from Osmington in those days. This visit to the romantic ruins of the Cistercian house above Southampton Water appears, from one of Constable's later water-colours, to have been prolonged into the moonlight.

---

[1] Southampton had already been mentioned when arrangements for the honeymoon were first discussed.

PLATE 4

WEYMOUTH BAY

1816, oil-sketch on millboard by John Constable

If that is so, Fisher had presumably gone ahead to prepare for his guests at Osmington. It seems to have been later on that he made extensions to the vicarage, at a cost of £600: and it must have been a tight squeeze for the two honeymoon couples who were now to share it for the next six weeks. The village of Osmington lies tucked away in a fold of the Dorset downs, below the hillside on which the residents of Weymouth had in the previous year paid permanent testimony to their gratitude for George III's patronage of Weymouth by carving his figure on horseback in the chalk. On the other side the ground rises again to the cliffs overlooking Weymouth Bay and facing across to the Isle of Portland with its connecting link in the Chesil Bank. There were several paths leading down to the sea between the lobster-catching hamlet of Osmington Mills on the east and Bowleaze Cove on the west. The weather was kind to the visitors in November, and much time seems to have been spent on the beach.

Only one slight shade of melancholy may have spread itself across their happiness. It was within sight of this shore that the East Indiaman *Abergavenny* had been wrecked by the fault of a pilot when Mary Fisher was a young girl, and her cousin Captain John Wordsworth was lost after behaving with great courage, with two hundred of his men. The loss had deeply affected his family, and it remained in Constable's memory for many years afterwards.

There were also excursions to Weymouth and Portland as well as to the neighbouring village of Preston, from the tithes of which Fisher's grandfather had derived his prebend at Salisbury. Here there was a fine view of a natural amphitheatre from the heights above Sutton Poyntz. Constable took a sketch-book with him wherever he went.[1] He was even supplied with freshly ground paints, for Fisher was not a man to fail in his promises; and these he could use for rapid oil-sketches out of doors, employing the lid of his paint-box held on his knees for an easel. By way of a return for the Fisher's hospitality he painted or commenced the portraits of his host and hostess.[2]

From Constable's point of view it was an ideal holiday and it remained in his memory as a gleam of happiness. If the two young wives were often left together they had no reason to complain: they were closer together in age and social background than their men were and had plenty to talk about in the London fashions or common acquaintances, while housekeeping had not yet lost its novelty.

As November drew to a close it became time to think about the return to London; the original idea had been to leave Osmington about the middle of the month, or so a letter received by Ann Constable from Maria had suggested; but the Constables were able to extend their honeymoon a little longer. Salisbury lay on the way home so Constable took his wife to spend a few days at the Palace with the Bishop and Mrs. Fisher. Proceeding on their leisurely way the Constables broke their journey again to stay at Binfield in Berkshire with Dr. and Mrs. Cookson, parents of young Mrs. Fisher, where Constable made another pencil-sketch.[3] It was not till the 9th December that they eventually reached London in time to spend their first Christmas together.

---

[1] Some pages are in the Victoria and Albert Museum and others are in private collections, size about $4\frac{1}{2} \times 7$ inches: see *Connoisseur*, March 1952, pp. 3–8.

[2] Both passed to their grandson Edward Fisher by whose permission they are here reproduced. One portrait is mentioned by Ann Constable on 15th November, and on 8th December she gathered that Mrs. Fisher's portrait had been successful.

[3] Formerly in the Gregory Collection.

Constable began by taking his wife to share his old lodgings in Charlotte Street. Maria had capitulated without making terms, while her husband was under the illusion that women can put up with the same discomforts as men do in their bachelor days.

1817

On New Year's Day the Constables dined with Farington. Next day Maria went to dine with her father, who was reported to be personally very well disposed towards his son-in-law, though he still stood in awe of Dr. Rhudde. As the result of Maria's efforts Mr. Bicknell was soon brought round. Warm words had passed between him and Constable on the night before the marriage, which Mr. Bicknell now expressed his willingness to forget. There was even some modest entertaining at 63 Charlotte Street. When Mr. Farington dropped in one evening for a dish of tea he found a party of young people present, chatting of such matters as the conduct of the Duchess of Richmond at the time of Waterloo.

My dear Constable

That you may not think that I neglect you, I write these few lines, just to say that I am so incapacitated from all kind of exertion by my complaint that letter writing is a labour to me. I cannot think—Time & abstinence will only cure me. I got it as you suspected by my journeys—My wife sends her best compliments to Mrs. C. I do the same. Success attend you in all your undertakings.

Dear Constable

yours very sincerely

John Fisher.

I congratulate you on your being on friendly terms with those whom it [is] as well should not of all people be your enemies.
Weymouth. Febry. 1. 1817.

Lambs have been dropt this fortnight!

The recent succession of events had not left Constable with much time to prepare for the Academy exhibition, and earnings were badly needed. Fortunately he had by him the studies which he had made in Suffolk during the previous summer. One of these was chosen out on Farington's advice; and such was the exhilarating effect of matrimony that Constable was able to complete before long the first of his series of larger paintings, exhibited at Somerset House in May under the title of *Scene on a navigable river*.[1] To this he was able to add the portrait which he had done of his friend Fisher, the painting of Wivenhoe Park on which he had been engaged when Fisher's last letter reached him, and another Suffolk scene.

The usual return to East Bergholt in search of fresh material had to be postponed till the autumn, Dr. Rhudde, after going as far as to drop cards at the

---

[1] *Flatford Mill, on the River Stour*, now in the National Gallery.

Constables' lodgings during their absence, had gone back to preserve a dignified silence at the rectory. The summer had to be spent in house-hunting; for there were indications that the Constable family might presently require less restricted accommodation than the lodgings provided. With £200 a year from his father's estate, and the allowance of £50 which Mr. Bicknell was making to his daughter, Constable calculated to be able to bring his income up to £350 a year at least by means of his earnings; but even so the utmost economy would be needed. Constable was at first inclined to take one of the large houses in Charlotte Street, which would have swallowed up nearly a third of his means; but from this he was dissuaded by the more prudent Farington, and ended by taking a smaller house, the rent of which would just bring his expenses to the level of his income. This was No. 1 Keppel Street, off Russell Square, where the land round still preserved something of a countrified aspect. Fisher gave the new abode the name of 'Ruysdale House' in jesting reference to his friend's admiration for the Dutch artist, with whose work that of Constable was coming to be compared.

On the 6th July Constable called in Seymour Street and found the Bishop poorly, but when he called again a day or two later the invalid was much better and was out. An invitation followed.

Dear Sir

Could you call upon us tomorrow morning & take your breakfast with us, as we must leave London the next day.

I am, my dear Sir,

yours very truly

J. Sarum

Seymour St. July 10, Thursd: 9 o'clock.

The following letter,[1] written to Dr. Cookson while he was staying at Osmington, shows that the Bishop was still looking after his nephew.

Palace Sarum July 28

My dear Friend

I am most happy in having the opportunity given me of placing the young Couple we are interested for in a situation of *thorough comfort*. I have a high opinion of John & a most affectionate regard for him.—but had he been a single man—I should not have thought it necessary *at this* time to have done more for him. But having married the Daughter of an old & intimate friend I have been most anxious to give him better Preferment for the sake of our dear Mary & her Parents. I suffered much in mind in not being able to do it sooner . . . —but all is now well. I have stretched a point to do it now—which I will explain to you when we meet.

---

[1] In the collection of Mr. John Fisher.

I cannot but admire my Nephews luck. This piece of good fortune reaches John at a pleasant time—when both the Fathers are present to share in the joy of the young Couple.

I have not time for another word.

Dear Sir, yours very truly

J. Sarum

Sarum, July 28, 1817

Of young Fisher there is no news till the 17th November, when a still younger Fisher was born. The infant was christened Osmond ten days later, in honour of the patron saint of Osmington; and this important event was soon followed by another, showing that the Bishop had still not forgotten his nephew, in spite of his departure from the Palace. On the 6th December John Fisher was installed Archdeacon of Berkshire, then a part of the widely-flung diocese of Salisbury. On the same day he had licence to hold with Osmington the rectory of Winfrith Newburgh with West Lulworth, 'worth £380, and contiguous'. In return for this it seems that he was required to surrender his first living at Idmiston, but he still gained thereby. The good news was announced in his next letter.

Dear Constable,

You will think me the most ungrateful man alive. But change your opinion on my own representation & call me the most idle. Your portraits are hanging up in the room in which I am now writing and are by the few judges I can procure to look at them much admired.—I myself & my wife are delighted with them. I enclose you with this, three pounds to discharge the bill for the frames & beg you to send me a few spirit colours as ordered in another part of the letter.

I have just returned from Salisbury whither I have been, to be installed Archdeacon of Berks. The emoluments are nothing: the honour something.[1] I have moreover exchanged a living in Wiltshire, for Winfrith in this neighbourhood. Lulworth Cove is in the parish, & is from the downs above all exclamation beautiful. By the buy my Archdeaconry will bring my up to London every year about the time of the Exhibition. Moreover do you know my wife has made me a present of a fine little boy, in the early part of last month? We kept her ignorant of the sad event at Claremont till two or three days ago.

I have been painting a little & will bring what I have done up to town for your inspection.—A paper I send with this will amuse you. Paste it up near your easil.

---

[1] At the time of the Survey the archdeaconry was rated for first fruits at £54 18s. 6½d.

PLATE 5

Collection, Mrs. O. P. H

OSMINGTON VILLAGE

1816, by John Constable

You painted me a little picture of Osmington[1] which was not in your box? Do you want it? or may I claim my own? Perhaps Mrs. Constable has taken a fancy to it. If so I must waive my right.— How are you circumstanced in Spring Garden? Let me know. Call tomorrow at the Charterhouse & do not neglect your best friends. Write to me under cover to the Bishop. Beleive me Dear Constable

your very faithful friend

John Fisher.

Osmington. Decr. 15. 1817.

The reference to the house in Spring Garden Terrace shows that the two friends had been getting out of touch with each other. No doubt they had both been too fully occupied with their new duties to have much time left for correspondence. It is also evident that Fisher had not been informed that Constable was himself a father by this time, his eldest son having been born already on the 4th December. The child was christened John Charles Constable, the second name being a tribute of respect to Mr. Bicknell, now that a happy reconciliation had taken place. We are told that the infant was to be seen almost as often in his father's arms as those of his nurse, or even his mother. 'His fondness for children,' says Leslie of Constable, 'exceeded that of any man I ever knew.'

'The sad event' which had to be kept back from young Mrs. Fisher was the death of the Bishop's old pupil, the Princess Charlotte. She had died in child-bed at Claremont, the house which had been made ready for her after her marriage to Prince Leopold, whom she had come to love. Mary Fisher must have known the Princess well in her Windsor days, and that Fisher's apprehensions had not been without some foundation is shown by the fact that Lady Albemarle, a daughter of Charlotte's governess Lady de Clifford, was so deeply affected by the news that it led to a miscarriage, from the results of which she did not long survive. The event, indeed, came as a shock to the country as a whole; and it was followed by a scramble among Charlotte's uncles (if so undignified a term may be used of Their Royal Highnesses) to see which of them could soonest fulfil their long-neglected duty of providing the throne with another heir-presumptive. It may have been some slight consolation to the Bishop that the race was won by another of his old pupils, the Duke of Kent, who before long gave the expectant nation a second heiress, with an equal sense of her responsibilities, but with a more prudent susceptibility in matters of the heart. 'The English love a Queen', remarked the infant's grandmother. It was not, however, until after the Bishop's death that his pupil's daughter came to the throne as Queen Victoria.

1818

Osmond's father, as forecast, came up to London for the Academy exhibition in the spring of 1818. His next letter was sent round by hand to 'Reuysdale

---

[1] Probably that of the village: the vicarage can be seen in the distance to the left.

D

House'; it is on the back of a cover directed to the writer at the Lodge, Charter-house, and postmarked the 29th May 1818.

Dear John

Send me by bearer a few skins of paint: flake white: blue: naples yellow: vandyke brown; brown pink: brown oker: a phial of boiled oil & another of linseed oil. I will return them in a day or two.—I have got your Osmington sketch book & want to copy one of your views. When do you leave town? and how are you. Yours truly

John Fisher.

The following note, slightly more correctly directed to 'Ruysdale House', must have followed a few days later.

My dear Constable

I return you your colours with many thanks: and have to request that you will accept of the accompanying present as a testimony of the gratitude of your

very faithful

and obliged

John Fisher.

I hope you will not find my present too fat for use.

On the 1st July Dr. Fisher seems to have been in London, for Constable dropped in at Farington's to say that he was on his way to Seymour Street, where he was to give 'instructions' to one of the Bishop's daughters. This was a high compliment from one who had himself in his younger days given drawing-lessons to one of the daughters of King George III. Little has so far been heard of the Miss Fishers, who were presently described by Constable to Farington as 'women grown and agreeable'. From one of Princess Charlotte's letters, in which she speaks unkindly of lunching with the Bishop and his *lovely progeny*, it may be inferred that the princess did not then consider them to be as well endowed in the matter of looks as she was herself; but that had been some years ago, and time may have remedied the defect.

The one now chosen for instruction was the elder sister Dorothea, known in her own family as Dolly, who later on became Mrs. John Pike. The following letter may have been written by her to Constable at about this time, possibly on the 6th July.

My dear Sir

I send you back your Easel & your stick, with many thanks for the loan of them. I likewise send the two pictures, Papa begs if it is no inconvenience to you, that you will keep mine for a short time, he has ordered Smith to make a frame for it, which he has desired to be sent to your house & when that is arrived he hopes you will have the goodness to forward both frame & picture to Salisbury. Allow me once more to return you my thanks for your kindness to me, with kind remembrances to Mrs. Constable, Believe me to remain

Dear Sir

Yours much obliged

D. Fisher

Seymour St.
    Monday
        Papa desires me to send one of my sea pieces, to forward in the same box to Salisbury; if they are both ready & would be the better for varnishing. Papa begs you would have the kindness to do it if they are at Salisbury by the 15th: or 16th: of August it will be very good time.

The next letter must have been written in this year, for the portrait of Dr. Wingfield[1] is dated 1818. The other portrait to which Miss Fisher refers may be that of Dr. Walker, which bears the same date.

Dear Sir
        We all return you many thanks for the sight of the two portraits. The Bishop bids me tell you that he is very much pleased with them both & we all anticipate the satisfaction we shall have in the possession of an equally good portrait of the Bishop.—
        As we are not acquainted with the originals we cannot judge of the likeness but I am sure they must be like because there is so much character in both the countenances. There is a playfulness in the eye of Dr. Wingfield as I suppose he is, which pleases me extremely (The one in the Gown & Cassock).
        If we do not see you again before we leave London our best wishes attend yourself Mrs. Constable & little Boy

Believe me Dear Sir

your truly sincere friend

& much obliged

D. Fisher

If the idea had been that Constable should paint a new three quarter length portrait of the Bishop like that of Dr. Wingfield to match other portraits in the Palace at Salisbury it does not seem to have been carried out. Constable, however,

---

[1] Dr. Wingfield was Headmaster of Westminster School and Canon of Winchester Cathedral. The portrait is in the collection of Professor W. G. Constable.

seems to have gone down to Windsor this year since there are sketchbook drawings by him of St. George's Chapel there,[1] possibly because he had gone to meet Archdeacon Fisher on his first visitation of Berkshire.

There is yet another note addressed to Constable at Keppel Street which may have been written on the 10th July.

My dear Sir

You will do me a favor if you will accept for your little boy the accompanying little trifle.

Allow me once more to return you my best thanks for all your kindness to me, & believe me to be my dear Sir

Your most obliged

D. Fisher

Seymour St. Friday.

The letter below bears the postmark of 14 July 1818.

Salisbury. July 13.

Dear Sir

The day I left London I sent to your house two Pictures of my Daughters painting. When they are properly dry I beg you will have the goodness to varnish them—& when they are in a proper state for travelling you will have the goodness to send them to Salisbury. I wish you to send to old Smith. He has some other frames in hand for me & he will send them all down together.

My Ladies are all very busy preparing Dresses for Guernsey for which Island we set out tomorrow. They beg to be kindly remembered to you & your Lady.

Adieu, my dear Sir,

yours very truly

J. Sarum

The Bishop was going over to the Channel Islands on a commission from Bishop North. While there he is said to have confirmed four thousand candidates in four days, this being the first time that the islanders had enjoyed an episcopal visitation since they had been placed under the See of Winchester.

Sarum. Aug. 21.

Dear Sir

We returned to this place on Monday last after a five weeks excursion to Guernsey & Jersey.

---

[1] Victoria and Albert Museum nos. 167 and 168, of which the former is dated 1818 by the artist on the back.

We hoped to have found upon our return Dorotheas Paintings which you kindly took charge of. But as they are not here I am inclined to think you have kept them till you heard of our return from our excursion.

Have the goodness to send them as soon as possible.

My Ladies all unite in kind regards you & your Lady with

                    Dear Sir

                         your faithful Servt.

                         J. Sarum.

                                        Palace Sarum. Sept. 6.
Dear Sir

        I must trouble you again about my Daughter Dorotheas Paintings. They are not arrived: I have written twice to old Smith about them—but I can get no answer to my Letters.

Have the goodness to enquire for them, & send them without loss of time.

Remember us very kindly to your good Lady & believe me

                    yours very truly

                         J. Sarum

My Nephew John & his Lady have been here the last ten days & left us to return to Osmington on Thursday last.

                                        Osmington. Oct: 5, 1818.
Dear Sir

        We have been great wanderers this summer. We were five weeks in the French Islands—two weeks at Farnham Castle & Winton, and we are now confirming in Dorsetshire.

On Wednesday we return home—there to stay. Can you & your Lady with her little one come to us at Sarum for two or three weeks? You may take that opportunity to paint my portrait again—you & Dorothea also may paint together.

This is become a very pretty place. The master & mistress of it join in best remembrance to you with, Dear Sir,

                    yours very truly

                         J. Sarum

Kindly and considerate as the Bishop was, he was evidently unable to see that the prospect of painting in the company of Dorothea might not be so great a temptation to Constable as he supposed it to be. The invitation does not seem to have been accepted, as Constable had to go down to East Bergholt to settle family affairs later in the month.

These is nothing to show the year in which the following note was written, but it seems to be connected with Miss Fisher's anxieties of this time. (As it is addressed to Keppel Street it must have been written before 1822.)

Dear Sir

Can my Daughter see you this day? A Note was sent by the Twopenny Post by mistake—a Servant was ordered to carry it & to wait for you answer. If you come to day let the Servant know the time.

If you cannot come to day we hope to see you very early on Thursday— as that is the only day we have to stay in London.

I am, yours very faithfully

J. Sarum

Tuesd: 10 o'clock.

On the 4th December a daughter, Mary Emma, was added to Archdeacon Fisher's family.

1819

In the meantime Constable had worked up one of his Osmington sketches into a fairly large finished picture which was shown in the early part of 1819 at the British Institution under the title of *Osmington Shore, near Weymouth*.[1] It may have failed to get into the Academy exhibition of the previous year because of its gloomy appearance, for it was now described by the *New Monthly Magazine* as 'not a very happy performance, but a sketch of barren sand without interest, and very unlike the artist's other pleasing works of home scenery'. The effect of desolation was not unintentional, for when Constable sent a friend a proof of the mezzotint by Lucas he recalled the wreck of the *Abergavenny* and quoted Wordsworth's line—

The sea in anger, and that dismal shore.

The year is not given on the following invitation, but the paper used is similar to that of the next letter from the Bishop.

Dear Sir

Have the goodness to favor us with your Company at dinner on Sunday next at ½ past five.

I am, Dear Sir,

your faithful Servt.

J. Sarum

Seymour St. March 12.

---

[1] Now in the Louvre, engraved by Lucas while still in the Bullock Collection under the title of *Weymouth Bay*.

The contents of the next letter, taken with those that follow, leave no doubt that it was written in 1819.

Dear Sir

We are all going out of town for a few days—but we intend returning the beginning of next week. I must then intreat you for you attention to my Daughter for a few Lessons. She is to have the companion of the Picture of Mr. Douglas's that she has already copied—& she will also copy your Claude.

I wish you would have the goodness to order two canvas's to be got ready & primed against our return. You know the size of your own picture. The size of Mr. Douglas's is $17\frac{1}{2} \times 14\frac{1}{4}$.

I am Dear Sir, yours faithfully

J. Sarum

April 12

Meanwhile further advancement was falling to the Archdeacon's lot. Canon Douglas of the 'great dinners' died on the 19th March and was laid to rest by the side of his father in St. George's Chapel at Windsor. As befitted the son of a Bishop of Sarum, he held or had held a somewhat bewildering variety of ecclesiastical offices. In his lifetime he had surrendered to make way for others two livings, one prebend, and an archdeaconry. At the time of his death he was still a canon residentiary, Prebendary of Fordington with Writhlington, Chancellor of the Diocese, Precentor of the Cathedral, and Vicar of Gillingham in Dorset. He enjoyed in addition a prebend at Westminster and was Master of St. Nicholas Hospital—an institution of a type which will be familiar to readers of Trollope's book *The Warden*, maintaining six Brothers and Sisters, with a Master and a Chaplain to look after them.

These accumulated spoils were now to be distributed among the living. The Precentorship, a dignity second only to that of the Dean, very properly went to the Bishop's own brother, Dr. Philip Fisher, who already occupied a prebendal stall in the choir. After all, if a Bishop of Salisbury could act as Precentor for the province of Canterbury, the benefits of which might be seen in the widespread adoption of the Use of Sarum, why should not a Master of Charterhouse regulate the services in Salisbury Cathedral? St. Osmond and earlier precentors had done their work so well that there can have been little left for a later precentor to do; and there is certainly nothing to show that the services of the cathedral suffered in any way from his absence.

His son John now ceded the prebend of Hurstbourn and was installed on the 31st March as prebendary of Fordington with Writhlington, estimated after all reprisals at a value nearly three times that of his previous prebend. Fisher had already succeeded Douglas as a canon residentiary. This was of even more importance, for the resident canons, now limited to six, shared with the Dean the everyday administration of the cathedral, forming as it were a chapter within the chapter. Residence, from being an intolerable burden, had grown to be a jealously guarded privilege, and in the ordinary way it would have been for one of these to call a newcomer into residence; but to this rule there was one exception. When the cathedral had been removed from Old to New Sarum, only a few of the canons had been able to comply with the requirement that they should build 'fair houses of stone, near the wall of the close, or the river that compassed the close'. The Bishop had then been kind enough to provide one; and in return it had become the practice for the Bishop first to collate one of the prebendaries to this house, and then to issue letters patent requiring him to be admitted as a canon residentiary.

So anxious was the good Bishop to see his nephew back by his side again in Salisbury that the necessary steps had already been taken on the day when Douglas died. The canonical house of which Fisher had thus been granted the use for life was called Leydenhall,[1] *Aula Plumbea*, and had originally been built by Elias de Derham, traditionally said to have been the architect of the cathedral. It was a spacious building, situated in the south-western part of the Close, with a pleasant garden running down to the river, over which rose an unusually high alder-tree. From here there was a wide view across the Avon and the water-meadows to Harnham Ridge in the distance.

Such a residence, as Fisher would say, was 'something'; nor was the burden of residence very great, involving only three months' residence in the year. There was, however, one drawback. The old rule required a canon, on entering the close, to 'entertain the bishop for forty days, the dean for thirty, and each of his brother canons for thirty'. The rule had gone, but the tradition of hospitality remained. Those who chose to reside in the close were still expected to spend their days in dining at each other's tables, regardless of the tax on purse, time, and the human constitution. Preferment, as the Bishop had once pointed out, was liable to be a costly business. Fisher told Constable seven days later that it had cost him £4,000 to step into Douglas's shoes.

Perhaps he was not expected to meet his new obligations without some financial assistance, for these favours were followed on the 26th April by another gift from his uncle when he had licence to hold with Osmington Douglas's vicarage of Gillingham, then worth £1,000 a year. Gillingham, now larger than its parent Shaftesbury, was then a quiet county town, hardly more than a village. It was situated conveniently near to Salisbury, but for the time being Fisher preferred to go on living at Osmington.

Constable was able to report to Farington on the 10th March that Miss Fisher was now qualified to paint landscapes 'prettily' in oils; but he was not finished with her yet.

Dear Sir   Seymour St. April, 22.

We have procured the Landscape from the late Mr. Douglas's. As we can have it but for a few days we must be expeditious; & I am very anxious that my Daughter should copy it under your direction. You will oblige me much if you could come to her tomorrow at an early hour, and begin upon the picture at once.

I am, Dear Sir, your faithful Servt.

J. Sarum.

---

[1] There are various spellings. It has now become Leaden Hall, a school for girls and small boys. The South Wing was demolished in this century.

In spite of all these interruptions to his own work, Constable had been able to get his next painting ready for the Royal Academy. This marked a new stage in his progress, for it was the first to be painted on a 'six foot canvas', one of those feats of endurance by which an artist had to prove his prowess before he could expect his work to be taken seriously by the world at large.

The subject was again one of his Suffolk scenes. It showed a sight common enough in those parts when the tow-path crossed over from one bank to the other and the barge horses had to ferried across the stream. In the exhibition catalogue the picture was given the not very distinctive title of *A Scene on the River Stour*, but it has since become better known as *The White Horse*.[1] Constable, it may be noted, had not yet sold a single picture for a decent price. It was seen by the public at the beginning of May and was well received by the press.

On the 6th May Constable went down to East Bergholt, returning to town about a week later, so that his direction of Miss Fisher's painting had to be suspended, and he found another note from the Bishop waiting for him when he got back.

Dear Sir

I hope this will find you safely returned, & that you will be able to go on with the Picture immediately as I fear we must part with it soon for the Sale.

I am Dear Sir, yours truly

J. Sarum

Seymour Street. May 11.

In a letter from Constable to his wife, probably written on the 21st May, he speaks of having had the Fishers with him all day the day before, and no doubt they paid a visit to Somerset House to see Constable's *White Horse*. In the same letter Constable says, 'I hope I have quite done with Miss F'. This hope was not to be fulfilled.

May 25.

My dear Sir

The Bearer of this Mr. Rham a Relation of my poor deceased friend Mr. Douglas—is anxious for an opinion of the Pictures which are to be sold on Saturday. You would oblige us all if you would look at them & give your opinion as to the value.

Yours very truly

J. Sarum

This was presumably a sale to be conducted in London of the better pictures from the collection.

---

[1] Now in the Frick Collection at New York. A full-size study is in the National Gallery of Art at Washington.

Seymour Street. June 6, Sunday.

Dear Sir

The time of our leaving London is fast approaching, & as my daughter is very anxious to finish her Picture, before we go—she hopes it may not be inconvenient to you to come here tomorrow soon after 12 o'clock.

Should you not be able to come, she wishes you would mention some other time.

I am Dear Sir, yours very faithfully

J. Sarum.

My Dear Constable

Will you have the goodness to tell me what price you put on your great picture now in the exhibition. We will call it if you please 'Life and the pale Horse', in contradistinction to Mr. Wests painting.[1] Did you not express a wish to have it on your easil again to subdue a few lights and cool your trees? I think you said so. Because the gentleman who meditates the purchase does not immediately want it. Do not forget my commission respecting your Claude. Would you part with your copy of your Reysdale? not for myself. & price.

Douglas's rubbish sold today for £600! People here wonder it fetched no more.—It makes me mad to hear them talk. Morlands Pigs brought 37 guins. Is it an original? The man in the middle ground has a red waist-coat & carries a bundle of very green grass on a fork. Miss Bensons copy of Ugolino[2] brought 6.6. Mr. Rhann told me, that cut off a piece of the 'Gaspar Poussin' & it would be a fine picture. Now He is called a judge. Get me the Cousins.—[3] I reckon to be settling in my house[4] by the first of August. If you do not come & pay me a visit this Autumn I will never forgive you. Recollect I never come to London without coming to see you, nor travel from the West End of the town to the Charterhouse without calling at the half way house. So much the worse say you for my time & patience. Let me know when your wife is out of her troubles & how your boy goes on. Mem. I have a painting apparatus complete. Brushes clean & pallet set. Colours fresh ground every morning &c &c—I leave Salisbury on Monday next the 5th & return the 12th—Believe me

most faithfully yours

John Fisher.

Palace Salisbury
July 2. 1819

It is only now that we come to the first of the letters from Constable to Fisher: he

---

[1] *Death on the Pale Horse* was one of Benjamin West's most famous paintings, and is said to have fetched 2,000 guineas at the sale of his works in 1829. Fisher has here written *pale* over *white* deleted.

[2] Probably the Reynolds picture of that name.

[3] The younger Cozens.

[4] Leydenhall.

must have written to his friend several times before, but Fisher had not apparently thought the letters worth preserving.

1 Keppel Street, July 17, 1819.

My Dear Fisher

    I fear you will think me very dilatory in replying to your friendly letter. I shall be happy to give you a good account of my Wife. She is however quite well and as we have every comfort about us, we hope for the best. Our boy is charmingly and the great amusement of the whole house. I should like of all things to make you a visit in the Autumn—though I cannot allow myself to be sanguine, yet it is cheering to think about it. Such a visit would have many charms for me—your society—the Cathedral—the walks—and those mines of art Longford & Wilton[1]—to which you could procure me admission to make some studies. The price I have fixed upon my large landscape is 100 Guineas exclusive of the frame. It has served a good apprenticeship in the Academy and I shall avail myself of it by working a good deal upon it before it goes on a second to the British Gallery.

    I should hardly like to part with my copy of Ruysdael[2]. Its being an old school exercise (of which I have too few) gives it a value to me beyond what I could in conscience ask for it. We will talk about the Claude when we meet. I have procured the drawing by Cousins for you—and could pictures choose their possessors you would have had many like it long ago. Mr. Woodburn[3] was unwilling to take less than his first price for it seven Guineas which is certainly not dear—and it has a good frame and glass—when shall I send it you. I do not wonder at what you tell me of poor Douglas's pictures—such collections and judges always make me melancholy. I neither visit them nor talk about them if I can help it—but such things are driven down the throats of Ignorance by Ignorance still more overbearing backed by the bye with good dinners. I have got over my difficulties with my Norman Warrior[4]—I have had a hard battle. His being in compleat armour made him almost too much for me.

    I have made a sketch of my scene on the Thames—which is very promising. My Wife unites with me in best regards to yourself and Mrs. Fisher. We hope your children are well—

I am

My dear Fisher

Yours very sincerely

John Constable.

---

[1] Wilton was the Earl of Pembroke's seat, also near Salisbury.
[2] Four copies after Ruisdael were still with Constable at the time of his death.
[3] Either Allen or Samuel Woodburn, both of whom were dealers: the former was used by Constable to sell his own paintings. See S.R. IV, p. 166.
[4] Constable had been asked by Henry Greswolde Lewis to paint a panel of a Norman warrior for Malvern Hall: his difficulties lay in finding a correct description of the appropriate armour. An oil-sketch of the subject belongs to Colonel John Constable. See S.R. IV, pp. 62–3.

The 'scene on the Thames' (the word *embankment* here has been deleted) requires a special mention. The subject was Waterloo Bridge, which had been opened by the Prince Regent two years before and which must have been a familiar sight to Constable on his visits to Somerset House. He had presumably been present at the ceremony: the colour and the sparkle of the scene had left a deep impression on his memory; and they presented him with a problem with which he was to wrestle for many years before he could get his painting just as he wanted it. The sketch now mentioned was intended to show the river as it appeared on the day of the opening. Constable took it round to Farington on the 11th August, and Farington then objected that Constable had made it too much of a 'bird's eye view', thereby lessening the magnificence of the bridge and the buildings.[1] Before then, however, Constable had heard again from Fisher—on a matter of great importance to them both.

Palace, Salisbury.
July 19. 1819.

My dear Constable,

        As I have painting materials here of every sort, you have only to put yourself into the Mail any day & come down hither. When your great picture is finished & you can spare it from the exhibitions I wish to become the purchaser. I will order tomorrow my bankers to place 7 guin: at Stephensons Remingtons & Co Lombard Street to your name. You may have the money by calling at that house any day after Thursday next. You may send me the Cousins immediately. I wish your wife very well. Beleive me

yours very sincerely
John Fisher.

Why talk about the Claude?

Would you copy me the Lord Radnors? instead?

Constable's reply to this letter is lost. It is clear, however, that he had not realized that his young friend was the would-be purchaser when he first named the price for *The White Horse*, and that he countered Fisher's request to buy it with an offer to sell it for less. The same letter probably contained the news that Constable now had a daughter as well as a son. Maria Louisa Constable was born on the 19th July, and named after her mother and aunt. Like John Charles, she soon became a great favourite with her father, and was known in the family as 'Minna' for short.

Leydon Hall, Close, Salisbury.
Augst. 11. 1819.

My dear Constable,

        I told you I beleive to call at Messrs. Stephensons & Co Lombard Street & state that you came from Messrs. Brodie of Salisbury & that they

---

[1] The only attempt of this description is a pencil drawing in the Victoria and Albert Museum: but Farington distinctly speaks of 'a painted sketch'.

would pay you the £7 s7 for the Cozins. But I never wrote to Stephensons to say you would call & I fear that you had a fools errand. Amid the multiplicity of my business I forgot it. If you *now* call you will find the money there—I thank you for the purchase. I hope that your wife & child are doing well. Let me hear of them. A man with an ugly face the name of Shepherd has been sketching the Bishops Palace to illustrate Bp Burnets history of his own times.[1] I thought him but an every day man: but he spoke well of your works without knowing that I was acquainted with you—Pray come hither for a day or two if you can. I like your conversation better than any mans—and it is few people I love to talk to. Life is short let us live together while we can: before our faculties get benumbed.— When we have got settled, you must come on a regular visit with Mrs. Constable, till then pay me a short batchelors visit. Why am I to give you less for your picture than its price. It must not be. I ordered a frame at Tijous[2] for my little Sarum view. Was it ever paid for? If it was not dun me for the money when we meet.

Beleive me most sincerely yours

John Fisher—

1, Keppel Street.[3] Aug. 13. 1819

My dear Fisher,

I was happy to receive your friendly letter yesterday. Nothing would give me greater pleasure than to make you a visit, and I hope to be able to accomplish it ere long. I am under an engagement to paint the portraits of General and Mrs Rebow at Wivenhoe Park about this time. I have written to him to know if it is still his wish & when I have his answer you shall hear from me again. My wife thanks you for your kind enquiries after her and her infant. They are both well and a more lovely little girl at a month old was never seen. We are so proud of her and at the same time so ambitious as to be induced to ask a great favor. It is our united wish to be allowed to name you for her Godfather. We shall take her to Church in a few days and shall be happy to hear from you.

I have been so much occupied that I delayed for some time sending you the Cozens—but I ordered a case and saw it packed on Tuesday & I hope by this time it is arrived safe.

Collins[4] left London today for Sir Thos. F. Heathcote's at Embley near

---

[1] Shepherd was much employed by Mr. and Mrs. Sutherland to illustrate the histories of Clarendon and Burnet in Graingerized form. Sutherland died in 1820 and the two books, with further additions thereto, were presented to the University of Oxford by his second wife in 1837. Gilbert Burnet was Bishop of Salisbury.

[2] The Tijous were framers and restorers in Greek Street.

[3] The original letter is now in the collection of Mr. C. J. E. Marshall, who has kindly made it available.

[4] William Collins, later R.A., a neighbour of Constable's in London.

Rumsey.[1] He intends passing a day at Salisbury in the middle of next week. He would be happy to receive a note from you (at Sir Thomas's) as he would be greatly disappointed at not meeting with you.

I shall not forget to call at Tijous.

Believe me, Most sincerely yours

John Constable.

My dear Constable,

I shall be delighted to be enrolled godfather on the first page of your family bible. I will endeavour to do my duty as such: and as a reward shall go down to posterity when all the relics of 'John Constable' are eagerly bought up as was the arm chair of Huntington & the easil of Sir Joshua.[2]

I expended my last sheet of letter paper in writing to Collins. Cousins has not yet arrived. What was the conveyance? Mrs. F. congratulates Mrs. C. on her nice little girl.

Yours

J.F.

Close

Augst. 14. 1819   turn over

Pray order me at some good painters warehouse 1 hundred of white lead & 3 galls of good boiled oil. It is for out door painting which I intend doing myself. Let them send it down by Russells waggon & deliver the bill to you which you may send by Post.—

It seems possible that Constable received another invitation from the Bishop to visit him at Salisbury this autumn, since he wrote to his wife from East Bergholt on the 26th October, 'I wrote to Fisher on Sunday, hoping I had not given offence by not coming to Salisbury to copy Miss Fisher's drawings'.

One of Constable's frustrations had still to be removed. For many years past he had been standing for election as Associate of the Royal Academy, only to see younger and inferior artists passed over his head. To take one example, William Collins was a landscape-painter much his junior, being of the same age as Fisher; but he had already been elected A.R.A. in 1814. The omens were now more favourable. On the 17th August the Academician Thomas Philips told Farington that Constable had produced his best picture in *The White Horse*, and though he was still an artist unsettled in his practice, yet what he did was 'his own'. On the 1st November Constable was at last elected an associate, defeating by eight votes to five another of the younger men—the American C. R. Leslie, who was destined to become his closest friend after Fisher.

---

[1] Sir Thomas Freeman-Heathcote, who had just succeeded to his father's baronetcy, was a patron of Collins.
[2] Constable himself purchased Sir Joshua's palette when it came up for sale in 1830: his own relics were piously preserved by his children.

To Constable the relief must have been great: not so much for his own sake, as for that of Maria, who had risked the displeasure of her family by throwing herself away on an unsuccessful painter. Mr. Bicknell and Mr. Farington exchanged compliments; and Constable went round with his wife to Charlotte Street, to thank Farington for the assistance he had given in the election. The Fishers were down in the country, but sent their congratulations as soon as they heard the news.

Close, Salisbury. Novr. 4. 1819.

My dear Constable,

The Bishop & Mrs. Fisher bid me with my own, present their congratulations on your honourable election. Honourable it is: for the Royal Academy is in the first place an establishment of the great country such as to be held in great respect: and in the second place you owe your place in it to no favour but solely to your own unsupported unpatronised merits.—I reckon it no small feather in my cap that I have had the sagacity to find them out.—

I am satisfied that you would have paid me your promised visit if it had been in your power.—And I am sorry that illness should have been the cause of prevention. Taking a house at Hampstead must with Apothecarys bills have been a heavy expense. But let us now hope that A R A will add a few guineas to the price of your pictures & enable you to live as comfortably as you could desire.—

I am myself for the present thrown into difficulties by an expensive & tedious Law-suit. It will be decided by Xmas. But I am going to return to Osmington for a year or two to recruit my finances. I shall rusticate for about three years.

I will send you a draft for your money about Xmas. Will that serve your purpose? If you wish it sooner or want it sooner I will give you a bill for the money immediately. Let me know.—With Mrs Fishers & my own best compliments to your Lady, Beleive me

my dear Constable

yours faithfully

John Fisher.

My compliments to Mr. Collins
who is a very sensible man.[1]

This letter calls for several footnotes, inasmuch as it appears to be a reply to another missing letter from Constable. In the first place, it seems that the sale of *The White Horse* to Fisher at the original price had now been concluded, the only modification being that the money was to be paid in instalments. By this

---

[1] Constable spoke to Farington of William Collins a little later as 'having a good disposition and being religiously inclined'.

generous and impulsive act, at a time when he himself needed all the money he had, the Archdeacon became the artist's first patron of any real importance; and it was something that Constable was to remember with gratitude for the rest of his life.

Secondly, the reference to Hampstead indicates that Constable's life was coming under the shadow of a cloud which grew darker as the years went on. The move to Hampstead at the end of the summer could only mean that he was becoming anxious for the health of his family and that it had been considered advisable to give his wife and children a breath of fresher air than London could provide. The Heath on the heights above was soon to rival Suffolk in his affections as a field for open-air painting; and already on the 2nd November he had been able to show Farington two studies done there. As against this new worry, however, his financial anxieties had been for the moment relieved. He had at last received his share of the estate left by his father; and Maria had inherited from Dr. Rhudde that portion for the sake of which their marriage had been so long delayed.

The precise nature of Fisher's lawsuit, which led indirectly to the purchase of another picture from Constable, is not known. That it had something to do with the collection of tithes on which the main part of the Archdeacon's income depended appears from a letter written to Constable by his brother Abram, just over a year later, when the case had been finally decided: for it seems that Fisher had been optimistic in supposing that his troubles would be over by the Christmas of 1819. 'I notice what you say about Fisher's Lawsuit', wrote Abram; 'they generally end in favour of the Clergy, & throw heavy burdens on the already depress'd agriculturist. The Clergy get in their sheafs & make memorandums, & entries of money recd. & if they get the farmer to overlook the modus & include all in a general agreement, their "*Successors*" come in & do away the right, independently of the difficulty of establishing a modus. I don't mean to say your friend had acted in this way, but you know it is done. I am glad he acts so much your friend. I believe him sincerely attach'd to you & has a high opinion of you as a Man and an Artist, & I like him for liking you.'

The congratulations of the Bishop and his wife were repeated in a letter from their younger daughter Elizabeth, posted on the 8th November.

My dear Sir,

It was with great pleasure we heard of your Election at the Royal Academy, & Papa & Mama desire me to offer you their sincere congratulations on it, in which we all join, as well as in kind remembrances to Mrs Constable and good wishes to the Babes.

I am dear Sir

Your very sincere

E Fisher

Palace Salisbury.

Something that looks like 'Dolly' has been added before the signature.

It was in 1819 that the Bishop suggested to Edward Duke of Kent that he should spend Christmas at Sidmouth in Devon. Edward broke his journey at Salisbury, caught cold, and then settled his family at Sidmouth. It may have been on this occasion that Baron Stockmar urged Edward to make his unfortunate will whereby he nominated John Conroy as his equerry.[1]

1820

Delays in the settlement of the action probably prevented Fisher from carrying out his promise, since the following letter may be taken as referring to the payment of the first of the instalments on *The White Horse*.

My dear Constable

If you will call on Tuesday March 14 at Messrs. Stephensons & Co you will find £50 there to your name on acct of Messrs. Brodie & Co Salisbury.

Yours sincerely

John Fisher.

Charterhouse
Saturday March 11.

On the day that Fisher's note was sent round, Constable lost one of his oldest friends in the President of the Royal Academy who had given much kindly advice as a student. Objection was taken to Benjamin West's interment in St. Paul's Cathedral on the ground that there was no proof that he had ever been baptized. The Bishop of Salisbury then intervened on behalf of the artist whose works he so greatly admired, saying that he had often seen Benjamin West at church in Windsor, that West had been married at St. Martin's-in-the-Fields, and so on. Even then the dispute took some time to settle. Sir Thomas Lawrence was elected as the new president on the 30th March.

Another death in the same season was that of Fisher's father-in-law Dr. Cookson, who succumbed to a painful malady which had made it necessary to give him a hundred drops of laudanum a day. He was able to leave four or five thousand pounds to each of his children, thereby relieving Fisher's immediate difficulties. Mrs. Cookson and her unmarried daughter Elizabeth then went to live at the Archdeacon's house in Salisbury; and this presently led to another marriage in the family. Some reference to these events is contained in Fisher's next letter, which also alludes to Constable's keen support of the Artists' General Benevolent Institution, to the council of which he had been elected in 1818.

Close, Salisbury April. 14. 1820·

My dear Constable,

Now that the funeral of your late President is over, and the dinner eaten by the members of the Artists fund, you may have time to read a

---

[1] See p. 25 above.

E

few lines of letter writing. In the first place, have you received your fifty pound? Because the Bankers of this place came to my wife for your direction in my absence, and she gave it Keppel Street *Bloomsbury*. Did you likewise procure your £7. s7. from Stephensons in Lombard Street as I directed you? When you have answered these questions I shall like to know how the picture proceeds & when it will be committed for trial at Somerset House. And when do you propose shipping off my picture? How has Collins done this season & what says the new President?—But most important of all when do you think that you shall be moving this way on your visit to Salisbury? Because I intend to keep myself open and disengaged to be at your service the whole time. Which perhaps you will reckon no small bore. The Bishop is at Oxford. My wife & brats are all well. Poor Mrs Cookson is however in a very precarious way. I beg my kindest regards to Mrs Constable in which my wife & Miss Cookson join me. Kiss my Goddaughter for me & beleive me

yours most faithfully

John Fisher.

Constable's new picture, which Fisher must have seen in progress during his visit of a month before, was another of the large Suffolk landscapes, even better than *The White Horse*. It was again a view of the Stour taken this time from the side of the water-mill which then stood at Stratford St. Mary near Dedham; and since it included Constable's favourite *motif* of boys fishing (Sir George Beaumont said of the larger of the boys that he was 'undergoing the agony of a bite'), it was later engraved by Lucas under the title of *The Young Waltonians*.[1] When it appeared at Somerset House, it was simply called a *Landscape*, and received 'a very flattering criticism' in one of the newspapers, which Constable at once took round to show Farington. This may have been the notice in the *Examiner* which said: 'The *Landscape* by Mr. Constable has a more exact look of nature than any picture we have ever seen by an Englishman, and has been equalled by very few of the boasted foreigners of former days, except in finishing.' Even so, it failed to find a purchaser at the exhibition: but more will be heard of *Stratford Mill* later.

The 'sea-coast windmill' mentioned in the next letter, of which we have only the extract given by Leslie, was *Harwich Lighthouse*.[2]

April 19th, 1820.

My dear Constable,

I am under obligations to an architect here who has retired from business. I want to make him a present of something near £20. I would rather give him one of your pictures, if I thought he would appreciate it.

---

[1] The original painting, which fetched the record price of 42,000 guineas when it came up for sale at Christie's in 1951, is now in the collection of Major R. N. Macdonald-Buchanan.

[2] Either the version now at the Tate Gallery, or that now belonging to Mrs. Ashcroft, which is on loan to the Birmingham City Art Gallery.

See what you can do for me. . . . Do not part with your London and Westminster view without apprising me, as I rather think I shall like to have it, in case I am strong enough in purse. At any rate, *I* can do no harm by saying *no*, if I cannot purchase. I am infinitely obliged by your purchase of the Claude. You can send it me down with the picture. You did right in sending the sea-coast windmill to the exhibition. Pray come as soon as you can, and stay as long as you can.

The next letter is whimsically addressed to 'John: Constable Esqre A R A. &c &c &c'.

My dear Constable,

Constables 'White Horse' has arrived safe. It is hung on a level with the eye, the lower frame resting on the ogee: in a western side light, right for the light of the picture, opposite the fire place. It looks magnificently. My wife says that she carries her eye from the picture to the garden & back & observes the same sort of look in both. I have shewn it to no one & intend to say nothing about it, but leave the public to find it out & make their own remarks. I am quite impatient to see you here & wish that your young family would permit your wife to join the party.

Yours most truly
John. Fisher.

Close Salisbury
April 27. 1820.

Have you mentioned to Segur[1] Sir G. Knellers head of Dr. Tho's Burnett Author of the Theory of the Earth &c &c, at the Charterhouse.[2]

Constable himself, writing at a later period to one of his relations, called his picture 'one of my happiest efforts on a large scale, being a placid representation of a serene grey morning summer'. The next two letters presumably relate to the completion of the payment for *The White Horse*.

Close Salisbury. June 22. 1820.

My dear Constable,

If you will have the goodness to call at Stephensons & Co. Bankers Lombard St, you will find £50 lying to your account. Your walk into the city will save either you or me 12s.—

I return from Berkshire on Monday 10th July. I do not wish to lose an hour of your society, so beg that you will set off on the 7th or 8th. that I may find you here on my return. My people will receive you. Mrs Fisher is delighted with the thoughts of seeing Mrs Constable & her little boy.

---

[1] William Seguier, Manager of the British Institution and later Keeper of the National Gallery.

[2] Dr. Thomas Burnet, whose *Telluris Theoria Sacra* appeared in 1681, became Master of Charterhouse in 1685. A three-quarter length portrait of him by Kneller is still at the school.

We have a capital nursery for him. Bring some good drying oil with you.—

You are to stay as long as you find it convenient. Do not forget the Claude book.

Yours faithfully

John. Fisher.

My dear Constable,

I sent you some days ago an order to receive £50. I am anxious to hear that the letter reached you & that the money has not fallen into improper hands

yours very faithfully

John. Fisher.

I have just met with the following observation in Leonardo da Vinci

"One painter ought never to imitate the manner of any other, because in that case he cannot be called the child of nature, but the grandchild."

My dear Constable,

If you do not mind the expense bring your babe with you: we have plenty of room.

Yours in short

John Fisher.

Close Sarum.
June 30, 1820.

This arrived on the 1st July and was endorsed by Constable on the cover: 'Wednesday morng. leave town—if we arrive Thursday.' It meant taking small children by coach for sixteen hours at a stretch, but the journey was safely accomplished.

Leydenhall served as headquarters for excursions into the country round, the wives being presumably left behind in the Close. Old Sarum was seen, and there were outings to Stonehenge on 18th July and to the New Forest on 4th August. At the end of July there was a short visit to Gillingham to see Fisher's other new house: a drawing called *Entrance into Gillingham* shows the small spire on the church tower removed in 1838, but omitted before then for the sake of composition from Constable's painting of *Gillingham Bridge*.

One of Constable's sketchbooks[1] has a free translation by the archdeacon of certain Latin lines subsequently used by Constable for the frontispiece to his book of mezzotints by David Lucas—

This spot saw the day spring of my life,
Years of happiness and days of Joy.
This place first tinged my boyish fancy
with a love of the art,
This place was the origin of my fame.

Close Salisbury August 8 1820.

---

[1] Musée du Louvre, no. 08701.

A distant view in oils of Harnham village dated August 1820 was probably done from one of the upper windows of Fisher's house.[1]

The last of the Salisbury drawings is dated 22nd August, so it was two months before Constable could finally tear himself away and return to his work in London. It may be noted that this was his only visit of any length to Salisbury during the summer, until we come to his last visit in 1829. There must have been many long and serious discussions on 'the art' between the two men; and Fisher was again able to supply Constable with materials for painting in oils on the spot, the easel being set up just outside Leydenhall or in the Bishop's grounds.

My dear Constable,

     I send you a letter which arrived after your departure. I hope you all got safe to London. You have left a very fine impression on the Salisbury world. By Friday's Salisbury Mail you will receive a print of Ostade by Vischer: if you could get me a duplicate I should be obliged to you. If you can pray pack the one you receive up & pay the carriage & send it to Mr Adams Lambs Inn Wallingford. If you can *not* get me a duplicate, send Mr Adams *any* print of *any* master of the same size. You need not be particular.

     I will add these expenses to our running account. I move to Osmington with my family on Saturday Sep 2. Direct *Weymouth*. Go on with Waterloo bridge. Macte virtute tua vir optime My wife sends all those sort of messages which womenfolk deal in.

Yours to the purpose

John. Fisher.

Thursday—Augt. 31. 1820.

     Dolly has finished her Claude. The Bishop don't know it from yours. I have not received your copy yet. But I will go to the Palace about it tonight & get it if possible in time to send with my Ostade—They are *gone again* today. A glorious sky today. Paint the eclipse on the 7th.

We must go back a little way to explain the introduction to Constable's next letter. The Bishop's old friend, George III, had died at the beginning of the year. Queen Caroline, who had gone abroad after Charlotte's flight to her side in 1813, returned to England in June to claim what she considered to be her rightful position by the side of her husband. Since then events had moved quickly. On the 5th July a bill had been brought in to deprive the Queen of her title and dissolve her marriage; and Farington had noted in his diary that the 'Queen's busines irritates & agitates the people—the Mass disposed to cry against Government, the Public mind very discontented'. Constable and Fisher, as staunch Tories, were strongly on the side of the King.

---

[1] A misreading of the name in the catalogue of the Isobel Constable sale of 1892, lot 243, as 'Hailsham' has led to an unnecessary supposition that Constable went home by way of East Sussex, but the view is easily recognizable. The painting was with Mrs. Roger S. Warner at Boston, Massachusetts, in 1946.

Keppel Street Sepr. 1 1820

My Dear Fisher—

I have just received your very kind note enclosing the letter[1] which did not arrive in Salisbury in time for me. You should have heard from me much sooner—but I found much to do & have settled my wife & children comfortably at Hampstead. I am glad to get them out of London for every reason—things do not look well though I fear nothing—but the Royal Strumpet has a large party—in short she is the rallying point (and a very fit one) for all evil minded persons. I hear the Duke of Wellington was yesterday in the most imminent danger—& had nearly lost his life by the hands of an *Old Woman*.

We had a pleasant journey to London—in truth we were all made far more fit for such an exertion by the unbounded kindness and hospitality of yourself and Mrs. Fisher—& our good friends at the palace—indeed my dear Fisher my wife & myself feel quite at a loss how to speak to you of those things.

I have a case made ready & your Claude dusted to be sent to you but I have not yet had time to pack it. We did not think you were going so soon to Osmington—or it certainly should have gone from here before— let me know when you would like to have it. The print shall come at the same time & Miss Webber's drawings.[2] My Salisbury sketches are much liked—that in the palace grounds—the bridges—& your house from the meadows—the moat—&c. I am putting my river Thames on a large canvas. I think it promises well. I am glad that person had not my picture which was in the last exhibition. I hear he had so little prudence, that his family have interfered, and obliged him to sell most of his '*Old Canvasses*'— which have brought him about an eighth of what he gave for them. He had a very large hot house & has been known to give 50 Guineas for a weed.

I am just returned from a walk to give some little relief to the poor old organist whom you once saw at my door—he is almost in a [state] of starvation with his wife & 7 children—2 out. He is taken for an *Italian* (but a Swiss called Fontaine) and is in consequence in *danger in the streets* —& if he ventures out he gets nothing. I shall venture to give him 5 shillings for you & add it to your running acct. I have had a letter from a lady, Mrs. Heaviside, giving an excellent character of him. The late Bishop of Winchester allowed him 3 shillings per week—a great loss indeed. Ever most truly with best regard to Mrs F & Mrs Cookson & family.

John Constable

Pray excuse the hasty writing of this letter but I came in late—as I was wishing you should have it before you left Salisbury. Excuse likewise the

---

[1] Probably one from Abram Constable, see S.R. I, p. 189.
[2] Harriet Webber was a young lady of Salisbury, later Mrs. Heniage.

PLATE 6

THE GARDEN AT LEYDENHALL, OR
SALISBURY CATHEDRAL FROM THE RIVER

1820, by John Constable

facing p. 56

PLATE 7

Collection, Sir Harold Wernher

HARNHAM BRIDGE, SALISBURY

?1820 (or ?1829), by John Constable

subject of the latter part of it—but poor Fontaine has seen better days as
has his wife. I visited his wretched dwelling in . . . Lane, Grays Inn Lane.
The four children I saw were very fine children & one in arms—the post
man is at the door. I shall now keep to my work. I hear something of a
job of 3 portraits—I will do them if possible—for the childrens sake. We
are fearfull my wifes brother will not live—he is a very superior young
man—of great promise & elegant manners. Once more my dear Fisher.
Adieu.

The brother-in-law just mentioned was Samuel Bicknell, already dying of consumption, though only about twenty-two at this time. Of the sketches mentioned
earlier in the letter, one must have been the painting of the garden at Leydenhall
now known as *Salisbury Cathedral from the River*.[1] 'The bridges' would be views
of or from Harnham Bridge not far from Fisher's house. The sketch made in the
grounds which the Bishop had tended so carefully seems to have been the original
study for the important painting called *Salisbury Cathedral from the Bishop's
Garden*.[2] This is another picture of which much more will be heard later; and it
is possible that the commission for the finished picture, which was done to Dr.
Fisher's order, had been given already before Constable left Salisbury. The
Archdeacon duly responded to Constable's appeal.

> Fontaine is not the only poor starving foreigner.
> All the 'image boys'[3] are distressed in ye same way.

My dear Constable

> Your letter reached me just as I was moving to Osmington & I have
been too busy ever since to reply to it. Your poor organist is welcome to
his 5s. & another such sum when you think fit to give it him. Pray do not
forget to execute my paltry Wallingford commission. I was much amused
& delighted with your letter. Pray write to me now & then. Get rid of
your *two* houses as soon as ever the hot weather is over & paint some
portraits, you will then keep yourself independent of the world & may
consult your own taste only for Landscape. This place is beautiful. It is
covered with golden balls yclept apples. Write in haste. Yours most truly
> John. Fisher.

Osmington nr Weymouth Sepr. 11. 1820.   turn over

> Look into the Courier for a letter.
> I quite forgot to say what was the purport of my letter that your kind
present of the Claude may be sent to Salisbury, & my wife would like to
[be] entrusted with a sketch book to copy if you dare lend it to her. Love
to your wife & children.

---

[1] National Gallery, no. 2651, here reproduced.

[2] A small sketch of the subject was formerly in the T. W. Bacon Collection, but this
may be a later compositional study. There is also an oil-sketch of the Cathedral from
the front of the Palace which is said to have been done this year, Victoria and Albert
Museum, no. 318.

[3] Italian vendors of plaster statuettes.

Miss Fisher's next letter bears the Bishop's frank of the 8th October 1820. From this and the letter that follows it appears that Constable had informed the occupants of the Close of his intention to proceed with the subject of Waterloo Bridge on a larger scale.

My dear Sir

I must write a few lines, to acknowledge the safe arrival of the beautiful frame & also to thank you for the trouble you have had about it, the picture is now hanging up over the sideboard in the dining room, & with the help of its magnificent dress makes a respectable figure.

John is not here at present to take charge of his own print, but I hope it will be safe in this house, till he returns to Salisbury.

Papa desires me to say, he hopes you will finish for the Exhibition the view you took from our Garden of the Cathedral by the water side, as well as Waterloo Bridge.

With our kind regards to Mrs Constable, believe me to be

My dear Sir, yours much obliged

D Fisher

If it is not a very unpleasant task, you may give each of your little ones a kiss from me.

Saturday. Salisbury.

Osmington. Weymouth. September 28. 1820.

My dear Constable,

As you have got your Waterloo Bridge on a large enough canvass I have sent you a print I picked up the other day which may be of service to you. I think it is remarkable for the simplicity & breadth of its effect.

I am down here with my wife & family waiting the confinement of the former.[1] When that is over I shall return to Salisbury alone & keep residence till the new year. I have just been reading a gossiping sort of book 'Cumberlands Memoirs'.[2] But it is amusing & contains anecdotes of a class of people that you would like to know something more of than their mere names. This season of the year with its volumes of rolling clouds throw the finest effects over this beautiful country. A large black misty cloud hung to day over the sea & Portland. The Island could be but just discerned. The smoke of Weymouth was blown off towards Portland & was illuminated by the Western sun & releived by the dark cloud. As I rode home a complete arch of a rainbow came down to my very feet: I saw my dog running through it. Your old friend and crony the little fat

---

[1] William Fisher, hereinafter called 'Belim', was born on the 22nd October.
[2] The *Memoirs* of Richard Cumberland the dramatist, described as 'very loose, dateless and inaccurate', had appeared in 1807.

housekeeper got a little drop more than usual a night or two ago, & danced & sung to the edification & amusement of the whole kitchen. Who is to paint the Queens picture for the common council?

Is the enclosed paragraph (from today's Courier) a puff rogatory? Send me a few scraps of London news or R A politics.

I have now written out my whole stock of materials sensical or nonsensical, unless I were to tell you that I am building a potatoe house & that Farmer Wallis had two barley ricks burnt by some people he forbad leasing. So no more at present from

yours faithfully
John. Fisher.

The enclosed cutting runs: 'Mr. HAYDON, the Historical Painter, requests us to state, that he is not the Mr. HAYDON who has been getting up Addresses to the QUEEN: the latter is an Auctioneer'.[1]

Constable took his new attempt on Waterloo Bridge round to show Farington on the 21st November; but Farington was evidently of a different mind from that previously expressed by Fisher since he advised Constable to proceed on and complete for the next Academy Exhibition a subject more nearly corresponding to that of the successful picture exhibited last May.

An empty cover from the Bishop to Constable[2] is dated 18th December 1820. It may have contained the letter from the Archdeacon to which Constable's letter written early next year is a reply.

1821

The letter from Constable to which Fisher's letter below is a reply has been lost.

Close Salisbury. Janry. 3. 1821

My dear Constable:

I am very sorry that I know none of the fellows of Dulwich college or any thing of the institution except the pictures. I am doubly sorry: because I cannot comply with a request of yours: & because I cannot show my esteem for Mr. Collins & his connexions.—

I have been living in a whirl since you last wrote me: and you must think me very ungrateful in not having acknowledged the receipt of the Claude the Ostade the Sketch book & above all your kind letter. In Novr. I was so alarmed at the aspect of publick affairs that I could think of nothing else. I have been very active since in getting up addresses in the South. On Queens Thursday I was up at the head of 80 Constable till

---

[1] It was Benjamin Haydon of whom Constable had once said to Farington: 'He is possessed with a notion that the eyes of all the world are upon himself.'

[2] In the Leggatt Collection.

three oclock the next morning. My great cause will be tried the third week of this month. I shall be in town on the thirteenth—You shall go down with me to the Court. My wife is at Osmington with new brat a *very* fine boy—

The Bishop likes your picture 'all but the clouds' he says. He likes 'a clear blue sky'. Dolly has borrowed the Claude to copy & has cut the tree to paint them only—I met the other day a man driving a pig in a string with a pair of spectacles on his nose. He was very grave about it & did not seem to think that there was anything incongruous in his appearance. My kind regards to your wife.—A Mr Francis fellow of Caius Coll Cam will call upon you at my recommendation.

Yours faithfully

John. Fisher.

We come now to a letter which requires some explanation. There may have been a missing letter in which the Archdeacon disclosed his intention, should the lawsuit reach a successful issue, to reward his lawyer by presenting him with one of Constable's paintings (as he had suggested doing to the architect): or the matter may have been discussed while Constable was down at Salisbury. The lawyer was Mr. John Pern Tinney, a native of Gillingham, who had been a solicitor in Salisbury since 1800 and was for many years an Alderman and Magistrate of that town: and the picture chosen for the purpose was *Stratford Mill*, the successful picture mentioned by Farington. The letter was sent round by hand as soon as the case was decided.

My dear Constable:

Get your picture finished: for Tinneys chimney peice is put up & the cause is won.

Yours

John. Fisher.

Saturday Eveng.
6 oclock. Jany 20.

The date given in the heading of the next letter is at first sight perplexing: but the London postmark is the 2nd February, and it is clear that the Archdeacon had overlooked the change of the month.

Salisbury. Janry 1st. 1821.

My dear Constable

Mr Tinney has decided to take the present frame in which your picture stands on my representation of its handsomeness and the expence to which a new one would put him.

It is *probable* that he may be in town before you send it down. If he is, take the papering off the frame: as the white of the paper gives the lights a brassy look & first impressions are everything.—

In a day or two the *case* will be sent up to you. The sooner then the picture is down the better. Only do not part with it till your new frame is made.—

Woolcotts Salisbury waggon sets off from Castle & Falcon Aldersgate Street, on Tuesdays at 10 oclock A M.—

Do not forget to get me the impression of the Coliseum, with the shepherd & his flock in it. I never saw anything that gave me an idea of its magnitude before. I go to Weymouth tomorrow.

Beleive me

yours most faithfully

John. Fisher.

It will be recalled that Fisher's father-in-law had died about a year before this. Mrs. Cookson did not long survive the shock of her husband's loss. She had been suffering from a weak heart for the past ten years and her end came on the 12th February, in her sixty-eighth year.

1. Pulteney buildings Weymouth.
Feb. 14. 1821.

My dear Constable,

I am here paying the last duties to my wife's mother. She died silently & suddenly, on Monday Morning at 3 oclock. Rather a singular accident happened to me in consequence of her death. I was in the Church at Osmington with the old clerk alone, pointing out the site of her grave, when the old man suddenly exclaimed, "I cannot stand Sir", & dropping into my arms, died.

When you next see Stothard tell him the following anecdote. I went to call upon a poor Curate living in one of our mud villages on a lonely part of this coast & was shown into a dark low underground parlour.[1] Casting my eye round the comfortless walls it was refreshed by spying in a corner a most charming bit of light & shadow: & walking up to see what else it contained I found Stothards Canterbury Pilgrims with the morning light breaking over the Dulwich hill. The poor man little less than worships the print.

Pray get at your circulating library, "the diary of an invalid".[2] You will be much amused with it: for it is written in a lively easy manner. And when you come to his critiques upon painting & statuary you will find another corroboration of our often repeated opinion, that persons of the highest education in the sciences are mere children in their knowledge of the *art*.

---

[1] Probably at West Lulworth. Constable had been with Stothard when the Pilgrims were actually painted: but here a print is meant.

[2] By Henry Matthews the traveller: the book appeared in 1820.

When will Tinney receive his picture? And how thrives the "hay wain"?

As soon as the Spring arrives, I will make a correct sketch of our ferry house at Portland[1] & send it you. I saw it the other day standing in sea bleached desolation.

This cold weather has given my babes terrible colds & coughs. How thrive your wife & yours. With my kindest regards to her

Beleive me

faithfully yours

John. Fisher.

The following note was probably sent with the above letter. It will be seen that the price of Tinney's picture is not yet included.

Is the following a correct state of our account up to Feby. 1821? Constable

Cr.		Dr.	
Claude.	6.6.0.	Draft.	50.0.0.
Packing.	5.18.0.	Draft.	50.0.0.
Picture.	105. 0. 0.	Draft.	20.0.0.
Frame.	22.10. 0.		

Constable at this time was going on from strength to strength, freed at last, thanks to Fisher's patronage, from the depressing thought that his great canvases would only remain on his hands to collect dust in the Keppel Street studio. With the several studies he made before proceeding to final execution, even one such picture must have taken up most of his time and energy during the winter; and the disturbing fear so far had been that, by neglecting smaller works with a greater chance of sale, he might be jeopardizing the prospects of his family, should the great work remain unsold. The theme on which he was now working, in consequence of Farington's advice, was a view taken from the platform in front of his father's water-mill at Flatford, looking down-stream over the mill-race to Willy Lott's cottage. This is the picture which Fisher, who may have seen the large rough preliminary study,[2] here calls *The Hay Wain*, the name by which it has been known ever since, and to which Constable refers in his next letter.

1 Keppel Street, 1821

My dear Fisher—

My wife and myself had the pleasure of dining with the Bishop yesterday when Miss Fisher gave my [wife] your letter. We condole with you—and Mrs Fisher—on the death of poor Mrs Cookson. From the New Times on Saturday we learnt, that this excellent person was removed

---

[1] Until within living memory Portland could be reached only by boat or on foot across the shingle of the Chesil Bank.
[2] Now in the Victoria and Albert Museum.

from a scene of great suffering and with little prospect of ever enjoying anything in this world. Your poor Clerks sudden death was really shocking—and must have called for a great exertion of your fortitude and piety of which so much of both belongs to your character.

It was singular your meeting with Stothards pilgrims in such a situation.

My picture is getting on and the frame will be home in a 3 weeks or a fortnight when I shall despatch Mr Tinnys picture. The case is arrived. Beleive—my very dear Fisher—I should almost faint by the way when I am standing before my large canvasses was I not cheered and encouraged by your friendship and approbation. I now fear (for my family's sake) I shall never be a popular artist—a Gentlemen and Ladies painter—but I am spared making a fool of myself—and your hand stretched forth teaches me to value my own natural dignity of mind (if I may say so) above all things. This is of more consequence than Gentlemen and Ladies can well imagine as its influence is very apparent in a painters works—sometimes the '*Eclats*' of other artists occasionally cross my mind—but I look to what I possess and find ample consolation.

Do not forget to send me the drawing of the ferry house—it is a "*blessed spot*" but that is its value. I have got you an impression of the Coliseum & the Teniers—the Mill in a flood of light. The Good Bishop & Mrs. F. "attacked" me about Martins "*pantomime*",[1] again yesterday—but I spoke my mind—as the shortest way. I could not sacrifice myself to [such] gross ignorance.

We lament to hear of your children having such colds—we have kept ours within & they have [caught] nothing.

My wife begs to join with me in kindest regards to yourself Mrs Fisher & Miss Cookson.

I remain

my dear Fisher

always most sincerely yours

John Constable.

You have stated the event very nearly. I have put all particulars on the cover.

Poor Colnaghi's son in law, Scott, has had a duel with one Christie a Barrister, a friend of Lockhart.[2]—They met at Chalk Farm ½ past ten Friday Evg—& Scott was shot through the body. He still survives—the ball extracted on Sunday morng—Mr Scott has two lovely children. You saw the boy.

---

[1] John Martin's picture of *Belshazzar's Feast* was hailed as a masterpiece when shown at the British Gallery in the spring of 1821.
[2] Scott, son-in-law of Paul Colnaghi the printseller and editor of the *Champion*, had made an attack on Lockhart.

Close Salisbury. March. 6. 1821.

My dear Constable,

I was as much shocked at poor Scotts catastrophe as if he had been a friend of my own. When the proper time comes pray tell Mr Colnaghi that he has my most sincere condolencies. I first heard of Lockhart & Scotts quarrel from Wilkie[1] the morning I called on him with Collins.

I am reading for the third time White's history of Selbourne.[2] It is a book that should delight you & be highly instructive to you in your art if you are not already acquainted with it. White was the clergyman of the Place & occupied himself with narrowly observing & noting down all the natural occurrences that came within his view: and this for a number of years. It is most elegantly written. I fear the book is scarce. But if you can procure it, buy it for me & keep it by you. I am quite earnest & anxious for you to get it, because it is in your own way of close natural observation: & has in it that quality that to me constitutes the great pleasure of your society.

You must send the *frame* with the picture to Tinney at my expence. If therefore he says any thing about the former you must only reply that the picture with its frame is a testimony of gratitude.

Let us hear when Mrs Constable is out of her troubles. Mrs Fisher is anxious to hear of the event. I think that I acquainted you with the death of my poor Mother in Law.

I am appointed a steward to the Society for promoting Xtian Knowledge. This will bring me to town in May: when I expect to see the Hay wain in a good light. The first week in June I go my visitation. Will you accompany me free of expence. I shall take Oxford in my way.—

Yours faithfully

John. Fisher.

In his previous letter Fisher had recommended *The Diary of an Invalid* by Henry Matthews for Constable's reading. Here he for once showed himself lacking in his usual tact: or perhaps he had overlooked the comments which it contained on the collection at the Doria Palace. 'Gaspar Poussin's green landscapes', wrote Matthews, 'have no charms for me. The fact seems to be, that the delightful green of nature cannot be represented in a picture. Our own Glover had, per-haps, made the greatest possible exertions to surmount the difficulty, and give with fidelity the real colours of nature; but I believe the beauty of his pictures is in an inverse ratio to their fidelity; and that nature must be stripped of her green livery, and dressed in the browns of the painters, or confined to her own autumnal tints in order to be transferred to canvas.'

All this was, of course, the direst heresy to Constable's mind, and contrary to everything for which he had been and was still striving. The traveller's offence

---

[1] Sir David Wilkie, R.A.
[2] *The Natural History of Selborne*, by the Rev. Gilbert White, was published in 1789.

was not lessened by the fact John Glover, the most prosperous landscape painter of his day after Turner, was a true gentlemen and ladies' painter, enjoying just that form of success which had been denied to Constable. The passage continued to rankle for a long while in Constable's mind, and in his next letter he gave vent to his feelings.

1 Keppel Street, April 1. 1821.

I trust my dear Fisher you will make every allowance for my occupation and various anxieties in my seeming neglect of you—but I am now releived of by far the greatest of my anxieties by the safe confinement of my wife who produced a beautifull boy about 2 o clock on Thursday last.[1] Both are thank God doing well. She was unusually large this time & our children have been ill—and many circumstances have happened to distress her—but God has helped me where I could not have helped myself—and all the rest of my (pictorial) anxieties are giving way to the length of the days and my own exertions—

My picture goes to the Academy on the tenth. At the same time (as the window on the stairs must be taken out) I shall send Mr Tinny's picture to Mr Woodburns—to be packed as the large case is there. The present picture is not so grand as Tinny's owing perhaps to the masses not being so impressive—the power of the Chiaro Oscuro is lessened—but it has rather a more novel look than I expected. I have yet much to do to it—and I calculate for 3 or 4 days there—

I hear of so many clever pictures for the exhibition especially by Ex members,[2] that it must be a capital show. They are chiefly in the historical & fancy way—I hear little of Landscape—and why? The Londoners with all their ingenuity as artists know nothing of the feeling of a country life (the essence of Landscape)—any more than a hackney coach horse knows of pasture. Collins requested me to return with him to see a landscape by himself for the Exhibition—it was beautifully painted—& I thought the subject might be about the neighbourhood of Bagnage Wells[3]—but he named a scene in the most romantic glen in Westmorland as the identical spot he had painted. This I am sure will never do as Landscape painting —but I stand on ticklish ground—though that ground is my own—and one might get involved in jarring—& make ones life uncomfortable. Friendship, and a well regulated mind, are things worth attaining if possible.

How much I am obliged to you for the mention of the books. The Diary is delightfull. It has given me new information on subjects that I have

---

[1] Charles Golding Constable was born on the 29th March.
[2] Exhibitor members, a term said to have been applied to A.R.A.s.
[3] Bagnigge Wells, now King's Cross Road, was a favourite suburban resort for Londoners.

heard of all my life. There is no doubt but that the Invalid is a clever fellow—but these Italian Tourists think they must talk about pictures & relate anecdotes of painting—I would recommend them always to mention the story of Alexanders visit to the painting room of Apelles.[1] He mentions the landscapes of Gaspar Poussin (whose works contain the highest feeling of Landscape painting yet seen—such an union of patient study with a poetical mind). The Invalid (indeed he deserves the name if disease gives it) imagines defects in the Landscapes that he may afford an opportunity to *"our own Glover"* of remedying them—this is too bad and one would throw the book out of the window—but that its grossness is its own cure —and one is led on for the fun of the thing—to be amused with the novelty of shapes which Ignorance appears in—

The mind & feeling which produced the "Selborne" is such an one as I have always envied. The single page alone of the life of Mr White leaves a more lasting impression on my mind than that of Charles the fifth or any other renowned hero—it only shows what a real love for nature will do—surely the serene & blameless life of Mr White, so different from the folly & quackery of the world, must have fitted him for such a clear & intimate view of nature. It proves the truth of Sir Joshua Reynolds' idea that the virtuous man alone has true taste. This book is an addition to my estate—Carpenter[2] got it for me 2 Vol Octvo.

Stothard was amused with your mention of his pilgrims—but said he believed many of his prints were to be found amongst the Hottentots.

I dined last week at Sir G. Beaumonts—met Wilkie, Jackson & Collins.[3] It was quite amusing to hear them talk about Martins picture. Sir G. said some clever things about it—but he added, even allowing the composition to be something (its only merit), still if the finest composition of Handel's was played entirely *out of tune* what would it be. It was droll to hear Wilkie say *"Gentlemen* ye *are too severe"*—and then say something ten times worse than had yet been said. Sir G. says he will not go out of town without painting me a picture—

My best regards to all your family—beleive me

my dear Fisher

always most sincerely yours

John Constable.

Dr Gooch[4] has just left my door. He says all is going well up stairs—

---

[1] 'One would imagine', said Apelles, as the horse neighed in appreciation of what he took to be a fellow creature, 'that the animal is a better judge of painting than Your Majesty'.

[2] James Carpenter, the bookseller of Bond Street.

[3] David Wilkie, John Jackson and William Collins were all younger men than Constable, but had already been elected full members of the Academy.

[4] Robert Gooch, the gynaecologist, who later became Royal Librarian.

Seymour St. Ap: 12, 1821.

Dear Sir

Now your Picture is gone to the Exhibition—before you engage in any great work, perhaps you may be somewhat at leisure to give a little attention to your old friend and scholar Dorothea. An hour or two from you will set her going again, for she at present is at a stand.

Can you drop in upon us some morning? Will you breakfast with us on Saturday at ½ past 9—precisely?

I am dear Sir

Yours very truly

J. Sarum

The Hay Wain[1] appeared at Somerset House in May under the title of *Landscape —Noon*, descriptive of the effect Constable intended to produce. It had a good reception in the press, but still failed to find a purchaser. The Bishop was at the private view, and his nephew came up to see the exhibition at the beginning of June. He and Constable went round to call at Farington's house, where Fisher maintained that there would be no coronation that year, saying that there was apprehension of a hired mob.

It is of more importance that the exhibition was also seen by two French visitors. One was the painter Géricault. The other was Charles Nodier, who wrote a little book on his experiences called *Promenade de Dieppe aux Montagnes d'Écosse*. The most vivid of these experiences seems to have been the sight of *The Hay Wain*, the only picture in the show which he mentions. 'The palm of the exhibition,' he wrote, 'belongs to a very large landscape by Constable with which the ancient or modern masters have very few masterpieces that could be put in opposition.' Then, after some description of the painting, he added: 'It is water, air and sky; it is Ruysdael, Wouwerman or Constable.' The repercussions of this were still to come.

Probably knowing nothing of Nodier's visit, and certainly quite unaware that fire had been set to a beacon which would throw its light over the still young nineteenth century, Constable was preparing to accept his friend's invitation to join him on his archdeaconal visitation.

They went through Berkshire together at the beginning of June. The area of the Archdeacon's jurisdiction was divided into four rural deaneries, at Newbury, Reading, Wallingford, and Abingdon; and at each of these places it was Fisher's duty, as *oculus episcopi* or the eye of the bishop, to inquire into the state of the churches and the way in which services were conducted, as well as into the life and conversation of the clergy, while instructing the priests to live well and learn the duties of their functions. The conclusion of one of Fisher's addresses has been preserved for us by Constable, who used it many years later to wind up one of his own lectures.

'In my present perplexity,' said Fisher, 'the recollection comes to my relief that when any man has given an undivided attention to any one subject, his audience

---

[1] Now in the National Gallery.

F

willingly yield him for his hour the chair of instruction; he discharges his mind of its conceptions, and descends from his temporary elevation to be instructed in his turn by other men.'

If they went down together from London, they may have gone first to Wallingford, one of the rural deanries, though there is no record of their presence there; and this would account for the somewhat tortuous route they took. The first record comes from Newbury to the west, which they had reached by the 4th June staying at the Pelican Inn. Here Constable must have been delighted to find a canal along the Kennet, complete with a lock and a watermill for him to draw, as on his own river the Stour. On the 6th they struck east again, passing from Newbury to Reading, where Constable sketched the ruins of the once great abbey. From here they headed north along the Thames valley to Abingdon, where Constable found another abbey to draw, besides sketching the town from the river. For these drawings he used a larger sketchbook than those which he had taken with him on his previous visits.

Duty thus performed, Fisher was able at last to share Constable's holiday. On the 8th June they visited Woodstock together, and Constable made a sketch of Blenheim Palace in its grounds. On the 9th they were at last in Oxford. Here Constable appropriately chose for the subject of his next drawing the college of which Fisher's father had once been Tutor, with the High Street where Dr. Philip Fisher had exercised his own jurisdiction by asking errant undergraduates for their names and colleges.[1] After this Constable could no longer bear to be parted from his family, and the two men parted company. It had been a pleasant excursion, and Constable wrote at once to his brother Abram, saying how much he had enjoyed it and hinting that it might be productive of profit at one time or another. Plans were made, either now or presently, for another meeting later on in the year.

The year of the next letter is given by the reference to the coronation in the connected letter which follows. Constable had probably gone up to Hampstead when the Bishop called.

Seymour St. July 10.

Dear Sir

I called at your house last week with Dorothea, but was not lucky enough to find you at home. We will call again any morning this week when we are sure of finding you.

Let us know whether or not we may see you tomorrow at an early hour —or any other day. Fix your own time, & we will endeavour to make our time agree with yours.

Dorry wishes you would have the goodness to arrange & set in order her Painting Box.

I am dear Sir, yours faithful Servt.

J. Sarum

---

[1] The drawing is now in the British Museum.

My dear Sir

    Papa & I called at your House the other day but finding you were out of town, we only left the drawing you were kind enough to lend me.

    We talk of leaving London immediately after the Coronation, & have already began to think of packing up, I have been looking over my painting Box, & should be much obliged if you would replenish for me, the colors I should like to have are as follows

1 bladder of Naples yellow
Do — of light ochre
Do — of Burnt Ochre
Do — of White
Do — of black
Do — of burnt Umber
Do — of Raw Umber
Do — of Burnt brown Sienna
Do — of Blue Black,

if you think they will keep well when the bladders are opened.

    When it is convenient to you, perhaps you will have the kindness to procure these colors for me, & let me have the account of the other things, you have been good enough to get for me.

    I hope Mrs Constable & your trio have escaped colds this wintry whether. Perhaps we shall have the pleasure of seeing you before we leave Town.

Believe me to be, dear Sir,

yours much obliged

D. Fisher

Seymour St. Friday.

    Papa desires me to add, if you would let him know when you are likely to be at home, he should like to call upon you.

The next event of interest was the crowning of the new king at Westminster Abbey, which passed off peacefully in spite of Fisher's prognostications. The Queen, it will be remembered, was refused admission to the Abbey, and died soon afterwards. Constable, now back in Hampstead, noted the fact of the coronation on the back of a sketch made on the evening of the same day.

Close, Salisbury. July 19, 1821.

King George the IV crowned this day!

My dear Constable;

    Your picture is hung up in a temporary way at Tinneys till his new room is finished. It excites *great interest* & attention. The work has got much together. How does the hay wain look now that it has got into your room again? I want to see it there. For how can one participate in a scene of fresh water & deep noon day shade in the crowded copal atmosphere of the Exhibition: which is always to me like a great pot of boiling varnish. We are not come, but coming to this place in a few days. The immediate object of this letter is to ask you in your visits to the Thames to purchase me a cheap wherry for the river here. I would not go to the expence of many pounds. You as a millwright of course are a judge of the state of repair of a boat. There is a little effort of expiring radicalism in the place today: but it will come to nothing. I preached before the Mayor & Corporation today & got credit. We dine together in ½ an hour and tomorrow I return home to Osmington: whither you must direct your answer. Mind, the boat is for the use of Miss Webber & Miss Cookson, so exert yourself for ancient love's sake. Dont let your wife see that last sentence.

Yours very sincerely
John. Fisher.

I expect you here any time between 1st September & 1st January. Begin your picture *earlier* this year, & let your mind have time to work. You never allow yourself opportunity for correction & polish.—

With reference to the next letter Leslie explains that it was then the practice of private collectors to lend their pictures to the Royal Academy for artists to copy. John Julius Angerstein, a London merchant of Russian extraction, was one of the leading collectors of his day, whose pictures eventually went to the founding of the National Gallery. Constable had already been to his house in Pall Mall on Farington's advice, for the purpose of studying the Claudes. The one here mentioned must have been that now called *A Seaport at Sunset*, originally painted for Cardinal Giorio.

No 2 The Lower Terrace, Hampstead
August 4. 1821.

My dear Fisher

I had the pleasure of receiving your letter dated the day of the (glorious as it proved) coronation of G. IV. I shall reply to it in order first.

I have attended to your request of a boat, which is not without its difficulties—as you cannot have all perfections in one. That which I have fixed upon (subject to your decision) is a *skiff*, sixteen feet long, & 5 feet wide. It will carry six "sitters" with either one or two rowers, is new & well built, *safe*—sound—and *steady*. The price 25 guineas, including oars & skulls. Sails would be an additional expense.

I had a friend with me and we saw many. We both agreed that there was nothing else likely. It will last for ever. But whatever you decide upon will you let me know as soon as possible, as they (Godfrey & Searl near Westminster Bridge) will keep it for me. There were some beautifull funnys but they are so crank they will drown your ladies, & there will be no fun in that. Will you write to me at this place according to the direction above, as it will reach me a day sooner. I am as much here possible with my dear family. My placid & contented companion with her three infants are well. I have got a room at the glaziers down town as a workshop where is my large picture—and at this little place I have [sundry] small works going on —for which purpose I have cleared a small shed in the garden, which held sand, coals, mops & brooms & that is literally a coal hole, and have made it a workshop, & a place of refuge—when I am down from the house. I have done a good deal of work here.

I have fitted up my new drawing rooms in Keppel Street & intend keeping them in order, hanging up only decent works. My large picture looks well in them but I shall do more to it—indeed you will be surprized at the good looks of all my concerns, & still more when I tell you that I am going to pay my court to the world, if not for their sakes yet very much for my own. I have had experience enough to know that if a man decries himself he will find enough to take him at his word.

Sir G. Beaumont is going abroad, to Italy. He has presented me with a beautifull little landscape, a mill (the same mill is in Tinny's picture). It is a Rembrant full of tone & chiaro oschuro. He has given it to me as a mark of his regard, and my old acquaintance. Collins is going into Devonshire. . . . &c. &c. He has just finished a "Landscape" I expect him tomorrow with his mother to see us.

There is some hope of getting a landscape, from Mr Angersteins—the large & most magnificent Marine, one of the most perfect pictures in the world—should that be the case, though I can ill afford it, I will make a copy, a facsimile—a "study" only will be of value but to myself—the other will be real property to my children and a great delight to you & me—the very doing of it will almost bring one in communication with Claude himself & with whose great spirit I may seem to hold commune.

Lawrence told me that should I really wish it, it would stimulate him to further exertions to get it of Mr. Angerstein.

When I left town last evening it was strongly reported that the Queen was dead. I have not had it confirmed today. Manning[1] said her symptoms were bad. I most [greatly] wish this "ill fated lady" (Walter Scotts expression) was in heaven. I hope they will bury Alderman Wood with her dead or alive—he was for once abashed by being hissed & hooted, & called "blackguard"—in the procession.[2]

We are quite alarmed for poor Catherine, who is we fear going to follow poor Sam, in a decline.[3] She has many bad symptoms which she

---

[1] An apothecary who lived near Constable.
[2] Queen Caroline had gone to live with Alderman Wood in South Audley Street after her return in 1820.
[3] Catherine Bicknell, Maria's sister: their brother Samuel was already dead.

has had long. They are going to try Cornwall. I have just read a copy of poor Sams will. He divides his property equally among his 3 sisters, after his "*debts*" are paid.

Will you be able to read this unconscionable letter? My wife desires her best regards to your Mrs F & Miss Cookson in which I most sincerely join. I am my dear Fisher

Yours truly,
J Constable.

Pray lose no time in writing to me. The boats on the Thames [sketches of each type are given] are a wherry—next a funny—next a skiff—which though not so fast is more steady & safe—uniting all qualities. In the room where I am writing are hanging up two small drawings by Cousins, one a wood, close, & very solemn—the one a view from Visuvius, looking inland, over Portici, very lovely. I borrowed them from my neighbour Mr Woodburn to keep me awake. Cousins was all poetry—& your drawing is a lovely specimen.

Ever your sincerely
John Constable.

Fisher's next letter is mutilated, the reason being that the top half of the first sheet contained a draft, which has been cut out for presentation at the bank.

My dear Constable:

Above I send you a draft, as a pittance towards the liquidation of my debt to you.—I thank you for your exertions in the purchase of my boat. If I had not supposed that your Waterloo would carry you down to the Thames frequently, I would not have hampered you with the commission. The skiff is just the thing but too expensive for me. I do not intend to give more than £10 or 12 pound for my boat. And my idea was, that you might see at Roberts's a second hand . . . [back of draft missing] . . . similar importance & necessity . . . Cicero's copy. For any body could transcribe that has patience, but very few can copy Claude. I exhort you to it by all means. It will be securing two or three hundred pounds to your family & will furnish *us* with an inexhaustible store of pleasure. I get impatient to know whether your wife will allow you to run down here this Autumn. Any time from Sepr. 1 to Janry 1 will be convenient to me & you need not be at any expence *at all*. One night in the Mail & you are here. The assizes are holding: and Coleridge[1] is here. Your letter lay on the table. He said that there were *some parts* of your last picture good, I told him that if (he) had said that *all* the parts were good, it would be no compliment, unless he had said the *whole* was good. Is it not strange how

---

[1] Sir John Taylor Coleridge, later a judge, was presumably now on circuit as a barrister, having been called to the bar in 1819.

utterly ignorant the world is of the very first principles of painting? Here is a man of the first abilities, who knows almost every thing, & yet is as little a judge of a picture as if he had been without eyes. There's Matthews again with "his own Glover". I am going to dine with the Judges. Adieu. My kind regards to your wife & my god-daughter. My wife joins me.

Yours very sincerely

John. Fisher.

Close. Salisbury
Augst. 6. 1821.

Constable's next letter introduces a new character, young David Charles Read, a drawing master of Salisbury, whom he seems to have met and encouraged in 1820—with unfortunate results, as things eventually turned out.

Hampstead, Sepr. 20 1821.

My dear Fisher,

I have been every day for weeks past intending to write to you, and my constant occupation I cannot offer for neglecting to reply to your last kind and *considerate* letter. The draft for 20 £ on Twinings came most opportunely. I have worked hard on several *jobs*[1] merely for something for my family to meet our additional expenses here, amounting to about 50 or 60 £, but have not been able to get the money for any one of them. Sir Thos. Neave came the nearest who did write to *know* what he was in my debt, but he is gone to Italy (without paying) as I hear.[2]

I am fearfull I disappointed you about the boat—had I known your price I could have succeeded immediately as I have since seen several second hand boats that would have suited you—a funny is the same price as a skiff but calculated for rowers only as there is no seat for another person.

How much I should like to come to you and I cannot say I will not. But I know I must go into Suffolk soon on account of a *job*.[3] But I will not say no, for I long for your company. You are my grand stimulus to exertion—and I have little regard for popularity, or to be run after by Ignorance. I work for excellence—and independent of my *jobs* I have done some studies, carried further than I have yet done any, particularly a natural (but highly elegant) group of trees, ashes, elms & oak &c—which will be of quite as much service as if I had bought the feild and hedge row, which contains them, and perhaps one time or another will fetch as much for my children.[4] It is rather larger than a kit-cat, & upright. I have

---

[1] The term implies an irksome commission, usually for a portrait.
[2] Of Dagnam Park, Essex. It will be found that the money was duly paid.
[3] Probably for the purpose of securing a commission for an altar-piece about which his brother Abram had written to him.
[4] This is generally supposed to be *Trees near Hampstead Church*, bequeathed by his daughter Isabel to the Victoria and Albert Museum: the estimate of its value is perhaps not far out.

likewise made many *skies* and effects—for I wish it could be said of me as Fuselli[1] says of Rembrandt, "he followed nature in her calmest abodes and could pluck a flower on every hedge—yet he was born to cast a stedfast eye on the bolder phenomena of nature". We have had noble clouds & effects of light & dark & color—as is always the case in such seasons as the present.

The great Claude does not come to the Academy this year. You will smile at the cause which hinders it—"*a young Lady*" is *copying* it—but they expect it another year. It would have been madness for me to have meddled with it this season—as I am so much behind hand with the Bridge, which I have great hindrances in. I cannot do it here—& I must leave my family & work in London—and I can hear nothing from Savile, who I believe is crazy.[2] All that family are come to ruin—so awfully just is the scripture—for a bigger rogue than the father never came to or escaped the gallows.

While sitting at breakfast the other morning we were surprized by the appearance of a singular figure with a portfolio under his arm. His waving locks on his shoulders, white hat, long great coat, large shoes with small buckles on the sides &c. surprized all my females, but it was poor Read the Salisbury artist—he is anxious to do something & I am glad to hear that the Miss Salesbures are kind to him. His studies have merit— could you show him civility? He has been shamefully treated by his friend (& *brother Baptist*) *little Linnell* the *artist*.[3] I wish to lend him my little copy of Tenniers (will you mention it to the ladies at the palace) when it [is] at leisure. Has Miss Fisher copied it? It is a pretty tone but rather too hot. Read is going to send me some copies he has made at Lord Pembrokes —I want to see how they are.

The beautiful Ruisdael of the "Windmill and log-house"[4] which we admired at the Gallery is left there for the use of students—I trust I shall be able to procure a memorandum of it—& there is a noble N. Poussin at the Academy—a solemn, deep, still, summer's noon—with large umbrageous trees, & a man washing his feet at a fountain near them—through the breaks of the trees is mountain scenery & clouds collecting about them with the most enchanting effects possible—indeed it is the most affecting picture I almost ever stood before.[5] It cannot surely be saying too much when I assert that his landscape is full of religious & moral feeling, & shows how much of his own nature God has implanted in the mind of man. It is not large—about 3½ feet—and I should like, & will if possible

---

[1] Henry Fuseli, the Swiss Professor of Painting at the Royal Academy.
[2] The son of one of Constable's uncles by marriage, formerly Christopher Atkinson.
[3] For Linnell's side of the story, see A. T. Story's *Life of John Linnell*, 1892, Vol. I, pp. 125–127, 131–137.
[4] *Evening Landscape a Windmill by a Stream*, bought for the Prince Regent, and still in the Royal Collection.
[5] Leslie says the picture went to the National Gallery: if so, it must be *Landscape with Figures*, no. 40, presented by Sir George Beaumont in 1826.

possess a fac simile of it. I must make time—the opportunity will not happen again. If I cannot come to you I will send you the *results* of this summers study.

My wife with the children are all well—we have not had an hours illness all the summer. She begs to join with me in best regards to yourself Mrs. Fisher and all your family. I am dear Fisher

always yours John Constable

My best compls to Tinny—does he like the picture? Bloomfield[1] wrote to Mr Bicknell to say that it was time the King should get away from Ireland, as they were getting so very free. The good nature of the King was so great—one man pushed through the crowd & was prevented shaking hands with the King—but the King saw him & put his hand out of the window & reached him, which so delighted the man that holding up his hand he vehemently exclaimed—"*by Jasus—this hand shall never be washed again*".

'The Bridge' to which Constable refers is the wooden foot-bridge up-stream from Flatford Mill, already introduced into one of his earlier pictures. As with *The Hay Wain*, he was now engaged on one of his large rough studies[2] by way of a preliminary to the finished picture which would appear in next year's exhibition. This sketch was engraved by Lucas as *The River Stour, Suffolk*.

Of greater interest, perhaps, is the reference to the studies of sky effects which Constable had been making. There are a large number of cloud paintings done at Hampstead in the late summers of 1821 and 1822, inscribed with careful notes of the time and the direction of the wind. Leslie had twenty of them, on one of which (belonging to the following year) Constable had written: 'Very appropriate for the coast at Osmington.'[3] Constable's interest in the sky is generally attributed to early training in a windmill, and no doubt this quickened his observation: but the influence may have been exaggerated, and Dr. Kurt Badt has shown the possibility of another explanation.[4] It was Luke Howard who laid down the fundamental classifications of cloud structure, and his work had been communicated to a wider public for the first time between 1818 and 1820. This, however, has little to do with the Fishers—unless Constable and the Archdeacon had been discussing the subject on their recent tour. It was evidently, as they say, 'in the air'.

On the 26th September, says Leslie, Fisher wrote to tell Constable of the objections made to the sky in Mr. Tinney's picture, by a 'grand critical party' who had sat in judgment on it. The letter went on:

After talking in vain for some time, I brought them out of my portfolio two prints from Wouvermans and a Van der Neer, where the whole stress

---

[1] Sir Benjamin, later Lord Bloomfield, who had been a confidant of George IV as Prince Regent.
[2] Now at the Royal Holloway College, Egham.
[3] Now at the National Gallery of Victoria, Melbourne.
[4] *John Constable's Clouds*, 1950. Howard's book was *The Climate of London*, which begins with the *Essay on Clouds*.

was laid on the sky, and that silenced them. While in every other profession the initiated only are judges, in painting, all men, except the blind, think themselves qualified to give an opinion. The comfort is, that the truth comes out when these self-made connoisseurs begin to buy and collect for themselves. At Lord Shaftesbury's, about twelve miles from this place,[1] there is a daylight Van der Neer. When you come we will go and see it. I had nearly forgotten to tell you that I was the other day fishing in the New Forest in a fine, deep, broad river, with mills, roaring backwaters, withy beds, &c. I thought often of you during the day. I caught two pike, was up to the middle in watery meadows, and was as happy as when I was "a careless boy". What have you done with your "Midsummer Noon",[2] and what do you intend to do with it?

The main parts of Constable's next letter[3] are well known. It contains one of his most important enunciations of artistic principle.

Hampstead 23^d Octr. 1821.

My dear Fisher

I trust you will pardon this delay of mine in replying to your last long and very kind letter—I fully expected to have been with you at this time—but I have had many interruptions but what has prevented me has been a good deal of Indisposition in my family. which has made it almost impossible for me to leave home. Our time expires at this place this month —and when I have settled my family in Keppel Street I shall be able to make you a Visit for a few days, should it be then convenient to you to receive me.

I have not been Idle and have made more particular and general study than I have ever done in one summer, but I am most anxious to get into my London painting room, for I do not consider myself at work without I am before a six foot canvas—I have done a good deal of skying—I am determined to conquer all dificulties and that most arduous one among the rest, and now talking of skies—[we cannot but (*deleted*)]

It is quite amusing and interesting to us to see how admirably you fight their battles you certainly take the best possible ground for getting your friend out of a scrape—"(the examples of the great masters)". That Landscape painter who does not make his skies a very material part of his composition—neglects to avail himself of one of his greatest aids. Sir Joshua Reynolds speaking of the "Landscape" of Titian & Salvator & Claude—says *"Even their skies seem to sympathise with the Subject"*. I have often been advised to consider my *Sky*—as a *"White Sheet drawn*

---

[1] St. Giles' House.
[2] This refers to the title under which *The Hay Wain* was exhibited (*Landscape—Noon*).
[3] Presented by Sir Kenneth Clark to the Minories, Colchester.

behind the Objects". Certainly if the Sky is *obtrusive*—(as mine are) it is bad, but if they are *evaded* (as mine are not) it is worse, they must and always shall with me make an effectual part of the composition. It will be difficult to name a class of Landscape, in which the sky is not the "*key note*", the *standard of* "*Scale*", and the chief "*Organ of sentiment*". You may conceive then what a "*white sheet*" woud do for me, impressed as I am with these notions, and they cannot be Erroneous. The sky is the "*source of light*" in nature—and governs every thing. Even our common observations on the weather of every day, are suggested by them but it does not occur to us. Their difficulty in painting both as to composition and execution is very great, because with all their brilliancy and conse-quence, they ought not to come forward or be hardly thought about in a picture—any more than extreme distances are.

But these remarks do not apply to *phenomenon*—or what the painters call *accidental Effects of Sky*—because they always attract particularly.

I hope you will not think [me (*deleted*)] I am turned critic instead of painter. I say all this *to you* though you do not want to be told—that I know very well what I am about, & that my skies have not been neglec-ted though they often failed in execution—and often no doubt from over anxiety about them—which alone will destroy that [the ease of not (*deleted*)] Easy appearance which nature always has—in all her movements.

Again talking of criticism have you seen *John Bull* of Sunday week. Poor Ward (but he is too far gone) will certainly hang himself—as a man (to those who know him) is much liked—but he is not at all pitied in this great picture & catalogue (for they should not be mentioned apart.) It is grevious he should have had the temerity to [do it. Haydon has not escaped (*deleted*)] meddle with such things—poor Haydon who nobody either pities or likes,[1] has not escaped but though he deserves much he has in this motion—only got a lash by a chance swing of the whip. *Ja^s Ward Esqr. R.A.* has been an author before. He wrote an account of an Old Woman in Staffordshire who lived six months—on counting her fingers and sucking the bed cloths.

How strange it is that we should prefer raising up all manner of diffi-culties in painting—to truth and common sense.

How much I can Imagine myself with you on your fishing excursion in the new forest, what River can it be. But the sound of water escaping from Mill dams, so do Willows, Old rotten Banks, slimy posts, & brickwork. I love such things—Shakespeare could make anything poetical—he men-tions "poor Tom's" haunts among *Sheep cots*—& *Mills*—the Water[mist? & the Hedge pig. As long as I do paint I shall never cease to paint such Places.[2] They have always been my delight—& I should indeed have

---

[1] See S.R. IV, p. 234.
[2] Indeed, his last great painting, on which he was engaged at the time of his death, was of just such a subject—Arundel Mill.

delighted in seeing what you describe [with you (*deleted*)] in your company "in the company of a man to whom nature does not spread her volume or utter her voice in vain".

But I should paint my own places best—Painting is but another word for feeling. I associate my "careless boyhood" to all that lies on the banks of the *Stour*. They made me a painter (& I am gratefull) that is I had often thought of pictures of them before I had ever touched a pencil, and your picture is one of the strongest instances I can recollect of it. But I will say no more—for I am fond of being an Egotist, in whatever relates to painting.

Does not the cathedral look very beautiful amongst the Golden foliage, its silvery grey must sparkle in it. Poor Read has sent me some copies made at Wilton, the Claude & a Van de Velde—they are very far from bad, and very much better than I expected. I only wished you to call on him, nothing Else. Your advice, & notice of him could not fail of being of service to him, in a matter in which the World is led by appearances—I hope he is getting a living. He seems industrious. I have requested the loan of the little Tenniers at the Miss Fishers for him to Copy. It is a Good Tone but rather too hot on the Right hand side.

My wife and children are now quite well, the former & my eldest boy having been great invalids. We sincerely hope Mrs. Fisher & all your Children and relations our good friends at Salisbury are well. Is the *Portrait* of which you make such laughable mention, still running the Gauntlet at the Publick House. What can the Good Bishop be about. But you fully account for all the scrape—the worst I should fear is that some of the dignity of his High Station must go with it—but I will say no more—that *love of patronage* which you mention, brought me known to you, and your excellent family, & which has brought with it most of the great blessings of my life. I long to get to work. I shall do another large Work of my Own, & Savile's picture[1]—but that is a dead pall. He is not only a fool, but he is as Crazy as a fool can be.

My last year's work has got much *together*. This weather has blown & washed the *powder off*. I do not know what I shall do with it—but I love my children to[o] well to expose them to the taunts of the Ignorant—though they shall never flinch from honourable competition. I have just paper enough to say adieu—& add my Wife's (who is sitting by me) best regards to yourself and all your family. I am yours

John Constable

Close Salisbury. Oct. 24. 1821.[2]

My dear Constable:

I had a most agreeable breakfast this morning, your letter serving me in lieu of my newspaper which is much too dull now to read. I was

---

[1] See S.R. I, p. 201.
[2] This letter is in a private collection.

glad to see your hand writing so clear & smooth. A certain proof of a tranquil mind.

I shall be alone and disengaged on Saturday the third of November: and continue so untill 26th of the same month. I think the earlier you come the better: and that I may be disturbed by a visitor latterly who would be a tie upon our pursuits. I project if the weather be fine to go & see Winchester Cathedral. The roof has been nearly falling in: owing to the constant cutting the 4 great supporting pillars to let in monuments (of folly & bad taste). I am told that the *hire* of the timber to "shore up" the roof amounts to £400, some say £700.

I was delighted with John Bull & was going to write to you on the spur of the moment, but deferred it & so the enthusiasm went off. It was well done particularly the opening description of the difficulties of making even a *bad* picture.

Our Cathedral looks well this weather: but is not so much releived by the warm tints as you would imagine. Owing to the moisture of the season & the rapid decomposition of the vegetation there is a constant humid halo, which makes the shadows at all hours very blue & cold & gives the Landscape a cold tone.

I am sorry your children have been unwell. Mine are in high health & good humour. How many dinners a week does your wife get you to eat at a regular hour & like a Christian? My wife sends her kind regards—

My dear Constable, yours faithfully

John. Fisher.

The next letter[1] from Constable to Fisher is the only one which later on remained with the recipient's family.

Hampstead Nov[r] 3[d] 1821

My dear Fisher,

I had the pleasure of receiving your letter from Hungerford. It has happened that our stay at this place is prolonged a week, which has preventd my being with you today as I had intended but Mr Bicknell will send the carriage for my Children on Tuesday next, and I shall be really glad to see them once more housed in Keppel Street.

On Thursday I shall take my journey to you by the little Salisbury which Ellen tells me leaves S[t] Clements at 6 [morg] & arrives at 8 [Evg] at Salisbury —and I now really believe that before 9 oclock on Nov[r] the 8th I shall be enjoying my tea with you & Mrs Fisher laughing at all the anxieties I have left.

---

[1] In the collection of Mr. T. Besterman.

Talking of anxieties past, on Monday there will be two associates elected at the Academy.[1] I hear there is a more than usual tribulation, the candidates being both numerous and powerfull. Leslie passed the day with me here not long ago—had I a vote, I should be happy to have found him on the list of candidates as my conscience would have then been safe. Collins came to town on Thursday, he called on you as he passed through Salisbury. I think I shall be able to get you some information that may be usefull respecting the painted glass—as I know an excellent artist in that way who some few years ago came from Birmingham and fixed in Newman Street, and who was very much recommended to me by Mr. Lewis.[2] He often has large assortments of Antient Glass—& often Historical subjects. I hope the Chapter will meet with such as all the modern glass which I have yet seen, makes me sick. "It is new wine in old bottles". The antient *Gothick* Glass is very rare—that from Abert Durer and the Century onwards is the most common & rich (like Kings College) but still not equal in taste to the Gothick Glass. I have always heard the corosions you speak of attributed to the same cause as that Dr Fowler mentions. I will do all I can for you in this matter.

You are always in luck in the beautifull places you come to—and I have often said such are my delight. The mill at Gillingham was beautifully situated, but do not you run some hazard often? My wife was alarmed when she read an account of your fishing excurtion in the New Forest— "when Mr Fisher *got up to his 'Ancles'* . . . but she was glad to find you was safe" . . .

It is quite dangerous to attempt writing to you, I find I have so much to relieve my mind of on all subjects. I have lately read Miss Grahams life on N. Pousin[3]—much more might be said on such a glorious subject, but still it amply proves how much dignity & elevation of character was the result of such patient, persevering and rational study—no circumstances however impropitious could turn him to the right or left—because he knew what he was about—& he felt himself above every scene in which he was placed—but such is the officiousness of the world that even "*Nichola Pousin*" was not without his *advisors* and *patrons*—but he had some *real patrons*, elegant & superior men who were his friends and who thought themselves the gainers when they allowed his judgement to exceed theirs in that study in which he had been all his life successfully engaged. Nothing but the greatest vanity and assumption could have brought forward our own Glover to remedy the defects of such a painter as Pousin—

---

[1] The elections for Associates were always held in November. Leslie was elected.

[2] In 1818 Henry Greswolde Lewis had written to say that Mr. Lowe, successor and conductor of Eginton's painted glass manufactory at Handsworth, was about to take up his residence in Newman Street and had asked to be made known to Constable as a brother artist. Lewis had recommended him as 'a very ingenious clever man': see S.R. IV, p. 57.

[3] Maria Graham (Lady Calcott) published her *Memoirs of the Life of Nicholas Poussin* in 1820.

but we have seen it done & by a man of education—but who was unwilling to appear ignorant of a peculiar profession. My wife desires her best regards and believe me truly yours.

John Constable

I have not seen Collins but he speaks in raptures of his tour—I shall be glad to see his studies. Frank[1] is much engaged cleaning pictures—which he does most skilfully. I wholly recommend him now poor Mr. Bigg[2] is scarcely equal to what he already has. I shall say nothing about the glass to Frank 'till I have seen you.

The last day of Octr was indeed lovely so much so that I could not paint for looking—my wife was walking with me all the middle of the day on the beautifull heath. I made two evening effects. The panorama of this place include what I have named—and has the addition of the finest fore-

grounds—in roads, heath, trees, ponds &c & every description of mooveable—both dead and alive.

I open my letter again to say how much I shall like to see Winchester—should that be still your plan. Thank you for the mention of Sir Th^s Neave—they sent the money & an additional present of 4 shillings over—which like N. Pousin I cannot return. I have children, he had none.

Constable followed his letter down to Salisbury, presumably on the 8th November. On the 12th he and Fisher went over to Winchester, where Constable thought the cathedral the most magnificent he had ever seen, much more impressive though not so beautiful as the one at Salisbury. The town he found better suited for an artist than Salisbury and he made a few drawings in his sketch-book.[3] On the 13th they returned to Salisbury and the next day being fine he and Fisher walked over to Longford to see the Claudes.

The Bishop and his family, he heard, were away in Devonshire, where Elizabeth had indulged in what seems to have been a family habit of falling off a horse. Another absentee was Mr. Tinney, who had gone up to London in preparation

---

[1] Frank Collins, brother of the artist.
[2] W. R. Bigg, R.A. had been forced by poverty to make a living by restoring pictures: see S.R. IV, pp. 244-6.
[3] For example, Victoria and Albert Museum, nos. 237 and 238. The book measured $6\frac{1}{4} \times 9\frac{1}{4}$ inches.

for his marriage to a widow of thirty-two whom he had known since childhood. The lady was much approved by all his acquaintances except Fisher, who did not consider the match high enough for a gentleman of whom he held such a very high opinion—and deservedly so, added Constable, who was to change his opinion later. His liking was returned.

My dear Sir

I hope you will not have left Salisbury when I return next week as I am really anxious to express my gratitude to you in my own house. Nothing short of necessity would take me from home while you are here, but necessity acknowledges no superior power.

I should be glad to put the Archdeacon aside for then you would probably come to me.

At present I can only regret my involuntary absence and request that you will consider me as

truly and faithfully, your obliged

J. P. Tinney

14 November, 1821

It was not until Constable had been away for a week that he found time to write to his wife—very unlike the Bishop, he said, who had written every day to Mrs. Fisher when the Constables had been there the year before. 'Fisher has been to two great dinners, running,' he reported, 'which makes him very wild, restless and uncomfortable to himself—as you know.' There was to be a small party at Leydenhall on the 16th, over which old Benson was quite enthusiastic, but he hoped to be home by the 18th at the latest. Since, however, he did a small open-air oil-sketch[1] of the cathedral from Harnham on the 19th, the fine weather may have tempted him to stop on till Tinney's return from London.

Having returned to town, Constable was kept hard at work during the winter, engaged on his new painting of the bridge at Flatford.

1822

Fisher begins the new year with an omen in his suggestion of an excursion to Paris, though in fact the visit never took place.

My dear Constable

Have the goodness to put the enclosed into John Bulls box.[2] It contains money. Perhaps you will do it next time you go down to Somerset House. If the waters permit us, we intend to be in London next Tuesday.

---

[1] In the Peterkin Collection, U.S.A.
[2] *John Bull* was a weekly journal, specializing in libellous comments: its politics were ultra-Tory.

Coxe[1] has determined to publish his life of Corregio. I have half persuaded him to dedicate it to the President & Royal Acads.

Will you go to Paris with me next June for a week (if your wife will let you)?

Yours truly

John. Fisher.

Dodsworth[2] wishes to know whether Sir. Th: Lawrence will purchase his Corregio on *your* recommendation.

Close Salisbury. Jany 2. 1822.   I wish a good new picture this year.

In his reply, which has been lost, it appears that Constable referred to the newly elected Academicians.

The February elections at the Royal Academy had indeed provided something of a scandal. There had been two places to fill, and no great competition, so that Constable had seemed to stand a reasonable chance of being elected. In the first election he had been overwhelmingly defeated by Richard Cook, a student of the same year as himself, who married a rich wife and never exhibited again after 1819. When it came to the voting for the second vacancy, the Academician Thomas Daniell, a landscape painter known chiefly for his aquatints of the East, had been able to secure the election of his own nephew William Daniell.

Osmington, Weymouth. Feb. 16. 1822.

My dear Constable

When your letter reached me I was in the agonies of moving from Salisbury to Osmington. I am very sorry the Academy has injured the value of its diploma's so much, since I had always a feeling of respect for the body. As far as the members can bring to a level merit & impotence, Wilkie & Daniels are now upon a par. I say nothing of you: because the title of R A will never weigh a straw in that balance in which you are ambitious to be found heavy, namely the judgement of posterity. You are painting for a name to be remembered hereafter: for the time when men shall talk of Wilson & Vanderneer & Ruisdale & Constable in the same breath. And do not let your vision be diverted from this North star, by the rubs & ragged edges of the world which will hitch in every mans garment as he hustles through life.

I have often told you that you may judge of the state of a mans mind by the appearance of his hand writing. You may perceive that mine is very tranquil. This place acts upon me like a charm in allaying all irritation. I have been here now four days & have not seen one being except my own family. To day is bright & delicious. The sea a deep blue. The shingle bank a bright gold, & the cliffs in brilliant patches of green owing to the constant rain.

---

[1] The Archdeacon of Wiltshire.

[2] William Dodsworth was a verger at the cathedral, with a partiality for rum. Besides being a collector he wrote a book about the cathedral.

G

You have often talked of an emerald in a dish of rubbish.[1] Old iron, bits of rag, flints, broken glass or tarnished lace. Such is the appearance of your picture at Salisbury.[2] The room which in it's proportions is magnificent is furnished exactly like the best parlour of an opulent pawnbroker. An enormous brass chandelier with twenty branches: a clock stuck round with gilt cupids like the chimney peice ornaments in the breakfast scene of Marriage a la mode. And to crown all, the walls covered with pannels of brown varnish yclept "old masters".

The light on your picture is excellent, it receives the South sun standing on the Western wall.—[Sketch of the room, with *Stratford Mill* hanging on a level with the spectator's head below a Venetian picture from Canon Douglas's collection: on one side is "A Douglas lake peice copied by Miss Benson" and on the other a picture marked "rubbish".] However it puts out all the other pictures & attracts general attention & will do you much service.

Do not let the frivolous errands & jobs of Seymour Street divert you from your grand picture. You *must shame* the Academy. If you can run down here on the Mail any time this season i.e. before October I shall be delighted. Mrs F. is sorry she cannot ask Mrs. C to the honeymoon spot. But we lie here three in a bed. I shall put you out. By the bye I owe you for your Salisbury journey. Beleive me my dear friend

yours most affectionately

John. Fisher.

Coxe is going on with Ant. Allegro's life. I was glad however to escape him he bothered me so.

Osmington Weymouth. Mar. 25. 1822.

My dear Constable:

Not having heard of you lately my imagination has been lively. I have conceived that you have been hard at work on a six foot canvass, that you have outdone yourself: & having thus got the Royal Academy into a corner that you are poking your brush in their faces. This is at least what I wish you to do.

In your next walk pray call at Colnaghi's & desire him, with my thanks for his credit, to present my draft for payment. He will find it duly honoured. Coxe is on the eve of publishing Corregio: but he has got some sad stuff in it, about the manner in which he is supposed to have mixed his colours; & talks about his painting on gold leaf to produce a warm effect. He will send you by my advice the proof sheets of that part of his work which treats of Corregio's ART, for your correction. You will then have

---

[1] Compare the opening passage of the lecture delivered by Constable before the Literary and Scientific Institution at Hampstead on the 25th July 1836.
[2] That is, *Stratford Mill* in Tinney's drawing-room.

your name probably in the preface. When you have leisure, let me know what is doing in Suffolk: and whether these riotous proceedings are to be dreaded.[1] One word will satisfy me. Do you lose by the reduction of the 5 per cents? We have been all ill with fever cold & cough. Two of my children alarmingly so. But I got them safe through by the old plan. Calomel, Jalap, & the Warm Bath; and they now look as well as ever. My wife expects her confinement the first weeks in April. What is your family history? I go to my Visitation the 21st. 22nd. & 23rd. of May. I expect you to go with me.—Beg Ellen[2] to take the enclosed as directed. Criddle lives nearly opposite Longs hotel.

Mar. 26

The above was written yesterday. I left off, trying to recollect some anecdote I had to tell you. I have just recalled it to my memory. It is, as you know part of the apocalypse that Xt should reign 1,000 years, & then the consummation of all things. In consequence of this prediction, during the 10th century, there was an universal expectation that the world was about to end. The agitation of mens minds is described by contemporary writers as extreme. Among other effects which the expectation produced was the neglect to repair their houses & churches. So that when the dreaded period was past, their buildings were found to be in a most dilapidated condition. The 11th century was therefore much occupied in repairing rebuilding & beautifying. Hence we know, at least, that few of our buildings can be older than this period. And that the 11 century & beginning of the 12th C. is a probable period to which to refer back many of our most beautiful structures.

It was the same cause that enriched the Church & made it so powerful. Men expecting the day of judgement were glad to compound for their sins by granting away their estates (which would no longer be of use to them or their heirs) to religious purposes—

Under another cover I send you a communication for John Bull which I will thank you to put privately into his box. It should be done speedily. Mrs. F sends her kind regards to Mrs Constable & Emma hopes "Don Tuntable is bery mell".[3] Beleive me

yours very faithfully

John. Fisher.

Do you think of coming down
here any time this year?

The year of the following note is not given, but it must have followed the last, accompanied by another letter for *John Bull*.

---

[1] Agrarian unrest.
[2] A servant of the Constables.
[3] The message was probably to young John Constable, now aged four.

My dear Constable,

Pray send the enclosed to its destination. I do not apologise for troubling you in the good cause. I dreamt incessantly of you & your painting room last night. I had eaten grossly. You had nearly filled . . . & were particularly ostentatious of a new palette of most beautiful wood. Is this ominous. Or is the picture a good one. My wife sadly delays her accouchment.

Yours truly

John. Fisher.

Osmington. April 9.

Why did you not write to me on Easter Sunday?

We may now turn to see whither all these omens were tending. At the beginning of the year Constable had sent *The Hay Wain* to the British Gallery, where the price was apparently fixed at 150 guineas. It was there seen by John Arrowsmith, a picture-dealer of English origin domiciled in Paris. He had probably heard of it already from Nodier or one of the other numerous French visitors who had been coming over to England since peace was restored between the two countries. Arrowsmith then paid a call at Keppel Street with a view to purchase: but since it was generally understood that the prices asked at the British Gallery were not to be taken too seriously, he began with a tentative offer. This attempt at bargaining must have been all the more exasperating to Constable since he was at this time undergoing a more than usually severe financial strain. It is true that there had been welcome accessions to his capital, but there had also been additions to his family; he was naturally anxious not to break into the capital for the sake of which he had sacrificed so many years of married life, wishing to preserve it intact for the future protection of his wife and children; and now there had come the heavy expense of maintaining a second establishment at Hampstead during the summer. His chief fear at this moment seems to have been that a whole winter's work spent on one of his large pictures might prove to have been wasted: for he had not yet found another patron on the same generous scale as that shown by the Archdeacon in his purchases. It was in this despondent mood that he wrote his next letter to Fisher.

April 13. 1822.

My dear Fisher—

I have made many attempts to write to you—more than a fortnight since I sent to Seymour St. for a cover to you & did not succeed—and I find a letter of almost three sides dated the first Inst. which I did not send on that account—but I shall (on the receipt of your letter this morning) no longer delay sending this at once by post.

I received your letter (Mar 25.) on Friday 29 Mar: with the communication for John Bull—I walked down with it the same day—so that if there was anything he should have had before the delay was not mine. I shall go again this evening with the other. Ellen set off with alacrity for you with the note to Criddle, and I called on Colnaghi.

We are looking with anxiety to Mrs Fishers confinement and shall be glad to hear of it at first hand. We were concerned at hearing of the in-disposal in your family but hope all are now well—if your children are ever ill what is to become of mine—but thank God I have not had one of them ill a day since I saw you.

I have not yet seen any of the sheets of Mr Cox's Corregio—but I hear of a letter from him to Jackson mentioning a desire that they may be seen by *"his friend Mr Constable"*. There is no doubt but it will be interesting—and as to painting on gold grounds, some [rumours] are certainly afloat about it—but it is all over with the Alchemy of the art—I hope never to be revived again but dark ages may yet return and there will always be found dark minds in enlightened ones. All that relates to gold is this, if covered by opake colors it is of no consequence what the ground is. If used (for Glory &c) and made appear as a thing unconnected with the painting (& so far supernatural) it has always been done down as late as Carlo Dolci—where it sometimes appears very beautifull as blended with transparent color behind the formal saints &c—but still it looks like trick —but a Correggio was above all this. I do not beleive he ever resorted to any such nonsense to aid "his brightness"—which was indeed superhuman —with the exception of himself. I shall leave Correggio with his own words *"—and I too am a painter"*.

I have sent my large picture to the Academy. I never worked so hard before & now time was so short for me—it wanted much—but still I hope the work in it is better than any I have yet done—but hardly any body saw it. Collins told Manning, on his asking if it was not better than Con-stable had yet done, Collins said it was—that the sky was very beautiful and there were parts in it that could not be better—& finished the com-pliment by saying—"it is an acknowledgment in Constable that he was wrong before & that *we* were right, and I hope it will do him a great deal of good". Some of the parts were very nicely finished, but you see how painters compliment one another. His own pictures are unusually well painted this year—none better—but all complain of want of impression and sentiment—his canvas is certainly not affecting—though his pencil is firm and delicate but he is too great a man now for me to venture to anatomize.[1] Wilkies picture is gone to the Academy & Calcott sends two —Turner says none of his will be there. I hear of some excellent pictures of the Ex members.

I have had some nibbles at my large picture at the Gallery—it shuts on the 20th. I have a *professional* offer[2] of 70 £ for it (without the frame) to form part of an exhibition in Paris—to show them the nature of the English

---

[1] This refers to Collins's election as R.A. in 1820: it will be seen later in the letter that Constable was still smarting under his more recent failure to secure election in the past year.
[2] From Arrowsmith.

art. I hardly know what to do—it may promote my fame & procure commissions but it may not. It [is] property to my family—though I want the money dreadfully—

And on that subject I must beg a great favor of you (indeed I can do it of no other person) the loan [of] 20 or 30 £ would be of the greatest use to me at this time—as painting these large pictures have much impoverished me—if you can I know you will oblige me, if not say so.

This summer I shall devote to money getting, as I [have] several commissions—both landskip, and otherwise—but a large picture (& if possible a good one) was necessary this year—the next may take its chance. I hope, indeed I really beleive, I have never done anything as good as this one I have now sent—at least it has fewer objections that can be made to it. It is difficult to distinguish superiority in these things. Opie says of Titian— "if not the best painter he certainly has produced the best pictures in the world".

My brother is uncomfortable about the state of things in Suffolk. They are as bad as Ireland—"never a night without seeing fires near or at a distance", The *Rector* & his brother the *Squire* (Rowley & Godfrey)[1] have forsaken the village—no abatement of tithes or rents—four of Sir Wm. Rush's[2] tenants distrained next parish—these things are ill timed.

I am going into Suffolk about an altarpeice—a gift of compunction I hear from a gentleman who is supposed to have defrauded his family[3]— shall add this motto, from Shakespeare, "may this expiate".

Young Carpenters[4] wife has given him twin girls—poor fellow, he is quite low about it, but it has produced a conciliation with his iron father, which will help in the business.

It is delightfull for me to find my painting room a never failing source of amusement to you here or away. Dreams go there by opposites—I have not cleaned my pallet since the last picture. My Wife sends her fondest love to Mrs F.—& family. Tinney called here with his brother. I dined with them in Montague Place and was introduced to his [paper] wife—he had been a long time ill in London. He is annoyed by your designating his "Old Masters" *trash*—the proper name, he knows not how to estimate any others—he goes by the *rule* of "name".

---

[1] The Rev. Joshua Rowley had succeeded Dr. Rhudde in 1819 after acquiring the patronage of Brantham-cum-Bergholt and nominating himself as Rector. He was a son of Admiral Sir Joshua Rowley, and his sister Arabella had been the first wife of Peter Godfrey of Old Hall, Bergholt. The Rowleys owned land to the north of Langham Valley Farm.

[2] Sir William Beaumaris Rush had inherited an estate at Benhall in Suffolk, but preferred to live in Wimbledon.

[3] Edward Daniel Alston of Diss, a distant cousin of Constable, had offered to present the altar-piece to the parish of Manningtree: he was supposed to have got the better of a family dispute over property, but the true motive for the offer will be revealed later.

[4] William Hookham Carpenter, son of James Carpenter the bookseller: he later became Keeper of Prints in the British Museum: his wife, Margaret Sarah Geddes, the artist, was a sister of Mrs. William Collins.

Stodthard has published the beautiful etching of the shield—of Wellington[1]—3½ feet circle, 7 sheets, *price* 3.3.0—oblige me & my dear old friend
by purchasing one. He has been used infamously by Green & Ward,[2] who
wanted him to swallow his reputation—on the principle of their jewellers
or whitesmiths—wishing to make the world beleive that all art originates
& emanates from them.

My conscience acquits me as to any neglect of [my] last picture—I have
dismissed [it] with great calmness and ease of mind. Ever yours truly

my dear Fisher J. Constable

My close occupation soon made me forget the Academy business—I
have all the honor. I could not have got more—the disgrace was not mine,
but there was disgrace somewhere—Sir . . . told the Bp. "Mr C. ought to
have been elected".

The unposted letter of the 1st April which Constable mentions appears to have
contained a sketch of the changes which had been made in the composition of
the 'Bridge' since Fisher had seen the rough study during his promised visit in
January. Leslie, who describes the drawing as a beautiful pen-sketch having the
force of a mezzotint, gives it as part of the above letter, though it does not seem
to have been sent on to Fisher till the end of the month. He also adds the following extract, which does not appear in the original letter, but probably accompanied the sketch, and accurately describes the most notable differences between
the study (later the property of William Carpenter) and the finished picture:

"The composition is almost totally changed from what you saw. I have
taken away the sail, and added another barge in the middle of the picture,
with a principal figure, altered the group of trees, and made the bridge
entire. The picture has now a rich centre, and the right-hand side becomes
only an accessory."

Fisher meanwhile was having his own anxieties, his income having probably
been affected by the agricultural unrest of which a sample had just been reported
from Suffolk.

Osmington. Weymouth. April 16. 1822.
My dear Constable:

Mrs Fisher produced me another boy[3] on Thursday morning last,
& is now nearly recovered.

I send you the only disposeable 5 £ I have in the world. I am summonsed
to pay £500 on the 24 of June which has very much straitened me. But I

---

[1] Stothard's engraving of his own successful design for a shield commemorating the
victories of the Duke of Wellington, presented to the Duke in 1822 by the merchants
and bankers of London, who subscribed 7,000 guineas for the purpose. Stothard had
received 150 guineas.
[2] Green, Ward & Green of Ludgate Street, who executed the design in silver-gilt.
West had also objected to his treatment by them.
[3] Francis, born at Osmington on the 11th April.

have the prospect of a large sum of money soon of which you shall be a partaker. I take it kind & friendly that you have applied to me & hope that you will always continue to do so.

I wish you would write with a little more "force". Your letters melt into one another with beautiful & imperceptible gradation, that I cannot for my life make out your meaning. You will be too busy to go the Visitation with me? I am very much occupied preparing a sermon for the opening of Windsor Church.[1] I cannot therefore add more than that I am

yours very faithfully

John. Fisher.

Write to acknowledge this by return of post.

My dear Fisher

Keppel Street. April 17. 1822.

Accept my thanks for your very kind letters and our sincere congratulations on the safe accouchment of Mrs Fisher.

The contents of your letter will be highly usefull. As I told you I had been so long on unprofitable canvas that I was getting hard run—but I am now busy on some minor works which will bring things soon about again. We shall lose about 10 £ per an: on poor Sam's legacy (when we get it) as he was foolish enough to change not long before his death out of the 3 per cents.

My writing requires much apology—but I seldom sit down till I am already fatigued in my painting room and near the post hour. I must say of my letters as Northcote says of his pictures "I leave them for the ingenious to find out".[2] My wife has given me a new pen for this letter & made two or three fruitless attempts to read the last I sent you and the postman ringing his bell at the moment I dismissed it.

I have heard not a word of news from Somerset House whether my picture will do me credit or otherwise. I saw Collins & he said *nothing*— but last year he told me my picture wanted a "great deal". But the Council had not (when I saw Collins) been up stairs. They had been engaged in the examination of above 1400 works of the *Ex* Exhibitors—a cross is put on the *condemned* (in this place) and they met the porters bringing down a good picture which they well recollected having admired and passed— when they stopped the man who said it had the *cross upon it* "which was enough for them". They (Wilkie, Collins & Cooper[3] of the Council who

---

[1] Leslie tells us that the Archdeacon, after preaching one Sunday, asked Constable how he had liked the sermon, and received the reply: 'Very much indeed, Fisher; I always did like that sermon.'

[2] James Northcote, R.A., was one of Constable's older friends; his talk was better than his painting, and gave Constable continual delight. The latter's economy in the use of quills has indeed left many problems for the 'ingenious' to elucidate.

[3] Abraham Cooper, cattle and animal painter, elected R.A. in 1820.

chanced to be going through the hall) looked and saw the "cross": upon closer examination, it was the frame makers cement or whiting—which running down in different directions made [the] exact appearance which had been mistaken by these men—so much for chance in these things on which perhaps hung the peace & livelihood of some respectable artist.

I must work hard this summer—but I should like to take the Windsor coach to hear your sermon. But I can ill spare a day—and as I have now an opportunity of earning a little money I must take it a religious duty to do it.

Poor Tinney has had a relapse—and has been very ill indeed. His complaint is inflammatory—he has a shade over one eye. *Pray burn my last letter to you.* His brother sat near us at Church who told me this and I have called on him since, twice. I sent my children for Mrs Tinney to see but she was not at home—she is a great "shopper".

I shall not let the Frenchman have my picture. It is too bad to allow myself to be knocked down by a French man. In short it may fetch my family something one time or another & it [would be] disgracing my diploma to take so small a price & less by over one half than I asked.

I put the note into John Bulls box—in doing so I got wet to the skin, but did not like to send it.

Several cheering things have happened to me of late professionally. I am certain my reputation rises as a landscape painter—and that I am (as Farrington always said I should be) fast becoming a distinct feature in that way. I am anxious about the picture. Clint[1] my neighbour, who expects to be an Academician before me, called to see it—now he said not a word—but on leaving the room looked back and said he hoped *his picture* would not hang near it.

I trust you will come to London on your visitation. I shall be much disappointed if you do not.

I am about Farrington's house—I think this step necessary. I shall get more by this movement than my family in conveniences—but I am loth to leave a place where I have had so much happiness & good fortune and where I painted my four landscapes[2]—&c &c. But there is no end to giving way to fancies—occupation is my sheet anchor—my mind would soon devour me without it. I felt as if I had lost my arms after my picture was gone to the Exhibition—

My wife joins with me in best regards to yourself Mrs. F and family— Ever my dear Fisher yours most truly

John Constable

I have not ventured to read this letter over. Take it as one of my sketches.

---

[1] George Clint, painter of theatrical portraits, had been elected A.R.A. with Leslie in the previous year. He lived in Gower Street.
[2] *The White Horse, Stratford Mill, The Hay Wain,* and *A View on the Stour.*

Joseph Farington, Constable's old 'monitor', had died suddenly at the end of the previous year. The Constables had already been to look over the house in Charlotte Street in February, scarcely able to believe that they were no longer to meet his 'elegant and dignified figure' there.

As for Mr. John Arrowsmith, why should the Frenchman have *The Hay Wain*? Why indeed? Flattering as his interest might be, Constable must have felt that it was an English picture, painted for Englishmen like John Fisher who loved their own countryside—if only they could be persuaded that nature was worth painting in her everyday summer dress, of which so few seemed to appreciate the beauty as deeply as Constable did. Moreover, one of Constable's major anxieties was about to be relieved by Mr. Tinney, to whom he may have been pouring out some of his troubles during his visits to the sick man.

April 1822.

My dear Fisher,

We have a note from Seymour St. to dine there tomorrow. It enclosed a cover to you—and though I have written so very lately I cannot omit a line—indeed your very kind letter and enclosure required an immediate acknowledgement, and the business was uncertain.

I have been to Farrington's this morning—they are sharp about the house and wanted me to take fixtures (and such of the furniture as I may wish for) on *Lease* at a valuation. I have refused the latter as unusual and subject to caprice. So the matter rests at present. They mean to part with some things—not by auction. They will sell the *Wilsons*.[1] I said I should like to know the price they fix on them—they are well worth 60, 80 or 100 £ the pair.

An event has occurred that gives me infinite gratification—as it proves the value of your friendship for me—and (I trust) your calculations of me [and] my intellect—

Tinney is still confined to town by an indisposition. I have seen him often—and he views me favorably for your sake. He is determined to love painting as an intellectual pursuit of the most pleasing kind—in preference to dirt, old canvas & varnish &c. &c. and my late conversations with him have gone to clinch the nail which you have driven.

He has desired me to paint as a *companion* to his landscape, another picture—at my leisure—& for 100 Gns. [with the] stipulation that it must be exhibited (which will keep me to the collar). If however I am offered more for [it], even 100, I may take it & begin another for him. It will enable me to do another large work as a certainty—thus to keep up & add to my reputation. This is very noble—when all the nobility let my picture come back to me from the Gallery. I am going to see the private view of the water colors by Jackson.

---

[1] *Study at Maecenas's Villa, Tivoli*, and *Study in Adrian's Villa at Rome*, painted by Wilson in 1765 for Charles Price, M.P. They were eventually taken over by Constable, from whom they passed to Samuel Rogers, the poet.

We are delighted to have such good accounts of Mrs Fisher & your new baby—3 boys . . . The *stock* must last—

We hear nothing from the great house. This [season] is always very trying to me—1400 works of art passed in review before the Council—all of the exhibitors.

How much I should like now to be at Osmington—but work I must & will—but the very thought of a walk upon

"—The lonely shoar
"—Where none intrudes
"By the deep sea—
"—and music in its roar".

If I recollect the ashes have very beautiful mosses and the stems particularly rich in Osmington.

I never thanked you for your interesting account of [the] middle ages— the expectation of the last day—I was not aware that its influence was so enormous.

Pray do not mention this to Tinney—as he has particularly requested me not to speak of it to any one, not to *you above* all. But I could not in justice withhold it from you: I know it will give you the same pleasure that it does me—we must take care he does not ever suspect you know it.

I enclose you the little sketch that made part of a former letter I mentioned to you—but which I did not send.[1]

Constable never took advantage of Tinney's very generous offer. He says later that he had waived it, perhaps in the course of another conversation; and it was presently superseded by a new agreement between them. Grateful as Constable was at the time, circumstances changed, and he always hated to be under any sort of obligation when it came to painting.

The large picture of Flatford bridge, to which he had devoted so much care in order to avoid the usual criticism of his lack of finish, appeared at the exhibition in May with the title of *A View on the Stour, near Dedham*.[2] It received a favourable reception, not untempered by criticism. The critics were beginning to complain of his sameness, a point on which it will be found that presently John Fisher had something to say.

After the opening of the exhibition Constable went down to East Bergholt, probably in connection with the altar-piece he had mentioned to Fisher. While he was there his wife wrote to him to tell him what was happening at Charlotte Street during his absence.

'Yesterday the Bishop & Miss Fisher called,' she said on the 11th May. 'He was quite in raptures with your Waterloo, sat down on the floor to it, said it was equal to Cannelletti & begged I would tell you how much he admired it &

---

[1] Evidently the sketch given by Leslie as part of a previous letter.
[2] Now at the Henry E. Huntington Art Gallery, San Marino, California.

wondered what you could have been about not to go on with it. Your portrait he said was a very fine one. He rummaged out the Salisbury & wanted to know what you had done.'

The *Salisbury* was evidently the sketch from the palace grounds of which Miss Fisher had spoken in 1820. The subscription mentioned in the following letter from the Bishop was probably for the Artists' General Benevolent Institution in the affairs of which Constable took an active part.

Seymour St. May 14, 1822.

Dear Sir

The day that I was unfortunately prevented from dining with the Society of *Artists*, I sent a Note to the Secretary at the Freemasons Tavern, & requesting that I might offer my mite of Five Pounds to the Subscription, desiring at the same time to be informed where I might send the money. I did not enclose it, because I was apprehensive that at a Tavern in the bustle of a public dinner, my Letter might not have been delivered, and that I take to have been the case as the Secretary has taken no notice of my Letter.

I wish you would take an opportunity of speaking to him on the subject.

I am Dear Sir, yours very truly

J. Sarum

P.S. I admire your sketch of Waterloo Bridge &c—

Osmington. June 15. 1822.

My dear Constable,

That you may not be out of the way, I write to say that I shall be in London on Wednesday or Thursday next; & stay a few days to see your pictures—I hear that Milman was much indebted to Martin's picture for some of his finest thoughts on Belshazzar.[1] I have seen him standing before the velvet quite absorbed. I have been so much occupied in my sermon that our correspondence has dropped. I have finished to my satisfaction: more than I expected. Tuesday is the day.

Yours

J F.

We may now leave Constable to take his family up to Hampstead, where Isabel Constable was born on the 23rd August.

The Bishop set out on his travels again, this time to survey the mountain scenery of Wales.

---

[1] Henry Hart Milman, poet and scholar, later Dean of St. Paul's, published his dramatic poem *Belshazzar* in 1822.

Osmington, Weymouth.
September 14 1822

My dear Constable,

I write to remind you of your promise to pay me a visit during my three months abode there as a bachelor. I shall be in the Close on Wednesday Oct: 6. And I shall be glad if you will let me know by the next post, or the next to that, when I may expect you. If you come early we will go and see Fonthill during the Sale. I beg my kind regards to your wife. I am in but a bad humour for writing or I would say more. The Bishop is in Wales. Beleive me

Yours sincerely

John. Fisher.

Fonthill Abbey was the palace in Wiltshire on which the eccentric William Beckford had spent a fortune. There had already been a partial sale of the contents in 1807. The present sale, for which Christie had already prepared a complete catalogue, was after all postponed till a year later. The cover of the next letter is marked 'Immediate', which indicates that Fisher was growing impatient, but the contents are missing, and Leslie gives only a brief extract from what was in it. It seems to have contained a remittance to meet Constable's more pressing needs with some remarks on Constable's work in Dr. Philip Fisher's usual strain of dry humour.

Osmington, October 1st 1822

My dear Constable,

. . . Captain Forster, a gentleman of property near Windsor, is an admirer of your art. He is to meet you at Salisbury; he was first caught by a sketch-book of yours which I had. Your pencil-sketches always take people, both learned and unlearned. Get one done on stone as an experiment, unless it is derogatory from the station you hold in the art . . .

J. Fisher.

This time Constable answered promptly.[1] He wrote to Osmington; but Fisher had already moved on to Salisbury.

No 2 Lower Terrace, Hampstead
Oct. 4. 1822

My dear Fisher,

You have created a difficulty with me how to name a day to meet you at Salisbury. You say you shall be at the Close on "*Wednesday Octr 6*"—I can be with you on Thursday Oct. 10—or on Saturday the 12th—as I have made arrangement here to come to you at all events, and the sooner the better that we may have our walks in the beauty of the season.

---

[1] Letter in the Victoria and Albert Museum.

I received your letter yesterday and the drafts. I shall get a letter from you a day sooner by sending it to me here—as above—and will you give me one line by return of post to say if either of the days I have mentioned will suit you? I hope Capn. Forster can meet me. I like at all times Dr. Fisher's criticisms and sayings. Sour Crout is no bad digester—and after all the arts & poetry are made for such people.

Our paper, the Post, has been filled with Millmans Belshazzar—which I have seen. How fortunate I am not one of those who are expected to have read it all. This would be one of the consequences of having been at College.

I did not expect you were any thing in my debt. I have kept no acct. & thought all had been paid long ago.

I think I shall send my other large landscape to the Gallery next year. Though I did not sell the other it furthered my reputation much.

This place ruins me—but is quite as necessary as food to my children & wife. This did not come into my original calculations—when I married.

Best regards to all. Let me have one line directly if quite convenient & you are . . .—which I always regret when you are not.

> Ever my dear Fisher
>
> truly yours
>
> John Constable.

I am not aware that I [? appealed] for the drafts—but they are acceptable—quite so. Will Tinny be at Salisbury?

We are quite surprised at your finding fault with my writing. My wife looking over me could not help saying John how nicely you are writing— I said it is to Fisher—who is particular. I cant say much for this.

I shall come by the little Salisbury coach—let me know the day which will suit you.

If Constable had left on the 6th, as originally proposed, he might yet have had his holiday; but Fisher's reply reported a new hitch.

> Close Salisbury. Oct. 6. 1822.
>
> Sunday.—

My dear Constable:

On my arrival here I found the Cathedral being painted. It will not open till about the 20th of this month. I return therefore to Osmington tomorrow to stay till the 20th and hope that you will follow me there immediately. Tinney is here now. I shall be sorry if this fresh arrangement of my time will interfere with any commissions he may intend for you. But perhaps Oct 20 will be time enough for you to begin upon them. Pray lose no time in coming to Osmington. I shall have more of your company there uninterruptedly. Life is short: let us spend it as happily as possible.

If on your way to Osmington you like to stop at Salisbury a night there is a bed for you & a mutton chop. The Weymouth Union Coach leaves the Saracens Head Snow Hill: a *day* coach Mondays: Wednesdays & Fridays. A *night* coach Tuesdays: Thursdays & Saturdays. We are preparing our new West window. The reason I did not direct you at Hampstead, was that till your last you did not give me a full direction: and when I send money it behoveth me to be careful. You certainly did not give the remotest hint for the draft. But I suppose I may pay my lawful debts how & when I please without consulting your leave. I wish you could pay yours. Dodsworth met me yesterday & asked for "Mr Constables copy of Teniers". You cannot show your face here without it. I did not say your writing was not "nice" but only that it was unintelligible. Your last letter is worse. But *I* must not talk to day. You may depend upon it that Charlotte Street will agree better with your wife & children than the Giltspur Street Compter will with you. You have just missed Milman. He has been here with me these last two days visiting Fonthill. It is a strange mad place. Imagine a bad imitation of Salisbury Cathedral converted into a dwelling house: "the abode of a foul familiar spirit". It was suggested that the Irish Bishop should be made abbot of Fonthill Abbey. The collection of pictures is small & only cabinet pictures. The best there is the "laughing boy" with the flower & two green rushes growing out of his——. Salvators Job: 2 pretty Teniers's: a Sir Josh: (fine) 3 Stothards which kept their place well among the *old* masters: several portraits by Bellini, very peculiar & grand: the blanks of the rest of the wall are filled up with innumerable Berghems & Rottenheimers.—Milmans things are very heavy. They are like old fashioned drawingrooms gorgeous with gilding & marble but cold & comfortless to live in.—And now adieu. Any day will suit me you like to come. Only the sooner the better. The day you receive this if you like. I shall have a pound or two more for you when you go away. Which will further reduce my debt. My kind regards to your wife.

Beleive me

my dear Constable

very sincerely yours

John. Fisher.

Come on to Weymouth as the walk is short to Osmington. Do not mention it, but I do not like the accounts I hear of our Bishop. He is in Wales. I fear he breaks.

The delay in departure, as things now turned out, proved fatal.

Hampstead, Oct. 7. 1822.

My dear Fisher

Several adverse circumstances had yielded to my wishes and I had determined on meeting you at Salisbury on the day appointed— but things have changed again and I know not how to make arrangements to come so far as Weymouth.—The loss of 4 days on the road is serious, as I am now in the midst of a great struggle, & "Time is my Estate."

I have got several of my commissions into tolerable forwardness—especially two (kit-cat) landscapes for Mr. Ripley, and I am determined to overcome all my difficulties while I have a great deal of health, and some little youth still remains to me. I have got things here in train by following which [they] are made comparatively easy. Such a journey would turn me inside out—& a visit to your coast would wash my brains entirely. I must wait and still hope to meet you (when quite convenient to yourself) when you return to the Close.

I shall send you some picture to look at. I have been busy here. *"Green Highgate"* has now changed its form again and become a very pretty picture[1]—and deserves a better or at least a new *name*. I have made about 50 carefull studies of *skies* tolerably large, to be carefull. I mentioned the desire of meeting Tinney—for the pleasure of meeting him. We are free & independent of each other. His handsome behaviour toward me, in wishing for a companion to his picture, was appreciated though waived by me—as there was really no room to be found for it. He meant what he said and I was gratified by the manner in which it was done.

I do not regret not seeing Fonthill. I never had a desire to see sights—and a gentleman's park—is my aversion. It is not beauty because it is not nature. There is real wit in the appointment of the Abbot to Fonthill. The *people* have forgot that horrible business. A person told me who passing through the park about the time, that he saw several fellows *"running away"* at the moment a Bishop in his carriage was passing—there was a general cry of *"run Jack"* *"by God there comes a Bishop"*. There seems nothing fine in the picture way at Fonthill—the two fine upright Gaspars are at the Gallery & one as well as the Altiori Claudes in other & let us hope cleaner hands—*nature* must revolt.[2]

It is singular that I happened to speak of Millman. I dare say he knows something—but it is very unfair to *encumber* literature. The world is full enough of what has been already done, and in the art there is plenty of fine painting—but very few good pictures. I am told his is fine writing and as you say gorgeous—but it can be compared—Shakespeare cannot, nor Burns, nor Claude nor Ruisdael, and it took me 20 years to find this simple idea out—or at least to act upon it.

Collins has brought home his wife Smack—and there is the devil to pay —Frank & the old woman will not abide, and Manning tells me Collins

---

[1] This might be one of several views from Hampstead. *A View of Highgate* was in the collection of Constable's admirer Thomas Churchyard, of Woodbridge.

[2] 'Grave imputations' on the moral character of William Beckford are said to have led to his seclusion at Fonthill for the past twenty years.

is in a great rage.[1] I have not seen him. I shall let him cool a bit. I should think him ruined.

This is I hope my last week here—at least this season. It is a ruinous place to me—I lose time here sadly—one of my motives for taking [the] Charlotte St. house was to remain longer in London. In Keppel Street we wanted room—& were like "bottled wasps upon a southern wall"—but the 5 happiest & most interesting years of my life were passed in Keppel St. I got my children and my fame in that house, neither of which would I exchange with any other man.

I must raise two or 3 hundred pounds, by selling out. It is a pity. My wife's legacy from her brother is just paid & transferred into her name, 1050 £ new fours—would you advise me to settle it upon her—I apprehend it could now be lawfully done as 'tis in her name, & not mine.

Ever sincerely yours   John Constable.

We have succeeded in our indictments and the houses opposite me in Charlotte St. are cleared, I hoped not to be filled again with the same cattel but it is to be feared—and "*Hansel & Good Will*" is highly valued in these cases.

The postscript refers to an unfortunate *contretemps* which had arisen in the course of the removal to Charlotte Street. Some account of the difficulties which Constable experienced in making Farington's bachelor residence suitable for occupation by a family will be found in the next letter; but it had been a particularly disagreeable surprise to discover that the premises on the other side of the street were being used for the purpose of what is politely known as the oldest of the professions. On the 9th September Lucy Dale and Elizabeth Williams, widow, 'late of St. Pancras', having been indicted for keeping a common bawdy house, were tried before the Middlesex Justices at Clerkenwell Sessions House, John Constable being a principal witness. The victory was not quite so complete as the postscript suggests, since judgement was respited: but at the sessions held on the 2nd December Lucy Dale confessed and was ordered to enter into a recognizance with two sureties, to keep the peace and be of good behaviour for two years. Elizabeth Williams was discharged.

Leslie explains that the gloomy prognostications contained in Constable's next letter arose from the practice of the directors of the British Institution in allowing artists to copy the paintings by old masters exposed at their gallery.[2] The complaint may seem to come strangely enough from such an inveterate student of the old masters as Constable was; but it is evident that he meant only to deplore the quality of the works that were being shown, fearing that the

---

[1] The Collins family lived near Constable. Mrs. Collins senior had opposed her son William's marriage to Harriet Geddes, whom he married against his mother's will in 1822. William's brother Francis lived with them and worked as a picture-cleaner. Young Mrs. Collins was a sister of Mrs. W. H. Carpenter, the portrait-painter.

[2] A drawing by Rowlandson, and Pugin, showing students copying pictures at the British Institution, is reproduced in Whitley's *Art in England* 1800-20, p. 110.

H

work of young students might suffer from their copying such trash. It is to be suspected, however, that the depth of his gloom was due to ill-health and anxiety over money as much as to anything else.

London. Oct. 31. 1822

My dear Fisher,

We left Hampstead a fortnight ago last Tuesday—and I have not had my pencil in my hand one day yet. I got laid up by my anxiety to get to you—for which purpose I was attending my bricklayers & carpenters at 6 & 7 in the morning: leaving a warm bed for cold damp rooms, & washhouses—for I have had an immense trouble to get the house habitable. I am now however quite well & at work again.

I am aware that the time is now past in which it was convenient for you to receive me. It has proved a very great disappointment to me and I fear that my not coming has vexed you, especially as I have not heard from you.

I have got this room (the large painting room) into excellent order. It is light—airy—*sweet* & warm. I at one time despaired of attaining either of these qualities, especially the latter, but we discovered a real greivance—a hollow wall—which communicated with the floors of my room, opened & was immediately over—the *well* of the *privy*. This would have played the devil with the oxygen of my colours.

I shall begin immediately on Saviles large picture. It will be a great bore but it may help to save me from ruin. I shall want at least 400 £ at Xmas. He has mentioned the delay on my part about his picture. It was his own fault, he should have communicated with me. I wrote to him yesterday—he keeps the place open where it is to hang. A gentleman, who was with him the other day, called on me & told me this—and that as he was soon expected to take a penurious fit, Mr. Lea advised me to finish it out of hand. Considering all the circumstances & how much I have done with the composition—would it be unreasonable in me to ask a 100 £ in advance? But he is foolish & proud—and he might throw it up altogether—as he is fragile & irritable.

I have got an excellent subject for a six foot canvas, which I should certainly paint for next year but for Savile: but I have neither time nor money to speculate with, & my children begin to swarm.

I have now two six footers in hand, one of which I shall send to the Gallery—at 200 £, or keep it. The time will come they will fetch some *dealer* 500 £.

3 Associates are to be chosen next Tuesday out of 40 candidates at the R. Academy. They are at a loss entirely—there is not an artist among them.[1]

---

[1] As Whitley remarks, this was hardly fair on Etty, who was now standing as a candidate for the first time—and who was, incidentally, before long to defeat Constable for election as R.A.

It is recommended that the secretary put them into a bag. The art will go out—there will be no genuine painting in England in 30 years. This is owing to "*pictures*"—driven into the empty heads of the junior artists by their *owners*—the Governors of the Institution &c &c. In the early ages of all the arts, the productions were more affecting & sublime—owing to the artists being without human exemplars—they were forced to have recourse to nature. In the later ages of Raphael & of Claude, the productions were more perfect (less uncouth) because the artists could then avail themselves or rather *strengthen* themselves by the *experience* only of what was done before to get at nature more surely. They had the *experience* of those who went before—but did not take them at their word—that is, imitate them.

Beleive me

ever yours

most truly

John Constable

I am always vexed when I am led off into painting this way but could you see the folly and ruin this day exhibited at the Gallery you would go mad. W. Vandeveld—& Gaspar Poussin—& Titian—are made to spawn millions of abortions—and for what are the sublime masters brought to pull aside the lack of their . . . ? only to serve the purpose of sale—to bring a penny into the empty hands of . . . frauds. Hofland[1] has sold his shadow of Gaspar Poussin—for 80 gns—it is nothing more like Gaspar than the shadow of the man like himself on a muddy road. It is a beastly [thing]. It is a shocking scene of folly & ruin—headed by Lords &c.

The two 'six-footers' mentioned in this letter are probably the two which had remained unsold. *The Hay Wain* and *A View on the Stour*. The 'excellent subject' for another may have been the view of Flatford lock which is presently mentioned as having been begun. In the meantime, if he was to keep the wolf from the door, Constable had to get on with his commissions, of which it will be remembered that two were from the good Bishop. Of these the following letter may have served to remind him.

Palace Sarum. Nov: 4 1822

Dear Sr

We are all disappointed at not seeing you here at this time.

I am particularly so, because I was in hopes you would have taken another *peep* or *two* at the view of our Cathedral from my Garden near the Canal.[2] But perhaps you retain enough of it in your memory to finish

---

[1] Thomas Christopher Hofland, a landscape painter who had failed to get into the Academy, was supposed to have great influence with the directors of the British Institution.

[2] The conduit which ran through the Bishop's grounds for the purpose of draining the old fish-pond into the Avon on the west.

the Picture which I shall hope will be ready to grace my Drawing Room in London.

We returned home last week from a long tour in South Wales. We often wished for you & your Pencil.

My Ladies unite in best regards to yourself & Mrs. Constable

with

Dear Sr

Yours very truly

J Sarum

It appears that Constable wrote back on the 9th November to say that he now had *Salisbury Cathedral from the Bishop's Grounds* in hand.

Palace Sarum. Nov: 10, 1822.

Dear Sir

I received yours this morning. I am glad to find that you are about your View of Sarum for me.

I wish you to employ the *Smiths* Father & Son to make the Frame. They have set up a Shop together in Kensington very near the Palace. I wish to employ them for my own sake as well as theirs. They owe me a large Sum of money & I must be repaid by their working it out for me.

Remember us very kindly to Mrs Constable & believe me

Dear Sir, yours very truly

J. Sarum.

This letter was followed, according to Leslie, by another from the Bishop, dated November 12th. Dr. Fisher, who had doubtless heard of Constable's financial difficulties from his nephew on his return from Wales enclosed with the letter a draft, accompanied by the words: 'Lawyers frequently receive retaining fees, why should not painters do the same?' John Fisher wrote the same day, probably to make certain that Constable would not take offence.

Close Salisbury. Novr. 12. 1822.

My dear Constable:

During my residence my time is much occupied with attendance at Church in the day & on dinners in the evening, that I find no opportunity of corresponding with my friends. And what is not a little remarkable, so belly devoted are the good people here, that they look upon it as a sort of *duty* imposed on the Canons in residence, to dine out or give a dinner every day as punctually as he goes to Church.—However I have lately resolutely closed my mouth on meat & wine, so that these dinner attendances are only loss of time & loss of patience, without loss of health.

My house is always open to you. I never want even notice to say that you are coming. But I would not press you to leave London now: as time

is as you say money to you, & you want it just at present. I recommend
you to get on with the Bishops picture. He is quite eager about it. He asked
me last night whether I thought he should affront you by sending you part
of your price. I replied that I was of opinion he would *not* offend you: as
Sir T. Lawrence himself took earnest money. In the matter of Savilles
picture you must decide for yourself. In case he does not *at last* take the
picture would it do you service in your profession? would it sell? It depends much on the temper of the man. If you think it probable that he
may leave you at last in the lurch; & if the picture otherwise would not
be profitable, I would ask him for earnest money, on the plea of the length
of time it will occupy you. You were sufficiently irritable in your last letter,
in consequence of the transactions at the Gallery. I will increase your
irritability. A two fisted peice of machinery called Gray living at Salisbury,
has made a water-colour copy of the Rubens (the 3 boys) at Wilton. Lady
Pembroke[1] is going to dispose of it for him by *raffle*, for 100 guineas! The
Bishops name is down of course. You see wealthy people regard artists as
only a superior sort of work people to be employed at their caprice: &
have no notion of the mind & intellect & independent character of a man
entering into his compositions. They regard the art as they do needlework
& estimate it by its neatness. I have Fuseli's M. Nights Dream hanging in
my room. At a dinner I gave, I was obliged to sit for an hour patiently &
hear Fuseli criticized & found fault with, by acclamation & this from a
party of men sensible & clever in their way: but who were no more able
to measure Fuseli's height than I to dispute with the Duke of Wellington
on Tactics. These men would not have criticized a clock or a spinning
Jenny. Because they do not understand those peices of machinery. And
yet they will teach a painter. What is so absurd or outré in Fuseli as the
figure of CHARON giving a Ghost a back hander with his scull in the picture
of the LAST JUDGEMENT.[2] Gray has taken down the Bishops picture:
ashamed of it at last. I found Calcotts card on my . . . when I came here.
If you see him say I was sorry not to have been in Salisbury. I met with the
following striking case in a medical review last night. Major Leonard aged
65 died after long disease of the chest. On dissection the lungs were found
most extensively diseased. The heart the original seat of the malady. When
the *cause* came to be debated, it turned out that he had been a remarkably
abstemious man. They were all at fault: untill a relative mentioned that
the Major L had been long in desperate habits of deep gambling. Hence
violent agitation: hence the disease. During the French Revolution death
from disease of the heart, was very common. Dr. Pemberton you probably
know died of the Tic Doloreux.[3] On disection a small spicula of bone was

---

[1] Catharine, daughter of Count Woronzow, second wife of the eleventh earl.
[2] Fuseli was compared by Sir Thomas Lawrence to Michelangelo.
[3] Christopher Robert Pemberton, physician extraordinary to the King, had died on
the 31st July: he suffered intensely from facial neuralgia, but his death was actually due
to apoplexy.

found projecting over the longitudinal sinus. Send Dodsworth your own copy of Teniers & make yourself another at your leisure. He is a man that I should not like being under an obligation to. My compls. to Mrs. C. Yours ever. J F.

Hume[1] "likes your clouds & your water. But he does not like your trees". "Your trees in Tinneys picture are shocking". I thought it important to advise you of this.

We now come to the results of Constable's appeal on behalf of young Read.

Close, Salisbury
Saturday. Nov. 30. 1822.

My dear Constable,

I cannot live without communication with the art; so in default of your company, I have cultivated the society of "Read with the flowing locks". He has really something of the sincere love & feeling for the art about him. He has just finished a laborious careful study of an old Shepherd & wishes to get it if possible into the British Gallery. He has begged that I would apply to you for your assistance & advice. If he sends it up carriage paid will you try & get it admitted? And if you cannot get it in, will you give it wall room for a short while till he can make up his mind what he should do with it? He is amazingly improved. Yet the Shepherd I think a failure: & tried to persuade him to stick to landscape. But he is at present wild, & talks of Raphael & Domenichino & universal art. His sketches this year are very interesting & have some genuine feeling in them. The principal merit of his "Shepherd" is the feeling & sentiment with which it is conceived. The Execution is meagre & starved. The truth is it has all those qualities which will never be felt at *the Gallery* & none of those qualities which are alone appreciated.—He talks of coming to London & getting into the Academy.

If I have in this matter brought trouble & bother upon you, you may thank yourself. You first introduced him to my notice. I have bought a little landscape of his.—

Look at Rembrandts descent from the cross. The man on the ladder has a great rent in his breeks, & a large peice of his a—e apparent.—Is not this *gratuitous* vulgarity? I see that Mr Lane Fox has brought Mr. D. Guests picture of the Duke of Wellington; & that Mr Guest is now painting Madame Vestris, & doing something between whiles I suppose.[2] I was

---

[1] The Rev. Thomas Henry Hume, only son of Bishop Hume, was Treasurer of the Cathedral. He had two sons with Wiltshire livings, but the reference is probably to their father.

[2] George Lane-Fox had succeeded his father at Bramham Park, Yorks, in 1821: Douglas Guest had been with Constable an unsuccessful candidate for the rank of A.R.A. in 1811: Lucia Elizabeth Vestris, the actress, had made her first appearance at Drury Lane on the 19th February of this year.

told yesterday & the information came I *think* from Calcot, that he gets his bread by painting pictures of another description. Representations of the manner in which the world is peopled.—It was the man's a—e that made me think of Guest & his doings. The palace party do nothing but talk of your picture that is coming. Put in some niggle to please the good people. We have had a glorious victory at Cambridge over the Whig-Radicals. Two government candidates stood. One polled 480. The other 280. Scarlett only 200. Or more than six to one.[1] Dodsworth desires me to thank you for the Teniers: and I thank you for returning so punctually the Osmington Coast & my little Salisbury Cathedral.[2] I am quite resigned. I shall *never* have them again. Luckily my great picture is too bulky or you would purloin that too.—I wish you would send me word of the real state of the case of St Pauls Cathedral. It is reported that to preserve the surface of the interior, Sir Ch: Wren put 4 coats of paint on it: and that it has now been breeches-balled in imitation of the original painting. How is this. Enlighten us in the country. Do you recollect a coarse painting at the Charterhouse of a caravan crossing a brook with a cock on top of the waggon? It is a bad copy from a beautiful Woovermans at Fonthill. But no more like the original than I am to Hercules.—What genuine things the etchings of Waterloo are. Are they scarce or common? The laughing boy was at Fonthill. Do you recollect the *place* the flower seems to grow from? [Sketch of a boy with a flower rising behind his posterior.] Let me hear from you soon. Beleive me my dear Constable

yours very sincerely

J F.

Constable was at last at work on the Bishop's picture, and the addition of Read's business was far from welcome; but the request was one that he could hardly refuse outright.

Charlotte St. December 6. 1822.

My dear Fisher

There is nothing so cheering to me as the sight of your handwriting —yet I am dilatory in writing to you. Your last letter required an immediate answer but this week has been a very troublesome [one] to me. The trial of one of our *opposite* neighbours whom we indited was to have taken place—and we were at Clarkenwell several days—but to day the infamous old woman has suffered judgment to go by confession, & [we] have agreed to pay all expence, about 30 £. The inmates have long since fled, some of whom were the old womans *daughters*—& we hope the business is well done. Both houses are clear.

---

[1] James Scarlett, later 1st Baron Abinger, had resigned his seat at Peterborough to contest Cambridge University as a whig candidate, with two tories opposing him.

[2] The coast scene is here reproduced: the small Salisbury Cathedral is not traceable, and may have been 'purloined' later on.

I will gladly do all I can for Reads picture but you know I can only give it its chance.—I possess neither affection nor favour at that wretched place. It shall go with my own—I shall mention his to Young.[1] Is it not possible to dissuade him from coming to London—but perhaps he prefers starving in a crowd, & if he is determined to make the adventure let him by all means preserve his flowing locks. They will be sure to procure him employment, and cannot fail of making him known—they may do him more service than even the talents of Claude Lorrain, if he had them.

Dodsworth may have his picture when I shall find an opportunity of sending it with your two. I have grimed it down with slime & soot—as he is a connoisseur and of course prefers filth & dirt, to freshness & beauty.

Which of the Huns (Humes) has ventured an observation on any of my pictures?

I am getting on here and am busy. The Cathedral is advancing—& Smith has the frame in hand. Does the Bishop come to town [at the] beginning of next month—for the parliament?

My altarpeice, for the chapel at Manningtree, is gone by—the man would not have it. He says I had harmed his future—but my brother tells me, "the whole concern of these brewers was a low sneak to Archdeacon Jefferson (who could license or not their blackguard publick houses) & on his death[2] they were glad to get clear of as much of the expence as they had not actually incurred, as they could." This is a loss to me. The frame is 5 £, being of mahogany without a joint, and of large dimensions.

I do not think my chance at the Academy so good as it was last year, when I was not elected. I am afraid they are not without their *sneaks*. I have nothing to help me but my stark naked merit, and although that (as I am told) exceeds all the other candidates—it is not heavy enough. I have no patron but yourself—and you are not the Duke of Devonshire—or any other great ass. You are only a gentleman & a scholar and a real lover of the art, whose only wish is to see it advance.

Your account of provincial arts—& artists, or as Vasari called them, the Itinerants—is very amusing—and the goodnatured amiable girl Lady Pembroke helping them on. Could more have been done for the paper-hanger to repaint your Water Closet?

An old friend of my wifes passed the evening with us Thursday (Mrs. Cipriani[3]). She is an old friend of General Slade's. She says there is a

---

[1] John Young the engraver, Keeper of the British Institution.
[2] Joseph Jefferson, Archdeacon of Colchester, had died on the 28th December 1821. In spite of what Constable here says, the altar-piece, which has for its subject the Resurrection, was made over to the church of St. Michael at Manningtree, where it was to be seen until the church was dismantled in 1965. Cleaned and reframed, it now hangs in the church of Feering, where Constable's old friend Walter Wren Driffield was fifty years resident curate. The picture will be reproduced in *Constable's Discourses*, to be published shortly in this S.R. series.
[3] Possibly a daughter-in-law of the artist G. B. Cipriani.

great family feud there caused by a marriage of the old blockhead's with a young girl—was it a *"runaway"* match?

I hear of much illness amongst children. My wife wishes me to ask how all yrs are. Ours are quite well. We take great care of them. This house is delightfully healthy & convenient. I hope to God I shall be able to keep it. I shall be better able to tell after X'mas.

I have been to see Davids picture (mass) of the Crowning of Bonaparte & his Empress. It is 35 feet by 21. As a picture it does not possess any thing of the language of the art much less of the oratory—of Rubens—or Paul Veronese.[1] It is below notice as a work of execution—but still I much prefer it to West—only because it does not remind me of the *schools*. West is only hanging on by the tail of the shirt of Carlo Maratti & the fag end of the Roman & Bolognese schools—the last of the . . . the Altorum Romanorum, and only the shadow of them.

I could not help being angry when I last wrote to you, about the patrons. Should there be a national gallery (as it is talked)[2] there will be an end to the Art in poor old England, & she will become the same non entity as any other country which has one.

The reason is both plain & certain. The manufacturers of pictures are then made the criterion of perfection & not nature.

Your letters (though I do not desire them) do me good. Write to me as often as you can. I am harassed & anxious but I hope to weather all. This house has almost upset me.

Ever yours my dear Fisher very truly

J. Constable.

Then, to complete the upset, almost the whole of Constable's family went down with illness at Christmas.

A letter from the Bishop's brother Sir George Bulteel Fisher may be given here since it was probably written about this time and there is nothing to fix the exact date.[3]

Charlton, Kent. One o'clock.
My dear Sir

If you should not have set off before this reaches you I write to beg you will be so good as to postpone your visit to us for the present in consequence of an alarming accident that has happened here to night.

---

[1] Constable was to see other pictures by David in 1835. 'They are indeed, loathsome', he wrote to Leslie.

[2] A paragraph had appeared in *The Times* on the 29th October, to the effect that the King had expressed such a wish, and had promised to contribute: *The Times* supported the project and hoped that Parliament would lend its aid.

[3] The paper bears a watermark which appears to be part of '1821' and notepaper (unlike the paper of sketch-books) was generally used about a year after that shown in the watermark.

The Childs bed caught fire & Mrs F in extinguishing it has burnt both her hands so dreadfully that she is in the greatest possible agony & I fear will be laid up for some time.

We have been in the greatest agitation—

believe [me] yours truly

G B Fisher

1823, January to June

It was not till the second month of 1823 that Constable had so far recovered from his upsets as to be in a mood for letterwriting. Fisher, too, had his reasons for silence.

London. Feby. 1. 1823

My very dear Fisher

You are negligent and unkind to him who esteems you far indeed beyond all other men in the world. You have written to me but two hasty half sheets for the last three months—and those were to incumber me with the "*wretched Read*" and his *wretched pictures*. I wanted little to add to the state of depression I have been in for some time past. Ever since X'mas my house has been a sad scene of serious illness, all my children & two servants being laid up at once—things which are now thanks to God looking better, but poor John is still in a most fearfull state. I am unfortunately taken ill again myself—but to day I feel better & determined to write to you.

Poor Read I am uncomfortable about. 'Tis true I excited your neighbourly benevolence towards him for the sake of his innocent family—but that certainly would not have been the case—had I thought it would have brought him one step nearer this dreadfull *feild of battle*, in which so much worth, and innocence, are doomed to perish.

None of his pictures are received at the Gallery. No one for a moment who saw them expected they would. Thus has he involved himself in no small expence to get rid of his little local reputation. The feild of Waterloo is a feild of mercy to ours. Would to God you & Mr Benson, that really good man, would endeavour to use it to the advantage of his family & prevail on him to quit a profession which he cannot fail to disgrace—

The truth must now be told *you*—which is that, he is ignorant of every rudiment of art—without one grain of original feeling—without one atom of talent—and—able only to do *something*—worse than *nothing* at *thirty years of age*.

When the Old Shepherd was laying on his back at my door with a mob of 50 people about it I would have thanked any body to have set my house on fire—though my wife and children were at the drawing room windows. I have ordered them back in the night.

With anxiety—watching—& nursing—& my own present indisposition I have not seen the face of my easil since X'mas. It is not the least of my anxiety that the Good Bishop's picture is not fit to be seen. Pray my dear Fisher prepare his Lordship for this—it has been no fault of my own. Add to it that I can make nothing of the wretched Smith's, to whom I gave the order for the frame more than 2 months ago—I think—I know not if it is even in hand—as they have never noticed one of my notes.

Your excellent Mother & family hearing of our distress most kindly called here—the sight of Mrs. P. Fisher always does one good. Her looks say we should patiently submit to all things, and confirm it in herself that she can.

My wife begs to join with me in best regards to yourself, Mrs J. Fisher & friends

and beleive me

my very dear Fisher

always most sincerely yrs

John Constable

We hope Mrs F & the infant are re-covered—& that all your family are well.

Dear Sir

    We arrived safe & well on Monday in Seymour Street and are anxious to see you. Can you dine with us on Sunday?

I am dear Sir, yours very truly

J. Sarum

Thursday, Feb: 6 – 23.

Fisher met Constable's attack of nerves with sympathy, at the same time bantering Constable about Read.

Osmington. Weymouth. Feb. 7. 1823.

My dear Constable:

    I am very sorry indeed to hear of the continuance of the illness of your family: but still more so of yourself. Women and children are the natural prey of the Apothecary, but a man has something else to do than to keep his chamber & look delicate. You may depend upon it that the plan I have adopted is the true principle of health. In all this precarious winter we have not had *a single* person ill, child mother or servant.

I have been incessantly occupied ever since October, as you will learn if you make enquiries in the proper quarters: and have had my thoughts so completely directed on one or two points only, that I suffered painting to become a minor object. But though I neglected the art, I assure you I often thought of the friend.

You seem to have been something ruffled by poor Reads intrusion & my recommendation. But really Constable it was your own fault. You spoke to me of him as a man of feeling for the art & brought his sketches for me to admire; & recommended him to my notice. I took you therefore at your word, & thought he *was* an artist. Not knowing any better, I had formed magnificent notions of the "old Shepherd" & little expected that the "Gentlemen in Pall Mall"[1] would reject it. Is it really bad, or are you jealous & they ignorant?

Dodsworth is hugeously delighted with his Teniers, & is in admiration & astonishment, how you could make it look so exactly like an old master. I made him angry by saying that the best plan is to put the picture up the chimney.

The first week in April I am settled at Gillingham & have always a bed & painting room for you there. The only grievance attending our marriage's & families is that they unavoidably keep us separate. In what state are your finances? I am woefully off. Owing to defalcation of income I am £1200 in debt. It must tell with your profession for gentlemen can never afford to buy pictures. Certainly not at a remunerating price.

The vulture of reform is now turning its eyes on the Church & is preparing to fix his talons in her fat. We shall have a rough time of it this Sessions. There is a party who wish to reduce the clergy of this country to the level of the Scottish Kirk. No incomes larger than £180 per annum. The consequence of this will be that no gentleman or man of intellect will enter the profession. The liberal, literary, & learned body to which I unworthily belong, will disappear: the universities will be converted into charitable seminaries, & the illiterate offspring of grocers & tallow chandlers will fill the pulpits. This I am told the great Lords wish to be the case. We tread too close upon their kibes. Whether it will be better for the country at large remains to be proved. The Americans know our value. All the old folio divinity (Tillotson, Stillingfleet &c &c) is bought up for America & is not to be had now at the booksellers but at an enormous price.—See the necessity of stimulus & encouragement to science. What have the Scottish clergy ever done in the way of literature & divinity. Is the name of any one of them known except Blair[2] & Home. And Home was excommunicated by his *brethren* for writing innocent "Tragedy of Douglas".[3]

---

[1] The Directors of the British Institution.
[2] The published Sermons of Hugh Blair, the Scottish divine, long enjoyed extraordinary popularity.
[3] John Home was minister of Athelstaneford: his *Douglas* (produced at Covent Garden with Peg Woffington in the cast) was regarded as an outrage by the ruling party in the Kirk, and he was cited before the presbytery of Haddington.

I wish you particularly to get the 4 no of the New Monthly magazine. It is for April 1821. Printed by Colbourne, Conduit St. Hanover Square. At the end is an excellent critique, on Mr Haydon & Mr Martin. "Mr Haydon will be regarded by posterity as the chief regenerator of elevated art in our time. Mr. Barry & Sir J. Reyds. excited a relish for high art & their names will be remembered with *respect*. But their works have not possessed sufficient depth of science or of what is best in art &c—Mr Haydon has awakened the best energies of artists. He & Mr Martin have set at rest the long established doubt of the supposed inadequacy of the natives of our Islands to lofty & refined attainments in the arts.—Mr Martin paints to the imagination . . . Mr Haydon on the contrary has an accomplished eye for colour light shade & mechanism of his art. The soul shines through his corporeal forms. In his pictures & brief but vigorous writing on Art he has created a new energy on the subject. He has added to the stock of genuine talent. His graphic hand is an index which points out to artists the proper pursuit of the profession—it points to the philosophy of Painting taught by his own example & reflecting a brightness from its intellectual splendour that will we confidently beleive, shine out through a long futurity."—There is more of it. I suspect Milman, It is like his manner.

The letter is (perhaps mercifully, if there was to be any more in Milman's manner) incomplete. The reforms which Fisher feared were approaching, but did not materialize till after his death, when the Cathedrals Act of 1840 swept away the prebendaries in all but name. Some echo of his opinions may be found expressed by Canon Jones in his *Fasti*: while the abuses of plurality and non-residence are there admitted, it is suggested that there may have been something to be said for a system which granted some of the greatest divines the independence and leisure whereby they were enabled to give themselves to their works.

To add still further to Constable's depression, he was again defeated in the February election for Farington's place in the Royal Academy. That he should be defeated was something to which he was perhaps by now growing reconciled; but it was a bitter pill to swallow when his successful opponent was declared to be his erstwhile friend, Ramsay Richard Reinagle, whole only claim to this distinction lay in his being the son of that nonentity, Philip Reinagle, R.A. Both father and son were involved in picture-dealing, and the son eventually lost his diploma for exhibiting a picture not his own.

The following fragment of a letter from Fisher bears a postmark of the 20th February, and probably belongs to this year:

Archdeacon Haris was very much delighted with your conversation, & asked my mother for your direction.

The bishop knows how ill you have all been. I will write to you again a post or two. Now the Bishop is in town we can write more frequently. With anxious wishes to hear a better account of you & yours.

Beleive me

my dear Constable

yours very faithfully

John. Fisher.

Charlotte Street. Feby. 21. 1823

My dear Fisher,

 I was cheered by your letter and kind enquiries of me & my family. I am now at work again and some of my children are better but my poor darling John is in a sad state. Indeed God only knows how it must end— Bayley[1] and Dr Gooch see him continually and are not at all without hope, but I am worn with anxiety and trouble of almost every kind. I often wish for your knowledge in medecine—but as I am entirely ignorant what can I do but send for aid—but the system is bad and the expence enormous—though Bayley & Gooch will not take any money of me. How happy you are to have your family all so well. Nothing has gone well with me since I have been in this house.

 I did not touch my pencil for a month or two, which has thrown me far back in my work. I am making it up now, but I am weak and much emaciated—they took a good deal of blood away from me which I could ill spare. I have fretted for the loss of time & being away from my easil— & for the waste of property in consequence—but most of all for my dear boy. But I will lease my house and go into any painting room. I have put a large upright landscape in hand, and I hope to get it ready for the Academy. I hope likewise to have the Bishops picture ready—I am stopped in its progress by the wretched Smith, who has & will plague me to death with the frame how vexing it is to be involved again with these wretches whom I had long ago turned adrift—for worthlessness, lies, and ingratitude: they have just put the frame in hand—after three months, from its being ordered.

 I am sorry to see that you are again haunted by that Phantom—"The Church in Danger"—it does not speak a just state of mind or thinking. That the Vultures[2] will attack it and every thing else, is likely enough— but you say they have failed on State—therefore it still stands between you and them & they can only fall together. The Nobility hate intellect— it is always in their way, and is the only thing they are really afraid of— but they know the value of it and endeavour to arm themselves from the same source as you—the Universities. And consider the ages they have

---

[1] Matthew Baillie, physician extraordinary to George III, who is said to have worked sixteen hours a day.

[2] The Whigs and the Radicals—from Constable's point of view.

stood, and the storms they have weathered. Let me hope your fears belong too much to yourself.

I was sadly ruffled with poor Read—as directly I saw his pictures I knew the weight of them. He never had an opinion from me but my fears were confirmed by all who saw them—and at the Gallery.

You are in a great scrape—and you feel it—& it is amusing to see how ingeniously you try to shake it off—by throwing all upon me & my introduction of him to you. But my introduction 2 or 3 years ago could have nothing to do with your judgement in this particular picture. In fact you very properly took great tiff at it, calling him *"Beast"* & *"Baptist"*—and tossed his sketch book round about the room—and further I could not have introduced him to you as an artist. I know that you knew better— but your consequence in Salisbury would have made any notice of yours of great value to him—or rather to his wife and children. My object was charity, thinking he would be content to vegetate in teaching where he was—and never to set foot in London—but his extreme ignorance—& vanity—& inordinate selfishness—make him capable of any thing. He has now moved his family and has written to Sir Ths. Lawrence under cover of the Bishop—to *"desire him call at* Mr Constable's to see these pictures"—& this without my knowledge as the pictures have not been returned to me. Read has ordered them to Sir Ths.'s & when he has *"done with them"* they are to be returned to me. O God. O God. The work you have made us here. The picture is entirely without hope—indeed how could it be otherwise. He is entirely ignorant of art—and a man sees nothing in nature but what he knows. Read tells me he has a landscape ready for the Royal Exhibition as fine as Lord Radnor's Claude—but not so grand. "*You see, Sir, because* we have *not such fine ruins in* this country".

That the *"Gentlemen"* at the Gallery may be ignorant, may be true—and perhaps it may be equally true that we artists are jealous—and even jealous of the Old Shepherd—this is capital—but it is better all things should have their course. I have sadly wasted this half side of my paper— but you did so with 2 sides, & that too with most idle and trumpery quotations—from some such learned fool as Milman—the most useless & troublesome of all beings. I wish you could see Martin's "Paradise" now in the Gallery—all his admirers should have been in it, & it would then have been a paradise of fools—but it is always best to give a man the rope. The artists always knew what he would come to, but they were considered jealous.

I have not yet called on the Bishop—and I wrote to him before to say, that he could not see his picture. How am I to know what you have been about. I look forward to come to you at Gillingham—and to do something at the Mill we went to. Yours ever truly

J. C.

You will see what they have been at at the Academy—Daniel's party have got in Reinagle—the most weak & undesirable artist on the list as you said.

The loss of over a month's work meant that Constable had no large picture ready in time for the Royal Academy exhibition. The upright landscape—which must almost certainly have been the preliminary study for *The Lock*[1]—had to be laid aside for another year. Its place was taken by Dr. Fisher's picture, which appeared at Somerset House under the title of *Salisbury Cathedral from the Bishop's Grounds*.[2] This won general praise and seems—for the time being, at any rate—to have given pleasure to the Bishop. Of the other pictures mentioned in the next letter, Turner's was *The Bay of Baiae, with Apollo and the Sibyl*: it was the subject of much controversy, and even Ruskin found it crude in colour. Wilkie's outdoor scene was *The Parish Beadle*,[3] again the subject of much criticism: his other painting was a portrait of the Duke of York.

Before we come to Constable's comments on the exhibition, it may be noted that there had been further changes at Salisbury this year, but for once John Fisher had not come in for a share in the distribution of prizes. The ruling Dean since 1809 had been Charles Talbot, a descendant of Bishop Talbot of Salisbury and grandson of the Lord Chancellor, who seems to have belonged to the tradition followed by Douglas and Coxe in their appreciation of good dinners. He died in 1823 and was succeeded by a very different type of man, Hugh Nicholas Pearson, whose chief interest so far had lain in missions to Asia. The Mastership of St. Nicholas Hospital, which Dean Talbot had held by way of a supplement to his stipend for the last year, now went to the Bishop's examining chaplain, young Tom Rennell, son of the older Thomas Rennell, Dean of Winchester and Master of the Temple, whom Pitt had once named 'the Demosthenes of the pulpit'. Rennell also received a prebend as a reward for his services—or possibly as a tactful form of wedding present from the Bishop in view of his impending marriage to Miss Frances Henrietta Delafield, a rich young lady from Camden Hill in Kensington, where he was Vicar. Constable did not allow his own preoccupation to prevent him from taking an interest in matters which affected the concerns of his friend. He may have thought that the academic attainments of such youthful prodigies as Milman and Rennell were tending to throw Fisher's more solid abilities into the shade, both in Fisher's estimation and that of others. Robert Southey, whom Constable had met on his visit to the Lakes in 1806 and was to meet again at Coleorton shortly, was beginning to take an interest in Church affairs.

Dear Sir

As *applause* will not pay Bills—I enclose to you another Draft on account.

Yours very truly

J Sarum

Seymour St. May 8, 1823.

---

[1] Now in McFadden Collection at the Philadelphia Museum of Art.
[2] Now at the Victoria and Albert Museum, and here reproduced. Leslie notes that Constable, as a mark of his fondness for everything connected with his native county, introduced cattle of the hornless Suffolk breed.
[3] *The Bay of Baiae* and *The Parish Beadle* are now at the Tate Gallery.

PLATE 8

SALISBURY CATHEDRAL FROM THE BISHOP'S GROUNDS

1823, by John Constable

May 9. 1823. Charlotte Street

My dear Fisher

We are bad correspondents—I have made many attempts to write to you during the present interesting season—but without effecting my purpose.

I had many interruptions to my works for the Exhibition as you know from various causes so that I have no large canvas there. My Cathedral looks very well. Indeed I got through that job uncommonly well considering how much I dreaded it. It is much approved by the Academy and moreover in Seymour St. though I was at one time fearfull it would not be a favourite there owing to a *dark cloud*—but we got over the difficulty, and I think you will say when you see it that I have fought a better battle with the Church than old Hume, Brogham[1] and their coadjutors have done. It was the most difficult subject in landscape I ever had upon my easil. I have not flinched at the work, of the windows, buttresses, &c, &c, but I have as usual made my escape in the evanescence of the chiaroscuro. I think you will like it but you could have done me much good.

I have been with the Bishop this morning for this frank. I am to *show* the young ladies the Exhibition on Monday. What a treat (it will be to them). I am vexed to see the Good Bishop looking ill. It may be a temporary cold—but he breaks, no doubt. This has been a fearfull winter for old & young. A gentleman told me last Monday, that he had witnessed at a burial ground in Spitalfeilds, 47 funerals one Sunday afternoon, when some others were sent home, as the clergyman was worn out.

I see Rennel has got another hitch from the Bishop, and Dr. Price[2]— dead—and so is the Dean.

I trembled for you—and more when I heard of the new appointment. The Evangelicals used to crow about him, but I verily beleive they had no reason—and certainly not latterly. Mr Coomb a medical friend (& an intimate friend of Dr. Burrow,[3] who exhibited March of Colchester) told me he (Pearson) had once rather got in among those people, but he was not at all tainted—and depend upon it if he was Burrow would hold no intimacy with him or any person that was so. The late Dean "*dug his grave*" with his teeth: & dropped down dead while he was preparing his dessert —as I hear. This is [?making] up a *fruit* tree.

Has not additional work fallen upon you, owing to so many imbeciles being in your Church—a Dean dead—Cox, blind—Jacobs old,[4] Price dead and Hume an idiot?

---

[1] The reference seems to be to the reforming politicians Joseph Hume and Henry Brougham (later Lord Chancellor as Lord Brougham and Vaux). Constable attacks them in his journal.

[2] Robert Price, Prebendary of South Grantham, and a Canon Residentiary, had died this year; it was his prebend which had gone to Tom Rennell.

[3] Edwin John Burrow, F.R.S., minister of a chapel of ease at Hampstead.

[4] John Henry Jacob, Prebendary of Ruscomb, died in 1828.

I

It is my wish to come to see you at Gillingham. I want to do something at that famous Mill, a mile or two off. You are in the midst of fine stuff. I am now busy both in portrait & landscape. And when my summer plans are arranged I will tell you of it, & meet you at Salisbury—I should not recognise you in any other place—and besides I have some of my children there—I have not yet seen Tinney's room.

I was glad to hear this morning that your infant is safe, and that you are all well. I have had a most anxious winter. My boy is getting about, but my wife is extremely delicate—and must be much attended to: my other children are all well, and beautifull.

Calcott admires my Cathedral. He says I have managed it well. He has a poor picture there[1]—and Turner is stark mad—with ability—the picture seems painted with saffron and indigo. Northcote gave him a sad trip up at starting. He was on my arm, when Turner asked him if he (Turner) was in his senses. Northcote said no—certainly you must be mad to do such a thing, but I can tell you over and over again, if you will persist in imitating "*Martin*" (Paradise Martin of British Gallery fame) you must be ruined. Turner has often spoke of this as a good *joke*—but as Southey would say, it *sticks*, as [it] is too sure & pungent to be laughed away.[2]

Wilkies pictures are the finest in the world. Perhaps the outdoor scene is too black. Fusili came up to him, and said "Vell—vhat dis is de new vay—dis is de Guercino. Vel I don't understand it".[3] Speaking of me generally he says—"I *like* de *landscape*—of Constable—but he makes me call for my great coat", & particularly he says, I am always picturesque— "of a fine color—& de lights always in their right places. He makes a good color"—&c. &c. This nonsense may amuse you when contemplating this busy, but distant scene. However though I am here in the midst of the world I am out of it—and am happy—and endeavour to keep myself unspoiled. I have a kingdom of my own both fertile & populous—my landscape and my children. I am envied by many, and much richer people.—

Let me hear from you—soon. I want to know of your movements, & whether you visit London this season—must you not do so "ex officio"?

I have work to do and my finances must be repaired if possible. I have a face now on my easil and may have some more. This is a great chubby boy, who has had an opportunity of running all over Italy, knows nothing of nature or art—being brought up at Oxford—and recollects nothing he saw while abroad—but that in Milan "*the Fantorini puppets* are as *large as life*".

---

[1] *Dutch Market Boats, Rotterdam.*

[2] The critic of the *New Monthly Magazine* may have heard of this when he wrote that Turner's mythological figures were 'as bad as Mr. Martin himself could have made them', and that the picture, if it did not have Turner's deservedly great name, might be mistaken for an early work of the former artist.

[3] Fuseli never lost his foreign accent, which was the subject of many jokes at the Academy.

"O dear. O dear. I shall never let my longing eyes see that famous country"—are the words of old Richardson.[1] Am I doomed never to see the living scenes—which inspired the landscape of Wilson & Claude Lorraine? No! but I was born to paint a happier land, my own dear England—and when I forsake that, or cease to love my country—may I as Wordsworth says

> "never more, hear
> "Her green leaves russel
> "Or her torrents roar"—[2]

I went to the gallery of Sir John Leicester[3] to see the English artists. I recollect nothing so much as a solemn—bright—warm—fresh—landscape by Wilson, which still swims in my brain like a delicious dream. Poor Wilson. Think of his magnificence, think of his fate! But the mind loses its dignity less in adversity than in prosperity. He is now walking arm in arm with Milton—& Linnacus. He was one of the great appointments to shew to the world the hidden stores and beauties of Nature. One of the great men who shew to the world what exists in nature but which was not known till his time.

Best regards to all *yours*. Yours most truly

J. Constable.

This lyrical outburst shows that the spring was bringing the blood back into Constable's veins again after his long depressing winter. Patrons might still be lacking; but at least he had never had to endure the poverty that Wilson knew in his declining days. And at the very time when Constable was writing this letter, Fisher was thinking of him, and planning how best he could tempt his friend to take the holiday he so badly needed to rest his nerves—that holiday in the country which was as much a spiritual necessity for Constable as the fresher air of Hampstead had become a physical necessity for his wife and children.

Gillingham Shaftesbury. May 9. 1823.

My dear Constable

We are at length settled at Gillingham. On my taking leave of Osmington, I thought of you, and brought away an old lobster pot & an assortment of our shore productions. These I have put into a box & sent

---

[1] A paraphase from Jonathan Richardson's apostrophe to Rome in *The Theory of Painting*.

[2] Adapted from the *Thanksgiving Ode on the General Peace*.

[3] Later Lord De Tabley, a man much respected by the artists of his day. Wilson had painted his *View of Tabley Hall and Park* while a guest of Sir John's father Sir Peter Leicester in Cheshire; but the collection also included a finer Wilson, *A View on the Arno*, which may be the painting of which Constable here speaks. Some writers, however, assume that he is referring to *Tabley House*: see W. G. Constable's *Richard Wilson*, 1953, pp. 186–189.

to you this day by the Old Salisbury, which rendesvouses at the Bell & Crown Holborn. I hope to see them some day in the foreground of one your sea peices.[1]

The old Salisbury Coach meets at Salisbury a western Coach which stops at my door at Gillingham downwards 3 times a week. Mondays Wednesdays & Fridays. When you can afford time we shall be delighted to see you: and if you think it will do him good, & can get trusted with the care of him we shall be glad to see little Johnny with you.

The more I see of this country the more & more I delight in it. It is genuine *home* scenery. The greens are most vivid & the foliage in the greatest luxuriance. It has the true flat Claude horizon broken occasionally by a distant hill. In my rambles I called the other day at a clergymans cottage. I found the room hung with very fine engravings. Among others Agostino Carracci's Christ stretching the chalk line. And over it, Loutherbourgs Snowdon with the coach flying over it, with sailors & their doxies enveloped in a cloud of Turnham green dust. I thought of your description "coaches where coaches never were" &c. I dined yesterday at the house built by Sir Godfrey Kneller. His descendant, a dandy, has just finished dissipating the fortune amassed by that man of wigs & drapery.[2] On the great staircase hung a beautiful portrait of Pope by Sir Godfrey: how unlike his usual efforts! I long to learn how you have succeeded in the Exhibition. The Courier mentions you with honour. "Constable has some admirable studies of landscape scenery" Courier May 6. I think to come to town about the last week in May on purpose to look at you, and to try to recover some of my property from you. What an ass was I, knowing you so well as I did, to trust you in the first place with those two sketches, & then to let go the "boat", instead of holding it as a pledge.—

I have in this short compass written out all that occurs to my mind. I hear & see nothing here, but old women, sick children, & quakers hats. With my kind regards to Mrs Constable. Beleive me

sincerely yours

John. Fisher.

Gillingham Shaftesbury. May 10. 1823

My dear Constable;

It was a pretty bit of sentiment, that we should be reciprocally thinking of one another & renewing our correspondence at the same moment, without either party setting the example. I have in truth been

---

[1] Constable used to collect a variety of natural objects for use in painting landscapes: the lobster pot would come from Osmington Mills.

[2] 'A few distinguished portraits and a small collection of pictures, principally formed by Sir Godfrey Kneller', had been sold from Donhead Hall, Wilts., in the summer of 1821, by order of Godfrey Kneller, Esq. The owner was descended from the artist's natural daughter Agnes, whose son Godfrey Huckle assumed Kneller's name on inheriting his fortune, and became possessor of Donhead by marrying the heiress, Mary Weeks.

too much occupied to sit down either to read or to write. A change of residence, getting rid of one curate & appointing another, a population of four thousand souls, & all the affairs of our invalid corps, have been employment for me more than enough. I like Dean Pearson exceedingly. I do not think (at present) that he is a Calvinist, or more serious than our cloth ought to be. At any rate be he what he may be the change cannot be for the worse. Any thing is more tolerable than the unhappy union one so often meets with, of incapacity and assumption. Now he is gone I may say that I never knew so weak & so offensive a man as he to whose grave digging you allude.

Sunday Eveng. May 18. It is 8 days ago since I wrote the above. I am just returned from Salisbury. Coxe showed me the proof sheets of his life of Corregio. It is really very nicely done. He has got over the initial part better than I expected. But he has evidently not quite a clear idea of chiaro oscuro. He has no notion that harmony & brilliancy of effect are connected with light & shade. Or that Corregio's great originality lay in that department. But still his work is well done. He proves I think satisfactorily that Corregio did not die in poverty or of the load of copper. He shows that he had bought houses & property in the city of Corregio. And what is more, *gold* was the currency of the country, & they never paid in copper. It would not have been a legal tender.

Your old friend John Foss the carpenter has been very ill with determination of blood to the head. He came to me in great distress to say that he could not bear to go into his shop, for he could not hear the sound of his own hammer. Mark Hardy an honest labourer in the Parish of Osmington has gained a chancery suit by which he gains $\frac{1}{4}$th of 1/17th of two millions of money which has arisen from the rent of estates which have been without a legitimate owner for two centuries. He has had his pedigree traced back to Edmund Ironside. His mother was an Ironside. All this is true, & no romance. I fear that the last fortnight in July & one week in August, I shall be with the Bishop on the Visitation. When do you think that you shall be here?

Tuesday. May 20. I have just appointed to be in town on Tuesday June 2. I shall call upon you that day. Why John Bull has run a muck at the Academy. What will Northcote say to his "pustules in progress". "The manner good the *matter* bad"? The Bishop is better. Poor man! nobody knows—!

Yours sincerely

John. Fisher.

The Dean was only fifty-four.

Fisher kept his promise of coming up to London at the beginning of the next month. Writing to his wife from the Charterhouse on the 4th June,[1] and

---

[1] Letter in the collection of Mr. John Fisher.

mentioning the pictures at the Royal Academy exhibition, he said: 'Constable has put the Bishop & Mrs F. as figures in his view very like & characteristic.'

A piece of news which Fisher does not mention in his next letter was that yet another member of the family had been brought into Salisbury. This was his youngest brother William, his junior by ten years, who had followed his father to Oxford and had been ordained priest in the previous year. In June 1822 he had tried his prentice hand by conducting three marriages in his brother's church at Osmington, where he must have met Mrs. Fisher's sister, Elizabeth Cookson. In 1823 he was presented to the living of Poulshot in Wiltshire, and on the 11th June he was collated to the prebend of Ilfracombe, which his father resigned in his favour. This meant that no less than four stalls in the choir of the cathedral were now occupied by members of the Fisher family. This in itself was a sufficiently striking manifestation of fraternal affection; but more was to follow. When Constable went down to stay with John Fisher a few months later, he learnt that his friend's brother was to be married to Mrs. Fisher's sister and was only waiting for the parsonage at Poulshot to be made ready for their occupation before that event took place. Before a year was out, William Fisher had married Elizabeth Cookson, and was presently brought into the Palace in his brother's old post of domestic chaplain. In due course he too became a canon residentiary, and was the last of the Fishers to be a voice in the Chapter when he died in 1874.

To look still further ahead, it may be observed that his son Herbert William Fisher kept the old Fisher tradition alive by becoming, while still a student at Christ Church, tutor to a grandson of the Bishop's old pupil Edward Duke of Kent: but this time the pupil lived to ascend to the throne as King Edward VII, and the tutor was rewarded with the ancient post of Vice-Warden of the Stannaries, of which he was the last holder. Memories of the past are evoked by the names of two of his sons of whom the eldest was Herbert Albert Laurens Fisher, Warden of New College, the famous historian, while the youngest was Admiral Sir William Wordsworth Fisher.

Gillingham. Shaftesbury. June 30. 1823.

My dear Constable.

Mr Arthur Drury, a fellow of Trinity college Oxford is candidate for the Mastership of Dedham school. If you can use any influence in his favour, you will confer a great favour on me. He is a gentleman & a scholar. Dr Hurlock votes.—[1]

Knowing how much you are tied down by your family, your portraits, & the necessity of carrying your dish between *fame* & *famine*, I almost despair of seeing you here. Let me hear what prospect I have of a visit & about what time. Coxe's Social Day came across my path the other day & I unexpectedly opened upon your Windmill.[2] The beauty of the thing

---

[1] Dr. James T. Hurlock, curate at and later Rector of the Bishop's church at Langham, who had been collated to Fisher's former prebend of Hurstbourn in 1821.

[2] A landscape engraved in line by J. Landseer in 1814 for *The Social Day* by Peter Coxe, not published till 1823. The original water-colour is in the Victoria and Albert Museum.

has sadly evaporated in the engraving. But what can the graver do with things that depend entirely upon feeling, freshness, & colour.

I wish you would procure for me that fruit peice in Covent Garden. That is if you will *let* me have it. I will send a draft immediately if you only say that you have secured it. It is a delicious plate of clean colours.

My kindest regards to your Wife.

Beleive me

my dear Constable

truly yours

John. Fisher.

1823, July to December

The turn of the year found Constable in better health and spirits. Two of the characters named in the following letter require a special word of mention. The Rev. Thomas James Judkin was for many years pastor of the episcopal chapel at Somers Town. He was himself by way of being an artist, holding the rank of Honorary Exhibitor at the Royal Academy, to which he contributed a number of views of the scenery round Southgate. Judkin entertained a passionate admiration for Constable, and the latter may for a time have found the incense of the acolyte acceptable: later on, however, he grew excessively weary of it, and did his best to shake Judkin off; but Judkin was not to be so easily discouraged, and reappeared in the end to preach the funeral sermon over Constable's grave.

Sir William Curtis, the banker and former Lord Mayor of London, was a bird of a very different feather. He was a great favourite of George IV, who had stayed with him in his house at Ramsgate two years before. He had another house, Culland's Grove near Edmonton, where Constable dined with him. Curiously enough, his wife bore the name of Anne Constable, but she does not seem to have been any relation to the artist. Sir William also, in his own way, took an interest in the arts.

Charlotte Street. July 3d 1823

My dear Fisher

I received your letter on Tuesday and on that day I wrote to my Brother urging him to use all his influence at Dedham in Mr Drury's behalf. Abram is not the man to lose time or spare exertion in our favor.

And as delays always are bad I set off immediately after the picture. To my surprize it was not gone, and it still improving upon me, I made an offer of eight guineas for it—but the barber was obstinate, for the price (10 Gns.). I assured him I was no gentleman, when he offered it at 9— but I procured it for 8 guins—which will help for a case, &c.[1] The size is

---

[1] The picture is now in the Fitzwilliam Museum at Cambridge, to which it was bequeathed by Fisher's son Osmond in 1914.

about 4 feet by 5 feet & a half. It has a gilt moulding which will clean—*glewed on the face of the painting*—about an inch & half wide. This is barbarous—but I fear it will not remove without injury.

It is a beautiful picture—and must at all hours give pleasure. Nothing can be more real than the things—and it is impossible to imagine a more delicious freshness in color, or correctness or elegance in shape.

I am anxious to come to you this year—& shall, and after this month, when I shall have got my jobs a little under. I leave it to you to name any week or ten days, in August or Sepr.

Let me hear from you soon—at any rate, as I can make but one visit this summer.

I have been a day or two at Southgate at Judkins. He is a sensible man —& you thought so—but he will paint. We dined at Sir Wm. Curtis's. He is a fine old fellow and quite a gentleman—it is his brother who is so woefully reduced & . . . for him. Sir Wm is now sitting for his portrait to Lawrence for the King,[1] who desired the portrait in these words—"Dam you my old boy—I'll have you in all your canonicals, when I can look at you every day". He is a great favorite—birds of a feather—
The last bell has rung.—

Adieu my dear Fisher Yrs

John Constable

My wife & children well—thank you for your kind regards. John is mending & we are afraid will remain . . .

A great row with Turner & Collins—but we are all square again—he[2] showed me a pretty picture he is now painting—but it is insipid—"far too pretty to be natural".

Let me know your wishes about the picture—and pray lose no time in sending the draft, for the payment of it has left me moneyless. You have hit my case—but I have the highest opinion of your skill in cases—I am struggling with *"fame & famine"*.

My best regards hope all are well. Let us be at Salisbury together either going or coming to Gillingham.

Gillingham, Shaftesbury. July 5. 1823.

My dear Constable;

Where *real* business is to be done you are the most energetic and punctual of men: in smaller matters, such as putting on your breeches,

---

[1] Sir William seems to have sat to Lawrence three times. The portrait here mentioned may be that which was inscribed 'G. R., to his faithful and loyal subject, Sir William Curtis'.

[2] Probably Collins. Collins's temper seems to have been spoiled by marriage, and another friendship was drawing to a close.

you are apt to lose time in deciding which leg shall go in first. I thank you heartily for the speed with which you have executed both my commissions. Below I send you a draft for £10,,10. If there is a frame to the picture and it is worth touching up I wish it to be done. If there is no frame I must beg you to procure me one. In the latter case perhaps it had better be now, as I shall hang the picture in my Salisbury house. But I trust in this as in other matters to your excellent judgment. I have never had this picture out of my eye since I saw it. Still life is always dull as there are no associations of ideas with it except to such men as Dr Browning. But this is so deliciously fresh that I could not resist it. If you have one of your coast Windmills[1] hanging up on your wall framed, I wish you would put it up with the fruit peice.

And now with regard to our meeting. I preach the Infirmary Sermon at the Cathedral in September. I am just beginning to put the colours on my canvass. I should be unwilling to have you here before the picture is finished as I must either neglect it or lose the pleasure of your company. Again I am unwilling to put your visit off to the old age of the summer when all the associations are those of decay. I will work hard & get finished by the 18th or 20th of August: about which time I will expect you. When you give me notice of your coming, I will drive over to Salisbury & give you the meeting. If this arrangement is not convenient to you, you may say as much & make it so. I care not how long you stay. I have discovered *three* mills, old small & picturesque on this river.[2]

Have you not some engravings for me? And were you not to bring some of Waterloo's etchings with you for me from Colnaghi?

I have a great desire to possess your "wain". But I cannot now reach what it is worth & what you *must have*. But I have this favour to ask that you would never part with it without letting me know. It will be of most value to your children, by continuing to hang where it is, till you join the society of Ruysdael Wilson & Claude. As praise & money will be of no value to you *then* personally, the world will liberally bestow both.—Tinney says that his picture is inferior to mine. He cannot find out that mine hangs alone; & that his is hurt (as is always the case) by villianous company. I dined the other day with our new puritanical Dean. He gave me Champagne, Hock, Constantia & Claret: but would not suffer *cards*. Poor blind Coxe was obliged to forego his game of cribbage tho his pricked pack of cards was in his pocket. I went afterwards to the Palace & found two Bishops & a Chancellor at whist. Yrs. J F.

(to be cut off)

Constable's answer bears the London postmark of the 10th July.

---

[1] *Harwich Lighthouse:* the reference suggests that Constable had painted at least two versions of this picture.
[2] The Wiltshire and Dorset Stour.

My dear Fisher,

I received your capital letter on Monday. I am always pleased with myself when I have pleased you. You have made an excellent purchase of a most delightfull work. It is a pearly picture but its tone is so deep & mellow that it plays the very devil with my landscapes. It makes them look speckled & frost bitten, but I shall make my account of it, as I am now working for "*tone*".

The painter is G. de Vris,[1] an artist cotemporary with Rubens—& de Heem painted his excellent fruit & flowers at that time, but this painters works are more scarce, and old Bigg thinks more excellent. I congratulate you, and I should have done so had you possessed it at almost any price.

I have stripped it of its barbarous & trumpery border, which was cemented on the very *surface* of the picture, and hid two inches of background all round, to the great injury of the composition,

I shall not involve you in much expence for a frame, but shall consider it more as a highly decorated panel, but I will not sacrifice the picture. It has cost me some trouble to make good the backgrounds at the edge, I speak of, but it is well worth recovering, as the want of an efficient feild crowded the composition.

You cannot think how much the picture is liked.

How amused I am with your letter. I am present at the deanery—and at the Palace. It is a laughable, but melancholy picture of some whom we well know. You are a great painter of manners.

I count much of our meeting. It will be my only holiday—and the only visit I desire to make. The time you speak of will do exactly for me without any thing, fortunate or unfortunate, occurs. Be it so. My wife is amused with your temptation—you think "*three mills*" irresistable, but it is you I most want.

I have a proposal to make to Tinney—he must let me have his picture & 50 or 60 Gs. and I paint him another—more for the ladies and old Hume.

Sir Wm. Curtis has a hankering—after my ["Wain"]. But I am not sanguine: and you I shall much prefer. We can talk about it. It was born a companion to your picture in sentiment. It must be yours. It is no small compliment to the picture that it haunted the mind of the Alderman from the time he saw it at the Institution, but though a man of the world he is all heart, and really loves nature. It does me a deal of good where it now is, therefore let it at present remain.

Should Tinney & I agree, it will enable me to paint another large picture for the Exhibition. I am hurt this year for the want of one—the Church should have been an offset only.

---

[1] The work is so signed: but little is known of the artist.

Lady *Dysart*[1] (*the last of the Tollmache's*) has a grand party to night. I was there yesterday.

The Exhibition closes on Saturday. It has not been so productive as last year, for obvious reasons—look on the walls. Academicians claim the places their rank gives them and you saw how the walls were filled. Old Daniel & young Daniel. Old Reinagle & young Reinagle—"Northcote", &c. &c. all of John Bull notoriety. I only fear the foundations of those walls are bad. If so it must tumble altogether.

Sir G. Beaumont has just left me. He is a capital fellow. He is pleased with a large wood I have just toned.[2] He said "well done". We shall in time drive the "Albanians"—from the feild. The civil war is at its highest in the Academy, the *white* & the *black Rose*. Collins, & the Sculpture & the portrait painters are for Turner, but it won't do. He is ruined in art— & he is watchfull & savage. Lawrence is *deep*, & sly, & cold.

The following letter is known only from the transcript printed by Leslie, who gives the year as 1822; but the Bishop's '2' is very like his '3', and Constable's next letter shows that he had only just received the news contained therein.

Malmesbury, August 3rd, 1823.

Dear Sir,

My daughter Elizabeth is about to change her situation, and try whether she cannot perform the duties of a wife as well as she has done those of a daughter. She wishes to have in her house a recollection of Salisbury; I mean, therefore, to give her a picture, and I must beg of you either to finish the first sketch of my picture, or to make a copy of the small size. I wish to have a more serene sky. I am now on my visitation, and shall not be at Salisbury till the 20th, but my letters follow me.

J. Sarum

Elizabeth Fisher, the Bishop's younger daughter, was engaged to John Mirehouse, a lawyer connected with the Old Bailey. As he had a family estate at Brownslade in Pembrokeshire, with a town house (though a small one) in Orchard Street, and was reputed to enjoy an income of £3,000 a year, it was regarded as a good match in every respect. It is true that Mr. Mirehouse's manners were rough and that he was not at all a polished man, but he was clever and much respected. He had been struck by the amiable character of Elizabeth and had fallen in love with her. After conveying their congratulations to the young lady in person three weeks later, Constable told his wife, 'She

---

[1] Louisa, Countess of Dysart in her own right, who had succeeded her brother in 1821. Hoppner's portrait of her as Lady Louisa Manners had been copied by Constable in 1807, and the copy is still to be seen at Ham House. Constable's description of her as the last of the Tollemaches is not quite correct, for her descendants were allowed to take the name of the family which she represented.

[2] Leslie says this was a large sketch for *A Dell in Helmingham Park*, of which there are several versions.

respects the man, but 'tis the Bishop's doing, for support'. It will be noticed
that the Bishop now speaks of the view from his grounds as 'my picture'.

As was Fisher's custom, a draft for money on his bankers was written at the
top of the next letter. This has been cut out for encashment, taking with it part
of the letter on the back; but the missing contents have been added in Constable's
writing, with the omission of the archdeacon's improper anecdote. The address
and date have also been removed, but the postmark shows that the letter was
delivered at Charlotte Street on the 15th August 1823.

My dear Constable.

I have been looking into our account & find that I am £12. 8s. in
yr debt of which I send you £6. 6s. 0. We will close the account when I
see you here. I shall be at Salisbury next Tuesday the 19th. Inst. on which
day I must beg you to be there, or you will have to come on to Gillingham
alone. Have the goodness to have the Fruit peice packed up & sent down
to Salisbury by Woolcots waggon Castle & Falcon Aldersgate St. so that
we may look at it together. I am anxious to see it, as I know it is as difficult
to get a picture out of a painters room as a title deed out of an Attorneys
office. I beg also more earnestly that you *let* me have one of your Windmill
coast scenes framed and that it may come down with the great picture. You
promised also to let me purchase your duplicate Dutch school engravings.

That ever Sir G. Beaumont should have got into Chancery to recover
one of Haydons pictures![1] This is only a letter of business. Adieu till we
meet. *I don't expect you to come.* I wish you could see old Dean Rennell[2]
& our Bishop together. One skipping about his garden shewing his improvements which 'tother dont care a sixpence for. The Dean, hobbling
along, spouting Greek & spittle, both which the Bishop holds in equal
detestation.

Yrs.

J F.*

*I cant sign my name to the above anecdote. Before you pay away the
draft obliterate my writing at the back. I forgot myself.

The letter below was addressed by the Bishop to Constable at Stamford Lodge,
Hampstead,[3] which the latter had taken for his family during the summer.

Devizes. Aug. 17.

Dear Sir

I am now nearly at the end of my Labors. The Visitation will end
next week, & on Thursday I shall hope to dine at Sarum.

[1] Haydon, as Constable told Farington, had once been Beaumont's 'hero'. The reference may be to the insolvency from which Haydon had just been discharged.
[2] The Dean had presumably come down for his son's marriage.
[3] The cover, which has become divorced from its contents, is now in the Leggatt
Collection.

I understand that you are expected at Gillingham about that time. I therefore write to beg you will come to Sarum on that day, & stay with us till the Monday following on which day we must leave Salisbury.

My Daughter Dorothea has much to consult you about, & we all wish to see you.

I am, Dear Sir, yours faithfully

J. Sarum

Dear Sir

Lest you should not be at Hampstead to which place I have directed a Letter to you—I write again to express our hope of seeing you at Sarum in your way to Gillingham where we hear you are going. We return home on Thursday & leave Sarum on Monday.

With respect to Smith I wish you to engage to pay the Ornament maker his two Pounds—& also to advance him a pound or two for the Gold Leaf—or rather to buy for him as much gold Leaf as he may need for my Frames.

I am Sir, in a great haste, yours

J Sarum

Devizes, Sunday.

Constable's next letter is headed with a triumphant announcement of his impending reunion with Fisher.

Astley Cooper[1] often arrives an hour sooner than the time fixed for performing an operation by which the patient is spared the anticipation of the approaching moments . . . ! ! !

Charlotte St. Aug. 18. 1823

My dear Fisher

I had fixed "*Wednesday* the 20*th*", to come to you—I now make it "Tuesday the 19th". I have taken a place with the little Salisbury coach and shall arrive in the evening. I must regret that by a mistake of my servant here I did not receive your welcome letter 'till 9 o clock on Saturday evening. Your beautiful picture had "*left*" my *house* but it will not arrive soon enough at Salisbury to meet us. I have had much trouble & delays in getting ready, all of which I shall explain. The frame is my own invention & has gone through many hands and coming only occasionally from Hampstead has been delayed. I think you will like what I have done—it is not expensive—at least I hope you will not think it so—about £4.4.0— but I shall bring all the accounts with me—of the case, packing &c. &c.

---

[1] Sir Astley Paston Cooper, F.R.S., the hard-working surgeon under whom Dr. Gooch had trained.

You will not grudge it. The picture is lovely, It always puts me not only in good humour but in the humour for painting—I regret its departure—

I have not a sea peice[1]—or "*Windmill Coast Scene*" "*at all*". I gave it to Gooch for his kind attention to my children. Half an hour ago I received a letter from Woodburne to purchase it or one of my seapeices—but I am without one—they are much liked—you have my sketch of Osmington.[2]

I have much to say which must be deferd till *tomorrow*—

I have had some troublesome letters from the Bishop—one of which walked me off from Hampstead to Kensington—after the wretched Smiths. The Bishops frame for the Salisbury remains in the same state it was at X'mas—wood much injured at the Exhibition. The Bishop wants another Salisbury, for Elizabeth who is going to be married—to whom? I wish they would take my frame & let my copy be the same size as that & so use the Bishops frame.

I leave my family with "*great pleasure*", they are all so well. Tomorrow my tall nurse [is] leaving us. I regret to part with so excellent & fine tempered a woman, but we found an excellent situation for her—& it spares me all but 70 £ a year—or 60.

I have done a great deal of work since I saw you—what I could take up to Hampd with me I did there.

I was at the Countess of Dysarts (*the last of the Tollmache's*) fate champetre at the old House at Ham. I have pleased her by painting 2 portraits lately—she sent me half a buck.

I have received Coxes Corregio "from the Author".

My wife laughed half an hour, at your expression—"but I don't expect you to come". What a trio you have like described to me—old Majendie's[3] bawdry—old Rennell's snott & spittal—and the Bishops very gentlemanly manners—excellent.

yours most sincerely

J. Constable.

On the 19th August Constable came down inside the coach to Salisbury and arrived in time to be sitting down to dinner with Fisher at six o'clock in the evening. He received a very friendly reception from the Bishop and his family, who were anxious that he should stop on over the following week-end; but Fisher was in a hurry to get back to Gillingham where he had left his wife, who was expecting another baby, to look after the children without her sister's help.

Constable, however, was able to make a sketch of the cathedral on the 20th

---

[1] A *Yarmouth Jetty* had been shown at the British Gallery earlier in the year: this seems to have been sold already.

[2] *Osmington Bay*, here reproduced by the kindness of the owner.

[3] Perhaps the Bishop of Bangor, said to have been a most enlightened Bishop: but several members of the family were connected with Salisbury.

PLATE 9

WILLIAM FISHER ('BELIM')

c. 1823, by John Constable

August[1] and he found time to transact his business with Tinney. 'Tinny is most kind & friendly,' he wrote to his wife, 'and wants two landscapes the size of the Cathedral upright—at 50 guineas each. Had I not better do them than get back the other to paint another for it?' In his next letter he seems to speak of the matter as settled, and refers to the painting of the two pictures as a nice employment for the winter.

On the 22nd August he was driven over to Gillingham by a different road from that taken on the last visit, going by Mere and passing Fonthill Gate. In spite of the beauty of some of the scenery he found Gillingham itself a melancholy place, with the corn in the fields around beaten down by the rain, and Fisher evidently was not enjoying his residence there. The local people, chiefly small farmers and cattle dealers, looked upon him as their natural enemy, and among the four thousand odd inhabitants he and his wife had not yet found a single friend with whom they were on visiting terms. The villagers were incredibly dirty, and as there was not one doctor in the whole large parish Fisher spent much of his time effecting cures, thereby enhancing Constable's already high opinion of his medical skill.

From Gillingham Constable was able to send his wife the description of the Fisher children with which it seems that she had asked to be supplied. Osmond, in long trousers and waistcoat and blue jacket, with a large shirt collar and frill, was a fine boy, larger than the Constable's John: he was now shedding his first teeth, stammered very much, and was constantly in one kind of trouble or another. Emma, wearing little trousers with a frill to them, was a dear little meek creature, bashful and quiet, with her hair flowing in ringlets.

Constable's favourite, beyond any doubt, was William, with his fair skin and blue eyes. 'Belim', as he was usually called, was a strong robust boy nearly three years old who reminded Constable of his own Charley and seems to have spent much time on his elderly friend's knee. 'He kisses like a marrow pudding', said Fisher. Last of all came little Frank, nicknamed the Master of the Charterhouse after his grandfather. He was a delicate child with silky hair quite white in appearance, who was always losing things.

On the 28th August Constable was taken over to Fonthill, where the sale postponed from the previous year was now due to be held. In the meantime, however, Beckford had sold the house and most of its contents to a gunpowder manufacturer; and the sale was made over to Christie's old clerk, Harry Phillips of New Bond Street, an enterprising man who made many additions to the previous catalogue. A full account of this visit was given by Constable in a letter to his wife dated the 29th August.[2]

I was at Fonthill yesterday. It was very good-natured of Fisher to take me to see that extraordinary place. The ticket to admit two persons is a guinea, besides impositions afterwards. Fisher says, there have been great changes in the articles since last year; so that it is quite an auctioneer's job. Many superb things are not now there and many others added— especially pictures. One of the latter (or I am greatly mistaken), a battle

---

[1] Victoria and Albert Museum no. 256, 7⅛ × 10⅛.
[2] The transcript is Leslie's, with the names restored.

by Wovermans, I saw at Reinagle's just before I left town. Yesterday, being a fine day, a great many people were there. I counted more than thirty carriages, and the same number of gigs, and two stage coaches; so that, in spite of the guinea tickets, there was a great mixture of company, and indeed very few genteel people. There was a large room fitted up with boxes like a coffee-house, for dinners, &c., &c. Mr. Phillips's name seemed here as great as Buonaparte's. Cards of various kinds, and boards, were put up, "Mr. P. desires this", "Mr. P. takes the liberty of recommending the following inns for beds", &c., &c. But I observed many long faces coming away from the said inns.

I wandered up to the top of the tower. Salisbury, at fifteen miles off, darted up into the sky like a needle, and the woods and lakes were magnificent; and then the wild region of the downs to the north. But the distant Dorsetshire hills made me long much to be at dear old Osmington, the remembrance of which must always be precious to you and me. The entrance to Fonthill and the interior are beautiful. Imagine Salisbury Cathedral, or, indeed, any beautiful Gothic building, magnificently fitted up with crimson and gold, and ancient pictures, and statues in almost every niche; large gold boxes for relics, &c., and looking-glasses, some of which spoiled the effect. But, on the whole, it is a strange, ideal, romantic place; quite fairy-land. The spot is chosen in the midst of mountains and wilds.

We have had such sad weather that I have been able to but little, but I have made one or two attacks on the old mill.

Some idea of what Constable meant by 'an auctioneer's job' may be gained from the fact that, according to one account, Phillips had extended Christie's original list of pictures from 115 items to 415; and it will be seen that the recently elected Royal Academician was not above joining in the fraud when it gave him the chance of selling one of his 'old masters' at a profit.

On the 1st September Constable had what he described as a magnificent ride with Fisher to Sherborne. He thought it a fine old town, and considered the collegiate church finer than Salisbury Cathedral. They must have spent the night there, since a drawing of the church by Constable is dated the 2nd September.[1]

In consequence of these excursions and the poor weather in August Constable had been able to do little in the way of sketching when he wrote to his wife on the 5th September, though he had managed to produce a little oil-sketch of Belim[2] before his favourite was taken off by his mother that morning to see his Aunt Cookson at Bath. By this time the weather had turned uncommonly fine; but though there were some beautiful evenings, the extreme heat and the glare from the sun made it difficult to work out of doors during the day.

Already on the 24th August Constable had written to say that the mills with which Fisher had tempted him were pretty, and one of them wonderful old and

---

[1] Victoria and Albert Museum no. 354.
[2] Formerly with Agnew's.

PLATE 10

THE BRIDGE AT GILLINGHAM, DORSET

romantic. His letter of the 29th shows that he had already made some attempt to depict the one that attracted him most, and on the 5th September he wrote, 'I have done something from one of the old mills which you will like'. This, it may be presumed, was a small study for the oblong *Gillingham Mill* of which, as will be recorded later, he promised to let Fisher have a finished version.

Fisher as usual would be able to supply his guest with the necessary equipment for painting; and his son Osmond, now nearly six, retained a clear recollection in later life of having seen Constable sitting with his easel during the visit at the right-hand corner of the picture known as *Gillingham Bridge*.[1] This must be the work to which Constable refers when writing to his wife on the 7th September as an excuse for the further prolongation of his absence from home: 'It will enable me to make a little picture of this village rather more compleat. It is for Fisher, a present to his mother—I shall bring it to London—this is to be paid for.'

On the same day Fisher wrote to his own wife:[2] 'We four dine together every day at two oclock: & Mr Constable likes his company so much, or your absence, that he stays till Wednesday. I conclude that the latter is the reason for his good humour, in as much as he fixes to go the day before your return. . . .

'We had all of us a delicious walk beside a pretty stream on the left of the Mere Road on Friday evening, Frank & all. There a tree thrown across on a bridge. Over this Osmond ran, & Frank skipped to their great delight. Belineen was seized with a pain in the middle & cried, "Oh I shall fall in come & help me Papa." Mr Constable painted,[3] Harriet gathered flowers & Christie hunted Water Rats. . . .'

The letter closes with messages from Belim, one of which runs: 'I make tea for Papa & have dinner with him & Mr Constable & Osman too. Only Mr Constable never comes in to dinner till the night.'

The weather did not prevent Constable from attaining his main objective, which was that of doing something with the 'old Mill' that had first attracted his attention as the subject of a possible picture when he drove over with Fisher to Gillingham three years before. This was an undershot water-mill worked by a branch of the Wiltshire and Dorset Stour, and belonging to Matthew Parham, which lay about a mile to the north of the town, just off the road to Mere: it is still in working order, though rebuilt since Constable's visit. It was (and still is) known as 'Perne's Mill', thus bearing Tinney's second name; and Tinney, who originally came from Gillingham, seems to have had some ancestral connection with the mill. The fruits of Constable's struggles with the mill will be mentioned in their proper place.

Mrs. Constable's patience was beginning to wear more than a little thin by this time, for her husband had been talking of coming home in a day or two since the end of August; but he found it hard to tear himself away from the

---

[1] The original sketch is probably that in the Tate Gallery. The version on which Osmond Fisher's note is written, and formerly taken by me to be the original, may be a copy of Constable's work by Dorothea Fisher.

[2] Letter in the collection of Mr. John Fisher.

[3] The original study for Perne's Mill may be a small oil-sketch formerly in the Salting Collection and now with the Earl of Haddington. No preliminary study for the upright version is known, though one may have been done on the spot.

K

vicarage which was, he said, a world in itself. 'Fisher is my best friend in the world', he wrote in one of his letters, and in another, 'Fisher is indeed a valuable and most intelligent friend—he esteems me as highly as one man can another for every thing—& Mrs F. says in her letter, "I am a most amiable man".'

In his last letter he spoke of waiting till the 10th September to hear from his wife before arranging for his return journey. Another of the Archdeacon's letters to Mrs. Fisher shows that Constable was still with him on the 10th; and as Friday fell on the 12th it may not have been until a day or two after then that he at last rejoined his family in Hampstead.

The time for Elizabeth Fisher's wedding was now approaching, having been fixed for October; and before Constable left Gillingham the carriage which was to convey her to her new home had already arrived and was standing in great state at the Bishop's palace, to astonish the natives of Salisbury, which Constable found laughable but imputed to the bridegroom's lack of polish. The year of the Bishop's next letter is fixed by his reference to the forthcoming event.

Palace Sarum. Sept: 24.

Dear Sir

I wish you would finish the small Picture of Salisbury as soon as may be. It is to be placed for the present in the back Drawing Room in London & opposite the Chimney Piece. Elizabeth after her marriage is to occupy our house in Seymour Street till we settle in town. I wish to have your Picture finished & placed in the house to surprize & to greet the Bride on her arrival in London.

If Smith should not have the Frame ready, I will no longer be trifled with—I will arrest him.

I am, my dear Sir,

Yours very truly

J. Sarum.

Constable had already heard during his visit that the Bishop was very angry with Smith, to whom he had advanced four pounds.

It was only after his return to London that Constable found time to thank Fisher for his hospitality.[1]

Charlotte Street Sepr. 30. 1823

My dear Fisher

I should have thanked you before now for my delightfull visit: but I found on my return so much occupation that my writing has been too long delayed. But I trust forms will weigh as little with you as with me in a friendship which is at once the pride—the honour—and grand stimulus of my life.

---

[1] The letter that follows has twice appeared at Sotheby's and was sold with the Westley Manning Collection in 1954. A photograph is in the Fitzwilliam Museum.

We have heard of you and Mrs. Fisher by the papers amongst the visitors at the sale—"Archdeacon & Mrs. Fisher"—and was you the Revd. Mr Fisher who so nobly stemmed the fire at Salisbury? I have just received a letter from the Bishop to forward my small picture of the Church,[1] that it may be ready to "greet and *surprize* the Bride" on her arrival in Seymour St. I had fortunately got it very forward. When must it be ready?

My Gillingham studies give great satisfaction. Old Bigg likes them better than any I have yet done. Collins not so. He has made some pretty parchment coloured things at Hampstead. Linnell has likewise been up there and has made some very cunning studies. I hear that Fuselli is dying —at the Academy, but is now . . . water on the chest—I shall lose an admirer.[2]

I found my wife and children all well, better than I have ever had them —since they belonged to me. They wish for a little longer stay at Hampstead—but [it] sadly unsettles me—to be torn from my painting room— and the work I do by littles up there is of no avail. I am now pretty full handed. I have begun putting Tinney's pictures compositions together, and I have several pretty minor things to do—but my difficulty lies in what I am to do for the world, next year I must work for myself—and must have a large canvas. If you are at Salisbury let me know, as I want to write to Tinney about his large picture, which I want up—I shall be glad of it frame and all, and I must of course pay that expence.

Pray let me know how you liked yourself on the 18 Sepr. at the Church —and if your sermon answered the purpose. Pray likewise tell Osmond that his boot-jack excited considerable admiration and in John astonishment. I have no other & it is in dayly use with me at Hampstead—I have been mostly here by day—and have got all my commissions on canvas.

The draft you gave me for the £15.1.8. I should have found of the greatest service on my return—but [on] taking it into the City I found it was drawn on the Salisbury bank—and not payable at Walters—will you have the kindness to bear this in mind shortly?

The English Claude[3] is painting at the Gallery, copying one of the broadest of Sir Joshua's works (Lady & Child), with a crow quill fitch [sketch of the artist at his easel]. He has on a French yellow-brown fur cap—&c. He has (as well as his copy) attracted much notice—and if possible become much more known. He has commenced "*portrait painter*".

Since writing so much I am returned from over the way. Reinagle asked me to see his *diploma* picture. It is such art as I cannot talk about—heartless—vapid—and without interest. In landscape this is abominable—his is a landscape.[4]

---

[1] Salisbury Cathedral.
[2] Fuseli, however, lived on till 1825.
[3] John Glover.
[4] *Landscape and Cattle*, No. 294 in the Diploma Gallery.

I was on Saturday at the private view of the "*Diorama*"—it is a trans-
parency, the spectator in a dark chamber—it is very pleasing & has great
illusion—it is without the pale of Art because its object is deception[1]—
Claude's never was—or any other great landscape painter's. The style of
the pictures is French, which is decidely against them. Some real stones,
as bits of brown paper & a bit of silver lace turned on a wheel glides
through the stone—to help. The place was filled with foreigners—& I
seemed to be in a cage of magpies.

How are your children—I cannot get Belim out of my head. My best
regards to Mrs. F. Ever yours [truly]

John Constable

The mention of the Diorama takes us over to France again, for it was thence
that the novelty had come to London. It was a variation on the Panorama, so
fashionable at the beginning of the century, when Colonel Fisher had taken
some part in it, the attraction lying in the way the effect of the pictorial views
was heightened by the changing lights thrown upon them as they passed by.
The show had been brought across from Paris to Regent's Park by no less a
person than Louis Jacques Mandé Daguerre, who is said to have been a brother-
in-law of Arrowsmith and who was himself a painter, though he is now better
known for his pioneer work in photography. Also concerned in the Diorama
was the landscape-painter Charles Marie Bouton, whom Constable was to meet
in less than a year's time.

Fisher's next letter[2] gave Constable a piece of good news.

Close Salisbury. October 2. 1823.

My dear Constable;

I thank you for your amusing & agreeable letter. I shall often make
mistakes in our money matters that I may hear of you more frequently. If
you, or *bearer*, present my draft at Messrs. Stephensons in Lombard
Street, it will be honored.

Tinney returned home yesterday from Paris. Of his visit & account of
things by & bye. He consents to let his picture & frame come to London.
I will see them packed. But he does it, he confesses, because he can deny
you nothing. He dreads your touching the picture. This of course is not
his own thought, for he would not discover any alteration you might make.
But it is the suggestion of Lewis the engraver.[3] "There is a look of nature
about the picture," says Lewis, "which seems as if it were introduced by
magic. This, when Constable gets it on his easil, he may in an unlucky
moment destroy: and he will never paint another picture like it, for he

---

[1] Leslie adds: 'The art pleases by *reminding, not by deceiving*.' This may have been
taken from another letter, or from Constable's conversation.
[2] The letter has been split up into two portions: the first part of it is in the Constable
Collection, while the last sheet, from 'I am delighted to hear', is in the Fisher Collection.
[3] Frederick Charles Lewis, landscape painter and engraver.

has unfortunately taken to copy himself." You must take the sweet & the bitter together. Lewis seemed to speak, Tinney said, as if he reported the opinion of other artists as well as himself. I leave you to digest the criticism as you may. If it is just, it is right you should know it: if it is erroneous it will put you on your guard.—

I should repeat to you an opinion I have long held; that no man had ever more than one conception: Milton emptied his mind in his first book of the P[aradise] L[ost], all the rest is transcript of self. The Odyssey is a repetition of the Iliad. When you have seen one Claude you have seen all. I can think of no exception to this observation but Shakespeare: he is always various; however mannered.

Mrs F and I were certainly at Fonthill with ten other people in the sale room. The goods were China, selling absurdly cheap. I suspect though many of them stale London articles. I laid out a few punds to please my wife, & got three lots of old china. One of them I bought on the speculation of *swapping* it with you for one of your little sea peices.

I was moreover the Mr Fisher who worked at the fire. The house burnt was an old wooden one of the date of Edw: III near the council chamber & of this fashion [sketch of a half-timbered building with pointed gables]. It caught fire about 9 on a bright moon light evening. The lathe & plaster all burnt first, & then I saw the skeleton of a wooden house filled with fire. It illuminated the Market place (in which it stands) & made it look like a Canaletti. When the house fell, an immense black cloud of smoke rose between me & the house obscuring the object: the light breaking gloriously from the edges. The firemen all got drunk & we gentlemen turned to supply water.

We expect that the Lady will be married in about a fortnight, but the precise day is a profound secret if the Bishop can hold water for so long. —I have given her a handsome peice of plate which has delighted all parties.—

I forgot while on the subject of Fonthill to tell you I got into chat with Mr Philips.—"How came your Woovermans at Reinagle's?" asked I. It was never there quoth he. "Oh yes it was," I said.—"Aye by the bye it went to be cleaned. If you want a picture cleaned I can recommend Mr Reinagle."—I suspect that the pictures will go very cheap.[1] I shall keep my eye on the *snow* storm Woovermans. It was a *snow storm* I found afterwards; not a chalk pit as you supposed.

The Bishop thinks Fuseli will be no loss to the art. He wants you to alter the trees in my large landscape because they stick to the sky.—He hopes that you put your *marriage* picture of Salisbury into a little sunshine. Neither he nor any of the girls nor my Aunt will suffer a word to escape their lips about our fruit-peice. My wife & I have puzzled ourselves often with guessing at the *megrim* that occasions this ominous silence.—

---

[1] The sale was to last for 39 days in all.

My sermon went off very brilliantly. Marsh praised it which was all I wanted. He is my Stothard or Fuseli. Even the Dean liked it. I did not myself. It was not on a *real* subject. It was factitious from one end to the other & contained nothing either *true* or *new*.—But it was as good as the subject allowed of—

Our new West window succeeds admirably. The middle compartment is up & looks gloriously. Rather too pale is the fault. Chantreys monument to Lord Malmsebury is all the gaze. [Sketch of the monument.] A recumbent figure. The left arm, elbow half buried in a pillow holding a book. The right half-extended in the act of speaking. Over the lower half of the figure a drapery is thrown in great & simple folds. It is to me a noble sedate impressive figure. But as you say I am no judge of *stone*. Tinney says he don't like the notion of a man reading in bed, on a monument, with a blanket thrown over him. This criticism has driven the Bishop out of his mind.—

By the bye this monument making is but absurd nugatory work.— What is the figure there for? What has it to do with Lord Malmesbury? What story does it tell? Is it meant for a likeness? Because, it no more gives one a notion of little, peevish, old, wizened Lord Malmesbury[1] in a flexen caxon than it does of Charon—The figure looks as big as M. Angelo's Lazarus.

I am delighted to hear that you found your wife & children so well. Greatly for their sakes, but something because you have found that you can be away from them & they notwithstanding well. Tell Mrs Constable to give my Goddaughter a kiss for me.—You had better I think write a short note to Tinney asking formally & positively for his picture & frame. I will then see it is packed up.—I must send you his account of his tour another time. I am tired now of writing.—Your account of the English Claude is delightful. I wish I had one of his landscapes to hang up near yours to see what the world would say—But what is the world, but a flock of sheep following their leader. And Glover is the old Ram with the bell just at present. I dont think Dodsworth will last long. What will become of the "Dodsworth collection"? Will it come to the hammer? A Salisbury man told me the other day that he thought his picture was no Corregio, because there was some discrepancy between it & the print. I said that I thought there were also some other reasons equally good. With my kindest regards to Mrs Constable

Beleive me

my dear Constable

truly yours

John. Fisher.

---

[1] The first earl, known as a diplomatist: his grandfather James Harris belonged to the close at Salisbury.

From the following letter[1] it will be seen that the Bishop, for all his many virtues, was not a very patient man.

Palace Sarum. Oct: 10, 1823.

Dear Sir

Elizabeth in her new capacity will be in my house in Seymour Street before the end of this month. Is her Picture finished? I wish it to be placed in the back Drawing Room opposite the Chimney to greet her arrival.

I wrote some time since to Smith at Kensington to order him to send the Frames (both of them) to your house on or before the 10th of October —in default of which I should cause him to be arrested for his debt to me. I hope he will save me the trouble & disagreeable feeling.

When are we to see you here?

I am
yours faithfully
J Sarum.

Constable did not at once reply to the letter. Fisher took it that he was offended by his remarks, and sought to tease him back into a better humour again.

Will you get one of Reads six foot canvasses into the Exhibition? It will be kind of you?

Close. Salisbury.
Oct. 16. 1823.

My dear Constable;

I am afraid my last letter annoyed you. I debated with myself whether I should communicate to you its contents. But decided on the score, that every sensible man would desire & could endure to hear what is said of him.

We married Lizzy Fisher to Mr Mirehouse this morning at the high altar in the Cathedral. The Bishop performed the service. Less exuberance of feeling on all sides than I expected. More state, but more lugubriosity than when we brought Mrs Constable to the stake at St Martin's. Much impatience on the part of the Bishop to know when you come to paint Tinney's portrait. Tinney went to see Denon's collection of pictures.[2] It is the Stafford Gallery of Paris. "Sad trash! I assure you", said he, "I had rather have my humble collection".—Read (I mean Raphael Read of

---

[1] Letter in the Leggatt Collection. Here again the final figure of the date looks very like a '2' in the Bishop's writing.

[2] The *cabinet* of Baron Denon, the sale of which provided drawings for the collection of Sir Thomas Lawrence. The Marquis of Stafford had one of the finest collections in England, and was the first collector to admit the public to his gallery (at Bridgewater House) in 1806.

Salisbury) seized me this morning to shew me a six foot canvas he has just covered with paint. Imagine a tint composed of blacking, rust of iron & cabbage water laid on with a scrubbing brush. In the very center stares the Sun. In the distance Southampton buried in an atmosphere of mud. In the foreground, plashy beach (like Collins) with the Sun reflected; a boat on her beam ends: & three of Collins's boys playing with dead fish. I wish he could see to what his lay figure has come. Another six foot canvass contains: a black foreground, a bright yellow cornfield of the colour & consistency of N. Wiltshire cheese: deep blue distance, dark rusty sky, & a rainbow—that must be seen to be conceived. In the same room is an original Titian he has just bought, & a copy of Rubens's boys at Wilton by himself. He smelt of Ginn, shook his locks enthusiastically & talked of future fame being preferable to present flattery. You are jealous of this man, Constable.

Tom Rennell was married yesterday to £10,000.—Did I tell you that a clergyman remarked "that he read the Church-service as if it was his own composition".—The Bishop has been fishing up some old drawings of Bucklers[1] against your arrival in Salisbury. With the intent I guess that you should copy & improve them. Retaining so much of Buckler as shall exclude light & shadow (the Bishops detestation) & improving his rawness with some of your colour & facility.—"[If] Constable would but leave out his black clouds! Clouds are only black when it is going to rain. In fine weather the sky is blue". I only send you this nonsense because I have nothing else to say.

Yours sincerely

John. Fisher.

Read goes excursions into the New Forest with a drove of pupils at his heels. Young Shorts among them.

I have just bought a most beautiful POODLE dog in town. I have not seen it yet. I have directed the man to bring it to Charlotte Street: & beg you will receive him for a few days till my brothers servant calls for him.

This letter seems to have been followed by another—unfortunately lost—in which Fisher gave Constable an amusing account of the sale of the 'Fonthill treasures', so called. The sale had lasted for thirty-nine days, during which time Mr. Phillips reaped a full harvest from his enterprise.

Fisher's letter had to some extent the desired effect of soothing Constable down; and though the latter's nerves were hardly yet in a state to bear with much more of 'Raphael' Read, he contented himself with a mild protest in his next letter from Hampstead.

---

[1] John Buckler senior (1770-1851), to whom the Bishop had given a commission in 1812 for the execution of two drawings, one showing the west front of Peterborough Cathedral and the other a north-west view of Exeter Cathedral.

Ocr. 19. 1823

My dear Fisher

Thank you for both your kind—amusing—and instructive letters. I shall always be glad to hear any thing that is said of me and my pictures. My object is the improvement of both.

When Nat. Hone's malignant picture, "The Conjuror" (meant to ruin Sir Joshua Reynolds "fair fame"), came to the Exhibition, the members were for rejecting it.[1] "No" said Sir Joshua—"if I deserve this censure it is proper that I should be exposed."

Lewis [is] like most men living in the atmosphere of the Art—followers and attendants on armies &c. &c. are always great talkers, of what *should be*—and this is not always done without malignity—they stroll about the foot of Parnassus only to pull down by the legs those who are laboriously climbing its sides. Lewis may be sincere in what he tells Tinney—he would himself no doubt spoil the picture—and not being able to see so far as that, wonders at what is now done & concludes it cannot be made better because he knows no better.

I shall write to Tinney and request the picture but with a promise not to meddle with it, and if I should see a material thing while on my easil— I will not touch it without first informing him of my intention.

Only think of your wasting your time, talents, & paper, about poor Read—but you are joking about another "*6 foot*" coming to London— does he drink?

I hung up my "*bridal picture*" with my own hands yesterday in Seymour Street—to "greet & *surprize*" the Bride on her arrival.[2] Thank you for your information. It will be better liked than the large one, because it is not "too good".

At the time you receive this letter I shall be at breakfast with Sir George Beaumont at Colorton Hall, Leicestershire, near Ashby de la Zouch. I put off this visit for a week or more to compleat the picture for the bishop & would have deferred it altogether rather than have not done it as his Lordship so much wished it.

I look to this visit with pleasure and improvement. All his beautiful pictures are there, and if I can find time to copy the little *Grove*, by Claude Lorraine[3] (evidently a study from nature), it will much help me. Sir G. will not possess these things for longer than a room is ready in the Museum

---

[1] Now at Dublin. Hone's intention was to convict Reynolds of plagiarism. The picture was in the end rejected at the instance of Angelica Kauffman, who had her own grounds of offence.

[2] The picture underwent considerable repainting by Constable two years later. It was sold by the family in 1954 and bought by Agnew's.

[3] Now in the National Gallery, where it is called *Landscape, with Goatherd and Goats.*

to receive them.[1] He was very full of Irvine the Talker, when he left London. I hope he will not "harp on that string", still. I met Irvine in the street a few weeks ago. His walk was a swing—he held a quarto book in his right hand, its back edging up between the deltoid & pectoral of the same side—and had I not known him I should have said there goes an insolent coxcomb—but I am told by several Scotchmen that he is not that.

How strange is the behaviour of the Palace folks about your fruit peice. Several reasons may be assigned—is it not out of the Bishops pale?— "Subjects that never interest". Perhaps impressed with its great beauty thay may think of an imprudent purchase—a great sum—&c &c—and would it not be better (and I feel myself involved) to tell its cost 8 guineas. But do as you like, it does not signify. Poor Tinney & his collection—why he has not a thing that would fetch any thing like that sum in London. Then you amused us with Fonthill—I like old china myself but I have a sister who is rather cracked who doats on it.[2] Therefore pray let me come soon—& chuse among my pictures. I should judge the sale was blighted by the prices I saw named in the papers—there was a Wouvermans, named at 30 or 40 gns—was it the sand bank? How well impudence can get out of a scape. First a downright lye which could be met—then another which was equally evident but which could not be positively opposed. What a diabolical trick to alter the figures in the prices on the fly leaves of the books—which Carpenter assures me was done—as they would no doubt afford rules for the bidders.

After my delightful visit to you I should have been content, but Sir George so much desired to see me and it is such a fund of art, that I thought it a duty I owed myself to go—I leave tomorrow—am now waiting at Hampd—and shall leave my wife & children tonight.

Your dog shall be taken care of in Charlotte St. There is my cook—& 2 cats to amuse him. Poor fellow, he little—nay human nature cannot conceive what he is destined to undergo. Have you put new wadding on your seringe? Could Flushing have kept a diary for the benefit of his successors, how amusing it must prove to the new comer—it puts one in mind of the Emperor who purposely left full lists of intended executions and punishments among his attendants who were to be the victims.

I want to get to my easil in Town—& not to witness [the] rotting melancholy dissolution of the trees &c—which two months ago were so beautifull—& lovely.

My wife begs to join with me best regards—

Yours very truly

J. Constable

---

[1] Beaumont is known to have been constantly talking about the formation of a National Gallery from 1821 to 1823: the project was realized in the following year, and Sir George presented a selection of his best pictures in 1826.

[2] Mary Constable, whose collection still exists.

I want to write to you about Cox's book—"Life of Corregio".[1] He has made such stupid confusion and nonsense about *Art*, in the letter of A. Caracci—it is too bad—& the letter itself is so beautifull— . . .

Edward Irving, the 'Talker' mentioned in this letter, had arrived in London during the previous summer on the invitation of a small chapel in Hatton Garden, where his magnetic personality soon attracted an enthusiastic crowd of well-known members of London society. The feeling evoked by his apocalyptic oratory—he was famous for his expounding of prophecies—may be taken as a sign of the times, paralleled by the reception given to the paintings of Martin and Danby. Constable, it may be noted, disapproved of enthusiasm in religion; but Irving is said to have been an essentially honest and sincere man, though his self-esteem was at the moment inflated by the reception he had received. He is now perhaps best remembered as the unsuccessful lover of Jane Welsh, who married Thomas Carlyle.

It will be noticed that Constable in describing Irving had not forgotten the lectures given by Mr. Brookes at his Anatomical Theatre to students of the Royal Academy many years before. Fisher's next letter is addressed to him at Coleorton Hall.

Close Salisbury. Oct. 23. 1823.

My dear Constable;

I have just dined in company with my baby boy. If therefore I am nubilous you know the cause.

I have "wrung from" Tinney his slow consent. The case is made & tomorrow the picture will be screwed down & be ready for your orders. I have told Tinney that you only want to tone the picture down: & that you will not alter a line or leaf without consulting him. In this he acquiesces. —Poor Dodsworth has incurred a debt of £1600 by publishing his book.[2] He hopes I learn to wipe off this incumbrance by the sale of his Corregio. His donation to you I have little doubt was intended to make you instrumental to the sale of his picture. I should like to see you gravely puffing it off in an auction room. Corregio is such an awkward word to have hit upon.

As you have an aversion to Read, I will discontinue to write. The six foot canvass & poodle dog coming to Charlotte Street is all poetry.— The Irvine mania is very like the Roscius mania. The public appear to be subject every now & then to epidemic mental diseases, for which there is no accounting; & for which there is no cure, but time. Witness Titus Oates's Meal tub plot: the South Sea scheme: Spanish bonds: the Queen.

---

[1] Archdeacon Coxe's *Sketches of the Lives of Correggio and Parmegiano* appeared anonymously in 1823.
[2] *An Historical Account of the Episcopal See and Cathedral Church of Salisbury*, published in 1814 and illustrated with reproductions of two drawings of the Cathedral commissioned by the Bishop from F. Nash.

Young Roscius[1] and then Irvine.—No minds however strong are exempted, occasionally.

Oct. 25.

Your Tinney picture is down. I have lent him the "white horse" to hang in its stead.—I told the Bishop that I only gave £8 for my peice, but still no remark. The girls are as *pointedly* shut up, as if the subject were indecent. It is a megrim. The sand bank is called the "woodcutter". It sold for £70. It is a snow drift.

I am at this moment sitting opposite the print of the Narcissus which I have pinned on my wall.[2] I envy you seeing the original. Is the figure on the right (my print is not reversed) as white as in the engraving. Poor Benson has lost within this month two children William and Ellen.—I buried the poor girl yesterday.

Yours very sincerely

John. Fisher.

Coleorton Hall. Novr. 2d. 1823.

My very dear Fisher,

I was [made] most happy by the receipt at this place of your very kind letter and the good news it contained of the birth of your baby boy.[3] I wrote to my wife to inform her of it in case she might not have seen it in the newspaper. You can never be nubilous—I am the man of clouds—

Your letter is delightfull—and its coming here served to help me in the estimation of Sir George and Lady Beaumont. Nothing can be more kind and in every possible way more obliging than they both are to me—I am left entirely to do as I like with full range of the whole house—in which I may saturate myself with art, only on condition of letting them do as they like. I have copied one of the small Claudes—a breezy sunset[4]—a most pathetic and soothing picture. Sir G. says it is a most beautifull copy. Perhaps a sketch would have answered my purpose, but I wished for a more lasting remembrance of it and a sketch of a picture is only like seeing it in one view. It is only one thing. A sketch (of a picture) will not serve more than one state of mind & will not serve to drink at again & again —in a sketch there is nothing but the one state of mind—that which you were in at the time.

I have likewise begun the little Grove by Claude[5]—a noon day scene—

---

[1] William Betty, whose first appearance at Drury Lane at the age of thirteen had brought in over £17,000 in twenty-eight nights: his appearances in later life had not been so successful, and he was now on the point of retiring from the stage.

[2] *Narcissus and Echo*, one of the Beaumont Claudes in the National Gallery, engraved for the *Liber Veritatis*.

[3] A misunderstanding—Fisher's next child was not born till the following year.

[4] Leslie (who gives the word as *sunrise*) says that this was *The Death of Procris*, now in the National Gallery.

[5] Constable's copy, inherited by Clifford Constable from Isobel Constable, is now in the Art Gallery of New South Wales at Sydney.

which *"warms and cheers but which does not inflame or irritate"*—*Mr. Price*. [It] diffuses a life & breezy freshness into the recess of trees which make it enchanting. Through the depths are seen a water-fall & ruined temple—& a solitary shepherd is piping to some animals—

> —"In closing shades & where the current strays
> "Pipes the lone shepherd to his feeding flock."

I draw in the evening & Lady B or Sir G. read aloud. I wish you could see me painting by Sir George's side. I have free range & work in his painting room. It is delightfull to see him work so hard—painting like religion knows no difference of rank. He has known intimately many persons of talent in the last half century and is full of anecdote.

The Rector here[1] (the gift of Sir G.B.) is Mr. Merywether's uncle—he seemed anxious to talk about your late curate at Gillingham. However I was guarded—and said nothing to be repeated. He has a bad opinion of his nephew—& thinks he will never do any good. He is a great lyer and always plagued for money. A curacy was . . . here, by the gentleman who would not have him near.

Poor Dodsworth, what ruin. Did that unfortunate Douglas [get] around him? I am glad I cried quits and sent Dodsworth the picture, & it was his own fault & preferring dirt, that he had not one of my own pictures.

This is a magnificent country—full of the picturesque. You are fond of a joke—I thought I was going to fill my house with dogs and rubbish—& had given orders to receive them.

How odd of the bishop's people, about your picture—they must be struck dumb with its beauty.

The hall is now going to church. The family never miss twice on every Sunday—& have family prayers. I am glad to see this—but I am told the latter was not the case 'till Sir G had heard Irvine—last summer.

Some parts of the print are very like the Narcissus but the figure is as you say not so white—the print is reversed—Yours ever—

J. Constable

In the dark recesses of these gardens, and at the end of one of the walks, I saw an urn—& bust of Sir Joshua Reynolds—& under it some beautifull verses, by Wordsworth.[2] It is a magnificent view from the Terrace over a mountainous region—here is a Winter Garden, the hint taken by Sir G. from the Spectator—Sir George has just sent to ask me to a walk. Yrs. J.C.

You are very kind to take so much trouble with the obdurate Tinney. He is very goodnatured to me in this matter—tis ignorance only that

---

[1] The Rev. Francis Merewether: John Merewether had acted as curate at Gillingham from December 1819 to March 1823.

[2] The verses had been written at the request of Sir George in 1811, and the first stone of the cenotaph was laid in the following year. Constable made a drawing of the cenotaph, which was later used for the painting now in the National Gallery.

disables him. I will write to you on my return in about a week for the
picture as I should like to be at home when it arrives. It was a happy
thought and kind of you to refill the place on his walls. O, when I think
of the "Ancient Masters" I am almost choaked in this breakfast room.
Here hang 4 Claudes, a Cousins & a Swanevelt. The low sun in the
morning sets them off to great advantage.

Once again, resolution melted in the warmth of congenial company and sur-
roundings, and 'about a week' spread itself out over the best part of a month.
When Mrs. Constable was told that the homeward journey was being postponed, she wrote to say that, since it was for her husband's advantage, she must
put herself out of the question and submit without murmuring to her fate; but
she could not forbear from adding: 'Had you not been so long at Mr. Fisher's,
which was quite unnecessary, I should have thought nothing of this visit'. This
time, however, Nemesis was on Constable's heels. Although his host was daily
pressing him to come out riding or walking, his intense desire to go on copying
Claude—'Pray finish your Claude', said Maria, 'or I think you will never be
happy again'—kept him indoors to such an extent that his health suffered. By
the time that he got home towards the end of November Constable had succeeded in undoing what little good the holiday at Gillingham may have done
for him. A missing letter from him seems to have sought Fisher's advice as to
the subject for next year's Academy picture.

Close, Salisbury. Decr. 12. 1823.

My dear Constable;

     The "touchwood tree" leaves Salisbury this morning, & will be in
London on Saturday, i e tomorrow. It travels by Woolcots Van which puts
up at 112 Fore Street. I ordered it to travel on end.

I know not how to advise you for the Exhibition. Tinney expects one of
his uprights to go in. He expressed a wish for something from Gillingham
of which place he is a native. The Waterloo depends entirely on the polish
& finish given it. If I were the painter of it I would always have it on my
easil, & work at it for five years a touch a day.—The great storm played
destruction at Gillingham. It blew down two of my great elms, bent another to an angle of 45° with the ground: stripped a third of all its branches;
leaving only one standing entire. This I have taken down; & your wood
exists only on your mill boards. The great elm in the middle of the turf is
spared. At Salisbury we had extensive floods; but little wind.

Southey is a friend of the establishment: but in one point I think him
(with diffidence) wrong.[1] He would adopt the Methodist preacher into the
Church as an inferior servant. This was the very cause of the corruptions
& downfall of the Roman Catholic establishment. For the sake of peace
& unity they adopted enthusiasts received their errors into the Creeds of

---

[1] The reference is probably to Robert Southey's *Life of Wesley*, Coleridge's favourite
among 'favourite books', which was published in 1820.

the Church, & then had to *defend* them. You cannot make use of the *men* without receiving their *opinions*.

I am impatient to see your Claudes.—The Bishop is delighted at the thoughts of Dolly "having additional opportunities of improving her style by copying so perfect a master".—Mrs. Mirehouse is warm in the praises of your picture of the Cathedral. It is in agitation at the Charterhouse to apply to you to paint the Masters portrait. The one done in Virginia not giving satisfaction. But there is much difficulty in getting the Ox to the Slaughter-house.

My wife is gone down to Weymouth to lie in. I join her there on the 28th Inst. We return to Gillingham the beginning of March.

I hope, that on your return home, no evil accidents will result from your too long absences from your wife and family. I conclude that they are all well from your saying nothing on that head.—When Dean Rennell was introduced first to his sons intended who is not unlike Jane Frigg, he turned round and exclaimed, My Heavens! What a beautiful woman Tom has chosen.

The saints will lose us the West Indian Islands.[1] They will undoubtedly attempt to place themselves under the protection of America. Tell me in your next what is to become of Angersteins pictures?[2] Dodsworth has not yet sold his Corregio. A man called Varley is here teaching drawing to the young ladies.[3] Principles he says are the thing. "The warm grey", "the cold greys" and the "round touch".

Adieu

yours sincerely

John. Fisher.

In a sense, Constable may be said to have taken Fisher's advice, inasmuch as he continued to work on the subject of Waterloo Bridge for eight years or more before bringing it up to exhibition level; but this lay further ahead than he could for the moment foresee.

Tuesday Evg. Decr. 16. 1823.

My dear Fisher,

I felt desirous of writing to you immediately on receiving your kind and welcome letter. As usual it breathes nothing but good humour, friendship—and understanding. I wanted just such an one as almost from the

---

[1] The agitation for the abolition of slavery was finding support in Parliament.

[2] Angerstein had died earlier in the year. The Prince of Orange had been suggested as a purchaser for his pictures, but Sir Thomas Lawrence advised that they should be offered to Lord Liverpool on behalf of the Government, and negotiations were now going on with Angerstein's son.

[3] The vanity of John Varley, the water-colour painter, was well known: he once declared that there were only four artists in England, who understood light and shade, and that three of them were his pupils: he even told Constable 'how to do landscape'.

time of my return I have been laid up and though in perfect health am quite disabled by pains in the bones of my head and face, [which] probably originated in the teeth[1]—it began at Gillingham. However they condemned one this morning who, though perhaps not the principal, still was an accessory before the fact. Perhaps I may look for some ease—but I have lived on suction for the last fortnight.

I am looking dayly for the case—which I am indeed anxious for as the time nears apace. I shall tell you all my proceedings with it—& I will do my will with it, in spite of Mr Lewis or all Grub Street combined. Those insects about the hive, sometimes are all attention for a moment but they live but one summer's day.

I shall now turn to your letter to see what requires noticing—

1. I am settled, for the Exhibition. My Waterloo must be done, and one other, perhaps one of Tinney's, Dedham, but more probably my Lock. I must visit Gillingham again for a subject for the other next summer.

2. How much I regret the grove at the bottom of your garden—this has really vexed me—I had promised myself the passing of many summer noons in their shade. The figures met with there were perhaps not the most classical—nymphs darting out of a cotton mill[2] in parties—to add to the rippling of the stream—or to quote Shakespeare & be poetical—"augmenting it with"—not tears.

3. I am glad the great elm is safe.

4. What you say of Southey is wise—just, moderate and undeniable— Though he can say much, he could not gainsay that short sentence of yours—it marks you master of your own profession—and every hours experience proves to me, that no man not educated from his early youth to a profession, can fully & justly enter into it. I asked Sir G.B. if there was not likely to be a society of noblemen and gentlemen to regulate the offices of the Church—the Horse Guards—the medical world &c—and award prizes to the aspirants.[3]

5. I much doubt if Sir George will like to have these little Claudes mauled, mangled, smeared & begrimed by a Young Lady—but I will say nothing about it. I shall send them away when the lady arrives. Pray

6. Will you request the Bishop to write immediately to that wretched fellow Smith at Kensington, to cut the frame for Mrs Mirehouses picture. I would decline painting any more pictures for the Bishop if I am again to be saddled by that wretched lying young rascal. I was to have had the

---

[1] This trouble went back to a dental operation which Constable had suffered at the hands of the village surgeon in 1798.

[2] This mill, later a silk mill, and only recently demolished, stood not far from the vicarage and Gillingham Bridge.

[3] This refers to the constitution of the British Institution, which was governed by laymen.

frame in Sepr. I do not beleive it is even begun—& he told my servant I had countermanded it.

7. We wholly concluded from a former expression of yours that Mrs. F was already confined.

8. I found all well on my return. I shall leave home now with confidence. My wife is not well, & Drew got her into a real illness by beginning with tonics. I told him the best medical opinion I know (yours) said they were worse than useless. My children are beautifull and healthy.

9. You excell in anecdotes of dotage—but I am not interested about Vipers—old or young.

10. Dodsworths Corregio is worth five pounds with the frame—certainly not more. My fd Mr Durant in Bond Street bought of him his Salisbury large copy but made his escape from the Corregio—for the stupid old verger to persevere in dishonesty, can only be excused by his rum and water.

11. Mr Angersteins pictures will probably be national property—& after 150 yrs separation, you & I shall see the Narcissus and the St Ursula become united again[1]—a brother & sister and after so long an absence from their parental roof, on the Trinity di Monte. Welbore Ellis[2] will forward it in the House—as the nobleman who is in treaty for the collection, will resign on that account alone. Sir G. was in correspondence about them.

Now I must leave off—considering the pain I am still in. The devil of a rinch they gave me this morng—I have made an exertion for you.

I have a note to dine at the Charter House Saturday—I hope I shall be able—for if you are not there I shall hardly beleive you are not. I dread the job, of the Grand Master,[3] & shall not forward it myself [but] leave it to fate. He is a delightfull subject, after all.

"Anecdote". My fd. Revd Roberson[4]—a master of Merchant Taylors —had in his duty (2 months ago) to swish a stupid boy—he did so without bad temper & properly. The boys father was connected with the Observer, who published the case, describing the boy as paralyzed from the blows on one side. At Engleford [he was] attd by a surgeon, who made a long job of it. The persecution of poor Roberson continued in the Times, Morning Chronicle, &c &c. Mr Roberson paid some long bills for the boys cure, &c. A trial came before Alderman Adkins & trustees &c—the boys fds. attending & swearing to all—when an anonymous letter arrived

---

[1] Both these paintings by Claude are now in the National Gallery.
[2] George James Welbore Ellis, afterwards 1st Lord Dover, a close friend of Beaumont, had stated his intention of moving for a grant in July 1823 (Parl. Debates N.S. ix. 1359): but the suggestion was adopted by Government.
[3] The proposal that Constable should paint Dr. Philip Fisher's portrait.
[4] The Rev. John Roberson had been a curate under Dr. Rhudde at East Bergholt. He died on 3rd January, 1824.

L

to a quarter of an hour, & proved that this boy afterwards had an over-bound & was thrown out of a gig, and pitched on his shoulder &c &c &c. When Aldn Adkins closely questioned them they slunk off, and would not appear again—but in the mean time poor Mr R—whom I have known many years, the most kind & benevolent of men—is now so ill, that his life is in eminent danger. I long to get out to call upon him, but I fear the worst. All this you know is levelling at the Clergy by the diabolical prints.

J.C.

I am now anxious for the case—write to me.

I have no room to say any thing of the Tinters. The wretched Varley you speak of is one of them. I have much to say on that subject which will open yours eyes [to] art generally as a subject. The post rings.

Palace Sarum. Dec: 29.

Dear Sir

    We have all been much disappointed at not seeing you in the course of the Autumn—but were pleased to hear that you have been so well amused & so well employed at your friend Sir George's. Dorothea wished much for you to rouse her from a fit of Idleness.

I wish you would once more write to young Smith about the two frames.

I must also beg of you to let me know what I am indebted to you for your last picture of Sarum. As this is the Season when we are called upon to pay Bills—I will send you a Draft immediately.

We are all well, & unite in every good wish for you & yours with

Dear Sir

your sincere friend

J. Sarum

1824, January to June

Palace. Jan: 6, 1824.

Dear Sir

    I enclose to you a Draft to my Banker:—also a Letter to Elizabeths Servant in my house in town with an Order to her to deliver to you the Picture of Salisbury Cathedral.[1]

Dorothea flatters herself that you will allow her to study one of your new *Claudes*.

I married Will. Fisher this morning to Eliz. Cookson.

---

[1] This letter is in the Victoria and Albert Museum.

Our new year opens under many pleasing circumstances—*fine weather, returning Plenty*, public Quiet—& the appearance of general Peace.

May you & yours have many happy returns of such a year.

I am Dear Sir, yours very faithfully

J Sarum

The year 1824 was indeed a propitious one for Constable's ambitions, and the signs were not long delayed.[1]

17 Jany. 1824.

My dear Fisher,

The Frenchman who was after my large picture of [the] Hay Cart, last year, is now here about it again—he would I beleive have both that and the bridge[2] if he could get them at his own price. He had made me offers—for that one or both. I showed him your letter and told him of my promise to you. His object is to make a show of them in Paris—perhaps to my advantage—for a prophet is not known in his own country. Let me hear shortly from you, that I may be at liberty or not to talk to him about this picture, the "Vain". He most desires that as it has already a great reputation in Paris, and might more fully answer his speculation. *He* assures me that it will become the property of the French nation—& will be in the Louvre the ensuing exhibition—which happens once in two years.

It is long, too long, since I heard of you. We are anxious to hear of the arrival of your new baby. May we congratulate you on your brother's marriage with your sister?[3]

I want to see the picture of the Cathedral belonging to Mr Mirehouse in a frame, in order to [? tone] it. But the Bishop has involved me with that wretch at Kensington and therefore a frame is hopeless. I will not get another on my own acct. I do not think that Mr M. admires it—but speaking to a lawyer about pictures is something like talking to a butcher about humanity.

I shall not send the picture of Tinney's to the Institution. My heart has failed me—I am sure every man who has a reputation to lose is in hazard of it at that place. Consider who are our judges—Carr, the Magnus—Sir Cs. Long—Priapus Knight—none of them have any affection for *new* art. The latter gentleman called on me the day before yesterday—he admired (so he said) my pictures, called me a "most successful landscape painter" —saw me hard at work for my four infants—and went away—& that day gave "Sixteen Hundred Pounds", for some drawings or slight sketches by

---

[1] This letter is in the Victoria and Albert Museum.
[2] *A View on the Stour.*
[3] Sister-in-law is meant.

Claude.[1] I saw them—drawings—they looked just like papers used and otherwise mauled, & purloined from a Water Closet—but they were certainly old, & much rent, & dissolved, &c. but their meer charm was their age.

I have sent the Bishops Cathedral to the Gallery and no other. I must write to his Lordship to acknowledge the draft for the last picture.

I have just completed my little Waterloo bridge. It looks very well indeed—

I should like your advice about the large Waterloo—it is a work that should not be hurried. I am about my upright Lock & I hope for one of Tinney's new ones.

Your family did me the favor of telling me they were much pleased with my room. I only want to work harder to be comfortable—my success in life seems pretty certain, but no man can get rich by study, & the labor of his own hands only—I shall now leave off study—

Ever yours most affetly

John Constable

I know not where you are but shall direct to Osmington.

Constable's indignation with the governors of the British Institution was now reaching boiling-point. The Rev. William Holwell Carr, though himself an Honorary Exhibitor of landscapes at the Academy, was just the type of connoisseur-collector that Constable disliked, with a decided preference for old masters. Richard Payne Knight, who owed his nickname to a learned book on the Priapeia cult which had to be withdrawn on the alleged score of indecency, was one of the leading connoisseurs of his day; but he was also an archaeologist and numismatist, and his liking for Claude did not make up in Constable's eyes for his failure to patronize living art. Sir Charles Long, afterwards Lord Farnborough, was another collector of old masters. In spite of his personal affection and respect for Sir George Beaumont, Constable's bias against wealthy amateurs was leading him to the view that only professional artists should have a say in societies for the encouragement of art, as it was with the Royal Academy.

Weymouth. Janry. 18. 1824.

My dear Constable;

Thurtell said[2]—but perhaps you are as sick of his name as you were of the Queens, so we will change the subject to one more agreeable. Yesterday at 4 oclock my wife was delivered of another boy (for a 2nd time within three months according to your account).[3] A very large fair infant

---

[1] Knight is reputed to have spent this sum on 273 drawings by Claude which went to the British Museum on his death three months later. Most of these were from a leather-bound volume discovered at a bookseller's in Spain by Colnaghi's agent Mr. Binda, so Constable had probably heard this from his friend, Paul Colnaghi.

[2] The execution of John Thurtell for murder a few days before had laid a powerful hold on the public imagination, owing to his reputation as a sporting character.

[3] Frederick Fisher.

like your friend Belim. My wife, to use the customary phrases is "quite charming" & "*better* than can be expected". This is news for Mrs. Constable. I was very sorry to find that your face ache continued so violent that you could not dine at the Charterhouse. Did you use the prescription I gave you, & had tried on you so successfully? All diseases seem to arise from fullness of habit: & all seem to yield to depletion & abstinence. At least in early stages.—

How curiously we synchronise! Just as I had written thus far, your letter of the—no date, was delivered. I will dismiss it first. Let your Hay Cart go to Paris by all means. I am too much pulled down by agricultural distress to hope to possess it. I would (I *think*) let it go at less than its price for the sake of the eclat it may give you. The stupid English public, which has no judgement of its own, will begin to think that there is something in you if the French make your works national property. You have long laid under a mistake. Men do not purchase pictures because they admire them, but because others covet them. Hence they will only buy what they think no one else can possess: things scarce & unique.

How would it gratify Holwell Carrs vanity to possess one of your great pictures when a parson & attorney at Salisbury have two like it? & when more may be had for money?—"Priapus" Knight (how punishment visits a man in *kind*) bought these drawings for the sake of seeing a set of prints, underwritten "in the possession of R. P. Knight Esqr."

The lawyer you allude to is an overbearing Coxcomb. He thinks he knows too much, ever to know any thing. Are you quite well or hurried that your hand writing is so very indistinct? I *guess* half your meaning. In the last Exhibition of pictures at Paris there were four sea peices representing the capture of English ships by American ships. A note at the bottom of the catalogue stated the immense superiority of the English over the Americans in guns & men. My brother married Eliza Cookson. But they consulted nobody on the subject; & really you know as much about it as I do. They will do very well, if they are not extravagant. Mirehouse promised to call & *bully* Smith about the frame, Which threat I dare say, if reminded, he will execute to the letter. The Old Baily is a good school for the extraction of blood out of mill-stones. Did you know the fact in natural history, that Rooks prefer to build in Elm trees before all others: & that they seldom or never frequent Chesnuts? When we were felling our Elms at Gillm. some rooks flew over & were clamorous, whether deprecating our work of destruction or not I cannot tell.

In the new novel attributed to Sir Walter Scott, called St Ronans Well, is the following passage "There are very well bred Artists; said Lady Penelope: it is the profession of a Gentleman.—Certainly answered Lady Binks: but the poorer class have often to struggle with poverty and dependence. In general society, they are like commercial people in the presence of their customers: and that is a difficult part to sustain. And so you see them of all sorts. Shy and reserved when conscious of merit: petulent & whimsical by way of showing their independence: intrusive in order to appear easy: obsequious & fawning when they chance to be of mean spirit". Are either you or Collins acquainted with Sir Walter Scott? Hayley settled near Cyrill Jackson in the country. He expressed a desire to be on terms of intimacy with him. Tell Mr. Hayley said Dean Jackson that I have no objection to buy my butter of him: but I dont see what further benefit I am ever likely to derive from his neighbourhood[1]—Mrs. Brown is dismissed the Palace at the instance of the Son in Law! If this had been done 10 years ago as I advised, the Bishop would have saved £2000. By the bye Mirehouse is a *radical*. He told me that there was not a tittle of good evidence to convict the Queen. Another brother I guess is going to marry your *pupil* Dindle.[2] We shall have some amusing scenes yet in this family.

[I am] shut up in Lodgings here with the walls round covered with the "Old Masters". I suffer like the Martyrs of old who had their eyes put out with a hot brazen basin held before their face. But I am releived by one picture which I guess to be a genuine Vanderhayden. Is not that the name of the man who painted brick buildings so minutely? It is very true & delicate; & pretty light & shadow. But the sky is . . . burnt: as if it had been touched up. No one who could paint so well would I think condescend to *copy* a Vanderhayden.

The final portion of this letter is missing, and Leslie only gives a single sentence from Constable's reply of the 22nd January: 'I have done the little "Waterloo", a small baloon to let off as a forerunner to the large one'.

Seymour St. Feb: 10.

Dear Sir

Will you and Mrs Constable favor us with your Company at Dinner on Saturday at ¼ before six.

You will meet my Brother the Colonel.

I am Dear Sir, yours &c &c

J. Sarum

The date of the following note from Dorothea Fisher is uncertain, but it is likely to have been sent to Constable about this time. It is written on a small scrap of paper which probably formed an enclosure to one of her father's letters.

---

[1] Cyril Jackson, Dean of Christ Church, Oxford, and William Hayley the poet had both retired to live in seclusion at Felpham, near Bognor. The allusion may be to Hayley's poetry, which is said to have been the only thing about him which was not good.

[2] This may have been a pet name for Dolly Fisher: but if so, the Archdeacon's forecast was wrong, since Dolly married Mr. Pike. The brother-in-law was probably Thomas Henry Mirehouse, appointed domestic chaplain to the Bishop on the 26th July of this year.

My dear Mr Constable

May I trouble you once more, & ask you what are the Colors I am to use in my sky of the picture you were kind enough to lend me, of Sir G. Beaumonts place.

Yours much obliged

D Fisher

Seymour St. Saturday.

The young ladies of the Fisher family certainly kept Constable busy. In a letter to Francis Collins, not dated, but probably written about this time, he said: 'Will you ask of your Brother a great favor for me?... It is the loan of his study of the Infant Academy[1] for a week or so—to oblige my friends at the Charter House. One of Fisher's sisters (a pupil of Sir Thomas Lawrence) paints delightfully in miniature—& has begun one on ivory from the print with only memoranda of the colors made in writing while the picture was at the Gallery. I will guarantee its safe conduct, & that it shall be returned within the fortnight.'

Fisher's next letter is whimsically addressed to 'John Constable Esqre Architectural Painter', which may possibly have reference to the *Waterloo Bridge*.

Weymouth. Feb. 12. 1824.

My dear Constable;

You have already learned no doubt, why I have been detained here. My poor little boy Frank has been in the most imminent danger from the meazles. I never left him for three days & nights. Nothing but the most unremitting attention, & the applying remedies constantly, as the symptoms varied, could have saved his life. He is now safe.—

Have you perceived by the papers that our old friend "the Griffin" is the new Canon of Christ-Church?[2] You see they make Daniels & Reinagle's academicians in more professions than one. He was an old friend and Chum of Canning. Disappointed vanity has been to that man, like what bitter yeast is to a batch of bread; making unpalatable every enjoyment of life. I did not know a man whose face carried more the appearance of unhappiness. I go to my visitation the 2nd or 3rd week in June. Will you attend me as my chaplain? You will then see Oxford again.

I beg to congratulate you upon the appearance of your name in the newspapers. Do not despise them *too* much. They cannot give you fame, but they attend on her. Smoke gives notice that the house is afire.

I shall be in town Wednesday or Thursday next.—Till then adieu.

Yours very faithfully

John. Fisher.

---

[1] By Sir Joshua Reynolds.
[2] Samuel Smith, appointed on the 11th February.

Fisher came to town, he found Constable hard at work on the painting he had finally chosen for the exhibition; and after that Constable was too busy to write again until the upright *Lock* had been dispatched to Somerset House.

Seymour St. March 8.

Dear Sir

As you see by the enclosed sheet poor Smith is come to his Senses —I must beg of you to proceed in finishing the little Sarum, as the Mirehouses want it to ornament their Room.

I am, yours truly

J Sarum

Seymour St. March 30.

My dear Sir

I must beg of you to finish your small Picture of my Cathedral, because Mrs Mirehouse wants to hang it up in her Drawing Room on Monday morning as she has a large Party of her friends to dine at their house to whom she wishes anxiously to shew it.

Smith has again promised the Frame for tomorrow or Thursday. Should he again disappoint me I will thank you to lend me yours.

I am, my good Sir, yours faithfully

J. Sarum

Dear Sir

Smith brought to me this morning the expected Frame. I sent him on to you.

I made a mistake respecting Mrs Mirehouses request. Saturday is the day on which she wishes to have her Picture hung up—so that it should be finished on Friday & sent to Orchard Street early on Saturday Morning.

Yours &c

J Sarum

Wed: 11 o'clock. March 31

Dear Sir

I will send my Butler with a Coach tomorrow morning about nine o'clock to convey the Picture of Salisbury to Mrs Mirehouses house in Orchard Street—to be placed immediately to grace her Fête.

Yours &c

J. Sarum

The following invitation[1] may have been sent on the 1st or the 8th April.

---

[1] In the Leggatt Collection.

Seymour St. Frid. 9 o'clock.

Dear Sir

Can you favor us with your Company at dinner this day at 6 o'clock? You will meet a Lady *Paintress* whom you will be pleased with.

I am, Dear Sir, yours very truly

J Sarum

Charlotte St. April. 15. 1824.[1]

My dear Fisher,

I have been for some time very desirous of writing to you, but I was never more fully bent on any picture than on that on which you left me engaged upon. It is going to its audit with all its deficiencies in hand—my *friends* all tell me it is my best. Be that as it may I have done my best. It is a good subject and an admirable instance of the picturesque.

The Academy have got some fine pictures this year, but for some of the old (as well as some of the *new*) Academicians, I have much to fear. They talk of a pension to the senior Academicians—this would be no bad thing—were it granted only on condition of their relinquishing the easil.

The new society[2] is crowded with works of art, as they are called. Some hundreds have been rejected and amongst them a wholelength portrait by the "English Claude" [sketch of the artist]—he is very angry as he says the eyes of Europe are upon him.[3] The portrait was in *uniform*—but he has his revenge upon the society by a landscape 15 feet long—this is the gee of Humbugg (as John Bull says) or worse.

We have been much amused by the poor old crazy fiddling Canon of Norwich, Mr Smith. He availed himself of our newly-born intimacy at the Charter House,[4] to call the next day to borrow 5 £—I gave him that sum immediately but looked upon it quite as a forlorn hope (he said he quite forgot to ask Dr Fisher for it). However he punctually returned it.

Our acquaintance did not end here. He ordered a large case with a picture ("by Hogarth") to be sent from Norwich for my opinion—it was a present to the King, but such was the effect of court intrigue that he has great reason to beleive that none of his letters "*ever reached His Majesty*". The picture is a wretched daub of an old country Squire on horseback with a white wigg, blew coat, & some attempt [at] a part of one of Hogarths prints in the back ground.

On Saturday I shall go for a few days into Suffolk. I want to see what

---

[1] The original letter is at the Victoria and Albert Museum.
[2] The Society of British Artists, of which Glover was one of the founders.
[3] Glover had anticipated Constable by receiving a gold medal from Louis XVIII in 1814 and again in 1816: he had also been in Switzerland and Italy.
[4] Dr. Philip Fisher, it may be noted, was himself a Canon of Norwich from 1814 till his death.

they are about and Lady Dysart wants me to see the woods which she has given into the care of my brother,[1] that I may bring a report to her, as he cannot leave them.

Miss Fisher is going to copy Gillingham[2] and on sending it this morning I requested the cover for you. I dined there the other day—to meet a "lady paintress with whom I should be much pleased". As I expected, I found a laughing ignorant vulgar fat uncouth old woman, but very good natured and she gave me no trouble at all as she wanted no instruction from me. When she told me of an oil proper for painting I told [her] it would not do—but she assured me it would and she could give me no greater proof of it than that one of *her* pictures was painted entirely with it. I think they called her

Mrs. Mac; Taggett.

I have had the Frenchman again with me—we have agreed for price, 250 £ the pair, and I give him a small seapeice Yarmouth[3] into the bargain —his agent to pay the money in a fortnight and the picture[s] then to go to him on his return to this country in 5 weeks. I wish all this may turn out right. Colnaghi speaks well of him. At any rate I shall not let them go out of my hands 'till paid for.

Do you come to London before the Visitation—but I shall make you a visit to Salisbury at all events—

Yours most truly

J. Constable.

Savile[4] is expected in town. They will decide probably on my large picture.

The new picture was shown at Somerset House under the title of *A boat passing a lock*, but has since been more generally known simply as *The Lock*, as it is called in the engraving by Lucas. If this was the picture Savile was after, he had been too slow in making up his mind, for it was sold on the day of the opening, as reported in the next letter. A very favourable notice of the picture appeared in the *Literary Gazette*.

35 Charlotte St. May 8, 1824.

My dear Fisher

I hear your being in London with Mrs F and your children is not unlikely to happen—I hope it will be the case and we look for a visit to

---

[1] Golding Constable, for whom John had procured the post: the woods were at Bentley.
[2] Perhaps the version of *Gillingham Bridge* now in the Tate Gallery.
[3] *Yarmouth Jetty*, of which at least two versions are known: this would probably be a copy of that exhibited in 1823.
[4] An unfavourite cousin of Constable's: see S.R. I, 201 and p. 74 above.

Salisbury this year—for a few days to make a study or two for a picture for Tinney. We'll then concert it together—as I shall not be able to leave London before fairly late in the year.

I have just deposited my picture[1] in its place in the *back drawing room* in Seymour St. and opposite and as a companion to a *landscape* of *Mrs. Mac Taggett*. To what honors are some men born—

My French-man has sent his agent with the money for the pictures destined for the *French* metropolis, thus again are honors thrust upon me. The one was got ready and looks uncommonly well and I think they cannot fail of melting the stony hearts of the French painters. Think of the lovely valleys mid the peacefull farm houses of Suffolk, forming a scene of exhibition to amuse the gay & frivolous Parisians.

My picture is liked at the Academy. Indeed it forms a decided feature and its light cannot be put out, because it is the light of nature—the Mother of all that is valuable in poetry, painting or anything else—where an appeal to the soul is required. The language of the heart is the only one that is universal—and Sterne says that he disregards all rules—but makes his way to the heart as he can. My execution annoys most of them and all the scholastic ones—perhaps the sacrifices I make for *lightness* and *brightness* is too much, but these things are the essence of landscape. Any extreem is better than white lead and oil and *dado* painting.

I sold this picture[2] on the day of the opening, 150 guins including the frame. I have now at my bankers 400 £—I have a plan, as I want but 200 of it, to buy into the new fours where we have 42 £ a year and make it £ 50 per an. and settle it without delay on my wife. It will be something —she got much better after you left town but this warm weather has hurt her a good deal, and we are told we must try the sea—on Thursday I shall send them to Brighton.

I do hope that my exertions may at last turn towards popularity—'tis you that have too long held my head above water. Although I have a good deal of the devil in me I think I should have been broken hearted before this time but for you. Indeed it is worth while to have gone through all I have, to have had the hours and thoughts which we have had together and in common.

The wretched Edy[3] has turned up again at the Bishops, and they have bought some little things of him to keep him from the workhouse. There is certainly something honorable in this—but it is like being numbered with a girl of the town. Let me hear from you, and pray write soon.

I am in high favor with all the Seymour Street family—and so I ought to be—but I look continually back for the great kindness shown in my

---

[1] Presumably the Bishop's *Cathedral*, on its return from the British Institution.
[2] To James Morrison of Basildon Park, with whose family the picture still remains.
[3] Probably J. W. Edy, who engraved one of Colonel George Fisher's drawings in 1793.

early day—when it was truly of value to me. For long [I] floundered in the path—and tottered on the threshold—and there never was any young man nearer being lost than myself, but here I am & I must now "take heed where I stand".

"Our rivals"—*"the Society of British Artists"*—that is Glover—Hoffland —Heaphy[1]—&c &c—have made their exhibition. Glover has several *whole length* portraits hung up exclusive of those turned out. But they have a man dressed up like the ace of Hearts—holding a board—&c. &c. They are come to this—and I do hear of disagreements—& that Hoffland fought —in one of their disputations. Yrs. affectly J. Constable

My best love to all & to dear Belim.

The moment was ripe for a retrospect. With the sale of three of his large pictures to strangers, who could not be suspected of any desire to help him along, Constable might be said at last to have 'arrived'. It was time that he did so, for he was now nearing fifty, and beginning to grow weary on the road along which he had set out so hopefully and eagerly as a young man. But it was sad that this turn in the tide of his affairs should coincide with a decline in his wife's health, which rendered another long separation necessary.

Two days later there followed another event to which Constable presently refers. This was the opening of the new National Gallery on the 10th May, with Angerstein's pictures shown at his old house in Pall Mall; but the day was still far distant when *The Hay Wain* would return from France to join them, for Constable was not yet reckoned among the old masters. The next two letters from Fisher are lost, and we only have the extracts from them given by Leslie.

Gillingham, May 10th [1824].

My dear Constable,

I admire your lion-like generosity in passing over my long silence without vituperation. I am glad you did not ask me for a reason, for I can assign none, except that I was always thinking of you, daily intending to write, and daily neglecting to put my intention into execution. Your last letter is evidently written in a tone of great exultation, and with reason. Your fame and fortune are both advanced; and for both you are indebted to Providence and your own exertions. I am not surprised that "The Navigator"[2] sold on a first inspection, for it was one of your best pictures. The purchase of your two great landscapes for Paris is surely a stride up three or four steps of the ladder of popularity. English boobies, who dare not trust their own eyes, will discover your merits when they find you admired at Paris. We now *must* go there for a week. . . .

---

[1] Thomas Heaphy the elder, a water-colour artist: he was the first President of the new Society.

[2] Fisher's name for *The Lock* must refer to the prominent figure of a youth in the foreground opening the lock gates: the term was applied to men excavating canals at this period, and Fisher may have misinterpreted the gesture.

I generally leave you wiser than I came to you, and some of your pithy apothegms stick to my memory like a thorn, and give me a prick when I fall a-dozing. "A man is always growing", you said "either upwards or downwards". I have been trying to grow upwards since we parted. When I consulted you about the Lancastrian Sunday School[1] in my parish, you advised me to "be quiet and do all the good I could". I took your advice, and the Quakers have, unsolicited, dropped the offensive rules.

J. Fisher.

Gillingham, May 11th [1824].

My dear Constable,

. . . They have had one or two smart brushes at the Church in Parliament, but have been triumphantly defeated. One member said, "If half the industry had been used to bring to light the good done by the clergy, which has been used to malign them, the Church would need no defender". However, I am indifferent to such attacks, I am at my post, and intend to be found at it, happen what will. The people of this place are given to my charge, and I will discharge the duty, with or without the tithes. What has become of "Waterloo"? I am ready to receive you at Salisbury, at any moment. Will you go with me on my visitation?

J. Fisher.

Constable himself took his family down to Brighton on the 13th May (if he adhered to the day proposed), and returned on the 19th to Charlotte Street, where he had young John Dunthorne,[2] a maid and his goldfinch to keep him company. From the day of his return he kept a journal for the benefit of his wife, instalments from which used to be sent down to Brighton as a convenient opportunity offered. This journal[3] supplements our knowledge of his relations with the Fisher family and enables us to place some of his undated letters. The next letter to Fisher, for example, must have been written just after a visit to Seymour Street on the morning of the 27th May, when he found all the family at home, including Mrs. Mirehouse, and brought away a frank for East Bergholt, as well as his little picture of Gillingham.

Arrowsmith had been calling almost every day during the week after Constable's return, so anxious was he that the pictures which he had ordered should be ready for him to take away when he left for Dover on the 25th. On one of these occasions he brought with him a friend, 'a great dealer in Paris', who can be identified as Claude Schroth. A comparison of the journal with Constable's letter shows that of the seven pictures mentioned three were bought by Schroth,

---

[1] Joseph Lancaster was the founder of the Lancasterian System of education through pupil teachers: his name is not usually associated with Sunday Schools, but the Society of Friends was active in promoting such schools at this time.

[2] The son of John Dunthorne, glazier and plumber, with whom Constable had once shared a studio at East Bergholt: the younger Dunthorne had been acting since 1814 as Constable's studio assistant.

[3] The manuscript is in the Plymouth Collection, with a few pages missing.

while the other four represented further orders from Arrowsmith, who had evidently decided that paintings by Constable were just what Paris wanted. There had also been a call from Tinney on the 23rd, when Constable walked back with him to his hotel and found him 'a clever pleasant man'.

My dear Fisher

You know how delighted I am at all times to receive a letter from you. Yours of the 10th May, was more so than usual. I was at the Bishops (by the order of Miss D.F. to see her copy of my Gillingham)—when I heard of your lady's being in London & for what purpose and of the safety of your boy.[1] Let me congratulate you upon it.

I have counted on the pleasure of seeing Berkshire again with you—but that is not possible with me this year. I am more than ever involved in *business*. I have just now engaged to get seven pictures of a small size ready, for Paris by August—2, 20 by 30 inches: 2, 12 by 20 do.: 3, 10 by 12 do.—making in all an amount of about 130 £. My large pictures are packed off—the same case contained 3 others which I had ready, 50 £ more.

The large ones are to be exhibited at the Luxemburg—& my purchaser[s] say that they are "anxiously looked for at Paris". The director of the Academy at Antwerp (Van Bree) has been here—(from having seen my picture in the Academy). He says they will make an impression on the continent.

Tinney called on me on Sunday. His picture is now on my easel and will soon be at Salisbury. He is anxious to have his ancestors mill, and a view of Salisbury, which we are [to] look for when I come to you.

My wife & children are at Brighton—and I will say nothing more about it. We never shall be able to reach Gillingham, I should fear. Tinney wants to join us in a visit to Paris—I told him you had got leave. I have not yet—but a steam boat goes from Brighton to Dieppe.

The *National* (not natural) Gallery is open at Angersteins. Mr Segar as Sir G. Beaumont calls him has it of course, & the 200— . . . he has put in a needy nephew under him.[2] Seguier has done me a civility lately. This flux and influx of old pictures will bother the rising art—and will in my opinion suffocate & strangle all original feeling at its birth. But *you know* as well as any one how to think on the value [of] productions of intellect.

The Good Bishop is going into Suffolk for some benefit as he hopes for his cough. The change of scene he believes will help him. He is much worn with fits of coughing, which last him sometimes fourteen hours.

---

[1] The child had been brought up for an operation.
[2] William Seguier, received £200 a year as the first Keeper of the National Gallery. 'Nephew' may be a slip for his brother John, who did restoration work there.

I have seen Savile, and have shaken him off. In fact I have made a virtue of necessity—and we are independent of him, and clear to finish the picture unshackled & unencumbered by an employer—such as he— at least. I have got my friend Johnny with me who is squaring and working hard for me, & the canvas is now coming for the Waterloo. Poor Savile is a wretched object, and his folly now stares him in the face, but he has a wife who married him for his riches and will not let him retreat while any is left. I am glad I have no hand in sending him to the Workhouse or something worse.

Tinney mentioned a family greivance, his wife's sister having slunk off and married a nasty dirty stinking little Baptist preacher. What a calamity—

The other day (what is it that this great town does not afford) two people flew over our heads in a balloon—and were knocked on their heads in a park near Croydon.[1]

My love to dear Belim. He ought to have been in one and may yet be my pupil. Beleive me my dear Fisher always yours truly

John Constable

Leslie's picture[2] is the best in the Exhibition—but it has not procured him a single commission—but a copy of it, except it has doubly secured him the patronage of the excellent nobleman—Ld. Egremont.[3] I have as yet been able to see none of the London sights. Glovers whole lengths must be curious—think of his ignorant presumption in *attempting* (to paint) a child. Ought he not to be made to stand in a pillory.

I hear the bell—& must again bid farewell. The World is well rid of Lord Byron[4]—but the deadly slime of his touch still remains.

I saw the marriage of Millman—the Lord have mercy, on the woman. These poets seem nasty people, but I do not know one of them. The town is full of pictures, & foolish people to buy them. One Ruysdael 1700 £.

In the second instalment of his journal Constable records the following events on the 31st May: 'Came home & set to work—on Tinny's large picture, which is now ready when ever they want it . . . In the afternoon Dr Fisher of the Charter House and Mrs. John Fisher & Miss F. called—& were quite delighted to find that I was so busy. Dr F. said—"Sir, I hope you will give me great credit. When I was at the Exhibition, I exclaimed this is the best landscape in the room

---

[1] Thomas Harris made an ascent from the Eagle Tavern in the City Road on the 25th May, accompanied by Miss Stocks: he was killed when the balloon fell over Beddington Park, Croydon, but the girl was saved.

[2] *Sancho Panza in the apartment of the Duchess.*

[3] George Wyndham, 3rd Earl of Egremont, a most generous patron of artists, with whom Constable stayed at Petworth in 1834. Leslie had already painted a *Sancho Panza* for him in 1823.

[4] Byron had died on the 19th April: there may have been some mention of him in Fisher's previous letters.

—and on looking I found it was yours" . . . . . I should say that they were all quite vexed at finding my dear Fish[1] & all my babies gone. Mr J. F.'s child quite well from the operation. . . . J. Fisher comes to town 14th. Inst.' This piece of good news was confirmed by a letter which arrived from Fisher himself on the afternoon of the 2nd June, just after Constable had finished cleaning and doing up the frame of Tinney's picture, which he thought he had made to look 'uncommonly well'.

Gillingham Shaftesbury. May 31. 1824

My dear Constable

In parsons language, I shall observe, that "I gather three things from your letter". First, that you will *not* accompany me on the visitation: secondly, that you will *not* go to Paris: and thirdly, that you will *not* come to Gillingham. To which I shall add a fourthly: that as you will not come & see me, I will come & see you & that on Monday June 14.

I particularly wished to have seen you here, as we have been making several additions to our choir. Three anthems & another clarionet; with which the player accompanies the counter-tenor solo's most lustily. Farmer Jupe [sketch] has been declared bankrupt & literally been beside himself. He has returned however to his Post & sings as well as ever, except that he seems a little wild occasionally in his shakes. I never look at them, but I think of you; & long to read with you Irvine's description of the Village band in the sketch book. Do you know it. If you do not, *pray* turn to it. Vol. 2. page 58–59. My father went to the Exhibition the other day. On his return he said. "The best picture is by John's friend—I forget his name"—"Mr Constable Papa". Yes Mr Constable.—Always a little lemon with his sugar. Sadler the Aeronaut is a pensioner at the Charter-house.[2] How scheming, beggars a man. He was a pastry cook in good business at Oxford. He drank tea at the Lodge the other evening: being an old crony of my Father. He says he used all his powers of persuasion with Harris to abandon the voyage, for he knew him to be ignorant of the management of a balloon. Sadler has made 50 voyages. Did I tell you in my last that Rennell was supposed to be dying.[3] Farewell till we meet. My dear Constable

very faithfully yours

John. Fisher.

It makes me smile to myself when I think of plain English John Constable who does not know a word of their language being the talk & admiration of the French! That he should owe his popularity & his success to *Paris*!

---

[1] Constable's pet name for his wife.
[2] The 'intrepid' James Sadler, as Erasmus Darwin called him, was the first English aeronaut, having made his earliest ascent in a Mongolfier balloon from Oxford in 1784, by means of rarefied air. His son William became even more famous as an aeronaut.
[3] Young Tom Rennell.

PLATE 11

The Fitzwilliam Museum, Cam

GILLINGHAM MILL

1824, by John Constable

Washington Irving's description of the 'village band' may be given as a supplement to this letter, since it seems to have portrayed closely enough the musicians to whom Constable and Fisher had listened together in Gillingham Church. It is taken from the *Sketch Book of Geoffrey Crayon Gent.*, which had appeared in 1820, and occurs in the essay on Christmas Day at Bracebridge Hall.[1] 'The orchestra', wrote Irving, 'was in a small gallery, and presented a most whimsical grouping of heads, piled one above another, among which I particularly noticed that of the village tailor, a pale fellow with a retreating forehead and chin, who played on the clarionet, and seemed to have blown his face to a point; and there was another, a short pursy man, stooping and labouring at a bass-viol, so as to show nothing but the top of a round bald head, like the egg of an ostrich. There were two or three pretty faces among the female-singers . . .; but the gentlemen choristers had evidently been chosen, like old Cremona fiddles, more for tone than looks; and as several had to sing from the same book, there were clusterings of odd physiognomies, not unlike those groups of cherubs we sometimes see on country tombstones.' Those who have read Thomas Hardy's *Mayor of Casterbridge* may remember the choir of that Wessex town trooping into *The Three Mariners* after morning service, with their bass-viols, fiddles and flutes under their arms, and striking up the 109th Psalm to the tune of Wiltshire. A flute and a clarionet used by the choir are still to be seen in Gillingham Church.

On the day after he received the letter Constable got busy on a small version of *Gillingham Mill* for which Fisher had paid him when last in town, so that it might be ready in time for his friend's arrival. 'As he has paid me for it', Constable noted in his diary, 'it is fair it should be so—& he will be pleased'. So diligently did he work that the painting was completed by the 7th June, when the date was recorded on the back.[2] We also learn from the journal that Sir George Beaumont had called on the 3rd June and had helped Constable a good deal in 'toning and improving' *Stratford Mill*, for Constable could never leave well alone. The next letter is from the Bishop, who seems to have been made aware of Constable's prejudice against Smith of Kensington.

Dedham June 9

Dear Sr

Upon my arrival here last night I found the Letter which I now enclose to you.

I wish you would have the goodness to order a Frame for my Daughters copy of your Picture of the Gillingham Bridge. Let it be a modest simple Frame.

We shall probably be in town again by the middle of next week.

I am Dear Sr

Your faithful Servt

J. Sarum.

---

[1] Fisher has written *sketch book* over *Bracebridge Hall* deleted. Irving's *Bracebridge Hall* had appeared in 1822.
[2] The picture is now in the Fitzwilliam Museum at Cambridge, to which it was left by Fisher's son Osmond.

M

The Bishop's letter must have found Constable away, for he went down to Brighton as soon as Fisher's picture was finished; but he was back in time for Fisher's visit, returning to London by the morning coach on the 14th June. His journal may now be allowed to tell the tale of how they spent their time together, in excerpts pieced together after the manner of Leslie.

Monday, 14 June. Fisher had called on his way to the Charter House with his boxes, in a coach.

Tuesday, 15 June. On getting to work, Fisher called and we met as usual delighted with each other. We chatted a great deal, and then went down to the Exhibition. Returned to dinner, boiled mutton, and some nice sherry. Fishers sisters are returned from Paris quite pleased.

Wednesday 16th. A French gentleman & lady called, to beg permission to see "*de* Gallery of Mr Constable". He was wholly struck & delighted with the picture of Tinneys—which now looks so very beautifull on the easil. Fisher called on me & had some dinner, a poloney & bread & cheese & sherry—we then had coffee & tea—& Leslie called to ask me to pass the evening. He stopped to tea and Mr Bigg called. Fisher and Leslie had a good deal of talk about Irvine.[1] A new book of his is just out, I do not recollect the title[2]—Fisher is quite pleased with him. Fisher says that Capt Basil Halls travel in South America is a most interesting work.

Thursday, 17 June. Came home & set to work on Fishers picture— which I did very well. About ½ past one Fisher called. We had a nice leg of mutton ready at two, and after dinner & a glass or two of sherry we set off for Pall Mall, to the Gallery—& looked in at Christies. We saw there all Reinagle's collection of pictures & some copies by his son. We then went to the New Gallery—beautifull rooms but the most wretched display of pictures that it is possible to conceive—nothing in the world can be worse. Saw the R.I.C. Judkin's picture "*Stolen Moments*"—too bad & vulgar to look at. I called at Lady Dysarts in Pall Mall. We returned to tea & coffee, quite tired with our walk. On our way from Pall Mall at the top of the Haymarket we had a full view of the balloon—which looked so near that I could see the divisions of colored silk. On its rising higher we saw it on a clear blew sky looking like a golden egg—it then went into a white thin cloud—& then emerged from it with great beauty, one side so very bright—& the other so clear & dark—looked 'till it was hidden by other clouds. After tea we walked round by Islington to the Charter House. Parted with Fisher at the gates, & returned by Holborn.

Friday, 18 June. After dinner Fisher called. I was at work & had been all day—on the little Osmington Coast.[3] Fisher was on a fasting plan to

---

[1] Washington Irving had known Leslie as a boy in Philadelphia; and Leslie had done illustrations for the *Sketch Book* in 1823.

[2] *Tales of a Traveller*, published in Philadelphia in 1824.

[3] Possibly the sketch called *Weymouth Bay* in the National Gallery, which is quite different in style from the sketches known to have been made at Osmington.

day—but took coffee—he did not call 'till 6 o clock evg. At tea time Peter Cox called. Johny said I was at Brighton, still he came in—& we heard him talking loud in the painting room. Fisher got up and locked the parlor door.

Sunday 20th.[1] Fisher took away his little picture of the Mill with a frame. He is quite anxious that I should dine there tomorrow or he says he shall have the party. I ought to be at the Artists Fund as it is a particular night. He spoke very much of the new novel, the Red Gauntlett, and was not the least surprised when I told him of Sarah[2]—he said she looked like it, & that her constitution was now impaired & she would never be well again.

Monday, 21 June. Was not interrupted 'till 4 o clock. Fisher came in determined that I should dine at the Charter House. I forgot to mention that about 2 o clock Collins called. He was quite struck with the look of Tinney's picture. He hopes it will go to the Gallery. Fisher was so determined that I should dine at the Charter House—but I was unwilling because I ought to have been at the Artists Fund. Collins however said there would be enough without me, so I went—about 4. The day at the Charter House was very pleasant. I met Dr Irvine, a goodnatured young man, & my old school friend Bob Watkinson,[3] a lady—& the three Miss Fishers.[4] Mrs & Dr Fisher were quite agreeable. The 2 younger were returned from Paris. There was a display after dinner of bonnets &c &c. from Paris, which as they wore them passed the Custom House. They were very pretty—one pink, the other white. A Mrs Wolfe came in the evening. She is very pretty, & talks incessantly of all the arts & sciences. I did not leave the house 'till 12. I slept pretty well for so good a dinner. The dinner was salmon—& a quarter of lamb, veal stewed—& some savory side dishes. 2d course—large dish of green peas & 2 ducks—lovely puddings & tarts, beautiful dessert & I drank only claret. We had good talk. Some of them stayed till 2.

Tuesday, 22d. June. Fisher called about 2 o clock—dined with us on a new peice of roast beef. Walked with him to Pall Mall & to my bank.

Wednesday June 23d. Fisher came on his way to Piccadilly to the coach, so Judkin took his leave. I went with Fisher to the coach & we had dinner in the Coffee House—I drank ale, & 2 glasses of brandy & water. He did the same. We parted quite delighted with having seen so much of each other—he longs like me to get to his darling wife & children.

Fond as he was of the Archdeacon's company, Constable found these visits something of a strain. Writing separately to his wife he said, 'You know when

---

[1] The pages of the journal relating to the 19th and part of the 20th are unfortunately missing.

[2] One of the maids.

[3] The Rev. Robert Watkinson and the Rev. Andrew Irvine, B.D., were both masters at The Charterhouse.

[4] Mary, Frances, and Jane.

Fisher is in town I am not in possession of my time a moment for certain'; and after his friend had departed he wrote, 'I am almost glad Fisher is out of town.' While he was in London this time Fisher had the opportunity of exercising his medical knowledge on the case of a sickly maid who had been looking after Constable in his wife's absence.

After such ample opportunity for conversation it is not surprising that Constable did not feel any great need to write to his friend again till nearly a month later; but one more extract[1] from the journal may be given before we come to his letter.

June 25th. After breakfast called on the Bishop by his wish. He had to tell me that he thought of my improving the picture of the Cathedral, and mentioned many things. "He hoped I would not take his observations amiss." I said, "Quite the contrary, as his Lordship has been my kind monitor for twenty-five years". I am to have it home to-morrow. He says I must visit the Colonel, at Charleton,[2] this or next month, for a day or two; I do not wish it, as I begin to be tired of going to school. The good Bishop has been at Dedham, and found the wretched ——'s all at daggers drawn. He reconciled them, and insisted on their shaking hands, which they did. Mr. Neave[3] called. . . . He was quite astonished at the picture on the easel (Tinney's), and hoped that I would always keep to the picturesque.

1824, July to December

It was probably from the painting brought back from the Bishop's house that Johnny Dunthorne made 'a delightful outline of the Cathedral' on 12th July for Constable to copy. We also learn from the journal that Constable retouched Dolly Fisher's copy of Gillingham Bridge before sending it back, and that its new frame from Coward's followed presently in response to a note from the young lady. On the 15th July a Mrs. Hand[4] called, anxious to have a small picture of Gillingham Mill. Then after setting his affairs in order, Constable left London to rejoin his family at last on the 17th.

Even though they had not yet appeared at the Louvre, Constable's paintings were already the talk of the town in Paris. Arrowsmith had written on the 19th June to tell of the sensation they had produced among the French artists, and their arrival had been considered of sufficient importance to receive special mention by the Paris correspondent of *The Times* on the 8th July. The pictures were even paid the compliment of being violently denounced. Mr. Phillips, a new Brighton acquaintance of whom more particular mention will be made later, sent Mrs. Constable a translation of what one of the French critics had said.[5] The article sought to give a word of warning to those of the writer's

---

[1] The original page is missing, and the transcript is Leslie's.
[2] Sir George Fisher lived at Old Charlton in Kent, where he painted views of the Thames.
[3] Probably Sir Richard Digby Neave, with whom Constable stayed at Epsom in 1831.
[4] Possibly a widow or daughter-in-law of George Watson Hand, Prebendary of Westminster, who had been Archdeacon of Dorset from 1780 to 1801.
[5] Now in the Plymouth Collection.

compatriots who were in danger of being seduced from allegiance to Poussin, and had been heard to exclaim, 'A miracle!'. This is the notice to which Constable refers in his next letter, written the day after his arrival in Brighton.

Brighton. July 18. 1824
No 9 Mrs. Sober's Gardens
Western Place

My dear Fisher

I have been long attempting to write to you—but in London I have so many occupations & interruptions, that I was glad to put it off 'till arrived here—whither I am come to seek some quiet with my children.

I am harrassed with a number of small commissions which greatly annoy me & cut into my time & consequently into my reputation. I ought however to complain of nothing as that will help my family—but I have formed a plan, of receiving no commissions under 20 or 25, or 30 guineas—however small as the picture itself must be perfect—& the subject as good as one on a six foot canvas.[1]

"*We*" have received a letter from the Wise Men of the Institution[2]— they offer us a good thing (but how it is done will form an amusing conversation with you & me afterwards). It is to receive some pictures of the living artists which are in private hands, with which they mean to form an Exhibition, next year, instead of this of the "*Old Masters*". I have to beg that Tinney's picture may be one and as it is already in my possession it is convenient—I trust neither you or Tinney will refuse me a request (unreasonable to be sure), but it will be of real service to me.

I have got the picture of the Cathedral, from the Bishop's—and Johnny has made me a delightfull outline of the same size. He is an invaluable companion to me. We must not let the Good Bishop have the bridal in his hand again. He will ruin both our reputations—I mean yours & mine.

Your sister called & brought me the little drawing of the Windmill.

The French criticks have begun with me and that in the *usual* way—by a comparison with *what has been* done. They are angry with the artists for admiring these "pictures which have made so much noise in Paris—and which they shall now proceed to examine"—&c &c.

They acknowledge the effect to be rich and powerfull—& the whole has the look of nature, and color (their *chief excellence*) to be rich and true & harmonious—but shall we admire works so unusual for these excellencies alone—what is to become of the great Poussin—&c &c. Is this the only excellence to be looked for in the art of landscape painting— they then caution the younger artists to beware of the "seduction", those English works cannot fail to produce, when "*exposed*" &c &c—

---

[1] Constable eventually produced a printed scale of prices for landscapes; but this was not until 1826.
[2] The British Institution.

All this comes of being regular criticks. It is like Milman's poetry—made upon what has been. The execution of my pictures I know is singular —but I admire that rule of Sterns—"never mind the dogmas and rules of the schools—but get at the heart as you can". But it is evident something like the end has been attained in these by the great sensation they seem to have made on most people who have seen them here or abroad.

I have the paper and will send it to you—as well as two little works, on the Roman Catholicks by our old friend Smith of Norwich: the title of one is "*Cats let out of a Scarlet Bag*": but I will send them to you. This morning a letter reached me at this place directed to

> *Monsieur* John Constable
> Peintre paysagiste 35 Charlotte Street Fitzroy Square
> a Londre

Can there be anything more amusing than all this? But I have not the least thought of going[1] among them. I am planning some large land-scape, but I have no inclination to pursue my Waterloo. I am impressed with an idea that it will ruin me. I most of all want to see you at Salisbury —but how or when I know not. I am looking for a months quiet here— and I have brought with me several works to complete. What a blessing it is thus to be able to carry one profession with me. A medical man cannot take his patients with him or you your flock. Will you think when you see Miss D. Fisher to say that I recd the money she sent for the frame of Gillingham.

> Yours very truly   J. Constable.

My wife is much stronger & better—for this change.

Poor old Smith—in one of his books—talks of the "*flatus pro ano*"—of an old woman, &c. &c.

The following day was the birthday of Constable's favourite daughter, for whose sake he had made a special effort to reach Brighton in time; and an oil-sketch of Brighton Beach[2] done on the same evening bears on its back a mutilated piece of paper with the words: 'My dear Maria's birthday Your Goddaughter . . .'. This may possibly have formed part of another contemplated letter to Fisher. A number of other sketches were done on the shore, by way of relaxation from the work that had been brought down to be completed for Arrowsmith and Schroth. The good Bishop, too, was enjoying a rest with his family after the activities of the London season.

> Palace Sarum. July 23, 1824.

Dear Sr

I cannot enclose a Letter without adding a few Lines. We have been here about ten days enjoying fine weather in my beautiful place.

---

[1] Or 'gain'.
[2] In the Victoria and Albert Museum.

I hope you are laying in a stock of health.

When you return to town, I must consign to your Care an old Portrait of an Ancestor of Mrs Fisher—that wants to be cleaned & repaired.

With the best regards of my Ladies

I remain

Dear Sr

your faithfull Servt

J. Sarum

It is not known what was the letter forwarded from Salisbury—perhaps another note from Dolly Fisher. A letter from the Bishop's nephew arrived next day.

Gillingham Shaftesbury. July 24. 1824.

My dear Constable;

I go to Salisbury tomorrow when I will ask Tinney to grant your request. In the mean time grant me one. Lend me for a *month* one of your best pictures with a handsome frame to hang over my chimney peice opposite the White Horse. As all the world is coming to Salisbury at the Music meeting, it may do you good. I will bear all expences. It should be sent directly. Smith's "flatus in ano" I have read.—The critique of the french "rule & line" gentleman is amusing enough. To how few is judgement confined: & by how few is the taste of the world guided! When Domenichino *lived*, nobody understood him: the many, no doubt, abused him, as they do you: & now his name will sell a canvass not fit for floor cloth. Some-how or other, I do not expect to see you this year. *If* you come hither it must be in September: if you come to Salisbury, it must be after Octr. 1. I am going next week to Southampton, to marry *Harriet* Webber to Mr. Heniage! He has a landed estate worth £8000 per annum. I think one of your six foot canvass's should hang over her dining-room chimney peice. The Bishop has been very active lately, pouring hot water into every ones shoes around him. I came in for a very handsome sprinkling. A paragraph respecting your Paris pictures got into the Reading Mercury: & was copied into the Sarum Journal. "Mr. Constable the eminent artist" &c.—Your pet Belim grows handsomer daily. "I have just read" sayings & doings, by the Author of John Bull. He talks of the "pea soup atmosphere of London". Tell John Dunthorne[1] with my regards, that the *great* Hershell telescope was a *real* one, and no humbug. It is a reflector of extraordinary power for examining at extraordinary distances: & is not meant to be fit for general use.

I am just returned out of Berkshire whither I went on a clerical visit. The ruling fashion among my brethren is to pronounce panegyrics upon

---

[1] Johnny Dunthorne had a passion for astronomy: the elder Dunthorne once showed Leslie a large telescope which his son had made.

the memory of Rennell.[1] How little the world knew him. After one of these public encomiums, I said quietly to Milman, "was Rennell sincere?" "He was so at *last*", replied Milman.—I congratulate you on the repossession of the Cathedral. Have Buckler or Reinagle to make him a copy of it. I have written my write. What can a man have to say, living [in] Gillingham: & dining occasionally with a few routine parsons: who have 52 sermons & on new years day turn the Leaf. With my kindest remembrances to your wife, beleive me

my dear Constable

sincerely yours

John. Fisher.

There is rather an overdose of galls in my ink to day I fear.

Fisher's next letter was addressed to Charlotte Street, but had to be readdressed to Brighton, where Constable was still.

Close Salisbury. Friday Aug: 6. 1824.

My dear Constable;

Tinney readily consents to your exhibiting your picture when the gallery opens. But he begs that he may have it *till* then. He particularly wishes for it at the Music meeting, the 16th August. You will do well to send it directly or you will really disoblige him.

I am on my road to Southampton to marry Harriet Webber tomorrow. So that I have few minutes to write in. I have discovered a beautiful old Mill in a secluded part of our valley on the spot where Fielding wrote his Tom Jones.

Beleive me

ever yours

John. Fisher.

It would appear from the next letter that Constable had lent Fisher a picture later on called *The Lane* to grace the walls of his house in the Close during the influx of fashionable visitors for the musical festival at Salisbury, and that he had also allowed Tinney to have his picture back for the time being. The letter iş undated, but the postmark shows that it was posted at Brighton on the 29th, while Constable's anxiety to have news of the safe arrival of the pictures indicates that the month was August.

(The dignitary of the Church seems to have forgotten the dignitary of the easil)

My dear Fisher

I am disappointed at not having heard either from yourself or

---

[1] The younger Rennell, whose exceptionally promising career had been cut short by his death on the 30th June 1824.

Tinney of the safe arrival of my pictures at Salisbury. No doubt the pick-pockets and fidlers who have of late made your cathedral the scene of their depredations must have put all other thoughts aside.[1]

I was piquing myself how promptly I had obeyed your demands—did you like the picture I sent you to *show*? Had I recollected your objection to that picture (The "Nass"[2]) I should have sent you Hampstead.

I am living here but I dislike the place—& miss (in this my solitude) any letter from you especially when I may expect to receive one. I am however getting on with my French jobs. One of the largest is quite complete, and is my best, in freshness and sparkle—*with repose*—which is my struggle just now. A friend here wished Ld Egremont to see it. It was shown him. He recollected all my pictures of any note, but he recollected them only for their defects—so that my friends good intentions failed. But I will do his Lordship & myself justice. The truth is that landscape affords him no interest whatever.[3]

Brighton is the receptacle of the fashion and offscouring of London. The magnificence of the sea, and its (to use your own beautifull expression) everlasting voice, is drowned in the din & lost in the tumult of stage coaches—gigs—"flys" &c.—and the beach is only Piccadilly (that part of it where we dined) by the sea-side. Ladies dressed & *undressed*—gentlemen in morning gowns & slippers on, or without them altogether about *knee deep* in the breakers—footmen—children—nursery maids, dogs, boys, fishermen—*preventive service men* (with hangers & pistols), rotten fish & those hideous amphibious animals the old bathing women, whose language both in oaths & voice resembles men—all are mixed up together in endless & indecent confusion. The genteeler part, the marine parade, is still more unnatural—with its trimmed and neat appearance & the dandy jetty or chain pier, with its long & elegant strides into the sea a full $\frac{1}{4}$ of a mile [small sketch of the Chain Pier]. In short there is nothing here for a painter but the breakers—& sky—which have been lovely indeed and always varying. The fishing boats are picturesque, but not so much so as the Hastings boats, which are luggers. The difference is this [sketch of boats with different types of sail]. But these subjects are so hackneyed in the Exhibition, and are in fact so little capable of that beautifull sentiment that landscape is capable of or which rather belongs to landscape, that they have done a great deal of harm to the art—they form a class of art much easier than landscape & have in consequence almost supplanted it, and have drawn off many who would have encouraged the growth of a pastoral feel in their own minds—& paid others for pursuing it. But I am not complaining—I only meant to call to your recollection that we have Calcott & Collins—but not Wilson or Gainsborough.

---

[1] See next letter: Constable must have seen an account in the press.
[2] If this was a Suffolk subject, *The Nass* may have been the local name for a rustic lane: the writing seems clear.
[3] This hardly seems to be correct.

While in the feilds (for I am at the west of this city—and quite out of it), I met with a most intelligent and elegant man Mr Phillips[1]—we are become intimate & he contributes much to our pleasure here. He is a botanist —& all his works on natural history are instructive and entertaining— calculated for children of all ages—his history of trees is delightfull—I shall buy them—& I think you would if you saw them—

Our next door neighbour is Mr & Mrs Masquerier, a portrait painter[2] —retired from business with a fortune—she a Scotch woman, a niece of Ld Buchan's—vulgar—& clever—with the assurance of the devil. Masquerier & I have no one feeling in common on the Art. On the score of the Academy the grapes are sour, & although he has made a fortune in the Art, he enjoys it only as a thief enjoys the fruits of his robbery—while he is not found out. He would (I see) give half his fortune for half my reputation.

No 9, Mrs. Sober's Gardens[3]—so called from Mrs Sober the Lady of the Manor—& rich in estates here—which are more so now by their new buildings. She is of the *good*, and has built a Chapple in which she preaches herself. I have heard this story—a man was taken before the Magistrates quite drunk—when asked what he was, he said he was one of Mrs. Sober's congregation.

Last Tuesday, the finest day that ever was, we went to the Dyke—which is in fact a Roman remains of an embankment, overlooking—perhaps the most grand & affecting natural landscape in the world—and consequently a scene the most unfit for a picture. It is the business of a painter not to contend with nature & put this scene (a valley filled with imagery 50 miles long) on a canvas of a few inches, but to make something out of nothing, in attempting which he must almost of necessity become poetical. But you understand this better than me.

My wife & children are delightfully well. Ever yrs. most truly

John Constable.

Leslie says that Constable wrote on the back of one of his Brighton oil-sketches of this year: 'The neighbourhood of Brighton consists of London cowfields and hideous masses of unfledged earth called country'. His letter roused Fisher to a response.

---

[1] Henry Phillips, fellow of the Horticultural and Linnaean societies, whose *Sylva Florifera* had been published in 1823: from 1823 to 1825 he lived at Bedford Square, Brighton.

[2] John James Masquerier was settled in Brighton from 1823: his wife Rachel Forbes was a widow of Professor Robert Eden Scott; her aunt Margaret Forbes married the 11th Earl of Buchan.

[3] The street does not appear in the local directory for 1824. Mrs. Ann Sober was the sister of Thomas Read Kemp who owned a moiety of the manor of Brighton and had built the chapel here mentioned for his own newly founded religious sect. In other letters the address is more correctly given as Western Place.

Gillingham Shaftesbury. Septemb: 8. 1824.

My dear Constable:

I have accused myself an hundred times of great neglect and ingratitude in never writing to acknowledge the receipt of your pictures, &
of thanking you for the promptitude with which you attended to my
request. But the truth is, I dislike to sit down to write to you unless "I can
have my talk out": and I have been in such a perpetual bustle for the last
month that I have never had a tranquail minute. For the last four days
the Bishop of Bristol has been at my house on a visit, & confirming my
flock.[1] My wife has been at the same time ill: I had my young parishioners
to prepare for confirmation. My family to move to & fro Salisbury & in
short any thing has prevailed but peace & quiet which is necessary to the
exertion of thought.

Your "Lane", in spite of the want of the hat brush & pressing iron,
looked very interesting & tranquil & came out remarkably fresh when it
got a reflected light on it, which during a portion of the day was the case
with it. I requested to be introduced to Collins's friend, Sir T. Heathcote
during the Music meeting; & brought him up to see your pictures: but
though he spoke civilly, he is evidently one of those who prefer execution
to sentiment. He is remarkably like Collins: about 60 years of age & a
bachelor. He said he should invite me to meet Calcott, but I have heard
no more of him.—I met in my walks the other day in the Close, a bankrupt
tanner of your country who is going about reading *Lectures* on *Belles
Lettres*. He came either from Halstead or Halesworth. He said he knew
your mother, & had heard of your fame. He was evidently in poverty, &
I promised to subscribe to a *poem* he was going to print.—You recollect
probably a conversation we had with Leslie respecting Irvine. I said that
Irvine had not done justice to the present character of the Clergy. That
they were a class of men who much admired his works, & had literary
reputation much at their disposal. In his new work, "the tales of a traveller", he has made us ample amends. I copy the following sentence from
p 316 of vol. I. "He was a good man: a worthy specimen of the country
clergy who silently & unostentatiously do a vast deal of good: who are as
it were *woven* into the whole system of *rural life*: and operate upon it with
the steady yet unobtrusive influence of temperate piety & learned good
sense." The rest of the vol is on the same subject & gives a pretty picture
of the serene tranquillity & decorum of a Cathedral city: & a most amiable
hint at the character of a *Prebendary*. Is this accident? Or was our talk
repeated?—Take an opportunity to let Leslie know that the compliment
has not been lost upon the body.—Your Knoyle protegee brought for my
inspection a most atrocious portrait of a horse & another of his pretty

---

[1] The archdeaconry of Dorset had been separated from the church of Salisbury in
1542 and annexed to the newly formed see of Bristol; it was restored to the Salisbury
diocese in 1836.

cousin the Maid of the Mill who stood & looked over your shoulder as you painted.[1] (Does your wife see any letters?) He will I see come up to town to try his fortune; & will prove another Read to you. Mind, as *before*, the introduction was *your* doing not *mine*. The pickpockets of Salisbury after rifling the pocketbooks left them where they were found. I saw them opened & returned to their owners. Lord Pembroke's contained three prescriptions of Dr Fowler—all safely restored. Col Fishers had a little paper done up, powder fashion, inscribed "Calomel". Also *carefully* restored. The Dean lost his purse: but as he wore an apron, the question was *how* the robbery was effected. The apron must have been *up*: & the nights were dark. So the pickpockets excaped suspicion of this delinquency.—Great outcries from the robbed that no Bow Street patroles had been engaged. This piqued our Salisbury constables: who set to work & secured a man in the Bishop's closet, & brought him before *me* during the Hail-stone chorus: the only thing I wanted to hear. He turned out to be my brother's hatter at Devizes. The great tree in the middle of my lawn shews manifest symptoms of decay. We fear if the equinoctial gales come on before the fall of the leaf that he will split. I go into Bachelor residence at Salisbury on the 3rd of October. I shall be at Reading on the 1st & leave it on the 3rd. if you mind to meet me there & come on to Salisbury: but I say the thing more in the spirit of despair than hope. The country was never more beautiful. I have a great mind to dress up your description of Brighton & send it to John Bull. It is an odious place: though I only guess. I never saw it. I am glad your wife & children are all well. The brightness of your future depends upon the brightness of their looks. My wife I thank God is well & my brats blooming. My dear Constable

yours very faithfully

John. Fisher.

Arrowsmith was at the same time pressing Constable to come over with Mrs. Constable to Paris, where the exhibition at the Louvre was now open: but the elation which Constable had felt earlier in the year was succeeded by a descent into deep depression. For one thing, he was more than ever anxious that Tinney should let him have back *Stratford Mill*, which had done him so much credit with his summer visitors, so that he might use it to enhance his reputation still further at the special exhibition arranged by the British Institution for the following year. Secondly, he was regretting his engagement to paint the two uprights, for which the enforced change in his plans had prevented him from finding subjects, and which the pressure of his French commissions had left him no time to execute.

Novr. 2. 1824. Charlotte St.

My very dear Fisher

I am determined to write to you though I am so far from well that

---

[1] Probably one of the girls from the cotton mill mentioned above by Constable.

I am not equal to it. I have been knocked up to day owing to writing a long letter to Tinney yesterday, in which I had to [make] the exertion of asking two favors of him [and] to make if possible my motives for so doing not misunderstood.

All my indispositions have their source in my mind—it [is] when I am restless and unhappy that I become susceptible of cold—damp—heats—and such nonsense. I have not been well for many weeks—but I hope soon to rid myself of these things and get to work again.

I expect my family home tomorrow from Brighton—my children will amuse me.

Pray my dear Fisher help me in my request to Tinney. I am clearing my mind as much as possible of these inconveniences. I have bought off some—and begged off others. Even such a little thing as you requested of me in the summer, you little think the serious interference it was to me, and how much it cost me to get it done for you—certainly not less than 20 £ —but if I had never done another picture you should not have been disappointed.

Tinney's pictures I see no prospect of my being able to afford the time from the publick to—and after a time they become a burthen—dead weight —and even a reproach to my own conscience, and lay me indeed open to the observation of my friends (& those the best) when no allowance is made for the real difficulties I have to encounter, because they cannot be made to understand them—I mean the world generally, *not you—but Tinney* and such highly gifted *common sense men*.

Help me in these matters as you always do—

Of the wretched Fontleroy—no one seems to sympathise with him—a greater instance of moral depravity they say never existed. [He is] the only man that I ever felt I *could* see hanged—

Of his hurt to the arts, is the case of the poor Widow Muss.[1] I saw her on Saturday just leaving Smith of the Museum[2]—she was left last summer a widow—suddenly—pennyless. The King bought (as you know) all her late husbands enamels, finished and unfinished. She purchased at his house[3] £1700 exchequer bonds—she was anxious & went to him last week in prison—saw him with his brother & the jaylor. He assured her all was safe—she might be easy—& she would have full 20/- in the pound (all this as you may say with the halter round his neck). On Saturday evening when I saw Smith, she had just left Basil Montague who had gained access to the firm—& learnt that F. had sold them all by forging her name.

The Wests are in an alarmed state. They thought there was plenty of

---

[1] Widow of William Muss, enamel and glass painter: an auction for her benefit was held on the 29th and 30th November.

[2] Constable's old friend J. T. Smith was now Keeper Prints and Drawings, at the British Museum.

[3] The banking house of Marsh, Stracey, Fauntleroy and Graham in Berners Street.

money of theirs there—old West had always told them particulars of his property—but now—lately (just before his arrest) he produced a bond of old Wests for £6000, which they never dreamt of and which they were forced to find a friend to pay. They beleive it to be a forgery—yrs J.C.

Pray let me hear of you by return of post. I heard of the bishop 6 weeks ago—he was leading his flock over the mountains of Wales.

The case of Henry Fauntleroy, respected member of a reputable banking firm, was one which nearly touched the sensitivities of men like Fisher and Constable, whose hopes were centred on making secure provision for their families. He had for many years been selling out securities held in a fiduciary capacity by means of false authorities. On the previous Friday a grand jury had found true bills of indictment: on Saturday he had been tried and convicted of forgery at the Old Bailey, and sentenced to be hanged. His defence, if it can be called a defence, was that he had acted as he did to save his firm from ruin and that his partners were equally involved. This was used by a section of the press to evoke sympathy on behalf of the condemned man. There was a petition for mercy, and a legal point was raised which it took twelve judges to decide, and it was not till the 30th November that Fauntleroy was finally executed. *The Times*, agreeing with Constable, held that if there was anything to be said in favour of abolishing the capital penalty for forgery, this was not the case on which to put it forward. The Bank of England came to the rescue of some of the victims.

Begun. Tuesday Nov. 2. 1824.

My dear Constable;

Association of ideas is sometimes very singular. What is there in common between you, and Alderman Wood? And yet seeing his name at the head of a paragraph in a newspaper made me think of you. I found that his son had been elected to some living in the city & that *Judkin* had been a rival candidate. The name of Judkin called that of Constable to my mind by an intimate association: and so I "stole a few minutes" to write to you on the spur of the recollection.

Thursday Novr. 4. I had written thus far in facetious mood, when yesterday I received your distressing letter. I was very sorry to perceive both from the matter & the hand-writing that you were very much out of order. But I trust the cold weather & your temperate habits will soon restore nature to her healthy action. Your body is evidently acting upon your mind & you are as we are all apt to do, raising inconveniences into difficulties. However we will suppose them & treat them as real difficulties. I had a conference with Tinney yesterday. He was as usual very good-natured; & willing to do much but not all that you ask. The great picture he will not let you have *now*: but he will keep his promise for the exhibition. With regard to your engagement to paint him two uprights he said that he would let you off only with this reservation. That he must have two pictures of that size of your painting. You are to follow your own devices. Only when he sees on your walls what he likes, he is to have the option of purchasing. This seemed to be the *leaning* of his mind yesterday. If he has changed it to day I will write again. He does not admit the propriety of your sensations: but I think he apprehends what you mean. *I* beleive however that you are right. No man ever composed any thing racy & genuine with a shackle on his mind. Every body has been ill. (Abernethy[1] says that there is not a healthy man in London, such is the state of the atmosphere & the mode of life.) My wife my servants, myself, have been all out of order. I was very unwell indeed. But I am now recovering fast. The Bishop has returned from Wales quite a renovated man; and bids fair for great longevity. The newspapers are such liars by trade & admit any statement for money so often that one can never give credit to any thing one sees there. Did Fontleroy commit these forgeries to support as he said "the house" or was he the wretched slave of lust first described? Such villiany, & *security* when evident detection awaited him, has seldom been heard of. —Tinney has just been here & has read to me his letter to you. It is in substance much the same as I have written on the other leaf. He is a most amiable liberal man. If you paint a large picture he says & you cannot sell it for more, he will give you 100 guineas for it.—However your fame is your Pole star: & all other objects must be sacrificed to it.—I copy you a passage from Israeli's Anecdotes[2] in absence of news. "In all Art perfection lapses into the weakened state too often dignified as classical imitation. It sinks into mannerisms, wantons into affectation or shoots out into fantastic novelties. When all languishes in a state of mediocrity or is deformed by false taste, then some fortunate genius has the glory of restoring another golden age of invention." History of the Caracci's. Let me hear from you again soon, saying that you are better. My regard to your wife. Yours sincerely

John. Fisher.

Without knowing what was in the letter which Constable had written to Tinney, it is hardly possible to judge of the 'propriety' of the feelings expressed therein. Here is Tinney's reply.

Salisbury 4 November 1824.

My dear Constable.

I am exceedingly distressed at the whole tenor of your letter of the 31 October.

With respect to the beautiful Picture which is the principal ornament of our house, Mrs. Tinney says she will not consent to its being again removed as it was last year for so long a time. She reluctantly will permit me to send it for the six weeks of the exhibition but not to remain in London

---

[1] John Abernethy, the celebrated surgeon.
[2] *A Dissertation on Anecdotes*, by Isaac D'Israeli, published in 1793.

after the exhibition shall close nor to be sent till just on time for the opening of it. Now what am I to do in this case? It is very true that our best apartment appears unfurnished while that Picture is away. I cannot ask of Fisher again to unfurnish his withdrawing room to supply its place? I hope you will not think her unreasonable.

With respect to the two Pictures which you were so kind as to promise on my account—I never can enforce against a friend whom I highly esteem any species of obligation. I have long waited—patiently—for the acquisition of what I should highly value—both as specimens of your superior art and as tokens of that friendship which I hold in no mean account. I would continue to wait patiently for them—happy always in the anticipation of eventually possessing them. I exceedingly lament the present necessity. But must yield to it without reserve—and in doing so I seem to discharge a duty of friendship which though very painful I hope not to regret hereafter.

I had hoped that you would be able to come to Salisbury during the Autumn. You seem to have forgotten that I begged you to bring your Palate with you—and that I intended to request you to employ yourself in taking a Portrait of my good Wife, which might have paid all the expenses of your Journey, and have gratified me as coming from your hands and on account of its interesting subject. Will you be so good as to think of this hereafter.

I know my good friend that acts of kindness ought to be expected from no professional person in the line of his profession. I do not wish that this or any other matter relating to the Art should between us be considered merely with regard to the friendship which happily subsists between us and which I would improve and perpetuate. Let this and every other transaction of the same kind of treated between us on the principles of business. I am not afraid of sinking in your esteem by that arrangement— and I assure you that you will stand as regarding me exactly in the relation in which I wish to place you.

I wish you to recollect how the matter of the two Pictures originated between us. You were complaining of the disagreeableness of preparing a great Picture for the exhibition without the certainty of remuneration. I told you you might freely go to the work—that any such Picture which you might bring to the exhibition, I would call mine at the Price of one hundred guineas, if no one would give for it a higher price—and *that*, without reference to subject or publick opinion. You desired me to enter into a similar engagement for two smaller pictures at 50 Guineas each— this I readily did, imposing no condition as to subject or anything else. This engagement also you desire me to abandon. I can only say—be it as you desire. My original object was only to ensure to you the sale of your performances, though I was so selfish as to feel anxious to possess them out of personal regard to you—and for my own personal gratification.

Whenever an opportunity occurs I shall keep the same object in view and feel the same anxiety. In releasing you from your engagement I think I evince no kindness towards you and do you an injury rather than a benefit, but your solicitation must justify me.

I shall be very happy to hear from you that your view of the circumstances has changed your opinion and your wishes, and that our engagement should not be dissolved.

Pray present my best Compliments to Mrs Constable and believe that I remain with great regard

Yours most truly and faithfully

J. P. Tinney

If the considerate tone of this letter made Constable feel as guilty in conscience as it should have done, it is to be doubted whether it did much to appease his fretfulness: nor is the suggestion that he should return to the work he so much disliked, that of painting portraits, one which would have made him feel particularly grateful. Unwilling to give up the object which he had in view, it seems that he now wrote another letter to Fisher, asking whether he could not overcome Mrs. Tinney's objection by offering to furnish her withdrawing room during the prolonged absence of *Stratford Mill*, and offering to let Fisher have the loan of his Brighton Sketches.

Close Salisbury. Novr. 13. 1824.

My dear Constable;

This moist muggy weather, seems to have deranged every body: and among others your humble servant. I have been as the old women say "quite poorly" this last week & not up to the energy of a letter.

The obstacle to your getting a fresh loan of your picture, is not mine but Tinney's. His assertion that I should not like to have "the White Horse" again removed, was gratuitous. He did not ask me. However on the receipt of your second letter, I went & made the offer; stating what I guessed to be your reason for wishing to have it viz to "whip up" your present pictures by. But I met with no success. He will not part with it, until the time promised. The application is hopeless, though the refusal is politely worded. I assure you I did not need any bribe to induce me to comply with your wishes. I am indeed already in your debt for the loan of the "shady lane". But the offer of the virgin sketches is too tempting to be resisted.—Perhaps it will be as well if I return you "the Lane". I will send for the Carpenter & order it off; unless you write to forbid me. Would the following request interfere with your occupations? To make me a sketch of a gothic chair to correspond with our choir. Or would you get it done for me. We have at last ordered our altar on *Sundays* to be temporarily brought down between the two pillars at the end of the choir. We want the chair as an accompaniment [sketch]. Is my sketch compre-

N

hensible?—The Cathedral brings poor Dodsworth to my mind. He has had two paralytic seizures. The second has drawn one eye up into his head, & has left him a woeful figure. But he still toddles about with his silver stick on his shoulder. *After thoughts*. If the request about the chair occupies any thing but an idle minute, or gives you the least trouble forego it. It is of no consequence. It is generally reputed that there will be a grand explosion in Ireland next Spring.[1] Some popular prophecies (Pastorini's[2]) predict the year 1825 as the first year of Irish *liberty*. Every thing seems tending to a rebellion. And then it is the opinion I hear of the D of W.[3] that the country must be *conquered*. So much for the result of Opposition politics, ministerial conciliation, & Catholic Emancipation.

I hope that you will a little diversify your subject this year as to *time of day*. Thompson you know wrote, not four Summers but *four Seasons*.[4] People are tired of mutton on top mutton at bottom mutton at the side dishes, though of the best flavour & smallest size.

When you write again, give us a little history of your wife and children. Beleive me

yours always

John. Fisher.

Charlotte Street. Novr. 17. 1824

My dear Fisher

Thank you for your letter of yesterday. I wrote rather a long letter to Tinney a few days ago—which will I hope set all right about the picture. You are both mistaken as to my motives for desiring it so soon as I at first requested to have [it]—I wished for it not to "*whip up any other pictures by*"—my Lock which now hangs in my room, being far beyond it in that respect—but my anxiety was to have it in readiness and by me as an inducement for the Wise Men from the Institution, to receive it—should it fail after all I must trouble you for your White Horse.

See my letter to Tinney if you can? I have endeavoured to awaken him to some perception of the feeling which must govern artists and poets in their productions—but though he "*respects*" the thing, his constitution and all the *habits* of his life, make it quite impossible for him to enter into any work of "*imagination*". It is different with you and was so from the first. You saw at once the right things in spite of the milk & water of the Bishop, & the Colonel, and the dirt & varnish which begrimed the walls of poor Douglas's drawing rooms.

---

[1] Catholic Emancipation had long been in the forefront, and had upset two ministries: Canning, as a follower of Pitt, favoured the Catholics. In 1823 the Catholic Association had been formed by Daniel O'Connell: it had assumed vast proportions, and had almost superseded the government of the country. It was suppressed in 1825.

[2] Benedetto Pastorini, the stipple engraver.

[3] The Duke of Wellington.

[4] Constable was fond of quoting from Thomson's *Seasons* to amplify the titles of his pictures.

I am at work again & I have my friend John Dunthorne with me—he cheers & helps me so much that I could wish him always to be with me. He forwards me a great deal in subordinate parts such as tracing, squaring &c &c. This morning a gentleman called on me who has "*nine telescopes*". You may judge how thick they soon got. It is John's forte. He is to see them tomorrow.

I am planning a large picture—I regard all you say but I do not enter into that notion of varying ones plans to keep the Publick in good humour —subject and change of weather & effect will afford variety in landscape. What if Van de Velde had quitted his sea peices—or Ruisdael his water-falls—or Hobbema his native woods—would not the world have lost so many features in art? I know that you wish for no material alterations— but I have to combat from high quarters, even Lawrence, the seeming plausible arguments that subject makes the picture. Perhaps you think an evening-effect—or a warm picture—might do. Perhaps it might start me some new admirers—but I should lose many old ones—

Reynolds[1] the engraver tells me my "freshness" exceeds the freshness of any painter that ever lived—for to my zest of "color" I have added "light": Ruisdael (the freshest of all) and Hobbema, were *black*—should any of this be true, I must go on. I imagine myself driving a nail. I have driven it some way—by persevering with this nail I may drive it home—by quit-ting it to attack others, though I amuse myself, I do not advance them beyond the first—but that particular nail stands still the while. I can't mention one strong living instance of what greediness of trying every thing has brought his very original mind to.[2] No man who can do any one thing well, will ever be able to do another different as well—I beleive that from our physical construction no man can be born with more than one high & original feel—this in my opinion was the case with the greatest master of *variety*, Shakespeare.

I will leave this stiff work—and speak of what has happened to me— and about me. Judkin was a candidate with young Wood—old Wood had been long breaking the ground & had parallized all Judkins friends—but he stood well on the ballot. Williams who stood next on the list to Wood, in ballot, is an instance of what a dissenter can do—he was paid for a sermon on the Thursday at this church, had no more to do with the parish than you—and was hated by the Rector for his principles—when he called himself the faithfull servant of the parish for 16 years. He is owner of a dissenting chapple at Homerton in which he does all the duty.

A Calvanist is capable of any thing—the *Revd* Dr. Richardson of Dunmow, late of Dedham, was caught by Mrs Richardson—in bed with *their favorite* servant, Bridget Hursell. Nobody however is *surprized* at the circumstances but Mrs. R. herself, to whom he has been of late so very *affectionate*.

---

[1] Samuel William Reynolds, senior, was himself also a landscape artist.
[2] The reference may be to Turner.

Wilkies mother is dead. This event will distress him the more as he was absent—he was on the road home from a visit to Sir Walter Scott—Collins was looking out to inform him of it before he got home.

I am very sorry that you are out of order—Salisbury is a muggy place. Your account of poor Dodsworth is deplorable but I am quite unable to read it without laughing.

My wife is quite well—never saw her better and more active & cheerfull —but she is rather stouter than I could have wished. My children are lovely—and much grown. John I am sorry to say is a genius[1]—he is very clever—droll & acute—what he does & says is curious, he has a fine disposition—and all my children are good tempered. Your goddaughter is so much the little lady that she delights every body.

I met with two or three very superior men at Brighton. Dr. Yates a physician—Lawrence a surgeon[2]—& Young (brother to the actor[3]) a surgeon but in bad health & retired—these men are all on the Lithgow practice—& are ousting all the old hum buggs and water gruel makers— in the shape of Drs. and apothecaries—&c &c.

Send me the picture of the Shady Lane when you like—would you like any other? The sketchbook I am busy with a few days when I will send it —they are all boats—and coast scenes—*subjects* of this kind seem to me more fit for *execution* than sentiment. I hold the genuine—pastoral—feel of landscape to be very rare & difficult of attainment—& by far the most lovely department of painting as well as of poetry. I looked into Angersteins the other day—how paramount is Claude.

I am puzzled about the chair—were I with you I could do very well with it. Do you want it rich or a more simple thing? Would not Pugin[4] do it well? I could do you something & will send you some ideas. You do not write to [me] by the bishops franks and I will not. I am now free & independent of Tinney's kind & friendly commissions—these things only harrass me. You know my disposition, is this—in my seeming meakness, if I was bound with chains I would break them—and—if I felt a single hair round me I should feel uncomfortable.

Can anything exceed the villany of the newspapers? After saying everything villanous of Fontleroy, most of which is true, they are now endeavouring to turn justice from its course—there is no doubt but *of all* who have suffered from the crime for which he is condemned, he is by far

---

[1] This pronouncement proved to be justified.

[2] Probably Sir William Lawrence, Surgeon to St. Bartholomew's Hospital.

[3] Charles Mayne Young, then the leading exponent of the Kemble tradition; his brother George, who had studied under Boyes in Paris, retired from practice at the age of forty-five.

[4] Augustus Charles Pugin, the French architect of the Diorama and illustrator of Gothic architecture, whom Constable may have known at the Royal Academy School. His son, A. W. N. Pugin, settled in Salisbury in 1833: he designed the memorial cross to 'Belim'.

the worst & deserved hanging the most—yet see what they are doing—
Mr Impey[1] told me just now that his lawyers meant to put in a writ of
Error—but that would require the consent of the Attorney General—
which they will never be able to get.

I met several times *Sir Richard Phillips*[2] at Brighton—he is a strong,
ensible, stupid, clever, foolish vulgar Dog—very amusing—no doubt a
great liar—having been long carried about on the shoulders of the world
—and his mind filled with all the dirt of life.

My wife wants some account of Mrs. F. & your children

Yours truly

John Constable.

I fear you will be annoyed by this ill written rigmarole letter—but forgive
it, as it has afforded much amusement to my mind to write it. I wrote it
last evening—but added the last to day.   J.C.

Fisher meanwhile had suffered a relapse, which he naturally preferred to attribute
to the vagaries of the English climate, rather than that 'fullness of habit' which
he blamed for the ailments of others; and he was gone to seek comfort from the
healing waters of Bath.

12. Laura Place Bath
1824. November 21.

My dear Constable;

You are quite correct. Salisbury *is* a nasty damp muggy place; and
I have been compelled to run away from it. I have taken a house for six
weeks at Bath & under the care of my Uncle (the Physician) am drinking
the waters. I am much better & expect in a week or two to recover myself
entirely. My wife & family are with me.

I was delighted with your long, calm, well penned energetic letter. I
must yield to you in your argument respecting variety of subject as I
always am obliged to.—

Saturday. Nov. 27.

Since writing the above my inestimable wife has been dangerously &
alarmingly ill with an inflammation on her chest. It is only this evening
that we regarded her out of danger. A silly man I consulted misled my
better judgement by talking of debility, & we delayed using active measures
till the opportunity was almost gone. I had actually prepared my mind for
the worst. However, God be thanked, she is better.

---

[1] Archibald Elijah Impey, a barrister of the Inner Temple, who had married one of
Constable's Suffolk friends.
[2] Author, bookseller and publisher of the *Monthly Magazine*.

Wednesday Decr. 8. My letter is written at awfully long periods. But I have been so shaken by my wife's illness & my own indisposition, that I have lost some of my usual energy. She is now sitting by my side, convalescent. I do not think that Tinney will give way. I beleive the fact to be that Mrs Tinney is the obstacle. However if you fail with him you are entirely welcome to the white horse. Should you be afraid to send me by the Bath Coach one of your new sketch books? We are sadly at a loss for employment: and copying the leaves of your mind is a great source of amusement to my wife. Do not trouble yourself about the chairs. I have met in Bath with what I was looking for. Did you ever see Bath? Will you run down for two days? It is the finest city in the world. Moreover here are Altar peices by Tom Barker;[1] daily Auctions of the "Old Masters" & gothic churches with Grecian entablatures. You shall hear from me again soon when my nerves have recovered their tone. Beleive me truly yours

John Fisher.

Fisher's new invitation was tempting; but with Constable, as usual, his work had to take first place.

Charlotte St. Decr. 17. 1824

My dear Fisher

Your letter from Bath has given my wife and myself the greatest concern. We trust Mrs. Fisher continues to recover from the serious attack which you described. You promise to write to me again. Pray do so—for we are both in a state of great anxiety about you. We hope your own health improves. How much should I have liked to pass a day or two with you at Bath—but after such an interrupted summer and so much indisposition in the autumn—I find it quite impossible to leave London, my work is so much behind hand. We hear of sad illnesses all around us—caused no doubt by the excessive wet. I have just received a letter from Sir George Beaumont—he has been seriously ill & quite unable ('till lately) to touch a pencil for many weeks.

Every thing which belongs to me, belongs to you, and I should not have hesitated a moment about sending you my Brighton book—but I will tell you—just at the time you wrote to me my Frenchman was in London. We were settling about work and he has engaged me to make twelve drawings (to be engraved here, and published in Paris), all from this book, size of the plates the same as the drawing, about 10 or 12 inches. I work at these in the evening. This book is larger than my others—and does not contain odds, and ends (I wish it did), but all complete compositions—all of boats, or beach scenes—and there may be about 30 of them. If you wish to see them for a few days, tell me how I am to send them to you.

---

[1] Thomas Barker, the popular landscape painter (1769-1847): born at Pontypool, but generally known as 'Barker of Bath'.

I much regret that I could not write sooner, as probably if I had I should have heard from you again, but I am so entirely occupied and so often interrupted that though I have often made the attempt I could not save the post. Pray do not omit to write to us soon.

My Paris affairs go on very well. The pictures in the Louvre did not *keep* the *ground* they *first took*—but though the director (the Count Forbain) gave them very respectable situations in the first instance—yet on their being exhibited a few weeks, they so greatly advanced in reputation that they were removed from their original situations to a post of honor —the two prime places near the line in the principal room. I am much indebted to the artists for this alarum in my praise—but I will do justice to the Count. He is no artist (I beleive) and he thought "as the colors were rough, they must be seen at a distance"—they found their mistake as they then acknowledged the richness of the texture—and the attention to the surface of objects in these pictures.[1] They call out much about their vivacity and freshness, a thing unknown to their own paintings. A gentleman[2] told me the other day that he visited the Louvre—he heard one say to his friend—"look at these English pictures—the very dew is upon the ground". They wonder where the *brightness* comes from. Only conceive what wretched students they must have been to be so surprized at these qualities—the fact is they study (& they are very laborious students) art only—and think so little of applying it to nature. They are what Northcote said of Sir J.R.—in his landscapes (at first) made wholly up from pictures —and know about as much of *nature* as a "*hackney coach horse does of a pasture*". In fact they do worse. They make painfull studies of individual articles—leaves, rocks, stones, trees, &c &c singly—so that they look cut out[3]—without belonging to the whole—and they neglect the *look* of nature altogether, under its various changes.

I learnt yesterday that the proprietor of my pictures, askes 12,000 franks for them together (500 £). They would have bought one (the Waggon) for the nation—but he would not sell them singly—this he could often have done with either. *The proprietor tells me* the artists much desire to purchase them & deposit them in a place in which they can have access to them. This may be, but I am still more ambitious of *English* praise—and *Reynolds* (the engraver) who saw them in the Louvre says he was astonished at their power and the art & nature which appeared in them. He is going over in June to engrave them. He has sent two assistants to Paris to prepare the plates—they will be in mezzotint. He is now about my Lock.[4] I sent it to

---

[1] *The Hay Wain* and *A View on the Stour:* one of the Hampstead views was also included.

[2] William Brockedon, painter, author and traveller, had returned to London and had written to tell Constable this on the 13th December.

[3] This comment may be derived from Schroth, who uses the term *découpé* in a later letter.

[4] These projects came to nothing in the end, though *The Lock* got as far as a proof. Reynolds went to France in 1826, but only to engrave after French painters.

him last week and he is to engrave the 12 drawings. All this is very desirable to me, as I am at no expence about them, and it cannot fail of advancing my reputation. My wife[1] is now translating for me some of their criticisms. They are very amusing and acute—but very shallow and feeble. Thus one —after saying, "it is but justice to admire the *truth*—the *color*—and *general vivacity* & richness"—yet they want the objects more formed & defined, &c, and say that they are like the rich preludes in musick,[2] and the full harmonious warblings of the Aeolian lyre, which *mean* nothing, and they call them orations—and harangues—and highflown conversations affecting a careless ease—&c &c &c——Is not some of this *blame* the highest *praise* —what is poetry?—What is Coleridges Ancient Mariner (the very best modern poem) but something like this? However, certain it is they have made a decided stir, and have set all the students in landscape thinking— they say on going to begin a landscape, Oh! this shall be—*a la Constable*!!!

Now you must be tired—pray beleive that there is no other person living but yourself to whom I could write in this manner and all about myself—but take away a painters vanity—and he will never touch a pencil again. Ever my dear F. truly yours. John Constable.

I was at Carlisles last lecture at the Academy on Monday—he *very unexpectedly resigned the office*. This has I beleive put them to a "non plus". Several candidates—but no *name* has yet offered, to flatter their vanity. He is considered *insane* by those to whom the Academy is life and death.[3]

Will you on your return to Salisbury send me your large picture—it will be of service to me and I want to do something to it, to nourish it— not paint upon a touch. Send it without the frame. I will not molest Mrs. Tinney's room if I can help it, but I think that picture the most showing for exhibition. Yours is superior in sentiment. I can judge better by having yours—I will be at the expence of a case, which need not be larger than the picture except one or two inches all round & about 3 inches deep. You offered to be at the expence for the Shady Lane. Let it be put against the other.

My wife begs to join me in best regards to all.

All of us are in unusual good health. Ever yours John Constable.

In the Gentlemans Magne. of Augst. I read a high flown account of poor Rennel. It is all of a peice with himself—I beleive the man to have been as worldly minded as Brogham himself—but his deception was on the right side, and as he was doing good I never quarelled with him. It is

---

[1] Mrs. Constable was learning French before her marriage, and had found it 'very amusing'.
[2] The comparison with preludes comes from the notice by Delécluze, a supporter of David, in *Les Débats* for the 30th November 1824.
[3] Carlisle enjoyed creating a sensation at his lectures on anatomy, which he attended in full court dress, with bag-wig and cockaded hat.

possible however (& I agree with Millman) he might have talked this language 'till he beleived it. But I judge not—he is long before this in the presence of him who knowest our most secret thoughts.

I have painted two of my best landscapes for Mr *Scroth* at Paris.[1] They will soon go but I have copied them, so it is immaterial which are sent away. I am putting a 6 foot canvas in hand.[2] You will be pleased with the small ones. If I had had the Shady Lane I should have sold it. Tinney promises his picture, but I shall trust more to you.

1825

It was Fisher's turn to be in low spirits, and his reply to the last letter did not come in till the new year had opened. Knowing Constable's weakness for gossip he began with an attempt to be light-hearted by referring to the latest sensational scandal. Maria Foote the famous actress had become involved at Cheltenham in an intrigue with Colonel Berkeley by whom she had two children; but he failed to fulfil his alleged promise to marry her. She then accepted an offer of marriage from Mr. 'Pea-green' Hayne. This led to an action for breach of promise, as the result of which Miss Foote was awarded £3,000 against Mr. Hayne.

There followed a war of pamphlets and the actress had a mixed reception when she appeared at one of the shows of Bath in the following year. Indeed, it was not till several years later, when the scandal had died down that the unfortunate lady at last achieved respectability by becoming the Countess of Harrington.

12 Laura Place Bath.
Decr. 27. 1824

My dear Constable;

I have written to Salisbury to desire that both your pictures may be immediately sent to you. I am quite greived to have lost you a purchaser—I have (if you would *permit* me) half a mind to become one myself.

Who would ever have imagined that those two card houses in Keppel Street could have attained to such celebrity: the one by the exhibition of your works at Somerset House; the other by the exhibition of Miss Footes works at Westminster Hall. I think the carte & three letters of the Colonel & Lady the most amusing specimens of finesse I ever read. And then how delightful is the alteration of style when addressing Mr 'Pea-green' Hayne. From the above remarks you will discover, that I have been very diligent

---

[1] Two views of Hampstead, later in the Gibbons and Bullock Collections, when they were engraved by Lucas. The two copies were exhibited at the Royal Academy in 1825 and bought by Francis Darby.
[2] *The Leaping Horse.*

in reading the newspapers lately. I have further, extracted the following paragraph for you; it is an advertisement to recover a pet dog, the description is as follows. "Coat glossy & black; ears broad & pendulous; but *very bare* from *scratching*, its elbows are in the *same state*. Left hip rough & broken out into *dry pustules*: eyebrows & nose brownish in colour & also lower parts of the feet." Literally copied. J.F. There are members of the family I should think who will not be sorry that the owner of these ears & elbow & hip has disappeared.

My wife will feel obliged to you for any of your sketch books. I could not have conceived a large city like Bath so totally devoid of art, notwithstanding the residence of the "two Barkers".[1] I have been to every shop to try to get a landscape engraving for my wife to copy & not one can I find. The only things I have seen are Miss Bernes engravings of the M. of Staffords gallery, in which every particle of effect has escaped. Westall[2] glitters in gilt frames and muscular drapery in every shop, & I found Lutherbourghs "Windmill" in a low valley, backed by the loftiest hills. I send you an original sketch by my son Osmond[3] which has more effect in it than any thing I have seen in Bath. It is untouched by an one but himself.

January 1. 1825.

My wife & I wish you and your wife joy of the new year. To you the last brought fame & prosperity. To me it brought nothing but sickness. To our maladies we have had lately to add an intermittent fever which attacked my little Frank & has left him with a voice like a fly's caught in a cobweb. My wife gets no strength. I however am getting muscle again, though thrown back by a cold.—

I went into a book auction the other day to occupy an idle hour, & bought Burns's poems. But he makes me melancholly to read him. In one of his scraps I met a rural image that delighted me. He is describing late autumn: & says that the feilds are now bare, except where the bean-sheaf stands blacking & rotting in the watry sun. I think I have a sketch of yours of a bean field. I am pleased to find they are engraving your pictures, because it will tend to spread your fame, but I am almost timid about the result. There is in your pictures too much evanescent effect & general tone to be expressed by black & white. Your charm is colour & the cool tint of English daylight. The burr of mezzotint will not touch that. Your sketch books would I guess engrave well. When you write send me any London news you can pick up, for we live here sadly in the dark. Is John Bull dying? He is wofully dull. Why has Carlyle resigned? Is he ashamed of

---

[1] Thomas Barker's brother Benjamin Barker (1776-1823) was also a landscape painter living in Bath.

[2] Richard Westall, R.A. 'The School of Westall,' said Constable, 'makes painting rather an imitation of drawing than a practice of a higher kind.'

[3] Osmond was now seven and seems to have benefited from watching Constable sketch at Gillingham.

the Academy?—I took a large sheet because I thought I had much to say & now I do not know how to fill it. I have been so much out of the haunts of men that I have lost all my conversation. And we have had so much sickness that my imagination is filled with nothing but pill boxes, phials, & the state of the weather. Let me hear from you soon & beleive me

my dear Constable

yours very faithfully

John. Fisher.

Charlotte Street. Janry. 5. 1825

My dear Fisher

    I was glad to receive your long letter the day before yesterday. I was anxious to hear from you again—for I had heard of the alarming anxieties you must have suffered on Mrs. J. Fisher's account. But your energies and your valuable medical power with God's blessing helped you over what might have been the fatal consequence of inadvertence. The account you give of your sickness in general is grievous.

    I am just returned from conveying to the coach office in Oxford St. a box for your and Mrs. J. Fisher's amusement. I have sent you two books. Pullins the prints from which are from good pictures—I know not what to lay hands upon—I could not spare any Brighton book—and your sisters have borrowed ("for a friend") such of my sketch-books as you have not had. The box will reach you tomorrow morning from Nelson's coach office. I have enclosed in the box a dozen of my Brighton oil sketches—perhaps the sight of the sea may cheer Mrs F—they were done in the lid of my box on my knees as usual.

    Will you be so good as to take care of them. I put them in a book on purpose—as I find dirt destroys them a good deal. Will you repack the box as you find it. Return them to me here at your leisure but the sooner the better.

    I miss the books you have—one a good size—& the other small, a view of Oxford Bridge on the first page—Is it not so?

    Carpenter sent me a receipt for 10 £. We are delighted with Osmonds drawing—it has in it the unconscious seeds of the chiaro oscuro—tell him his boot jack is in constant use with me, my own being mislaid.

    My wife and I return your good wishes for the returning year. We had the pleasure of dining at the Charter House last Sunday week. The "*Master*" dined with Lord Stowel[1] on that day. This was a loss to me—for independent of his very superior understanding, the father is a continual source of amusement to me. I feel my-self so far an insulated being as to be out of the reach of his shafts *generally*.

---

[1] William Scott, 1st Lord Stowell, judge of the Court of Admiralty and a brother of Lord Eldon.

Old Crazy Smith has at length turned himself out of Norwich Cathedral
—perhaps the "flatus ex ano" of the old woman blew him out. Indeed he
seems to be unfit to be any where else than at St. Luke's.[1]

I am writing this hasty scrawl [in the] dark before a six foot canvas—
which I have just launched with all my usual anxieties. It is a canal scene
—my next shall contain a scratch with my pen of the subject. The postman
is ringing his bell & I make haste to conclude—but I cannot omit to thank
for the description of the lost dog—what would Juvenal have said to so
marked a specimen of the time & character of a strange age. I hear Miss
Foot plays tonight. She meets with universal sympathy—Berkley is de-
tested—& will not get over the . . . panels I hear—he has been black
balled at the Club.

J. Constable.

Constable may now have been working on the full-size study for *The Leaping
Horse*[2] which Leslie suggests may at first have been intended for the finished
picture. In spite of Fisher's advice, he had again chosen for his subject a View
on the Stour near Dedham, with a boy taking a barge-horse over one of the
barriers erected on the tow-path to prevent cattle from straying. This stretch of
the river was known as the canal, being separate from the main branch of the
Stour.

When Constable wrote to Fisher again[3] he had interrupted his work to stay
with Mr. William Lambert at Woodmansterne in Surrey, and his wife had just
forwarded a letter from Arrowsmith to say that King Charles X of France had
awarded the artist a gold medal for his pictures at the Louvre, and expressing
the hope that next time the King would make him a Knight of the Legion of
Honour.

Jan. 23d 1825.

My dear Fisher

    I am uneasy that I have not had a letter from you. I hope your
invalids have neither relapsed nor increased in number.

I write you this letter from Woodmanstone, a village six miles south
west of Croydon. I am painting a little family group[4] of three children and
a donky, the grandchildren of Mr Lambert a very old friend of my wife's
father, whose ancestors were fixed here in 1300. I am making a pretty
picture. It is to go to the parents in the East Indies. The children are sent
here for their education and spoke the language only imperfectly on their
arrival. The butcher was driving home a calf in his cart when one of the
boys exclaimed "Aunt—what for one *gentleman*—take away *cow* in *gig*."

---

[1] Probably a reference to St. Luke's Chapel at Norwich Cathedral.
[2] In the Victoria and Albert Museum.
[3] In the collection of Sir Kenneth Clark (transcript originally prepared for Lord
Plymouth).
[4] See *Burlington Magazine* for August 1950, where it is reproduced.

You may suppose I left home most unwillingly to execute this job, but it is my wife's connection and I thought it prudent to put a good face on it. The large subject now on my easil is most promising and if time allows I shall far excell my other large pictures in it. It is a canal and full of the bustle incident to such a scene where four or five boats are passing with dogs, horses, boys & men & women & children, and best of all old timber-props, water plants, willow stumps, sedges, old nets, &c &c &c.

I hope the books and the Brighton oil sketches reached you. Your picture and the Green Lane are now in my gallery. I was delighted to see your picture, it is so careful and so entirely unaffected in arrangement and execution. What some of the other large ones have in power this makes up in sentiment and truth. I shall not object (if you may not) to its going to the "Gentlemen" at the Gallery, but I shall try for Tinneys when the time comes as I think it has more qualities for an exhibition among others pictures.

My pictures in the Gallery at Paris "*went off*" with great "*eclat*"—I hope my reputation is on the advance. I have a letter this morning from Paris —informing me that on the King's visit to the Louvre he was pleased to award me a Gold Medal, for the merit of my landscapes, which is to be forwarded to me by the first opportunity—he at the same time made Sir Thos. Lawrence a Knight of the legion of honour. I have both a pride and satisfaction in relating these distinctions (if I deserve them) to you. At the same I can truly say that your early notice of me—and your friendship in my obscurity—was worth more, and in fact is now looked back to by me with more heart-felt satisfaction than all of these put together. I have added to the respectability of my family by making the family name a mark of distinction—and above all by being respectable myself and forming friendships with my superiors, not that any of these circumstances will make any difference in my habits. I know the difficulty of gaining reputation in the first instance—and I am dayly made sensible of the still greater difficulty of maintaining it.

My reputation at home among my brother artists [is] dayly gaining ground, & I deeply feel the honour of having found an original style & independent of him who would be Lord over all—I mean Turner—I believe it would be difficult to say that there is a bit of landscape that does not emanate from that source.

Reynolds has got off a proof of my lock—it looks most promising[1]— the size is 13 × 15 inches (the part engraved). As you say, they cannot engrave my color or evanescence, but they can the chiaro oscuro & the details & the taste and with it most of my sentiment. A bad engraver will not injure me to that degree you think—but it is as you say quite impossible to engrave the real essence of my landscape feeling.

---

[1] This was as far as the engraving got: *The Lock* was later engraved by Lucas.

I left home last Thursday & shall be back again I hope by the end of one week. Pray let me then or if possible before have a letter from you. When writing to the Bishop will you say that the picture of Mrs Fishers ancestor is in hand and though troublesome will turn out well. Ever my dear Fisher

Yours most truly

John Constable

I hope you will give us some good accounts of Mrs. Fisher and all your invalids.

My little group is a canvas 24 × 20. It makes a pretty little picture. In the background is Woodmanstone Church. [sketch]. I find this village like most others, all to pieces. Dr. Buchannan (the father in law of Coleridge the Barrister)[1] is at variance with all the parish, and it is perfectly ridiculous to see how they go on—the ladies however contrive to keep up appearances —but they visit with difficulty. Mr Lambert is the old Country Esqre. his "study" contains pictures of racers & hunters—guns, gaiters, gloves, half-pence, turnscrews, tow, gunflints &c &c.

Yours most sincerely

John Constable.

When my medal arrives I will send it to you & you may put an account of what it is like into the Saturday papers, if it is worth while.[2] Tell me if you think a print of the Cathedral (the Bishops picture) would answer enough to pay £20 or £30. I should think it might, it would make a good one, especially that which I am now about.[3] You cannot think how I regret being about this picture to the neglect of my large landscape, for every reason—besides I can make no part of art pay now so well as my own landscape. But I will not quarrel with kind friends & kick down the ladder.

A reply soon came in from Fisher.

12. Laura Place. January 27. 1825.

My dear Constable;

You have but too well guessed the cause of my silence: two of my children have been again ill with fever & inflammation of the windpipe. Poor little Frank dangerously so: & as this was the second attack within a month, he still is in a very weak & fragile condition. My wife, thank

---

[1] The Rev. Gibb Buchanan, D.D., was vicar of Woodmansterne: his second daughter Mary was married in 1818 to Sir John Taylor Coleridge, whose visit to Fisher at Salisbury has already been mentioned.

[2] The medal is illustrated in R. C. Leslie's edition of his father's *Life of Constable*, 1896, p. 166.

[3] The one for which Dunthorne had taken an outline in the previous summer.

God, is entirely recovered, & three of my children keep in excellent health.
For my own part, I have not been so well for years.

Your package arrived safe. Your Brighton sketches carried us down to
Osmington in imagination. I shewed them to an amateur artist living
here. He wanted to know "what colours you used?" The Choiseul Gallery[1]
has been of the greatest comfort to me. I have copied in pencil with the
greatest pleasure, Ostade's butcher killing the ox; the boy looking out of
window into the sunshine, & a Vanderhayden. Thanks to you for giving
me the *sixth* sense: the power of receiving pleasure from chiaro-oscuro. It
has wiled away many an anxious hour. I was impatient to hear how you
fared at the King of France's visit to the Louvre. Your medal could not
have given you greater exultation than it did me. Indeed I always consider
your fame as mine; & as you rise in slow but permanent estimation, pride
myself that I have formed as permanent a friendship with a man of such
talent. But these things are better felt than said. I think a simple paragraph in the Sarum journal will be fitter, than a description of the medal.
If Sir Thomas's honour is mentioned first, it will have more appearance
of accident. But you must decide: & I wait your decision.

I went to see Barker the painter a day or two ago. He has built himself
a house on top of one of the highest hills here, on the model of a temple
at Paestum: & is preparing the walls of his dining room for a fresco painting
by himself. He talked to me much of the Vatican, while shewing me the
room: & told me as a secret, that the subject he had chosen was the taking
of Scyros by the modern Greeks.[2] There is no art as you observe out of
London: & no doubt this poor man has lived with himself, & Bath Idol
worshippers, until he thinks himself quite equal to Raphael. London being
empty, we have here all the shews: the wild beasts, the infant Lyra,[3]
Bradbury the Clown,[4] Braham[5] & Der Freishüz, the rattle snakes, Martin's
Belshazzar, & the learned pig. There is a Venetian look about it. I do not
know whether it does not remind me of an easil picture of Corregio in
which St Jerome is a principal figure. The marriage of St Katherine? I
shall be running up to London soon when I shall get a sight of your new
six foot canvass. My wife observed that your enumeration of objects,
"carried her down to the river side". I do think that an impression of
your Cathedral would sell well at Salisbury. But it entirely depends on
the brilliancy of the engraving. If it be added at the foot, "from the original

---

[1] The pictures of the Duc de Choiseul were engraved by Basan in 1777.
[2] Bryan's *Dictionary of Painters* says: 'Perhaps the noblest effort of Barker's pencil
was the magnificent fresco, 30 ft. in length, and 12 ft. in height, representing "The Inroad
of the Turks upon Scio, in April, 1822", painted on the wall of his residence, Sion Hill,
Bath, and possessing merits of the highest order, in composition, colour, and effect.'
[3] A sketch of the infant Lyra was exhibited by Miss M. Ross at the Academy this year.
J. H. Anderdon speaks of her as 'a wonderful child who astonished the groundlings when
hoisted upon a music stool to play a harp'.
[4] Grimaldi's chief contemporary rival, whose 'leaps were of astonishing height'.
[5] John Braham, the German-Jewish tenor, was the original Max in Weber's *Freischutz*
on its production in England at the Lyceum on the 20th July, 1824.

in the possession of the Bishop of Salisbury" it would be as good as giving the Palace, a commission upon the character of the incumbent. If he does not know how both to bear and forbear, he is as often a brand as a luminary.

Beckford is here playing with bricks & mortar on the top of Lansdown.[1] The Somersetshire clods who were trundling his wheelbarrow & carrying his hods, suddenly struck work & insulted him by saying that they would not work for a ——r. He was going to leave Bath in a pet, but the *Master builders* persuaded him to stay & pacified the virtuous feelings of the man. Yrs.

J F

I began this letter two days ago. Since then I have carried my two sick boys up to a house on the top of Lansdown, & they begin to recover. There is (I now admit) something noxious in low damp situations. Do you recollect how sitting in the Gillingham meadows affected the nerves of your head & brought on the toothache? I hear that the Master of the Charterhouse is grown quite *fat*.

I have been reading much about the French Revolution lately. The Duc de Choiseul was principally but ignorantly perhaps instrumental in bringing it about—protecting & abetting Voltaire & Co. He little thought that in patronising their licentious pens, he was laying the foundation of that bloody insurrection which was to disperse his gallery of pictures & send them to be sold to the nation of "Shopkeepers". He it was who banished the Jesuits; the first & necessary step to bringing about the change. He died the year before the volcano burst.

Seymour St. Jan: 28, 1825.

Dear Sir

We arrived in town yesterday for our Winters Campaign. I hope to hear that you are about again.

The sooner you can call upon us—the better, as I have several little matters to talk to you upon. I hope you may be able to bring with you a good account of Mrs Constable & your children.

I am Dear Sir, yours very faithfully

J. Sarum

I wish to have my Picture sent home.

Fisher's next letter did not reach Constable till the 31st January.

On the 8th February the Bishop gave Constable a frank for one of his letters to East Bergholt. The year of the following letter is uncertain, but it seems likely

---

[1] William Beckford had gone to live at Lansdown Terrace, Bath, after leaving Fonthill. He was buried under the tower which he erected on Lansdown Hill, and the grounds were given by his daughter to form a public cemetery. The tower, intended as a repository for what was left of his books and works of art, was completed in 1827 and still stands.

to have been written after the Bishop had at last shaken off the Smiths of
Kensington. The French frame-maker might be Tijou, who had done some work
for his nephew in 1819, or a man named Cruzac, mentioned in Constable's
journals for this year as a cheap worker.

Seymour St. Feb: 26.

Dear Sir

I am very angry with your little French Frame Maker. I ordered
two frames which were promised to be done in ten days—Three weeks
are now elapsed & no frames. If they are not sent to me by Wednesday
next—I will not take them off his hands.

I am, Dear Sir, yours very truly

J. Sarum

The French Man did not tell me where he lived—so that I cannot send
to him without troubling you.

The date of the next note is even less certain, and it may have been written much
earlier, though not later than this year. There is a tradition that the portrait of
Alexander Hyde, Bishop of Salisbury from 1665 to 1667, was found in a cottage
and brought to the palace in Dr. Fisher's time.

Seymour St. March 2.

Dear Sir

I return you Mr Carlisles Book with many thanks. I am sorry I
have kept it so long.

Mr Biggs may clean and line my Picture of Bishop Hyde in its present size.

I am Dear Sir, yours very faithfully

J. Sarum

There can be no doubt as to the date of the following note, on which Constable
has himself written in pencil, 'The last note from the poor Bishop March 22, 1825.'

Dear Sir

If you can afford time to dine with us on Thursday, at 6 o'clock—
we shall be truly glad to see you.

I am Dear Sir, yours faithfully

J. Sarum

Seym. St. March 22.

The postmark shows that the date on the next letter is a mistake for April 6.

4 Belle Vue Bath. April 8. 1825

My dear Constable;

I rode yesterday out of the white atmosphere of Bath into the green

o

village of Bath-Easton; & found myself by instinct at the *mill*, surrounded by weirs, backwaters nets & willows, with a smell of weeds, flowing water, & flour in my nostrils. I need not say that the scene brought you to my mind, & produced this letter.

My poor dear wife has been lamentably ill again with inflammation of the lungs. She is now apparently recovering. But I have yet my fears for the final result. I have now been so long habituated to contemplate her as in danger, that I should submit to the blow with fortitude. But life would be a blank for the future; saving only the green spot of your friendship. Children are a dubious good.

I have not expected to hear *from* you, knowing how you were employed. But I have heard *of* you; by the repetition of one of those speeches which you have a talent at making. I mean, which a man cannot forget it he would. Mary White reports you as saying "that your wife and you are going to *exhibit* at the same time".[1] Which is to me as complete a history of your goings-on, as if you had written a volume.

I wil send you in a week or so, your sketches back & Pullan's Collection. In the same box I shall enclose as a sort of remunerating fee, 2 vols of Paleys posthumous sermons, which you may read to your family of a Sunday evening. They are fit companions for your sketches, being exactly like them: full of vigour, & nature, fresh, original, warm from observation of nature, hasty, unpolished, untouched afterwards. There is prefixed to a new Edition of his works a life of Paley by his son in which the inner man is laid open. If you can get it, there are parts that will delight you. He appears to have been a strong-minded, guileless simple hearted man who told the truth & declared his honest opinion to every man he met with, friend or foe. Hence he was *sometimes* in scrapes.

I hope to be able to get a peep at the Metropolis and your picture about the 20th of June. If I find I can leave my wife. We are going to set up our staff at Osmington immediately. I expect to be fixed there by the 20th of May.—In a letter I had from the Charterhouse some months ago it was mentioned that you were out of spirits seemingly & had lost your glee in conversation. What cog of the wheel wanted grease?—I have had a very tremulous letter from the Bishop informing me of my Aunts illness. She is better, but has been very severely handled. There is a junta in London who by various means contrive to distribute ecclesiastical fame, just as obtains among the painters. Rennell was the first hound of the pack. Bloomfield Bp of Chester succeeded him. They have two reviews in their pay, & the ear of the Bp of London & the Archbishop. If you do not *belong* to them, no mercy is shewn. They are just beginning to puff up Hale the * Preacher of the Charterhouse & you will see him a Bishop or Dean. Having vented this little morsel of professional spleen, I conclude

---

[1] Emily Constable had already been born on the 29th March: but for reasons which will appear presently, Fisher had not been informed.

with my heart much easier. My kind regards to Mrs Constable & wishing her well through her approaching "exhibition" Beleive me yours very sincerely

John. Fisher.

* one bit more. This is the party that brings the charge of "want of liberality" & "high Church" & "intollerance" & "priestly pride" on the establishment. Easier still.

The 'junta' to which Fisher refers was the High Church party, led by Henry Handley Norris from his chapel of ease at Hackney, and known as 'the Hackney Phalanx'. Norris is said to have been given first refusal of every vacant bishopric while Lord Liverpool was in office, with the request that he would nominate someone else if he did not want it himself, so that he became known as 'the bishop-maker'. Young Tom Rennell, as Fisher says, had belonged to this party. Charles Blomfield, who had been made Bishop of Chester in the previous year at the early age of thirty-eight, was translated a few years later to London: he is the bishop who so shocked a member of the royal family by appearing in the House of Lords without a wig, in a hat 'something like a butcher's.' The Preacher at Charterhouse, William H. Hale, was Blomfield's chaplain at Chester, and followed him to London: he did not rise higher than Archdeacon in the Church,[1] but he succeeded Dr. Philip Fisher as Master of Charterhouse in 1842. Fisher may have been brought in touch with the activities of this group through his service as a steward of the Society for Promoting Christian Knowledge, of which Norris was secretary.

My dear Fisher

I had been for some time looking for a letter from you—and I was very anxious to write but I had heard from the bishops family when I dined there about three weeks ago that you were in great trouble from Mrs. J. Fisher's having had a relapse. Let us hope for the best and that she is not apparently but really recovering—the season is in her favor & more than all an affection of the lungs has not been her previous habit— my medical friends tell me that circumstance is very material.

My own anxieties are not a few, exclusive of my pictures and pursuits in art—cares which come upon me dayly. I have had a good deal of sickness here with my wife—for these two months she has been suffering under a diohrea—which has at last brought on premature confinement (on the 29th. Febry.), but I hope all is going well. It is a nice little girl[2]—she is suckling her child but is in a sad weak condition—and we are obliged to watch her carefully—I hope all will go well.

I have worked very hard—and my large picture went last week to the

---

[1] Hale strongly opposed the abolition of burials in towns. 'I have two archdeacons with different tastes,' said Bishop Blomfield, 'one addicted to composition, the other to decomposition.'

[2] Emily, who died at the age of fourteen. There is an error of dating here. Emily was in fact born on the 29th March.

Academy—but I must say that no one picture ever departed from my easil with more anxiety on my part with it. It is a lovely subject, of the canal kind, lively—& soothing—calm and exhilarating, fresh—& blowing, but it should have been on my easil a few weeks longer. Nevertheless, as my most numerous admirers are for my mind in these things—I thought I would send it.

Turner exhibits a large picture "Dieppe"—Callcott nothing, as I know —his eyes took bad at the finishing—Collins a coast scene with fish as usual, and a landscape like a large cow-turd—at least so far as color & shape is concerned.

My medal is handsome & was given me in a handsome manner.[1] When my name was announced to the whole body of artists &c. as a gold medal, there was an universal applause. The Ambassador to whom I was introduced is a most pleasing unaffected man—he said the King his master was fond of these things—and my landscape he understood had particularly struck him—& he begged me to consider it as the reward of a competition. I am fulfilling many orders in small for Paris—Mr Schroth 3 more—M Didot (the great printer)[2] 3—Mr. Arrowsmith 2—&c &c—these all make income.

I am glad to hear you speak of Osmington dear Osmington. I will come to you there—should your state of things be able to receive me. The coast there—[the] air of which is a delicious mixture of warmth & freshness— cannot fail of setting dear Mrs Fisher to rights.

I shall be glad of my sketches—but I would not ask for them—will you recollect that you have 2 sketch books, a large one & one with Oxford Bridge as a frontispeice. Let me hear again soon. I am delighted to be drawn close to you—I was not out of sorts at the Charter House—but only wanted you or.... The "fool" Bob Watkinson (I only quote his name at school) was better than nothing.

The post waits

Yrs affcly

J.C.

He has just called for this letter.

4. Belle Vue Bath. April 10. 1825.

My dear Constable;

I am very sorry to find that while I was having my joke, your wife was in jeopardy. You may congratulate yourselves upon being so far well through, what might have been serious. *We* are going on for the present very prosperously.

---

[1] The function presumably took place at the French embassy, since the official intimation stated that the medal would be presented by the ambassador, now the Prince de Polignac.

[2] Firmin Didot, of the Rue Jacob in Paris, had called on Constable at the end of March with a letter of introduction from Arrowsmith.

Your voluntary offer to come down to Osmington, as soon as we are settled, have been the pleasantest words I have heard or read for the last melancholly six months. My mind & spirits have in truth been much shaken; & I received the promise with an exhilaration that I have been long unused to. We will wander home from the shore about dusk to the remnants of dinner as heretofore; & spend the evening in filling up sketches. There is always room for you. I am sorry our house is too cabined to offer your wife & children accommodation. Will you accompany me on my Visitation the 14th. 15th. 16th. June? & return with me to Osmington? Your sketches set out tomorrow. Paley will arrive from a London bookseller. The sketch books are locked up at Gillingham. When I go there next, I will remit them.

Why was not your picture on your easil a few weeks longer? I have looked over your letter, but find no other observation to make on it, so I will conclude with a quotation that will please you. By the bye you never answer my letters. You write as if you had never received them.—My extract is from Sharon Turners Hist of England Vol 1 p. 424. 4to. He is speaking of our classical education: that it stunts originality, contracts the mind, & makes men knowing only in *words*. It is a complete illustration of your saying, "that a good thing is never done twice".

"It has been remarked that great excellence has been usually followed by a decline. No second Augustan age is found to occur. A Virgil emerges, & as if he cast on his countrymen an everlasting spell, no future Virgil appears,—no second Homer, or Euripides—no succeeding Pindar Horace, Demosthenes, Thucydides, Tacitus or Cicero. The fact is remarkable. But it is to be accounted for, not in a *want* of *talent*, but from the *destruction* of talent by *injudicious education*.

"It is in Literature as in PAINTING: if we study departed excellence too intently, we only imitate: we extinguish genius and *sink* below our models. If we make ourselves copyists, we become inferior to those we copy. The exclusive or continued contemplation of preceding merit, contracts our faculties within, *greatly within* its peculiar circle, & makes even that degree of excellence unattainable, which we admire & feed upon. We become *mimics* instead of *competitors*: mannerists instead of originals. We are enclosed by a despotism from which we ought to have revolted". (Send this to the Somerset House Gazette.)

There is more to the subject equally good if you turn to the book. It is highly amusing work. Quite *original* itself.

yours faithfully

John. Fisher.

The Bishop keeps his bed. What is the matter?

What indeed could be the matter with one so active, who had been last heard of as leading his flock over the mountains of Wales at the age of seventy-six and bidding fair for longevity? Constable's next letter contained disquieting news of two of his oldest friends.

Charlotte Street April 13. 1825

My dear Fisher

Thank you for your second letter. The expression that "we are going on prosperously here" has set me much at ease respecting the health of your dear wife. It has released me from the sad feeling which has attended me ever since I read the second paragraph of your first.

The Bishop & Mrs Fisher have been both in eminent peril. Indeed on Friday and Saturday morning the Bishop was hardly expected to survive. He got cold in the loins riding in these easterly winds. This week his terrible cough caused such grievous pain in the diaphram and in all the . . . of the abdomen that inflammation was expected to follow.

I dined with Mirehouse on Sunday. Mrs M. was at dinner and has recovered [from] her lying in.

We are going on better but I have had great anxiety for her & the new infant. It will be some time before her strength returns. We are anxious for some of the children, John and our little Isabel—who show symptoms of the hooping cough—but they do not. . . . At any rate the season (should it prove that) is in their favor & they shall not want for care and nursing.

It is true I do not answer your letters—but I read them over & over & they generally form answers to mine. All your quotations are good & make for my grand theory—I have added much to it in practice and in theory since we met. It is the rod and staff of my practice—and can never fail or deceive the possessor—

While writing I have received the book of Paley's. The sketches are not yet arrived from Bath. This I mention because you said they would depart on Monday.

They are overwhelmed with large pictures at the Academy—what will become of mine I know not—but I am told it looks very bright.

My Lock is now on my easil. It looks most beautifully silvery, windy & delicious—it is all health—& the absence of every thing stagnant, and is wonderfully got together after only this one year. The print will be fine. I am so harrassed and interrupted that I must now conclude almost as abruptly as I did my last.

The visit to Osmington I much look to. Nothing shall readily occur to prevent [it]—I will give up Paris first. I have rather a cheering account of my picture at Somerset House (the . . . with its . . . is gone to the dogs). Its cheering original feel will support me through all inaccuracies—but they should not be there to make it more academical and to prevent the *learned vulgar in our art*, from blowing their noses upon it.

I am summoned to tea with my wife & new baby. She joins with me in kind regards—& I am always

my dear Fisher

truly yours,

John Constable

The Leaping Horse appeared at the Royal Academy exhibition under the unassuming title of *A Landscape*[1] and received good notices. It was accompanied by the two copies of Schroth's views from Hampstead, which were sold twice over, the final purchaser being another complete stranger, Mr. Francis Darby of Colebrook Dale. Leslie tells us that Constable was delighted with this sign of his growing popularity: but Constable's pleasure in the favourable reception of his pictures at Somerset House must have been marred by the unaccustomed absence from the private view of one who had been a regular attendant since he had first been an exhibitor, who had taken an interest in his progress since even before then, but who did not live to see this new proof of his assured success.

John Fisher, Bishop of Salisbury, died at his house in Seymour Street on the 8th May, 'after long protracted sufferings borne with exemplary patience'; and the seals of his office were sent to Lambeth to be broken. He left his bishopric no richer a man than he had come to it, for he had expended any surplus from the revenues of the see in acts of benevolency, living on his own private means. Just as he had once startled the collegiate world by a strange neglect of his own interests when he refused to break a promise once given, so now men marvelled at the altruism shown when he had refrained from renewing a lease of the best episcopal property, thereby rendering his successor £30,000 the richer.

Archdeacon Fisher came up to London at once and on the 14th May he wrote to his wife from the Charterhouse:[2] 'The poor Bishop's cough proved after all to be an affection of the lungs, & he died at last of consumption. His meat & wine & cayenne pepper had been poison all the time.

'I was with Constable yesterday evening. He is busy painting for Paris & has some beautiful subjects on his easil.'

On the 16th May the Bishop was taken, as he would himself have wished, to be laid at rest by the side of his predecessor in St. George's Chapel at Windsor, that smaller 'cathedral' of which he had tended the fabric with such loving care. His body was conveyed in a hearse drawn by six horses, caparisoned with velvet coverings of the episcopal purple, rich plumes of ostrich feathers, and armorial bearings. This was followed by five carriages of the royal family. Then came three mourning coaches with four horses each and the carriages of his own family. After the family came his fellow peers, spiritual and temporal. They were met by the Dean and Canons of Windsor on entering the chapel, where the clergy of his far-flung diocese were assembled. The burial service was read by the Dean, and the coffin was then deposited in its vault. So ended that unusual combination, a great and good man.

---

[1] Now the property of the Royal Academy.
[2] In the collection of Mr. John Fisher.

The loss of the Bishop continued for some time to weigh upon Constable's mind; and he must have been glad when the following invitation came round by hand to Charlotte Street, with its opportunity to talk over the old days at Salisbury.

Dear Constable

Will you and John Dunthorne come and drink tea with me at the "dark hour" when your painting is over. I will show the Charterhouse by moon light & will have some nice talk.

I am moreover sadly lonely. I see that those bright eyes that once dwelt on you with kindly feeling are set in death! Yrs

John. Fisher.

31 May. 1825

Work had to go on as usual, however. Tinney's picture arrived in London in time for the special summer exhibition of modern masters at the British Institution, and was sent round to the gallery along with Fisher's *White Horse* as an example of Constable's style at its best. Fisher's picture was then sent on, without its owner's permission, to another exhibition in France, to be held at Lille in August: but even Constable did not dare to take the same liberty with Tinney's picture.

At some time during the summer it seems that Fisher put in an appearance at Charlotte Street, when a visit by Constable to Osmington was more or less fixed up, and Fisher left his hat behind. Time slipped away with no realization of the promised visit to Osmington, until Fisher felt compelled to send his friend a reminder.

Then Constable wrote from Hampstead to say that his eldest and favourite son John had been seriously ill.

Osmington. Weymouth.
August 24. 1825.

My dear Constable;

It struck me after I had dispatched my blank memorandum, that the illness of yourself, or of some of your family, was the cause of your non-appearance here. Your letter with its uncomfortable details has just reached me, and I sit down on the instant to reply to it.

If you can get the consent of the mother, bring your poor boy down here directly; or send him down to my house at Salisbury & we will meet him there. He shall have the best advice the country affords, with sea air, sea bathing & good food. You must exonerate me of any responsibility if any thing happens, & if he does well we will see what can be done for him in the way of education. This will releive the mind & spirits of your wife who is not strong; & will give you more leisure for your easil. I would not make the offer, but that all my own invalids have quite recovered here, & my sickly boy & girl are quite robust & rosy. My wife also is herself again.—

I was getting so ill & nervous in town that I was obliged to leave it at a moments warning, while I *could*. But that I left my hat behind me was J.D.s wicked device. I have been recovering ever since & am at this moment as hale as ever I was; or indeed better than I have been for many years. A physician whom I consulted in London (Dr Farr of Ch: Square) recommended me in St Pauls words "to take a little more wine for my stomachs sake". And he was right. I have mended from that hour. Would not the same prescription do you service? It should be taken every day at the same hour or hours & in the same quantity. Say 1 glass at dinner & 1 at bed-time.

I am sorry to find that J.D. had failed. There must have been something peculiarly debilitating in last years weather & in the beginning of this. I would that he & you could pay us a visit here—Bring your boy down by easy stages—It will help your easil by quieting your mind—Or if you prefer it, bring one of your healthy boys & leave him here to take his chance. As for money matters do not make yourself uneasy—Write for any thing you want & send me any picture in pledge you think proper—Your family or yourself shall have the *difference* whenever it is called for—

Whatever you do, Constable, get thee rid of anxiety. It hurts the stomach more than arsenic. It generates only fresh cause for anxiety, by producing inaction and loss of time. I have heard it said of Generals who have failed, that they would have been good officers if they had not harrassed themselves by looking too narrowly into *details*. Does the cap fit? It does *me*.—

Propitiate your wife. I would have come to Hampstead, had I been able; but I was [so] very shattered & nervous that I had not the energy. I could sooner do it now & at this distance: & will come if I thought it would do you any good. Pity me. I am sitting in the shade with my children by me writing to you with a quiet stomach & cool head. I am obliged to leave all this to go 10 miles to eat venison & drink wine, with a brother officer whose head is filled with the same sort of materials, that his venison pasty is made of.—

Let me hear from you soon & beleive me always

faithfully yours

John. Fisher.

You want a staff just at present. Lean upon me *hard*.—

On the 31st August Constable took his family down to Brighton and returned to London next day.

Charlotte Street Sepr. 10. 1825.[1]

My very dear Fisher,

I was overcome by your kind and most friendly letter, which some changes here have prevented me replying sooner to. I have been much harrassed of late—and at the time I wrote you my disagreeable letter I was quite ill & out of sorts. I have now rallied again and thank God am once more at my easil.

Your kind offer to receive my dear boy—indeed all your friendly suggestions of help—are sincerely appreciated by my wife and me, and we cannot sufficiently express to you our sense of them—but we knew not what to do—the distance you are off is so great, and you have great charge of your own, but we rejoice in the good accounts you give of Mrs. Fisher and your children. We determined to give our boy the chance of the sea— and about a week ago I took them all to Brighton. We chose this place— it is cheaper than any other—it is near—and we have several friends there. John is certainly better, & he is now fond of bathing which we are told will help him—we can hardly judge yet of the effect it will have. It is better for me that they are so far off—if we must part—Hampstead is a wretched place—so expensive—and as it was so near I made my home at neither place—I was between two chairs—& could do nothing.

I am now thank God quietly at my easil again. I find it a cure for all ills besides its being the source "of all my joy and all my woe". My income is derived from it, and now that after 20 years hard uphill work—now that I have disappointed the hopes of many—and realized the hopes of a few (you best can apply this)—now that I have got the publick into my hands —and want not a patron—and now that my ambition is on fire—to be kept from my easil is death to me. My commissions press in upon my hands. I have sent for Johny who is uncommonly well—doats on me— and wants to be here again. I shall, I hope, turn some work out of hand. I shall find him a home out of my house—he is too good for my maids.[2]

---

[1] The original letter is in the Victoria and Albert Museum.
[2] This means that Dunthorne, with his country upbringing and natural refinement, was too unsophisticated for the company of the London girls who would provide his chief society in Constable's house.

Let me do him justice—it was my *"wicked device"*—not his (which I put into his mouth) about the *hat*. I plead guilty—& crave your pardon, but I see that pin stuck.

But I crave your forgiveness on a much more serious business—Your large picture ("Constable's White Horse") is now exhibiting at [the] Musee Royal in the city of *Lille in Flanders*—and that without your leave. Wilkie, Sir Thos. Lawrence & myself were each applied to by the Mayor of that city (who under royal authority is at the head of its establishments) for pictures. It will be safely returned about X'mas and they will be much obliged to us. Lawrence has sent some—Wilkie not at home. They have already been mentioned in a Brussels paper.

Of my finances though they are not prospering yet not worse than usual. I am going to do something in them. My brother[1] will send me £400—of which I shall apply 200 £ to the new fours whence my wife has 42 £ a year—I want to make it fifty, and *settle* it (naming you Trustee). This I can legally do—as it was her brothers and stands in her name. I lose by this 400 (4 £ an:) as my brother pays me 5 £. I have some debts, frame maker, colorman &c. 150 £ per cont. I am about 400 £ behind, but I shall get through some how. I wish I was more for money.

You remember the two small pictures in the R.A. sold to Mr Hibbert[2] —he wrote to me to dispose of them elsewhere if opportunity offered—as he had had great losses in India. A Mr Darby in Shropshire (of whom I had never heard) sent to know the price—and gave it without delay. Mr Hibbert is now very angry—*not with himself*—but with me, for not letting him know of Mr Darbys offer. But he is not so angry but he has ordered two others. Ever my dear Fisher, yours most sincerely

John Constable.

I am as you say tormented with details, but if a man is not equal to both great & small matters he will not be a great man. Old Russell[3] the soap boiler, had often his whole property embarked in speculations—yet *he broke up every lump of sugar* used in his own large family. Your father says "Life is made up of little things". Ld Wellington while *commanding* at Waterloo, blamed *"himself"* excessively for not thinking of *breaking a hole* in the wall in the garden at Huguemont, to supply his poor men with ammunition, who perished for want of it.

Leslie gives an extract from Fisher's reply.

---

[1] Abram, who managed the family business. Apparently John's share of his father's estate was regarded as capital invested in the business, bearing interest.

[2] Henry Hebbert, a merchant of the Strand. Constable omits to add that Mr. Hebbert was so accommodating as to cash Mr. Darby's bill for him.

[3] Jesse Russell of London and Walthamstow, whose son married Constable's cousin Mary Watts.

Osmington, September [1825].

My dear Constable,

. . . I despair of ever seeing you out of London, but I repeat that I have bed and board at your service. The news is, that Mat. Parham's (*alias* Perne's) mill is burnt to the ground, and exists only on your canvas. A huge misshapen, new, bright, brick, modern, improved, patent monster is starting up in its stead. Do you recollect the situation of Talbot's barn behind the old Manor House, near the church, at Osmington? It took fire on the 28th September, when it was surrounded by fourteen large ricks at the distance of no more than twenty yards. No water—no engines— straw on every side—the barn full of wheat—and thatched cottages and cornstacks in every direction. Talbot lost his presence of mind, and every body was at fault. The occasion called me out of my usual indolence. I took command, gave plenty of beer and good words, worked hard myself, and in twenty minutes we smothered the fire, with no other loss than that of the barn. It was distressing to hear the poor rats squalling at one end of the barn as the fire approached them. They could not escape.

Constable in the meanwhile had resumed the daily account of his doings for his wife, and from this we learn something of the work on which he was now engaged. First of all, before settling down to the winter's work, he had to clear off the commissions for which he had been paid, and at the beginning of October these included his second edition of *Salisbury Cathedral from the Bishop's Grounds*, with Mrs. Mirehouse's picture to be altered. *Waterloo Bridge* had been chosen once again as the subject for Somerset House, and of this he had already got the outline ready. He was able to report good progress by the end of the month, when he was busy getting in the large picture of Waterloo Bridge on the real canvas, after Mr. Stothard had suggested a 'very capital alteration', which Constable thought would increase its consequence and do every thing for it; but work still seems to have been going on with the two paintings of the Cathedral, which Constable had hoped to have finished a fortnight earlier. He then went down to Brighton on the 3rd November, and it was not till after his return that he found time to write to Fisher again. His letter is given by Leslie.[1]

Charlotte Street. November 12th 1825

My dear Fisher,

. . . What you say of Mrs. Fisher and yourself and family makes me very happy. I am just returned from Brighton, and am glad that I can give you a good account of my wife and children; my poor boy has gained strength and composure. I have been only occasionally with them, being very busy here, where I have done a great deal.

I am hard and fast on my "*Waterloo*" which *shall be done* for the next exhibition—saving only the fatalities of life. I have nearly compleated a

---

[1] The original was sold at Sotheby's in 1927, and the second paragraph has here been corrected from the extract in the sale-catalogue.

second Cathedral which I think you will (perhaps) prefer to the first—
but I will send them both to Salisbury for your inspection if you like.

I have much more to say about pictures, but you say I never answer
your letters. Your last delighted me. The account of the fire and the rats interested John Dunthorne and me alike. How fortunate that you were there.
I am vexed at the fate of the poor old mill. There will soon be an end to
the picturesque in the kingdom. I desire to come to Salisbury, if only for
two days, to renew our friendship in those walks where it first took so
deep a root. I *will* come. How did the fire originate? Write for me when
you wish for me. You set my mind at rest by the way in which you speak
of your picture being at Lille; they have sent to know the price; I have
set them right on that head. I am uncommonly well; never in better health
or spirits.

Something in the next letter requires a special explanation, since it led to the
final breach with Tinney. In England the Royal Academy, run by artists, had
come first, while the British Institution, guided by laymen, had come later. In
Scotland it was to be the other way round. There was already a Royal Institution
for the encouragement of the arts, but no Academy as yet, and artists could only
become associate members of the Institution. Early in 1825 some of the associate
members had begun to get restive and signed a circular setting forth their
grievances and hinting at the formation of an Academy on the London model,
to which the Directors gave a guarded reply. The Academy was not actually
formed till early in the following year, and the first exhibition was not held till a
year after that; but it would seem that Constable had already been approached
to know whether he would lend his support by contributing to the first exhibition.
It may well be imagined that Constable, holding the views he did on the management of the British Institution, would be only too glad to help. Constable had
written to Tinney to ask him to lend *Stratford Mill* for this purpose, and had
been snubbed. Tinney's letter unfortunately coincided with a visit from Arrowsmith and upset Constable completely.

Meanwhile *Waterloo*, which had 'promised delightfully' before he went down
to Brighton, was beginning to look less hopeful, and putting an end to any
chance of getting down to Salisbury that year.

Charlotte Street Novr. 19. 1825

My dear Fisher,

I am always a blest man when that my mind is full—I can write to
you. I should fear that my vision of happiness in making you a visit at
Salisbury—like most of my dreams of bliss—will be but a vision—I am so
hard run in every way that I know [not] which canvas to go to first.

My Waterloo like a blister begins to stick closer & closer—& to disturb
my nights—but I am in a feild that knows no flinching or affection or
favor. "Go on", is the only [voice] heard—"aut Caesar aut nullus".

I am in trouble about Tinney. I have trifled with the friendly [offers]
always so kindly proposed to me by that valuable man. I have no right to

expect a favor at his hands—I have only the right left of apologizing to him for the past—but if artists (creatures of feeling, visionaries) are to be judged of by every day usage—like pound of butter men—they must always be in scrapes and on the wrong side.

My name (though looked for) will not appear at the opening of the noble Institution in Edinburgh—I should have liked to have struck a blow in that quarter—but I must submit to circumstances—

My large work engrosses me—but the devil has begun his tricks even in this early stage of it—and almost ruined my well laid scheam of finance.

I had nearly by dint of pains & conduct & my brother's friendship laid in a sufficiency at my bankers, to keep my mind easy on that score during progress—when my French friend Arrowsmith, came here from Paris, and a most friendly meeting ensued—he finding his order in two landscapes compleated & to his entire satisfaction—still he had advanced 40 £ for works which he considered ordered—leaves that balance. He gave new orders, to the amount of about 200 £. The work being forward, he wanted delivery at X'mas half.[1] At his last visit with a French friend—an amateur —he was so excessively impertinent and used such language as never was used to me at my easil before—that I startled them by my manner of showing that I felt the indignity. He apologized, but I said I could not receive it & he left my house telling Johny that he would gladly have given 100 £ rather &c—& I sent him a letter withdrawing all my engagements with him—and enclosing him a draft for the balance (40 £) on my banker.

He was just that day on his return—he sent me a mild & gentlemanly letter: agreeing to my request & saying that he alone was the sufferer.[2] I have now written to him at Paris, to say, that as we were now on an equal footing, I was most ready to forget all—& to resume our friendship, assuring him resentment formed no part of my character, leaving it to himself, as to any further orders about pictures.

Thus like Marshall Tallard[3]—"I have lost every thing but honor". I am now on the research to supply my resources for the ensuing campaign. He was acquainted with all my possessions—which makes it the less delicate on his part.

I soon expect my family from Brighton, from which they have benefited greatly. I am so sound *body* & *mind*, *wind* & *limb* that I am manfully combating, the devil & all his allies. When *your severe* comments, are made on my impetuosity above—pray be so kind (for just, as well, you always are) to bear in mind that I have a high character to support in Paris.

John D & I are delighted with the true & full occupation we have.—

---

[1] The writing here is obscure, and Lord Plymouth's reading is 'went to Dover'.

[2] Arrowsmith's letter (in the Plymouth Collection) is dated the 16th November: the journal for the 15th is unfortunately missing.

[3] The saying is usually attributed to François I, and is said to have been quoted by Napoleon after Waterloo. The Comte de Tallard was defeated and captured by Marlborough at Blenheim.

He is calm—gentle—clever—& industrious, full of prudence—& free from vice. He is greived at his master having so much of the devil about him. J.C.

Tinneys letter has cut me deeply—but I deserved it. He treats my regret at having incurred his displeasure, with contempt. Is his old wife at the bottom of all this? But no matter—I am [reconciled] to myself—but still hearing the order above—"*go on*"—"*go on*".—

Arrowsmith has sold my "Vain"—the old home—for 400 £. Mr Schroth has been offered 100—for one of his small ones. Arrowsmith has a room in his house called Mr. Constable's room—I shall contribute no more to its furniture. He says my landscapes have made an epoch there.

To complete the story of this chapter in Constable's life, rumours of Arrowsmith's bankruptcy were already getting round, and negotiations were not resumed. Schroth went out of business six months later, thus terminating Constable's supply of resources from abroad. The scolding which he had anticipated from Fisher came promptly enough.

Close Salisbury. Nov. 21. 1825.

My dear Constable;

I cannot afford you a very long letter. Christopher Cookson[1] leaves me on the last day of the month. After that I am entirely at your service, and it will give me the greatest pleasure to see you, and John Dunthorne if he likes to come, here at my house. We are all given to torment ourselves with imaginary evils—but no man had ever this disease in such alarming paroxysms as yourself. You imagine difficulties where none exist, displeasure where none is felt, contempt where none is shewn and neglect where none is meant. What passed between you & the Connoisseur I do not know; if he took liberties, you acted quite right; & will probably raise yourself by vindicating (your) dignity. But poor Tinney you utterly . . .[2] tenacious of property & had rather see his picture on his own walls than hear of it in Edinburgh. He recollected my simile I dare say, & thought that getting his picture out of your hands was not unlike the gauze handkerchief in the bramble bush.—So he wrote to the institution. He says you are a develish odd fellow. For you get your bread by painting.—He orders two pictures leaves the subjects to yourself; offers ready money & you declare off for no intelligible reason. All this he says & thinks. But as for my wrath against you, or contempt for you, it is the shadow of a moon beam. Come hither before your wife & children arrive or I shall never see you. I hope the dose of bitters I have administered above will be of service.

Yours ever in all moods

John. Fisher.

. . . . have joined a large party.

---

[1] The eldest of Mrs. Fisher's three brothers.
[2] A line is here missing. The postscript is also mutilated.

In his journal for the 21st November Constable told his wife that he had been begging hard to get Tinney to lend him the picture to send to Edinburgh, and that Tinney did not like to do so as it had been so long absent: but this must refer to the exchange of letters already mentioned, and on the 24th 'the great Coxe' came round to pack up Tinney's picture, which quite spoilt Constable's day for him. After this *Stratford Mill* remained safely with Tinney for the rest of his life-time. Work on the second version of the *Cathedral* was still going on, and on the following day Constable noted in his journal: 'Painted all day on Mrs. Mirehouse's little picture of the Cathedrum—making in all, as pretty Minna says, "three Cathed*rums*"—but it now is so prettyly finnishd & looks so well that I shall let it go with more satisfaction.' Then, on the 26th, Constable sat down to write his last letter to Tinney and reply to Fisher's criticism of his conduct.[1]

Charlotte Street. Nov. 26. 1825

My dear Fisher,

Your prompt and very kind letter has done me a great deal of good. I had formed I trust strange notions about Tinney, and if there is any meaning in words I should still be warranted to do so with his letter before me.

I have sent him his picture. You got me originally into the scrape, by an act of friendship. You might have lent a helping hand to have got me out of it. There was once a time that I could have redeemed my poor landscape which was from the first more than thrown away, but as pictures cannot choose their possessors, or the painters of them for them, we must let the subject rest.

My new picture of Salisbury is very beautiful and I have repainted entirely that of Mrs. Mirehouse—I am now delighted with it, but when I thus speak of my pictures remember it is to you and only in a comparison with myself. These events have caused me to be almost abiding with you, so much does this city, by a singular chance associate to my life. I think it was unkind if not unjust in Tinney not allowing me the picture. I am now cut off from any prospects in that quarter and my name will not appear among them. This is no trifling matter with me.

It is easy for a bye stander like you to watch one struggling in the water and then say your difficulties are only imaginary. I have a great part to perform & you a much greater, but with only this difference. You are removed from the ills of life—you are almost placed beyond circumstances. My master the publick is hard, cruel & unrelenting, making no allowance for a backsliding. The publick is always more against than for us, in both our lots, but then there is this difference. Your own profession closes in and protects you, mine rejoices in the opportunity of ridding itself of a member who is sure to be in somebodys way or other.

---

[1] The letter to Fisher was sold at Sotheby's in 1927. The transcript is from one kindly supplied by Professor W. G. Constable.

I have related no imaginary ills to you—to one so deeply involved in active life as I am they are realities, and so you would find them. I live by shadows, to me shadows are realities. Tinney you say does not understand the motives which influence me in my whole towards the art. Tell him I do not understand his, but this I know, they will never be felt—by an iron head, and a cold calculation of 2 & 2 makes 4, which I beleive it does exactly.

You do not help me in these matters though you understand them better than anybody, and Tinney less.

I have been several times to Colnaghi. You had the Waterloos[1] away with you or they were sent to the Charterhouse. The book spoke of them & no where could they be found, not in letter F.

I am so engaged that Johny and I cant give up. I am in for a winters campaign & every day I feel the loss of. . . .

I do not regret my trimming to the Frenchman, but it is a serious loss to me. His attack on me was unexpected & undeserved in every part. It was one of those foolish trifles which often produce much mischief, and which is out of the contract of reason entirely, & they were insolent and took liberties with me which J. D. and his father (who were in the room at the time) said were too bad.

It has sadly deranged my finances & will I fear cause me to give up my large work. I cannot supply the deficiency. I am now beating about, but without success. I beleive it is no secret Grey . . ., he was discovered by his lady, with his valet, and so on for all the rest.

I have a half length of a lock in hand[2]—far better than usual.

I have just had a visit from Mr. Bannister[3] to request a landscape. He has long desired one of me, in which, he says, he can feel the wind blowing on his face. He says my landscape has something in it beyond freshness, it's life, exhilaration &c. I was letting two chimney sweepers out of my door when he came on the steps. "What", he said, "brother brush".

> Yours very truly,
> J. Constable.

Two days later, if Leslie's date is to be trusted,[4] *Waterloo Bridge* was again promising well. Though still only a sketch and outline, a friend was ready to predict that it would be Constable's triumph and that he would 'certainly set the Thames on fire, if any body could'. A month later Constable was able to shake off his worries by going down to Brighton to stay with his family over the new year.

---

[1] Engravings by Waterloo.
[2] That is, about 50 × 40 inches.
[3] Jack Bannister, the comedy actor, who had himself been a student at the Royal Academy. The visit was on the 23rd, and Bannister eventually bought a view, of Hampstead Heath, now in the Tate Gallery.
[4] The original page of the journal is missing, and several of the entries given by Leslie are wrongly dated (Bannister's visit, for example, is dated the 28th).

1826

Charlotte St. Jany 14, 1826

My dear Fisher

I begin this hasty note by wishing you a happy year to come—hoping Mrs. Fisher and all your children are well and bearing up against this (to me) dreadfull weather. All my family are at Brighton and I left them well on Thursday.

I staid a fortnight with them & did there one of my best pictures—the subject was the Mill (Perne's) at Gillingham—it is about 2 feet, and is so very rich & pleasing that if you are at Salisbury and would like to see it, I will beg the proprietor Mrs Hand (a friend of the Chancellor's[1]) to let me send it to you—*Mere* church is in the distance.[2]

I was yesterday at the Charter House. Your pictures are in the river—where they must wait on board 'till the ice breaks.[3] *Your* picture cost me an *oath* for the first time—Tinney's or rather his conduct with it, have cost me many. Your picture did me great credit at Lille. I am honorably mentioned in the final discourse of the prefect—and a gold medal was voted to me by the Jury, which I received yesterday. The discourse is curious. He speaks of the raciness and originality of the style—which he says being founded in nature is capable of much beauty—but dangerous to all imitators. So far the Exhibition has extended my reputation—& I trust you will forgive me what I did and prize the picture the more. There are generally in the life of an artist, perhaps one, two or three pictures, on which hang more than usual interest—this is mine. *All* things considered, the gold medal should be yours.

Much pleasure had I at Brighton—mixed with a sentiment of melancholy —by a book in French which my wife read to me while I was painting *"Parham's Mill"*—they were letters by Nicolas Poussin—now first published in Paris from 'till now undiscovered letters to his employers in Paris.[4] They are to me repleat with interest—my wife has discovered that painters now and painters then, were little different—the letters are apologies to friends for not doing their pictures sooner—anxieties of all kinds, insults —from ignorance. One of them speaks of "Strange news from England" —the beheading of Charles, &c, &c.

My large picture is at a stand—owing in some measure to the ruined

---

[1] Probably the Rev. Matthew Marsh, Chancellor of the Diocese: the Chancellor of the Cathedral was the Hon. Hugh Percy, at this time Dean of Canterbury.

[2] This detail enables Mrs. Hand's version to be identified with a picture of the same size in the Lewis Collection.

[3] Constable's exhibits from Lille had been consigned from Calais on the 28th December to Captain Margollé, master of the *Perseverance*. The bills of lading are in the Plymouth Collection. The letter suggests that two of Fisher's pictures had been sent: but this may be a slip.

[4] *Lettres de Nicolas Poussin* had come out in 1824, and Constable's friends the Strutts had ordered a copy from Paris in December.

state of my finances. My late friend Arrowsmiths business was unfortunate—it not only took away my French money—[but] has diverted a source of income for the future. I had that unfortunate morning received Tinny's——letter—it was laying with my brushes by me—and was such an one as I had thought he would not have written to me—or indeed to any one. It fell on poor Arrowsmith—& ultimately on myself—

It did not help me with Tinney—it has hurt my mind—as it is not at all as you say a thing of imagination—it is on his part a dog in the manger business—and he must re-win my good opinion, by some act of friendship —I want to copy the picture.

You richly deserve all that I think of you for your kindness about your picture—& Tinny likewise deserves all that I think of him—but I am now silent on that subject—you will I know treasure my poor picture the more. You are the person, the only person in the world to whom I could have wished this & all the circumstances attending it to have happened. My brother has had great losses in business—& he cant help me. Old Bicknell —would see all his grandchildren starve first—John Constable.

I am executing *all* my commissions amounting to 400 £—4 months will do them—God will help those who help themselves—J.C.

J.D. paints portraits in the country.

A letter from Fisher to Constable is evidently missing at this point.

Charlotte Street Feby 1, 1826.
My dear Fisher

Thanks to that ridiculous paragraph which has given me once more the pleasure of the sight of your hand writing—it is an old story (but spoilt in the telling) of poor Clennel & Edwin Landseer[1] when in the country, for the poor woman said "Lau! Sir, why I am *seventy*".

I had the butler here yesterday from Seymour Street—I did not know the family were in London—I must be disgraced and cannot face being thought neglectful. Mr. Mirehouse sent for the "*Cathedrum*" as your pretty goddaughter calls it—it is wholly a new picture and very pretty. Of Mirehouse—but stop, your own matchless power of discriminating character, has long ago anticipated every thing. One almost feels a desire to indulge in the comfortable or rather consoling wish—that all the good Bishop's family had been buried with him.

Your picture is now standing in my room, perfect & without a speck of injury—it is returned with an increased reputation—and with a gold medal on its back. I make no further mention of old greivances, but you may now fairly exult over Tinney—do not hurry its departure.

---

[1] Landseer was about to be elected A.R.A. at twenty-four, the earliest age then allowed under the rules. Luke Clennell was a painter, better known as a wood-engraver: he had lost his reason in 1817, but had partially recovered.

I am greatly distressed for a sketch book or two in your possession—I hope you have a large one & two small ones. The title papers of the small ones are—the Bridge at Oxford—& the shoar opposite Gravesend or Woolwich.

John Dunthorne has taken my place at the easil while I hasten to write to you—all this morning I have been engaged with a sitter a relation—and a dissenter—but without knowing why—only that his wife would not let him go to church.[1] I thought it would be a good thing was all the Church as by law established done away—I said if [so] that there would be an end of all sect and religion in the country—all however woefull & deplorable spring out of it—I asked if there would be any game in the country if preserves were done away!

How are your children and Mrs Fisher? You never mention my dear Belim.

Ever your

J.C.

Post waits. How are the days lengthened.

While we are on the subject of 'Cathedrums', it may be mentioned that the new version was finished this year, as shown by the date on it, and that this also passed into the possession of the Mirehouse family.[2] The fact is somewhat difficult to explain, but it has to be remembered that the Bishop's original picture was still apparently in Constable's studio, and it may be that his heirs preferred to take the revised version in exchange.

Osmington. Weymouth. Febry. 5. 1826.

My dear Constable;

I plead guilty to neglect & feel much humbled by the forgiving tone of your last letter. The truth is that my mind has been unusually occupied for the last six months. I do not affect the plea that I could not find *time*: but I could not find the disengaged *mind*. When I write to you, I do it with all my heart; & when its kindly movements are obstructed with care or business, I have no appetite for our agreeable correspondence.

I did not wish to speak of our common friend while you were suffering under irritation. But I may now say that he is a very altered man. He has of late sadly miscalculated life. He rose from a most embarrassed situation to his present place by abilities, friendliness & incorruptible integrity. He not only rose to the surface himself, but buoyed up all his family with him. He is now almost sinking as fast, & his bane is egregious vanity. He would

---

[1] Probably Mrs. Constable's cousin Henry Edgeworth Bicknell, a solicitor whose wife belonged to a dissenting family and who was sitting to Constable for his portrait at about this time.

[2] Now in the Frick Collection, New York. Miss Mirehouse stated in 1894 that it was bought from the artist by her father (described in the Holland Sale Catalogue of 1908 as 'Bishop' Mirehouse).

be the wealthy literary gentleman: not the able man of business. He has aimed at objects which have made him somewhat ridiculous, embarrassed his circumstances, hurt his character for legal knowledge by giving hasty and supercilious opinions, & married a woman who has reduced him to the alternative of giving up the society of the world or of his wife.

All this has soured his natural fine temper & made him morose & unapproachable. Paradoxical he always was. But he now, I observe, never gives an unbiassed opinion. The reason he was so refractory about your picture, was this: that he could not bear to see the walls of his "splendid" room disfigured by a blank frame. So much has he suffered vanity to mislead him, that he never acknowledged to the world that his picture was our joint gift, but left it to be concluded that *he* was your patron.

With all this, he has a store of *high* qualities which, if he would shake off his wifes dominion, & his egregious vanity, would soon reinstate his character. I have said all this to sooth, by shewing reason, your excited feelings. I would not have opened the subject to another man & beg it may go no further.

As your letters are generally about your pictures, I may in my turn speak of myself. Bishop Burgess has in a most flattering manner reinstated me in my old situation as *chaplain*, & I am just where I was in my Uncle's time. I sit at the bottom of the old table but I confess I painfully miss old faces. This is a very tall feather in my cap, & I am not a little elevated by it. My relative gave me preferment for blood's sake: but my new master has no such motives. So *you* have an answer for Collins when he tells you again that "he finds I am not thought much in my profession."—What a glutinous power has mortified vanity!! Ordination sermons and examining of candidates have been one reason for my long silence.—Enough of self.—

I shall be at Salisbury for some days at the end of this month. I should like to much to have Perne's Mill there to look at. You will never procure Tinneys picture in London either to copy or exhibit. You must come & pay me a visit in the summer on purpose to copy it, & bring Dunthorne with you to get in the outline. We shall be in the Close in June.

I have two of your sketch books, a large & a small one which I shall send up by the Magnet coach. You may feel secure that they are all that I possess, as I keep them carefully under lock & key. Mary White is going to be married to the Revd. Mr Cotton Precentor of Bangor. £3. I have a memorandum that this sum is owing to you by Mrs Fisher. Have you received it?

The poor Bishops saddle horses were brought away from Wales half starved and have been taken in by Mr Lear out of charity. The old servants shrug their shoulders. The man is as venomous as a poisoned rat.[1] I feel

---

[1] The reference may possibly be to Mr. Mirehouse.

on reperusal that I have been imprudent in my sketch of character. So I make it a condition that you burn this letter when read. You confidant with him at times.

You are welcome to my white horse till the end of the summer season. Your handwriting is getting *again* illegible, & I cannot afford to lose your agreeable matter. I send you a copy of some words I cannot decypher [an exact imitation of "established done away" in Constable's last letter]. How droll & true was your wife's remark on Painters.—

I travelled with a shrewd young lady in a stage the other day. We were talking of the inhospitable character of the Dorset Gentlemen: I said, I hoped when rents improved they would improve. "Oh no" she said "they are incurable. They *pique* themselves upon inhospitality." Do not betray me.

Ever yours

J. Fisher.

Dr. Thomas Burgess was a worthy successor to the good Bishop. He had been translated to Salisbury in 1825 from St. David's, where he is said to have performed his duties 'with a zeal worthy of the best ages of Christianity', of which this was evidently not considered to be one. By this time, however, his great energies were beginning to fail him, and he may have been glad of the Archdeacon's support. Constable by now had given up Waterloo Bridge, and was engaged on the large picture known as *The Cornfield*, which is described in the next letter.

Charlotte Street Apl. 8, 1826

My dear Fisher

I should not have remained so long silent after having received your last kind and friendly letter, had I been wholly without news of you and yours. I am glad to find from my friends in Seymour Street that you are all well & that I may expect to see you for some time continuance in London—"after the lylacs have blossomed at Osmington".

I will endeavour to reply to your letters in future but when I wrote to you I was so full of myself (which is indeed abominable)—but you must thank yourself for taking a greater interest in all that concerns me than any other human being does.

I have dispatched a large landscape to the Academy—upright, the size of my Lock—but a subject of a very different nature—inland—cornfields —a close lane, kind of thing—but it is not neglected in any part. The trees are more than usually studied and the extremities well defined—as well as their species—they are shaken by a pleasant and healthfull breeze—"*at noon*"—"while now a fresher gale, *sweeping with shadowy gust the feilds of corn*" &c, &c.[1] I am not without my anxieties—but they are not such

---

[1] From Thomson's *Seasons*.

as I have too often really deserved—I have not neglected my work or been sparing of my pains—they are not sins of omission. I at this moment, hear a rook fly over my painting room in which I am now writing—his call, transports me to Osmington and makes me think for a minute that I am speaking and not writing to you—it reminds me of our happy walks in the feilds—so powerfull is the voice of Nature. Yet it was only a small still voice—and that for once—

My picture occupied me wholly—I could think of and speak to no one. I was like a friend of mine in the battle of Waterloo—he said he dared not turn his head to the right or left—but always kept it straight forward —thinking of himself alone.

I hear of some fine pictures, which are gone. Callcott has three—Ward a fine battle—Collins's very fine but I have not seen them—his brother Frank has just left me. He says Lawrence has but one whole length— Shea[1] only one—Jackson only one—(Mrs. Heneage) Phillips none—so that there is a dearth of large canvas's—but let us hope intellect will carry the day. Leslie has a very fine picture—but a fearfull subject—Don Quixote in the mountains introduced to the donkeys (Dorothea), and as the picture is literal, he has made the Don without his breeches—he is in the act of stooping to raise the lady—and his back is towards the spectator.

I am not writing in the best of spirits—to day my boy is gone to Brighton to school[2]—John Dunthorne is gone with him—I rode as far as Charing Cross & left him to his fate, but I hope for the best—& that it will do him good—the air—independent of his gaining some knowledge.

I am much worn, having worked very hard—& have now the consolation of knowing I must work a great deal harder, or go to the workhouse. I have however work to do—& I do hope to sell this present picture—as it has certainly got a little more eye-salve than I usually condescend to give to them.

I have seen nothing—but John Bull contemplates a rush into Suffolk Street[3]—he is a great disperser of humbugg. There was a characature of Mrs. Fry[4], &c, and those who were planning some scheme for to rid the poor of pawnbrokers—the disputing moment is, who shall be the bankers to the new society—Mrs F is made to say, "I hate the 'Hoares' in Fleet Street—I should like Too-good-Rogers". It was bought up in two hours.

I dined with my Seymour Street friends at Mrs. Mirehouses—Mirehouse threatens me with having to paint his portrait—Angels, & ministers of grace defend me. He was hospitable—but there is a coarseness of manner about him that is intolerable—of his professional powers I hope I shall

---

[1] Sir Martin Shee, R.A.
[2] John had gone to stay with Mr. Phillips, whose wife kept a school.
[3] The Society of British Artists.
[4] Mrs. Elizabeth Fry, the Quaker philanthropist.

always remain in ignorance. Our dear Elizabeth, is a natural, but refined & sensible creature.

All that you have said about poor Tinny, has vexed me—I have thought much, but hoped I was mistaken. I should be sorry if any of my letters vexed him, but I was indignant—or rather irritated. We were charmed at your delicacy in saying that he has never acknowledged our *joint* present —it was solely yours.

I must now finish

with best regards to all I am

My dear Fisher

truly yours

John Constable.

The Cornfield[1] appeared at Somerset House with the simple title of *Landscape*. In spite of Constable's hopes it remained unsold, and reappeared in the next year at the British Gallery as *Landscape: Noon*, with a more correct version of the lines from Thomson's *Seasons* quoted in the letter above. It was accompanied by *A Mill at Gillingham in Dorsetshire*, almost certainly the picture painted for Mrs. Hand.

Fisher, in the meantime, was still cherishing the forlorn hope that he might tempt his friend down to Dorset.

Osmington, Weymouth.
April 22. 1826.

My dear Constable;

With this I send you the sketch-books so long detained. But they have been doing their work. They have propagated your name in heavy soils where your pictures would never be able to take root. My wife, to save the books from rubbing, sends some little memorandums of kindness to our Godchildren.—She is writing a few lines respecting them to Mrs Constable; but I cannot make out from your letter, whether she is in London or Brighton. I shall be in town on the 3rd of May with my family. But can only stay there 48 hours as I must return to attend the Bishops visitation. I shall return to town about June 1. This is a country, that the more you live in it, the more you discover its beauties. Did you ever look down the little wooded valley of Sutton and Preston from the spring-heads in the little amphitheatre formed by the hills??[2] It has a peep of the blue bay in the distance: and two forlorn ash trees in the foreground—[sketch of the trees]. The place is very sequestered & is frequented by kingfishers & woodcocks. But fellows from Weymouth with padded chests & vacant

---

[1] Now in the National Gallery.
[2] Constable had visited Preston near Osmington during his honeymoon. A drawing done by him from the hillside above Sutton Poyntz is in the Whitworth Art Gallery, Manchester.

faces come there, & let off guns; & disturb the still genius of the place. This is in return for your rook. When Belim repeats his catechism we cannot make him say otherwise than "& walk in the same *fields* all the days of my life". He might form a worse idea of happiness.—

I send you an original design of Emma's. Her great-grandmother had the same turn. I have seen the Thames frozen & the skaters done from her windows at Hampton with a pair of sizzars.[1] You put your paragraph about your not being in good spirits about poor John, between your stories of Don Quixote by Leslie & the charactature of Mrs Fry. You recollect Falstaff says "I am melancholly; come sing me a bawdy song", and Bounaparte caught a certain disease at Fontainbleau the night he signed his abdication. Do the public object to the exposure of the Dons glutei muscles? The picture *was* our joint present. At least I gave you *one* hundred & it was worth *two*. Have you a spare bed in your house or all full? With kinds regards to Mrs Constable

beleive me

ever yours

John. Fisher.

I dare say Mrs Constable secretly rejoices that I am coming to town only for two days & that "that Mr Fisher" will not keep her husband from her so much.

Charlotte Street April 26, 1826[2]

My dear Fisher

I received your letter and the book, and the kind recollections of Mrs Fisher and yourself towards your godchildren have afforded us very great pleasure. I hope Mrs. Fisher has received before this time a letter from my wife.—I shall proceed to *answer* your letter—firstly to say that you may have the comfortable room next to ours with either the feather bed or mattress as you please & for as long as you please. Roberts[3] is anxious to put it all ready for you directly so you will find all ready.

The spot you speak of above Sutton I well recollect. It is lovely—its sentiment must arise from the expanse around—contrasted with the recesses—and solitudes and haunts—below. But in general these subjects deceive on canvas. The anecdote of our dear "Belim" is very pretty. Depend on [it], the love of nature is strongly implanted in man, at least the pursuit of it, is almost a certain road to happiness.

Were you at all struck by my sobbing rook? His caw—(happening at the moment of writing to you) made me start: it was a voice which instantaneously placed my youth before me.

---

[1] This would be Elizabeth Laurens. The occasion might have been the great frost of 1763. Emma was Fisher's second child.
[2] This letter is in the British Museum.
[3] Mrs. Roberts was the children's nurse.

I have lately been into Suffolk[1] and have had some delightfull walks in *the same fields*—bless the dear boy—our ideas of happiness are the same, and I join with you in praying that he may never seek in less hallowed places.

When my mind is disturbed—it stirs up the mud. How could circumstances ever place me in a situation to write so much stuff—to an Archdeacon!—My agreable associations with Tinney's name are no more.—

I am now busy at the Academy—& am writing early as after breakfast I must be there—My wife is very good and is at the breakfast table at 8— it is now ready—As as I have much to do I must put this paper in my pocket and finish it at Somerset House. It is quite out of my power to describe the scene of dismay and devastation the rooms now present—I could quote Dante—Milton &c—"Dire was the Tossing"—&c—&c, but it is a delightfull show.

Turner never gave me so much pleasure—and so much pain—before. Callcott has a fine picture of a picturesque boat—driven before the wind on a stormy sea—it is simple grand and affecting—he has another large work not so good, rather too Quakerish—as Turner is too yellow, but every man who distinguishes himself in a great way, is on a precipice.[2]

Sir Thos Lawrence is very superior to himself in Peel & Canning—he has a lady playing a guitar—hanging by Turner & you seem to hear its imperfect sounds over his "wide watered shoar"—

But above all this harmony of sound and colour—hangs a most "*atrocious*" portrait of the King hideous to behold & of immense dimensions —its appearance poisons the Exhibition—it is done by some Irish fellow, who has influence at Court[3]—Poor Sir Thos. must be possessed for it is a loathsome characature of his & manner—& he has made the rod for himself—in *inventing that size* canvas, & the cunning Irishman knew that the subject commanded the best place—that is the center of the head of the Room. Canning is over the fire place, a dead Christ by Westall[4] at the bottom of the Room—and a Group of Naked Women & peacocks on the west side center.[5] The details of this show we shall soon anylize together —Chantry[6] loves painting (better perhaps than stone) & is "*always up stairs*" & he works now & then on my pictures—& shows me about—&

---

[1] This was a short visit to his brother Abram, who had been taken suddenly ill.
[2] Turner had four works in the exhibition: most of the critics agreed with Constable that they were too yellow. One was *Forum Romanum* for Sir John Soane's Museum.
[3] This portrait of George IV by Thomas Clement Thompson, R.H.A., led to a libel action brought by Thompson against the weekly journal *John Bull*, which accused the artist of deceiving the hanging committee by letting it be supposed that the portrait had been painted by command, and so must be given a good place. The action was decided in 1828 in favour of the defendants.
[4] *The Entombing of Christ*, by Richard Westall.
[5] *The Judgment of Paris*, by Etty.
[6] Sir Francis Leggatt Chantrey, R.A., the sculptor and founder of the Chantrey Collection.

yesterday he joined our group & after exhausting his jokes on my land-scape—he took up a large dirty palate rag & threw it in my face & was off.

Presently he came back & asked me if I had seen a beastly Landscape by Reinagle (R.A.)—it is so indeed.

The voice in my favor is universal—"tis my best picture".

ever dear Fisher truly yours

John Constable

The Colonel has some of his heartless atrocious landscapes in Seymour Street & has sent to consult me on them. How shall I get out of such an infernal scrape. Truth is out of the question. Then what part can I play—praise is safe—& the whole of no consequence—?

David Lucas, in a marginal note on this letter, gives one of Chantrey's jokes on the occasion to which Constable refers. 'When the picture of the Cornfield was at Somerset House previous to the opening of the exhibition,' he says, 'Chantrey came up and noticing the dark shadows under the tails of the sheep, suddenly said "Why Constable all your sheep have got the rot, give me the pallet, I must cure them." His efforts made all worse, when he threw the pallet at Constable and ran off.'

On the 16th May Constable wrote to his wife: 'Fisher's stay in town—and every thing else belonging to him is uncertain—but he will call tomorrow—& we shall then settle if he has my bed. He is going to Cambridge to canvas for the Solicitor General—Copley[1]—chairman of a committee.'

This opportunity for an uninterrupted talk between the two men seems to have rendered any more letters unnecessary until July.

On the 21st May Fisher appeared at Charlotte Street in the morning and stayed till two, when he went out to make calls. He came back at four, and Constable then walked back to the Charterhouse with him, from which we may conclude that Constable had not needed to give up his bed to Fisher.

On the 22nd Constable saw nothing of Fisher, who had gone to Greenwich, presumably to see his uncle the Colonel. On the 23rd Fisher called early in the afternoon and spent the rest of the day in Charlotte Street, making himself agreeable while Constable went on with his work.

Fisher's next letter shows that he had now acquired one of the various versions of *Salisbury Cathedral from the Bishop's Grounds*. The description of the spire as 'sailing away with the thunder-clouds' suggests that the Archdeacon had taken over the Bishop's picture from his uncle's estate; and if so, the Mirehouses may have accepted the new version in exchange.

Close. Salisbury.
July 1. 1826.

My dear Constable;

The two pictures arrived safe on Friday, & within an hour were up in their places; the white horse looking very placid & not as if just returned

---

[1] John Singleton Copley, son of the American artist, later Lord Chancellor as Lord Lyndhurst: he had already been returned for Cambridge in 1825 and was standing for re-election.

from the continent. It is wonderfully improved by Dunthorne's coat of varnish. The Cathedral looks splendidly over the chimney peice. The picture requires a room full of light. Its internal splendour comes out in all its power, the spire sails away with the thunder-clouds. The only criticism I pass on it, is, that it does not go *out* well with the day. The light is of an unpleasant shape by dusk. I am aware how severe a remark I have made.

The old frame & the smaller packing case return tomorrow by *Woolcotts* which picks up at the *Elephant* in Fore Street. *Browns* Vans go from the Castle & Falcon. Let me know the utmost that you have laid out. Enclose the amount of Dominics bill[1] & I will send the money. My wife is impatient for the "Dunthorne Wilsons". I write in haste

But am ever yours

John. Fisher.

Tinney is absent: but I will tempt him when he comes. I think you give the wrong name to Hugo Stevens's sham Bishop. Bp *Hyde's*[2] is a large & rather well painted picture.

Leslie gives the next letter from Constable.

Charlotte Street, July 7th [1826].

My dear Fisher,

You will receive Dunthorne's Wilsons to-morrow;[3] Mrs. Fisher cannot fail to be pleased with them. I have added a little to your batch of Waterloos, making, I think, a nice bargain for ten guineas. Have you done anything to your walls? They were of a colour formed to destroy every valuable tint in a picture. . . .

A poor wretched man[4] called to see me this morning; he had a petition to the Royal Academy for charitable assistance, it was ——. His appearance was distress itself, and it was awful to behold to what ill-conduct may bring us; yet calamity has impressed even on this man an air of dignity—he looked like Leslie's "Don Quixote". When I knew him at the Bishop's he wore powder, had a soft, subdued voice, and always a smile, which caused him to show some decayed teeth, and he carried a gold-headed cane, with tassels. Now, how changed! his neck long, with a large head, thin face, nose long, mouth wide, eyes dark and sunken, eyebrows lifted, hair abundant, erect, and very greasy; his body much emaciated and

---

[1] Presumably Colnaghi's account for the prints by Waterloo mentioned in the next letter. Dominic was Paul's son.

[2] Alexander Hyde, Bishop of Salisbury, 1665–67. There is a tradition that his portrait was found in a cottage and brought to the Palace in Dr. Fisher's time.

[3] Copies by Dunthorne of the two pictures which had been taken over by Constable with Farington's house: these are now with Mr. John Fisher.

[4] Probably Samuel De Wilde, the theatrical painter.

shrunk away from his black clothes, and his left arm in a sling from a fall, by which he broke his left clavicle. I shall try the Artist's Fund for him. I cannot efface the image of this ghostly man from my mind. . . .

Poor Mr. Bicknell is in a sad state; he had an attack of apoplexy about ten days ago; it was coming on when you saw him. . . . I have made several visits to the terrace at Lord Pembroke's;[1] it was the spot of all others to which I wanted to have access. I have added two feet to my canvas. My wife and all here are well. I trust we shall not need a country excursion, in which we leave this convenient house, and pay four guineas a week for the privilege of sleeping in a hen-coop for the sake of country air.

                                              Charlotte Street Sepr. 9. 1826
My dear Fisher

It is now a very long time since I heard from you—and I have now no means of hearing of you elsewhere. Let me have a line from you soon and dispel the thoughts that any thing may be amiss—or any part of your family out of health. You once said—"life is short—let us make the most of friendship while we can".

I have little to say on what belongs to myself, but that little is good. My children are well and my wife for her very tolerable. They are in a small house—at Hampstead, Downshire Hill.[2] I am but little there—but it is an easy walk from here. I am just returned from a day or two at Brighton, where I had been to return my boy to Mr Phillips's. My wife's father, is in bad health—about 2 months ago he had a severe attack of apoplexy— which was repeated. He is however by depletion quite recovered. He was under its influence when you saw him—which may account for his more than usual stupor. When first attacked he was not expected to survive many days—something then came out as to his affairs—he is worth little or nothing, but has a great many *bad* debts owing to him. As soon as he had got any money the "*great folks*" came and *borrowed* it of him, on little or no security. But they kindly asked him to "*dine*" frequently, well knowing how much he loved a "table"—these habits no doubt laid the foundation of this evil, but he is 74, and now better than ever he was. It is his fate to be devoured by strangers.

John Dunthorne is not returned from Suffolk, He has been very busy —his last job, "*a large sign of the Duke of Marlborough*".[3] I have written to him to hasten his return. He is wanted here by myself & others.

My last landscape [is] a cottage scene—with the Church of Langham—

---

[1] R. C. Leslie states that part of Lord Pembroke's house and terrace form the nearest objects in *The Opening of Waterloo Bridge*.
[2] No. 1 or 2 Langham Place, 'to the left of the new chapel'.
[3] Probably for the inn of that name still existing at Dedham, The sign seems to have been last repainted by Dunthorne senior in 1809.

the poor bishops first living—& which he held while at Exeter in com-mendamus. It is one of my best—very rich in color—& fresh and bright—and I have "pacified it"—so that it gains much by that in tone & solemnity. My friend Mr Phillips at Brighton is commencing a *Brighton literary journal*. He wants me amongst others of his acquaintance to contribute some paper on art—landscape of course—but general. *What do you say?*

And what do you say to this sonnet—which I have just received—the author tells me it is in imitation of the serious sonnets of Milton. But I make no observation—*only give me your opinion.*

To Constable
The English Landscape Painter
on his receiving a Medal from the King of France.

———

Well hast thou earned the triumph and the prize
    Thy course has been heroical: thine hand
      Hath carved from rock the pedestal where stand
Thy daring feet—despite the calumnies
That with unsparing anger needs must rise
    From that most ignorant and bigot band.
    Thy genius is the law of thy command
And doth enthrone thee with the great and wise
In Art—nor is it low, nor unmeet praise
    With gifts so masterfull and close allied
      To place thee at my Wordsworths glorious side
Alike for mocked at. Toils have been your days
    While Truth and Nature with a strifefull pride
Enwreath for either brow the living bays!

———

Rochfoulcaut says lovers are never tired of each others company because they always talk of themselves.

I am particular in requiring your opinion of this sonnet.

                    Yours

Post knocks.   J.C.

The new picture, known as *The Glebe Farm*, became one of Constable's favourite themes.[1] It is more or less a fanciful composition, as Leslie found when he went to the spot not long after, and was probably based on a much earlier sketch of a

———

[1] There are many versions, Constable's own efforts having been plentifully supple-mented by posthumous imitators. That mentioned may be the sketch now in the Tate Gallery.

cottage scene, with the tower of Langham Church added; but it would serve well enough as a memorial to the Good Bishop, recalling the place of Constable's first introduction to the Fisher family as viewed through the romantic mists of youthful memories. Fisher was wrestling with more practical, if not less spiritual, matters.

Maidenhead. Septemb: 27 1826.

My dear Constable;

Do not accuse me of neglect. You were never more occupied in the month of April preparing for the exhibition than I have been since the month of August. Last week there was an ordination, & I planned the Sermon which you will shortly see in print. You will participate in my pleasure when I tell you that I am beginning at last to make myself *felt*. I think that we shall both live to see ourselves, where Collins will neither wish nor expect to see us. I write this sitting in commission upon a dispute between a clergyman and his parishioners, & compose while the parties argue. There is a brother parson arguing his own case, with powder, a white forehead & a very red face: like a copper vessel newly tinned. He is mixing up in a tremulous tone & with an eager blood-shot eye, accusations, apologies, statements, reservations, and appeals, till his voice sounds on my ear as I write, like a distant waterfall.

Your correspondents sonnet is quite correct in its moral; & it is like Miltons in *shape* but in nothing else. The conception and execution are both prosaical, and the language is indistinct. The following you will see the fault of.

"thine HAND*
"Hath carved from Rock the pedestal where stand
"Thy daring FEET."*

Again, "Thy genius is the law of thy command" comes under that figure of speech termed *nonsense*.

Again "And doth enthrone Thee with the great and wise" in *Art*! is an anticlimax—setting you up to pull you down again. You would see the ridicule if the poet had been writing of Dr Baily,[1] and had said

"And doth enthrone Thee with the great and wise"—in *physic*!

The sonnet is however gratifying to you to shew how persons think of you. You are secure both of present & future *fame*; but never of *popularity*. Few men like Shakespear, Walter Scott & Hogarth unite the two. Do not be anxious about celebrity. It will find you out sooner sitting at your easil quietly than if you made any stir. And as for your Sonnetteer you must cry with Pope, "Oh! save me from my friends".

I am concluding this letter at *Abingdon*. The Bishop dismisses me on Saturday when I return to Osmington for the Winter.

---

[1] Constable's own physician, Dr. Matthew Baillie.

I am doubtful about your Brighton Gazette. You are in possession of some very valuable and original matter on the subject of painting, particularly on the *Poetry* of the Art. I should be very sad to see this seed sown on some unvisited feild where it would blossom in forgetfulness: while some theiving author, like a sparrow, would fly off with a sample & take the credit from you. Throw your thoughts together, as they arise (in a book that they be not lost) when I come to see you we will look them over put them into shape & do something with them. Perhaps we could illuminate the world thro' *the Quarterly*. Pray do not forget to put together the history of your life & opinions with as many of your remarks on men & manners as occur to you. Set about it *immediately*. Life slips. It will perhaps bring your children in £100 in a day of short-commons, if it does nothing else. Besides *I* have been all along desirous of writing your life & rise in the art.

Your account of poor Mr Bicknell is a solution of all our difficulties. His friendships account for his poverty, and his apoplexy for his apathetic stupidity. An *easy* man in this world, is like a perch with his back fin cut off, & thrown out for bait to a Jack. And a man *overfed*, is like a frog under a cruel experiment which physicians make. They blow him out as round as a ball & *sciure* the fundament. The wretch floats down the stream helplessly. He is too bloated to swim.

Friendship in the long run is better than love: there is the same opportunity for self-applause & it does not pall. It is a good proof of the superiority of mental over bodily gratification. A word or two now of MYself.

I live with our new Bishop as son with Father or brother with brother. Our habits of life similar, our pursuits similar, our modes of thought similar. Or only sufficiently different to increase the pleasure of communication. He evidently delights in my company & will hardly let me out of his sight. And I find a man who can appreciate my acquirements and understand my speculations. I have been unconsciously acquiring at Osmington in long winter evenings a greater stock of knowledge than I was myself aware of, & find that I have no reason to be discontented with the use I have made of my time. The Bishop improves me & drives me on in my classical acquirements; while in general divinity & comprehensive views of history, I find myself "in easy circumstance". He is urging me to overcome my indolence & shew myself in print—& before Dec. I shall be out. I have got my nerves steadier & my understanding more at my control.—My ambition is strongly awakened, and I see glimpses of light thro' the wood.

We have had at Salisbury a strange bird from the menagerie at Somerset House, "St John Long"[1] by name an *Irishman*! He lives near you &

---

[1] John St. John Long, an Irish engraver who had taken to painting a few years before.

manufactures views from the East with trees drawn after this fashion:
T T T T He came to take a view of our Bishop on his own sollicitation &
much against the poor Bishops will. Describe the picture I cannot, except
that the canvass was eight feet long. He told me secretly, when I remon-
strated upon the want of modesty & repose in the picture, that he intended
to impress the Bishop with a proof of his skill, which, saith he, his Lordship
does not fully seem to be aware of. I will paint this gallery *down*. Accordingly, next morning, I found the pictures most curiously deranged, as if
St Vitus had been among them. My poor uncle was hanging over Bp
Douglas next the ceiling, & this gingerbread abomination swinging in the
place of Northcote's cool colours.[1] When Mrs Burgess came down to
breakfast the struggle between her & the painter, the one for restitution
the other for the innovation was droll. However she gained the day. The
Gallery was restored to its former order. He dismissed. His picture sent
to a *back* room. And a thirty-guinea frame counterordered.

The bishop is a great man for restoring greek passages to their right
owners. The *habit* is so strong upon him, that he thinks he can prove Bp.
Hyde's spurious portrait to be a genuine picture, & supposes our friend
Hugo to be a very honest & sagacious man. Here you have the weak side
of an otherwise clear-headed man.—

I went some weeks ago to Salisbury tower.[2] There I saw a drawing by
Bp Fisher of Langham Church & valley with a great oak in the centre of
the picture. The drawing was really well planned. [sketch.] My wife &
children were never in better health.

Yrs ever

John. Fisher.

Abingdon. Sep. 29.

The schedule of money transactions was quite satisfactory—except that
I have a memorandum of a few additional pounds which I owe you. But
at present I cannot keep my promise of sending you a remittance—Owing
to the disturbance in the currency, I am quite hard run. I know you did
not *ask* for any thing—but I thought it necessary to say this in my own
defence.—

Constable's third son, Alfred Abram, was born on the 14th November. Constable, writing to announce the event, may have remembered how much he had
needed encouragement for his own ambitions at Fisher's age, in the days before
his marriage.

Charlotte Street November 28. 1826

My dear Fisher,

The rumour may have reached that I have another boy, making my

---

[1] Bishop Douglas was the previous bishop but one: Bishop Fisher had been painted
by Northcote, and the portrait is still at Salisbury.
[2] In Windsor Castle.

Q

number six, being 3 of each. It is an awfull concern—and the reflection of what may be the consequences both to them and myself makes no small inroad into that abstractedness, which has hitherto been devoted to painting only. But I am willing to consider them as blessings—only, that I am now satisfied and think my quiver full enough.

I gloried in your letter. Its friendship for me, was if possible forgot for the moment—in the delight at seeing you at length properly appreciating yourself—and you never need fear of indulging too much in that exulting tone which it breathes—& in which you are doing yourself no more than justice. Take care that you launch your boat at the appointed time, and fearlessly appear before the world in a tangible shape—that they may clutch you. It is the only way to be cured of idle vapours—and useless fastidiousness. *Bury no longer* your natural manliness of character, and great acquirements in study—but let mankind be the wiser and better for them, especially in this age—of cant and folly on the one side and Catholick despotism on the other. You are admirably situated between both—to attain [ultimate] success.

My wife is at Hampstead where she was confined. She has a beautifull son . . . and both are doing well, but it was a month before the time. I am endeavouring to secure a permanent small house there, to prevent if possible the sad rambling life which my married life has been, flying from London to seek health in the country. I have put the upper part of this house into an upholsterer's hands to let, and have made my painting room, warm and comfortable, and become an inhabitant of my parlors. I am three miles from door to door—can have a message in an hour—& I can get always away from idle callers—and above all see nature—& unite a town & country life. All these good things I hope to add to a plan of economy, for I will not live under the depression of exceeding my income. Neither my principle nor my pride will bear it—even Salvator Rosa was brought to a state of saving & reflection, when the horrors of debt and poverty were contrasted with his *own pride*, by his black servant—"Ah Master *you* are the last man to stand at a bridge with a *begging* box in your hand". "You are right, black philosopher" said the painter, & as extreams produce extreams in genius—he became a miser & died rich.

I passed the evening last, with Northcote. He enjoys a "green old age"[1] —& is as full of vivacity as ever. He is always delightfull, instructive & amusing. Taking excellence, he said, originality must be always first— bring something to light out of nature for the first time—something that in common life *a patent would be granted for*—an original invention or a decided improvement. Patents are not given for making a time peice or a telescope ever so beautifully, not differing from others—but inventing them first or adding to them what is usefull, [deserve] them of the gratitude of mankind.

---

[1] Northcote, now eighty, applied this to Constable's own work.

There has been sad work lately in the Academy—but it is too contempt-ible to talk about, as is usual in bodies corporate—the lowest bred & the greatest fools, are the leaders.

The *Sonnet* which you justly tore to raggs, was poor Judkins—he is anxious to know "*how you liked it*"—I shall never let him see, "*how you liked it*". He *will* dabble in poetry as well as in painting—and for the former he is woefully "*shown up*" in last Sundays "Monitor"—the subject of his poem seems something of the same as his picture of the "Stolen Moments".

I have taken your advice and have written nothing for the Brighton Courier. I must husband all the property I am worth—and you must polish my rude materials for the world & make them not only palatable but digestible for the benefit of my children.

I have seen an affecting picture this morning, by Ruisdael. It haunts my mind and clings to my heart—and has stood between me & you while I am now talking to you. It is a watermill, not unlike "*Perne's Mill*"—a man & boy are cutting rushes in the running stream (in the "*tail* water") —the whole so true clear & fresh—& as brisk as champagne—a shower has not long passed. It was beside the large one at Smiths[1]—& showed Ruisdaels compass of mind in landscape.

Northcote says the failures and difficulties of success in arts, are for the most part caused by our early habits & education. Virgil, he says, is drummed into boys as the height of excellence—whereas he is a "farthing candle" to Shakespeare. The first book he (Northcote) read was Jack the Giant Killer—& he still beleives it unequalled—at least it has sunk deep into his mind, and so on—

I have published my proposals for a print of Dr Wingfield,[2] James's brother in law. Do you know any stray Westminster birds? It is a guinea. Johnny quite well & busy.

I am delighted to see how you live with the bishop—that you avail yourself of his great worth and understanding, and that he does not use his "*rank*", or the "wisdom of age" to "trip up" and "overbear", the more valuable qualities of vigour & energy to be found in youth & middle age.

I have no doubt but Hugo Stevens is a scoundrel—but you are wise in leaving the bishop to find it out—one gets no thanks for making the dis-covery—because it must prove the duped, a fool, at the same time.

Love to all. Ever yours sincerely, John Constable.

I have received from Carpenter, your copy of Burnets light & Shadow —his etched specimens are delightfull, his letter press meagre—& with little information—but still it may inform many—and offer light to those who are wholly dark.[3]

---

[1] John Smith, the dealer of Great Marlborough Street.
[2] The engraving by William Ward of Dr. Wingfield was published in 1827. Dr. Wing-field was headmaster of Westminster School.
[3] John Burnet, Scottish painter and engraver, published his *Practical Hints on Light and Shade* in 1826. The publisher was W. H. Carpenter.

1827

Constable's last communication was followed by a long silence between the two friends. The intervening events may be briefly told. A sixth child, Adela, (later Mrs. Duboulay), was born to the Fishers on the 21st January. Constable had sent Mrs. Hand's picture to the British Gallery, together with a *Glebe Farm*, painted for George Morant.[1]

On the 6th April 1827 Constable wrote to Dominic Colnaghi from Downshire Hill in Hampstead: 'Our friend Fisher passed all yesterday with me here. He told me of his pleasant visit to you and your father.' Writing on the 11th to tell his wife of his visit to town, after his return to Salisbury, Fisher said: 'Constable's great picture is a view of the chain-pier at Brighton. It is most beautifully executed & in a greater state of finish and forwardness, than you can ever before recollect. Turner, Calcott and Collins will not like it.'

Constable's *Brighton*,[2] based on the sketches he had made of the marine parade and the chain pier there was sent to Somerset House soon after, along with another *Gillingham Mill*,[3] a small upright which Constable may have intended for Tinney before their relations were broken off. Once again a familiar figure was missing from the private view, for Sir George Beaumont, the last of Constable's kindly 'monitors' had died on the 7th February.

Constable's delay in writing to Fisher was due to his preoccupation with his wife's health, which had been rapidly deteriorating. He had been seeking to find a permanent residence for her in Hampstead, and it was not until this had been found in Well Walk that he took up his pen to write again.[4]

Sunday Eveng. Augt. 26. 1827

My dear Fisher

We sadly neglect much happiness that is placed within our reach—weeks and months have passed since we met and no communication since —I know not where you are and you know not what I have been so long about. Your cares lay far and wide apart, and I am not wholly without them. Still, we do amiss to remain inactive towards each other, for both our sakes. No worse account can be given of life at the last hour than to have neglected the social duties.

I am at length fixed in our comfortable little house in the "Well Walk", Hampstead—& we are once more enjoying our own furniture and sleeping on our own beds. My plans in the search of health for my family have been ruinous—but I hope now that my movable camp no longer exists—and that I am settled for life. So hatefull is moving about to me, that I could gladly exclaim—"Here let me take my everlasting *Rest*"—no moss gathers

---

[1] Later in the Wynn Ellis Collection and in the sale of the Armstrong Heirlooms, 1910. Whitley is mistaken in supposing that Morant could not have bought a *Glebe Farm*.
[2] In the Tate Gallery.
[3] In the Victoria and Albert Museum.
[4] The letter is in the Victoria and Albert Museum Library.

"on the rolling stone". The rent of this house is 52 £ per ann. Taxes &c, 25—and what I have spent on repairs 10 £, or 15 at interest, and money sunk on lease 23 gns. I let Charlotte Street at 82 £, to a very agreable man and his wife—Mr Sykes—he is a teacher in most of the genteel families here in the "dancing line": I have no doubt of their being very permanent. I retain my 2 parlors, large front attic—painting rooms, kitchen &c.

All this account of myself is a little prelude, to an entreaty on my part on you for help—can you let me have 100 £, on any account. If as a loan, I will give you security and pay full interest, or any way that you please. It is to pay my workmens bills—of painting—& repairs of various sorts to this house. I throw myself my dear Fisher on you—in this case—the weight of debt to me is next to the weight of guilt. *Help to establish me in this house!* It is indeed everything we can wish. It is to my wife's heart's content—it is situate on the eminence at the back of the spot in which you saw us—and our little drawing room commands a view unequalled in Europe—from Westminster Abbey to Gravesend. The *dome* of *St Paul's* in the air, realizes Michael Angelo's idea on seeing that of the Pantheon —"I will build such a thing in the sky". We see the woods & lofty grounds of the land of the "East Saxons" to the N. East.

I read Turners History continually—for two reasons—first I think thereby of you—and its information is endless and of the best kind. How delightfull & filled with high moral & religious feeling are all his reflections— do you recollect his depicting the nature of the human mind, *clinging to hope*, at the end of the life of Wolsey—Henry 8th.—

I have Burnett's book on color for you from Carpenter.[1] Where shall I send it, or shall I meet you at Sarum with it—"*during your durance*"— and make a few autumnal sketches on spots, now endeared [to] us both—

My Brighton was admired—"*on the walls*"—and I had a few nibbles out of doors. I had one letter (from a man of rank) inquiring what would be its "*selling*" price. Is not this too bad—but that comes of the bartering at the Gallery—with the keeper &c.

My Dr. Wingfield has paid—but nothing more—no one will buy a *schoolmaster*—nor is it likely. Who would buy the keeper of the tread mill, or a turnkey of Newgate, who has been in either place? *Mr Banister is my neighbour here*—a very fine creature he is, very sensible—*natural*—and a gentleman. He said that at Eton there were three brothers—masters there—of the neame of Heath. The boys named them, "Black Heath", "Blasted Heath", and the other (who flogged incessantly)—"*Arse-cutt* Heath"[2]

---

[1] Burnet's *Practical Hints on Colour* came out in 1827.
[2] Dr. Heath, Headmaster of Eton from 1792–1802, was known to the boys as Ascot Heath.

Collins is likewise my neighbour here—but I have made up my mind to rid myself of this unpleasant fellow—at least, if I see him again, it shall not be of my seeking. He is now at war with *some* members of the Academy —and hated by *all*. Many things are said to his disadvantage—and some have even appeared in the newspapers. A meeting of the Academy has been called but they decline interfering, between Pickersgill and him, who are at daggers drawn. Pickersgill told me (clenching his fist & teeth at the same time) that he would not forgive him 'till he was in his coffin.

"This is news of the Art"—but I confess I show you only the shades of the picture—the lights are more to be seen in the late sale at *Lord de Tabley's*—all *new* pictures. They sold there for 8000 £—2000 £ *more than he paid for them*. A landscape by Wilson—500 £. Query—had he 50—for this truly magnificent and affecting picture? But the voice of "Retribution" will at length break forth—and exclaim in the words of Shakespear "May this expiate"—but Wilson has joined the *"noble army of Martyrs"*—& who would not so join them—who would not "so equal him in fate could they equal him in renown"? He was aware of all this himself when he told Farrington that *"the country was not yet prepared for him"*—his natural dignity never allowed him to say more. His works were truly original. He showed the world, what existed in nature, but which it had never seen before. His fate accorded, for it is the nature of man to hate a benefactor, as in Galileo, Vasalius[1] (the anatomist) &c.

John Dunthorne has compleated a very pretty picture of your lawn & prebendal house, with the great alder & cathedral,[2] and he is now in Suffolk, painting the portrait of the Revd Richard Leeds, who has a fine place and estate there—but whose real name has been long lost, in that unpropitious one *"Dick Shitt"*. His ugliness is portentous—how John will get on I know not.

I laboured hard on a portrait of Mirehouses's father—it is detestable enough of course—still he expressed himself satisfied—but he has left it on my hands unpaid for. I shudder to think that a name so dear to me should have been merged into his—he will swallow up the whole family.

We long to hear news of you and Mrs. J. Fisher & your children. We are well here and in great beauty—my pretty infant soon after you saw him was seized with whooping cough. I find medical men know nothing of this horrible disorder, and can afford it no releif. Consequently it is in the hands of Quacks. I was advised (by an American) to hold the boy *down the privy* for a quarter of an hour every morning—as a certain cure. Another certain cure was to put him 3 times *over* & 3 times *under* a donkey. J.C.

---

[1] Andreas Vesalius, professor at Padua, burnt his books in despair in 1544 after the hostile reception of his *Fabrica* by the Galenists.

[2] A 'finished' copy of the oil-sketch made by Constable in 1820, now in the collection of Mr. John Fisher.

The sale mentioned in the above letter had been held by Christie on the 17th July. It excited great interest because Lord de Tabley, as Sir John Leicester, had filled his gallery with works by contemporary English artists. Richard Wilson's picture, *A View on the Arno*, which Constable had already admired at Sir John's house, was bought for 470 guineas by Jesse Watts-Russell, the son of the soap-boiler and husband of Constable's cousin Mary Watts.

> Close. Salisbury.
> September. 3. 1827.

My dear Constable,

     I would have replied to your letter by return of post, but I am utterly destitute of money; & I endeavoured to borrow £100 for you. I have failed. But if you can raise it elsewhere, I will lend you my name, & assist you gladly to liquidate the debt at a future day.—It cost me £4000 to get into Douglas's old embroidered shoes: & the act has made me I suspect a poor man for life. I paid £900 out of my income this year in liquidation.

I am elected a member of the Royal Literary Society & must appear in London in December to be installed. I shall then have an opportunity of seeing you at the bottom of "Well Walk". The arrangement is a good one in one particular. You will be less disturbed by morning flies[1] than in Charlotte Street.—

I rather repent having been elected into this society. I shall have to sit & coerce the elasticity of ones intellect, while subjects like the following are being read. "Remarks on *Brut Iysilis* a fabulous chronicle in the 2 Vol. of the *Myrvyan Archaeology of* WALES". I hate Wales & Scotland & Ireland & all their barbarous unintelligible incredible antiquities.

"My durance" is at an end. I return to Osmington next Friday the 7th Inst. I do not know any thing that will give me greater pleasure than to see you *there*. Prithee come. I will tempt you by saying, that by that time I may be able to negotiate a loan for you. I am worn to death with the incessant visiting, & the same persons, & the same prate, of this busy-idle place.—The whole of the Diocese is in my hands, I educate my boys (for who would send them to "Arscutt") & there you have sufficient reasons why I write so seldom.

As for Wilson, and the world not appreciating intellect, & all that sort of feeling, I have long discarded it. The world hates intellect & will keep it down as long as it can. Listen to Pope.

> In parts superior what advantage lies?
> Tell for you can, what is it to be wise?
> Tis but to know how little can be known,

---

[1] The morning visitors of whom Constable had complained.

To see all others faults, & feel our own,
Condemned in business, or *in arts* to drudge
Without a *second*, or without a *judge*.
Truths would you teach or save a sinking land?
All fear, *none* aid you, [and] *few* understand.
Painful preeminence! yourself to view
Above life's weakness, and its comforts too.

Essay on Man. Ep. 4. 1. 258.

This is you. Now listen to my case. "I have long had in view, of composing an essay on Theological studies for the use of young people. What gave birth to the project, was observing the strange averseness that grown men have for others making experiments in religion. So that I thought that it would be no ill scheme if I could draw the next generation to a more enlarged & liberal way of thinking, & make them do that for themselves, which they have an unwillingness from many *opposing passions* that others should do for them." Warburtons letters.

This is what I feel. I was always well read in the Scriptures, divinity & the early Church, but no one would listen to my views or accept my interpretation though they would praise my preaching. A very learned man comes, to take me by the hand & makes me his confidant. But thus it is: intellect is & is meant to be its own reward. Faber[1] writes to me & makes the same complaint. You say it, & I feel it. Johnson was only honoured because the dastardly world feared him.

Did you see a curious letter in the Morning Herald some months ago from Haydon dated Kings bench, complaining that his pictures were lying rolled up in garrets in Holborn. I have mislaid the letter, though I cut it out to send it to you. But in looking for it, I discovered a curious letter from that fellow West addressed to my Uncle, which I send you. It is a curious specimen of his ignorance & sycophancy.

I rely upon your paying me a visit at Osmington & that before the Autumn disappears. With my regard to your wife beleive me

most sincerely yours

John: Fisher

My wife & children are in perfect health.
Burn this letter for it savours vilely of vanity.

As usual, the hoped-for visit to Osmington had to be postponed. In October Constable was called down to Flatford to look after his brother Abram, and his autumnal sketches had to be made on the familiar banks of the River Stour. Fisher, however, was able to keep his appointment in town.

---

[1] The Rev. George Stanley Faber (1773–1854), a controversial writer to whom Bishop Burgess gave a prebendal stall at Salisbury in 1831.

Osmington. Weymouth.
Novr. 30. 1827.

My dear Constable;

I shall be at the White Horse Cellar[1] on Monday night next Decr. 3. I shall remain at that house, (or at E 2, *Albany buildings*), untill Thursday, when I intend to spend two whole days with you at Hampstead. I will sleep at the nearest Hotel.

I will bring up £30 which is all that I can at present command. I have paid off £1500 debt this last year. My wife & children continue quite blooming. I am in better health than I ever recollect. I hope to have the same report of you & yours. With regards

Beleive me

faithfully yours

John: Fisher

1828

Fisher's visit to Well Walk was followed by another long silence: and on Constable's side there was plenty to account for it. If he had lulled himself into a false sense of security over his wife's health when he had secured the new house, the ever more menacing symptoms of tuberculosis soon deprived him of his hopes. Yet another child was born at the beginning of the year, exhausting her enfeebled frame. In the spring Maria was taken seriously ill at her aunt's house in Putney; and when it was thought that she might derive some benefit from the tonic air of Brighton, she was found to be too weak to be moved.

Anxiety over money was removed when Mr. Bicknell died and was found to be much better off than his son-in-law had supposed; but Constable had other strains on his mind as well. Maria's life was now ebbing away fast, and she had still not been given the pleasure of seeing her husband enrolled among the ranks of the Academicians. Before the February election took place, Constable steeled himself to the hateful task of going on the usual round of begging visits to the powers that were—more for the sake of his family than his own, for he knew by now that his reputation depended on no diploma—only to be told that his favoured competitor Etty was much the better artist, while he himself had only the respect generally felt for his character to commend him. In the event it was Etty, at whom he had laughed as no artist not so long ago, who won the election by an overwhelming majority.

It was not until after the tumult of Somerset House, where he exhibited an upright *Dedham Vale* as seen from Langham,[2] and it had been found possible to send Mrs. Constable to the sea-side, that Constable found time to write to Fisher again.

Charlotte Street June 11 1828

My dear Fisher

Is it possible that I should have had little or no tidings of you since

---

[1] Now occupied by Hatchett's Restaurant in Piccadilly.
[2] Now in the National Gallery of Scotland.

we parted in November? We do a sad injustive to our friendship. But this silence is a bad thing and we wrong ourselves by it. It has so much annoyed me that I was determined not to let this (my birth) day pass without emancipating myself from what seems almost a spell, for I have never felt a greater desire to write or had in reality more to say to you (at least of myself) than now. For this has been to me a most eventfull year—half of which is scarcely past when, three things at least of moment to myself have occurred—

1t. The birth of a lovely boy whom we have named Lionel Bicknell— he was born 2d. Jany. 1828.

2d. Painted a large upright landscape (perhaps my best). It is in the Exhibition, noticed (*as a redeemer*) by John Bull, & another, less in size but better in quality, *purchased by Chantrey*.[1]

3dly and last though not least, Mr Bicknell has left us a fortune that *may be* twenty thousand pounds—this I will settle on my wife and children that I may do justice to his good opinion of me—it will make me happy —and I shall stand before a 6 foot canvas with a mind at ease (thank God).

The Exhibition is poor—but though the talent is so small its produce as is usual in individual cases as well has been very great—150 £ per diem, perhaps, on average.

I have little more to speak of it. Lawrence has many pictures, and never has his elegant affetuoso style been more happy. Jackson is the most of a painter but does not rank with him in talent. Phillips is bluff.

There is a grand but murky dream by Danby.[2] It is purchased by "*Beckford*"—the subject is from the Revelations but might pass for the burning of Sodom—500 gns—copyright to Mr Colnaghi 300—British Institution with a letter of thanks 200. I only wish you could see the work that has elicited all this.

Turner has some golden visions—glorious and beautifull, but they are only visions—yet still they are art—& one could live with *such* pictures in the house—[3]

Etty has a revel rout of Satyrs and lady bums as usual, very clear & sweetly scented with otter of roses—bought by an old Marquis (Ld Stafford)—coveted by the King (from description), but too late.

Some portraits that would petrify you—they are indeed, to use your own word, atrocious. Newton[4]—the Vicar of Wakefield—most affecting.

---

[1] *Hampstead Heath*, now in the Sheepshanks Collection at the Victoria and Albert Museum.

[2] *The Opening of the Sixth Seal*, by Francis Danby, A.R.A., who was then painting in the style of Martin, and was to prove a dangerous rival to Constable in the next election.

[3] Of Turner's four exhibits, *Dido directing the Equipment of the Fleet* and *Boccaccio relating the Tale of the Birdcage* are in the Tate Gallery: the other two were views of Cowes Castle (one in the Victoria and Albert Museum).

[4] Gilbert Stuart Newton, nephew of the American painter Gilbert Stuart, who became insane after his election as R.A. in 1832.

My wife is sadly ill at Brighton—so is my dear dear Alfred: my letter today is however cheerfull. Hampstead—sweet Hampstead that cost me so much, is deserted.

I am at work here—shall take my boy & pretty Minna to Brighton on 20th.

I have seen Mary White & her pretty infant. I have not seen Mirehouse this 12 month & hope I never shall (again)—he paid me.

Give me some account of yourself and family and what are your movements. *Evans*[1] wants to come with me to Salisbury to see you—he can appreciate us both—

Ever my dear Fisher

Yours most truly

John Constable

The post waits. It will out for so much haste. I dare not read what I have written—I cannot.

Close. Salisbury.

June 19, 1828.

My dear Constable;

The business, and cares of life grow round me so fast, that I lose my appetite for things that used to amuse and interest me. I have so many necessary letters to write on unpleasant topics, that I hate this occupation: all my friends complain, as you do, of my silence, & I now write to confess my mistakes and promise amendment.

Your legacy gave me as much pleasure as it could have done to myself. You will now be releived from the carking fear of leaving a young family to privation & the world. You will feel that your fame and not your bread are dependant on your pencil. To work with success, we must work with ease. All the most delightful productions of literature have been thrown off the mind, at an instant of leisure, and clear-headed tranquillity.

Bicknell paid you a high moral compliment. My plan of provision, is to leave a home & bread to eat, round which the weak and unsuccessful of my family may rally. Every family should have a homestead: perhaps this should be your plan.

Poor Coxe as you probably know from Peter,[2] is no more. He died of old age, unable to contend with two helps of Salmon & lobster sauce, washed down with large drafts of Perry. A dissentery ensued, & as Fowler expressed himself, "his long distended bowels, were unable to contract."

But while I smile at the poor mans foible "strong in death", I must do him justice. A more *irreproachable* friendly man did not exist. He was

---

[1] The surgeon now attending Constable.
[2] Brother of Archdeacon Coxe.

always benevolently employed, & at his funeral the congregation disturbed the service with sobs. After a great dinner, he used to steal into his kitchen, and give his cook a guinea. His domestics never left him. A silent but strong compliment from human nature. His regard to truth was remarkable. He is the author of twenty four quarto vols: & has hardly been convicted of a mistake. He was quoted as authority in his life time, an event of rare occurrence. For the prevalent feeling of men is jealousy of one another.

Hume bought a Ruysdael at Weymouth which was sold at an auction of a stone Merchants goods, in Portland. The master of ceremonies acted as pimp upon the occasion. When the picture reached Salisbury, it was shewn to Read, with long hair, who claimed it with triumph as his *own*.—

Of your picture I had a good account from Peter Coxe, both as to subject and place of hanging. Pictures bring Tinney to my mind. He has had a partial paralysis which has for the present deteriorated his intellect: but I trust that he will recover. This has probably been hanging over him for some time; and was the cause of his want of pliability in the case of your picture.—

Your remark on Danbys picture is irresistible. I have a curious bit of lore upon that subject, if you will put me in mind to tell it you when we meet. I retain the recollection of Evans in my mind with much vividity. I love that profession, & he as a sample of it. Look into one of the Souvenirs of last year for "*Ruth*" a canzonet by that choice marvel of intellect Mr Hook. It is *beautiful*! It evidently *painting* in print. Newton had a long and severe tussle with himself, whether he should give the Vicar of Wakefeild a "buz-wig" or not.

Hampstead is beautiful, but it keeps you out of *art*. Do you perceive that it is not *situation* that makes your wife ill? On the first of July I take my tour into Berkshire. About the 10th I return to Osmington where I shall be glad to see you.

Beleive me

ever yours most truly

John: Fisher.

In the meantime, Mrs. Constable's health had been steadily deteriorating: she had a cough which gave anxiety, and suffered from nightly perspirations. Her husband brought her back to Hampstead, and towards the end of August he was able to report some improvement in a letter to Dunthorne: yet he was still anxious—'she is so sadly thin and weak', he wrote. On the 15th September he told Colnaghi that he was greatly unhappy over his wife's illness; 'her progress towards amendment is sadly slow, but still they tell me she does mend; pray God that this may be the case!' By the end of the month, however, there was still no improvement to report. Constable then wrote to Fisher, whose reply was immediate.

Close, Salisbury.
Oct 4. 1828

My dear Constable,

Your sad letter has just reached me, and, I greive to say at a time that I fear I cannot move. I am expecting to be called into residence at this place, when I must be a fixture until January 1. But, if this be not the case, & I can get my liberty, I will come and see you soon. I fear your friendship makes you over-value the use I can be of to you; but what I can give you shall have. Trial is the lot of life. Poor Tinney has been visited most severely: he has lost his intellects! This must have been coming on for some time & accounts for his conduct respecting the picture. Whether the affection will be permanent only time can shew. I am much hurried about at the present moment. I began this letter at Salisbury. I finish it at Osmington, & tomorrow I start for Salisbury again. Support yourself with your usual manliness and beleive me always your most faithful & attached

John: Fisher.

The truth, which could no longer be disguised, was that Mrs. Constable was suffering from a pulmonary consumption which had by now almost run its course. Leslie was at Hampstead a month or so later, and found her lying on a sofa; Constable, he tells us, appeared in his usual spirits in her presence, but before Leslie left the house, Constable took him into another room, wrung his hand, and burst into tears, without speaking. She died on the 23rd November.

Of the letter which Fisher wrote on hearing the news, we have only the extract given by Leslie.[1] Ironically enough, it was written from the very house where that happy honeymoon had been spent twelve years before, and in the same month of the year.

Osmington, Weymouth, November 29th [1828].

My dear Constable,

I write with the hope and intention of giving you comfort, but really I know not how. Words will not ward off irreparable loss: but if there be any consolation to the heart of man to know that another feels with him, you have that consolation, I do sympathise with you, my old and dear friend, most truly, and I pray God to give you fortitude. I am additionally grieved that I cannot come and say this in person, but I am so entangled with my family and numerous affairs that I cannot reach London until December. Our new but estimable friend, Evans, paid me a most flattering visit. He travelled one hundred miles out of his way to come and see me in my Arcadia for twelve hours only. He arrived over night, and left me next day at noon; we had time, however, to exchange a great deal of mind. Our conversation turned, of course, much upon you; we agreed that for your comfort, during the trial upon you for the exercise of your patience, you should apply yourself rigidly to your profession.

---

[1] Another transcript in the Constable Collection adds a few words, which are here included.

Some of the finest works of art, and most vigorous exertions of intellect, have been the result of periods of distress. Poor Wilson painted all his pathetic landscapes under the pressure of sorrow. Set about something to shew the world what a man you are, & how little your powers can be depressed by outer circumstances.

Let us talk of other things. I met, in Schlegel,[1] a happy criticism on what is called Gothic architecture. We do not estimate it aright unless we judge of it by the spirit of the age which produced it, and compare it with contemporary productions. The Gothic Minster was the work which gave birth to that phenomenon, the Crusades, and realised that poetic beautiful monster, the mailed knight; who went forth in purity and honour to preach the Gospel with his mouth, while he broke its laws with his sword. The Minster was raised to hold such worshippers while still alive, and to contain their gorgeous tombs when dead; and we never look at the Cathedral aright unless we imagine mitred abbots and knights in chained armour, walking in procession down its solemn aisles. I have put Schlegel into our own language, and have enlarged a little on his notion, since he only hints the thing. What a propriety it gives to the tombs of the cross-legged knights! The monkish priests exacted the tribute of putting off the knightly spur when the Cathedral was entered. Our choristers fine anybody at this day coming in with spurs.

I do not know what to go on writing to you about. I live here apart from the world, and run into contemplative habits. Socrates considered life only as a *malady* under which the nobler spirit was condemned for a time to linger, and called living "the learning how to die"; he meant that the vexations of life render death not only light but desirable. The word *malady* explains the cock sacrificed to Aesculapius; death was curing him a his *malady*, and he sacrificed the fowl, in playful allusion to this, to the god of physic. It is singular, but this notion has helped me under some very vexatious circumstances of ingratitude. Christianity puts the argument higher, and makes the "malady" preparative to better and lasting *health*.

J. Fisher.

Osmington. Weymouth.
Decr. 7. 1828.

My dear Constable;

As soon as ever my Mother is fixed at Hampstead, I will come & pay you a visit, & help you to bear your privation. But the arrows of death have flown thick, & as I received the news of your loss, I heard of the demise of my Mothers only sister. It will shake her nerves terribly & I am in great dread of the result. I only wait therefore to hear of her arrival in London to pay an instantaneous visit. Evans letter was so far satisfactory that he reported you in a state of complete self possession—I

---

[1] The *Sämtliche Werke* of Friedrich von Schlegel appeared between 1822 and 1825.

entreat you to retain it, for you have need only to look within yourself, and find satisfaction. I wish if "Brighton" is not out of your possession that you would put it on an easil by your side, Claude fashion, & so mellow its ferocious beauties. Calm your own mind and your sea at the same time, & let in sunshine & serenity. It will be then the best sea-painting of the day.—I feel much for your situation, but I cannot put such feelings into words. You have a treasure in your new friend, who is always at hand.

Beleive me

my dear Constable

ever faithfully yours

John: Fisher.

My dear Constable;

I am ready to move on the 5th of January up to London. Could you give me & my boy a bed each in Charlotte Street for a week or so? Let me know in a day or two. This is the first moment I have been disengaged & able to leave home these nine months. I intend to stay in London a month, and shall devote the greatest part of that time to you & your painting room.

Ever my dear fellow

yours most truly

John. Fisher

Osmington
Decr. 25. 1828.

1829

From this time on, Leslie tells us, Constable never wore anything else but mourning. His most immediate care for the moment was the upbringing of his children, of whom the eldest had not yet turned eleven when they lost their mother. Satisfactory arrangements seem to have been made for the schooling of the eldest boy and the girls, but the younger children had to remain under his personal supervision with Mrs. Savage as housekeeper and Mrs. Roberts as nurse. The occupation which this gave him may account for the satisfactory tone of the letter to which Fisher refers in his reply.

Osmington. Weymouth.
January 8. 1829.

My dear Constable;

I had fully made my arrangements to be with you at this time, & had actually taken my place in the coach, when they wrote from the Charterhouse that my Mother was so much shaken by the death of her sister that she felt unequal to the bustle of seeing me & my boys. She requested me to put off my journey until February. So here I remain. I am sorry as this disappoints you; but I am not altogether sorry to postpone my visit; since this cold weather affects me very much as far as the lively use of my faculties goes, & so has always used me through life. And when I am with you, I always wish to be at my best.—

The tone of your letter to me was very satisfactory to my judgement: you appear to be smitten, but not cast down. I will lend you any assistance in my power in the education of your children. There is a little book published by the Society for Promoting Christian Knowledge, which is all you want for religious instruction: "Crossmans Introduction". To which you may add, "Nelsons practice of true devotion" 12mo. It is a most sensible book: which, I cannot tell why, is not usually to be predicated of these sort of books.—

I hope the Carthusians have thanked you for the offer of your house. But they had already taken one at Hampstead when your friendly offer arrived. To me your back drawing room in Charlotte Street will be invaluable, both in point of view of accommodation, & neighbourhood to you & your easil: but I will not trouble you, more than a day or two, with my *boys*. A servant I shall not bring: but will pay a little additional girl, for running on my errands.

I am too stupid to run into chat, but bright or dull beleive me always

yours most faithfully

John: Fisher.

If Evans sees my Mother & thinks ill of her, which her requesting *not* to see me makes me suspect pray let me hear from him or you—

An event now occurred which would have given Constable more satisfaction if it had happened a year earlier. Another vacancy at the Academy had arisen this year through the death of his old friend Mr. Bigg. This time, on the night of the 10th February, Constable was easily successful on the preliminary voting; but in the final ballot it was only by a single vote that he defeated the Irishman Francis Danby. Turner came round late at night to Charlotte Street to tell Constable the news, and the two men sat up talking together till one o'clock in the morning.

A note was sent round to the Charterhouse where Fisher had at last arrived to look after his mother; and Fisher had the pleasure of sending back another addressed to 'John: Constable Esqre R.A.'

Lodge. Charterhouse
Febry. 11. 1829

My dear Constable;

Although I fully expected the event, your note gave me the greatest pleasure in confirming the fact, that you are a Royal Academician. It is a double triumph. It is in the first place the triumph of real Art, over spurious Art; and in the second place, of patient moral integrity over bare chicanery, & misrepresented worth. Your rewards are beginning now to flow in upon you with full tide; although, as everything is ordained in a state of trial, the painful is mixed with the sweet. My Mother sends her congratulations which are worth the having. Tomorrow I go with you & call upon your friends.

The event is important to me, since my judgement was embarked in the same boat with your success. Most faithfully yours

John: Fisher

Turners presence was a high compliment. The great landscape painter by it claimed you as a brother labourer.[1]

Abram wrote up from the country two days later to congratulate his brother on becoming what he thought John should have been years ago and added: 'I am glad Mr. Fisher is with you, it adds to your happiness at all times & just now is a high source of pleasure & comfort, knowing as I do the account you set of his long tried friendship.' But as Fisher said, the painful was mixed with the sweet: and for John it was a cruel twist of fortune that the honour for which he had worked and waited as long as he had done for Maria should have come just when it was too late for her to share the pleasure with him. Nor was his bitterness made less when he called on the President and was told that he was lucky to have been elected, when historical painters of greater merit were waiting on the list.

Abram's letter shows that Constable had taken Fisher's advice about keeping hard at work and was already engaged on *The Nore*, a scene of stormy desolation in tune with his present mood.[2] The detached fly-leaf of a small quarto book given by Fisher to Constable on the 2nd March[3] suggests that the Archdeacon may have stayed on in town till then, but the cold winds from the north-east drove him away again before his intended month was up, to Constable's great disappointment, for the visit was doing him good.

The boy who is mentioned in Fisher's next letter as being brought up to town was Frederick, while the boy who was now about to go to Eton was Osmond. Mr. Haynes (or Haines) was one of Constable's medical men at Hampstead and Fisher had presumably met him during his visit to Constable on Downshire Hill in 1827.

My dear Constable;   Osmington. April. 22. 1829.

My little boy aged 5 is coming up to town to have a slight spot removed from his lip by Brodie.[4] Will you have the kindness to take him in for a couple of days with his maid, till the cautery has been applied. They will be with you in the course of a day or so from the present writing.

I am coming up to Eton again with my boy the first of May—when I have seen him settled I will pay you such a visit as a swallow pays a daisy on a grass plot. Can I not persuade you, now that you do not need any thing more than fame, to come & see me at Salisbury as soon as the Exhibition has been well opened. I will take you down with me if you like. Ask Evans to join the party. I will come once more & partake of the pleasant hospitalities of Mr Haynes dinner table if he will repeat his invitation.

---

[1] Turner may not, however, have been quite so pleased as Fisher took him to be: see S.R. III, p. 19.
[2] Probably the sketch for *Hadleigh Castle* in the National Gallery.
[3] In the Plymouth Collection.
[4] Constable had dined with Dr. Brodie's brother while staying with Fisher at Salisbury in 1821.

R

I write in much haste. The cares of life & six children damp my poetical energies & finer feelings as dead leaves in winter smother the green herbage.

Every yours poetically or prosodically

John: Fisher.

Charlotte Street. April 23. 1829

My dear Fisher

I am glad that you make this house serviceable to your family—on any occasion. My housekeeper here will provide all that is necessary—so that the sole attention of your servant can be devoted to your little boy. They could not have come more conveniently—my own family having left this house to day where they have been spending Easter. The beds & rooms are well air'd. Mrs. Savage (who is all that her name does not imply) proposes that the front bed room being large and having two beds be theirs—one bed is so large your boy can either sleep with or from your servant. A fire can be kept constantly there—or the drawing room is at large for them in the day. I live down here (the parlor)—and shall be not at all putt out of the way.

I have just got a letter from the Academy—the Pandemonium opens to the devils themselves on Saturday—in which they [are] allowed every excess for six days (Sunday excepted).[1]

Your sudden departure putt me out a good deal and made me angry, as well as you disappointed my friends in the Academy. Propitiate them on your return, and then you may leave me to myself. My conquest has made a gap in the rebels, I hear Collins says his diploma has fallen 50 per centum—this is very glorious, and it makes me enjoy mine exceedingly.

I was sadly ill when you left me. I never had so bad a cold before. It lasted 2 months. I got it leaving my room to sleep in a little cold back parlor—to make way for you when you did not come—& I could not leave it as you did not write to say your plans were altered—I left my bed at an hours notice. However Hampstead and a picture set me tolerably well up. I have sent the great Castle,[2] such as it is—and a rich cottage.

Evans was disappointed at not seeing you again—and Haines's face became still more "*contracted*".

Nothing shall prevent me coming to see you at Salisbury next summer—should we have one. Evans would be delighted—but he has suffering humanity on his hands—though he, & Haines divide the spoil.

I passed a day or two with my children at Ham House—the Countess of Dysart (the last of the Tollemaches). She was very kind to & pleased with my children—three of whom are with me.

---

[1] Leslie explains that this refers to the varnishing days allowed to the members of the Academy.

[2] *Hadleigh Castle*: the other picture has not been identified.

I went on to Wimbledon and saw poor Miss Bicknell that was[1]—she has sadly dished herself and I think she begins to feel it to be such—she cried & kiss'd the children a good deal. She seems to be just coming to her senses—or that her senses are just leaving her. I think she will go insane—& that she might without the step she has now taken. She has given away 35,000 £ from my children, for some blackguard out of the Academy. See the Chronicle of this day week last.[2]

Wilkie 8 pictures—Lawrence 8. Jackson & Pickersgill 8 each. Callcott, though not 8, one 8 feet long—a classical landscape. Turner has some. They have an immense crash in the hall—it is evident the Devil must vomit pictures all over London. Poor old Northcote, was at the edge of death—but revived. I saw him yesterday—his catheter drew blood instead of urine alone.

It seems that Frederick Fisher arrived almost immediately after this letter was written and that Constable at once wrote to report the result of the operation, offering the Archdeacon a ticket for the private view of the Royal Academy exhibition.

Osmington. Weymouth.
April 27. 1829.

My dear Constable;

I shall be at Eton with my boy Osmond on the 1st of May & must stay there to watch him for a fortnight. I cannot therefore avail myself of the kind offer of your ticket.

I thank you most gratefully for your kindness in receiving my little boy Frederick & his nurse. It is odd that neither you nor she say how the operation was performed; by knife or cautery; & whether the child is much disfigured.

I beg your pardon for using you so ill when in London. But the cold, bitter, North-East winds kept me in such a state of irritation, the whole of my stay in London, that I should have been a most unpleasant inmate to you, & have disturbed your serenity. I felt this, & staid purposely away. I gave you all of my company that I dare: & at last suddenly left London & its damp windy streets in a precipitate fit of desperation.

I have not yet recovered it. There is a deep cellar in the infernal regions which is reserved for the most desperate. London in March is a type of it. See Miltons cold Hell. Why did you turn out into an unwholesome room on my account? I cannot hold myself responsible for such instances of unwise hospitality.—Your life is valuable. There are many Collins's, & a few Calcotts; but only one Wilson, & one Constable, in a generation.—

Will you run down to Windsor for a few days between May 1 & May 14. You will find me there in Lodgings. Pray do; & let us walk over those delicious scenes again; scenes of natural & artificial magnificence, where

---

[1] Louisa Bicknell had married John Sanford on the 1st January.
[2] This contained a favourable notice of Hadleigh Castle.

parsons eat & stuff & dream of dirty preferment; where pedagogues flog little boys bottoms, talk burly, & think themselves great men in 3 cornered hats; where statesmen come, *not* to *flog* bottoms, but to kiss them; & where every body seems indifferent to the splendid scenes that surround them.

Ever yours

somewhat cynically

John: Fisher.

The reference to visiting Windsor again suggests that Fisher and Constable had met there before. Osmond, it may be observed, was going to Eton under the famous Dr. Keate: and he was present on the famous night when over a hundred boys were flogged after the riot following on the dismissal of Munro. He probably escaped punishment as a junior boy on that occasion; but he had the privilege of being swished himself for losing his Latin grammar.

The next letter is known only from Leslie's extract.

Osmington, April 30th [1829].

My dear friend,

I discovered in an old pocket-book this day an extract from Milton's prose works. *When* I made it, and from *which* of his works, I forget. But this I remember, that I meant to send it to you, saying what I now say: that it is the principle on which my friendship for you is founded. You know that I do not use words in mere flattery. "As to other points, what God may have determined for me I know not. But this I know, that if he ever distilled an intense love of moral beauty into the breast of any man, He has instilled it into mine. Ceres, in the fable, pursued not her daughter with a greater keenness of inquiry than I have, day and night, the idea of Perfection. Hence, whenever I find a man despising the false estimates of the vulgar, and daring to aspire—in sentiment, language, and conduct— to what the highest wisdom, through every age, has taught us as most excellent, to him I unite myself by a sort of necessary attachment. And if I am so influenced, by nature or destiny, that by no exertion of or labour of my own I may exalt myself to the summit of worth and honour, yet no powers of heaven or earth will hinder me from looking with reverence and affection upon those who have thoroughly attained to that glory.' . . .

My dear Constable, ever yours faithfully,

John Fisher.

There is a brother Artist here
a clergyman. Bring your best   Windsor, May 4. 1829.
Sketchbooks. in pencil.

My dear Constable;

I have here snug lodgings in the Canons Row in the Castle, the window commanding the vale of Eton, with the turn of the River & *the*

clump of Trees; with such glorious evening effects as would drive you wild.
Lose not a day [sketch[1]] & come & see it.

ever yours

John: Fisher.

Turner has been here
to visit Wyatville[2]

---

[1] Here reproduced, with the letter.
[2] Jeffry Wyatt, the architect, had changed his surname to Wyatville by royal licence
after his election as Royal Academician in 1824.

Certain turns of phrasing in the last two letters suggest that the two friends may have visited Windsor together before, during the Visitation of Berkshire, perhaps in 1818. There is nothing to show that Constable was able to accept this invitation to pay a pilgrimage to the Bishop's last resting-place.

In June Fisher came up to town again to see his mother, and left a note for Constable before going home again.

Charterhouse.

My dear Constable;
Wednesday. June 17. 1829

I leave town for Salisbury to-morrow morning, where I shall be happy to see you, but shall not see you.—You know Dr Sam Johnsons sentiment: make new friendships continually & do not let your old ones die a protracted death.

Yours faithfully

John: Fisher.

So many times had Constable vowed with firm determination that nothing should prevent him from joining Fisher in the summer, and so often had some family ailment arisen to interfere with his plans, that the Archdeacon may be pardoned for his scepticism. The last visit to Salisbury for more than a night or two had been in 1821, and many things had happened since then. Now Mrs. Fisher added her persuasions to those of her husband, extending her invitation to the two elder children; and this may perhaps have turned the balance.

Charlotte Street July 4. 1829

My dear Fisher

I was most happy to receive Mrs Fishers very kind letter, in which you are so kind as to see me with my children. I have taken places in the "little Salisbury coach" for Tuesday next, the 7th., and we 3 shall be with you at tea, I am told before 6 o clock, so that we shall be able to walk over the bridge before dark.

The weather may be more settled by the time I come to you, but the fine effects of such a season make ample amends for their inconvenience. My children are all well, and I think I never felt in much better health than I now am—thanks to Evans.

I took a farewell look at the Academy with Evans [on] Thursday. He is impressed with *my* Castle, and is horrified at the violence done to all natural feeling in *Turner*—one of whose pictures has been compared to a "spitting box" at an hospital. I now trouble myself little with other men. I leave these things to speak for themselves. Evans will be delighted to join us at Salisbury. His intellect & cultivation is as you discover of the first class, & his integrity invulnerable. I have just done a small portrait of his mother.[1]

---

[1] The portrait now belongs to a descendant, and not, as was stated in the 1952 edition, to Mr. Dudley Wallis.

PLATE 12

Victoria and Albert Museum

JOHN FISHER AND HIS DOGS

22 July 1829, ink and water-colour sketch by John Constable

If you have not your book of Claudes etchings at Salisbury will you procure it, as it contains his epitaph[1]—and some memorandums—and I am employed to give a sketch of his character to prefix to a book of engravings now making in the National Gallery here.

I passed the afternoon of yesterday with Jackson at his villa, alone. He used a term which was usefull & comprehensive. He said the whole object & difficulty of the art (indeed all arts) was "*to unite nature with imagination*": we were talking of Danby & Martin—&c—&c. The art is now filled with Phantasmagorias—ever truly yours

John Constable

More when "*we meet*"—

We may take it that Constable arrived with young John and 'pretty Minna' on the day fixed: and so far as John is concerned, it is not unlikely that this visit to the Close may have led in due course to his decision to follow in the Archdeacon's footsteps, and to adopt the profession which his father had rejected, by qualifying for the Church at Cambridge. The time was spent quietly at Leydenhall, and the furthest excursion was to Old Sarum, where the abandoned site of the once great city made a special appeal to Constable's romantic sentiment for the past.[2]

According to prescription, Constable spent much time sketching. His drawings were done in a larger sketch book and in a much freer style than on his previous visits. With Fisher's usual help, he was also able to make some small oil-sketches from the windows on the first floor of Leydenhall, looking out across the watermeadows to West Harnham. One of them is inscribed on the back in pencil: 'Fisher's Library Salisbury', with the date, Sunday July 12 1829.[3] These studies, which show the interest in cloud formations that had developed since the last summer visit of 1820, reflect the quiet serenity for which Fisher had been hoping. It is also possible that the beautiful small painting, *Water-meadows near Salisbury*, which shows the Avon flowing past the foot of Fisher's garden—perhaps the most gently placid of all Constable's works—was painted in the open air during this visit, while the mood still lasted—though its very serenity has led some to date it much earlier, along with some of the sketches, even where these bear their dates on the back. This was sent to Somerset House in the following year.[4]

That there were once again quiet rambles into the countryside is shown by a small drawing, dated the 22nd July, on the back of which is scribbled 'Fisher & his dogs';[5] and little imagination is needed to suppose that the long summer evenings were filled with talks about 'the art', while Mrs. Fisher was putting the children to bed. The last drawing is dated the 28th July, and on that day or the next Constable found it necessary to return to town, leaving John and Minna behind: but this convenient arrangement was immediately disturbed.

---

[1] The epitaph is given in a selection from Constable's papers at the end of Leslie's *Life* (1st Edn., p. 121), with some remarks by Constable. The volume under contemplation at the National Gallery does not seem to have come to fruition.

[2] See the letterpress to the Lucas engraving.

[3] Victoria and Albert Museum No. 311.

[4] Victoria and Albert Museum No. 321. For the curious story of how this picture was rejected when Constable himself was on the hanging committee, see S.R. III, p. 26.

[5] Here reproduced.

Close. Salisbury
July 30. 1829

My dear Constable,

I have this instant returned home & found my house so full, that it is out of my power to retain your children any longer. My eldest boy is just returned from Eton, two of my wifes brothers are come uninvited, one with his wife & a child, so that I literally have not a bed to spare, & your poor boy is reduced to a leathern sofa. Pray send Roberts for I am quite in a difficulty.

I have not one word of news having just come home from a Dorsetshire village. Only they were just beginning their hay-harvest.

Ever yours
John: Fisher.

John was presumably sent back to London; but it would appear from the next letter that Minna was allowed to stay on.

From the next letter it appears that Constable had made Fisher a present of one of his own works, of a fair size. Fisher seeks to convey his title for the picture by means of a rebus; but unfortunately his small sketch (which looks something like a horse-shoe or a belt or a collar) fails to convey his meaning. In a later letter he seems to speak of the subject as a boat, but even so it is difficult to guess to which of Constable's works he refers.

Dorchester; Aug. 9. 1829.

My dear Constable;

Your case containing the [sketch of a horseshoe-shaped object] arrived just as I was leaving Salisbury. I just got a glympse of its agreeable surface, & came away. I accept of it with the greatest pleasure, as a mark of your friendship, & to my eye, the best specimen of your peculiar art. It is not every man who could have made such a thing a pleasing picture. I intend to hang it over the piano-forte in the first drawing room, under the Claude when it comes. Let the frame therefore be handsome, & about £5. I hope Dunthorne will bestow a little pains to reconcile the sky & landscape in the right hand corner.[1]

Minna grows into favour every day. Her spirits get more buoyant, & she skips about like a gazelle. Her manners are naturally very good, & a little stay where she will mix with company will ensure them.

I detained your sketches of the Mill on the coast[2] & another—but overlooked your Wilsons which ought to have gone. But Roberts was come & gone like a flash of lightning. The great easil has arrived & waits his office. Pray do not let it be long before you come & begin your work.

---

[1] Dunthorne was now working as a picture-restorer, and this sentence evidently refers to Fisher's Claude.

[2] Probably one of the Brighton subjects (e.g. the mill at Rottingdean), but possibly *Harwich Lighthouse* which Fisher thought was a windmill.

I am quite sure the "Church under a cloud" is the best subject you can take. It will be an amazing advantage to go every day & look afresh at your material drawn from nature herself. You may come as soon as you will, we expect no more company.

My dear Constable

faithfully yours

John: Fisher.

The 'Church under a cloud' may be taken as referring to the first conception of *Salisbury Cathedral from the Meadows,* for which Constable made several preliminary drawings[1] during one or other of his visits to Salisbury this year, with his back to Fisherton Mill (which lies on the other side of the footbridge seen in the picture).

The postmark on the following letter from Mrs. Fisher shows that it was written on the same day as that on which her husband was writing to Constable from Dorchester.

Sunday.

Dear Mr Constable

Minnie and I had agreed to write to you to day before we saw your hand writing. I have to thank you for your very gratifying letter addressed to me some little time ago, and which I should have thanked you for before only that we have had our house fuller than it could hold (for we were obliged to borrow a room at our neighbour's) and I have consequently been entirely occupied with my guests.

Mr Fisher is now at Dorchester where he went for the purpose of preaching to-day before the Judges but I hear that the Calendar there was so light that their Lordships took their departure from thence yesterday and consequently did not wait for the spiritual counsel which he was prepared to give them. The picture arrived quite safe and is duly appreciated.

Minnie was much amused last week by being taken into court and hearing a woman tried for breaking into a house. I took her into the Judges box which was in itself an interesting circumstance and enabled her to see and hear in great comfort—She is quite well and as happy as possible—

Now that we are without company I have more time to attend to her education and I will endeavour that she shall not in this respect be a loser by not returning to school. I hope you will allow me to keep her some time longer. I certainly will not part with her till you come in person to fetch her. I have possession which is in itself nine points.

I have not been in the way of hearing anything of Gray, as for the sham lion he has not yet found an opening to get again within the fence. The

---

[1] One is in the collection of Mr. L. G. Duke, and the other, dated 1829, is in the Lady Lever Collection at Port Sunlight. The latter is marked as though for transfer of the design. Others are recorded.

real royal beast continues in a grand mood and has not yet condescended
to extend the paw of forgiveness to the offending bull dog. He found himself in the way to be cajoled by a certain episcopal fox last week and bolted
within five minutes of the hour when he was to have officiated as chaplain
at a feast given to the Judges.

Little Min is now ready to add her mite. Believe me,

your faithful friend,

Mary Fisher.

The note appended by Minna to Mrs. Fisher's letter is fully given in the volume
dealing with Constable's children. At this point it is sufficient to quote one
sentence from it: 'I am so happy here that I should like to stay here as long as
you like to keep me here.'

Close. Salisbury
Sepr. 3. 1829.

My dear Constable;

Many thanks for your continual remembrance of me which is
worth more than all: but nevertheless many thanks for your outward signs
of remembrance. Your venison,[1] and your revivification of the Claude.

I shall be at Windsor, on Saturday night Sepr. 5th with my boy. Now
either you let me see you there, or hear from you, to say you cannot be
there. I will then come on to town to meet you, & bring you back here. I
shall return to Salisbury, by its night coach on Friday the 11th Sepr.

I yearn to see you tranquilly & collectedly at work on your next great
picture; undisturbed by gossips good and ill natured; at a season of the
year, when the glands of the body are unobstructed by cold, & the nerves
in a state of quiescence. You choose February & March for composition;
when the strongest men get irritable & uncomfortable; during the pre-
valence of the NE: winds, the great distraction of the frame, & the gradual
cause in England of old-age. Then at such a season, can your poetical
sensitiveness have its free and open play? Sep: Oct: & Nov: are our
healthiest months in England. Recollect, Milton had his favourite seasons
for composition. The season you select for composition is the chief reason
of the unfinished, *abandoned* state of your surface on the first of May.
Your pictures look then like fine handsome women given up to recklessness
& all abominations.

I long to see you do, what you are fully capable of, "touch the top of
English Art." To put forth your *power* in a *finished polished* picture, which
shall be the wonder & the imitation-struggle of this & future ages.—
But any freak of imagination or anxiety distracts you. Now come & work,
& don't *talk* about it.

---

[1] Probably one of Lady Dysart's presents.

Your great boat[1] looks nobly in the center of the lesser Drawing Room. Minny is the nicest child in the house possible. Nobody would know of her existence if she were not seen. She improves in her French & other-wise—her *ear* is perfect; & she dances quadrilles with the chairs like a parched pea on a drum head.

Marsh and the Bishop have been together [on a] Visitation for three weeks; they have ne[ver] broken bread together, nor spoke together, nor I beleive seen one-another. What a mistake our Oxford and Cambridge Apostolic Missionaries fall into when they make Christianity a stern haughty thing. Think of St Paul with a full blown wig, deep shovel hat, apron, round belly, double chin, deep cough, stern eye, rough voice, & imperious manner, drinking port wine, & laying down the law, of the best way for escaping the operation of the Curates Residence Act.

I need not I beleive sign my name. My hand is pretty well known to you.

Yours most truly.

Close. Salisbury.
Oct. 21. 1829.

My dear Constable;

My only reason for not writing to you is really & in good truth, I have nothing to say. My thoughts are so compelled to run in the current of mere pounds & shillings, that I have little to communicate upon other subjects. You have said for the last three months that you were coming here, & I have been patiently expecting you. But I am sorry to say that the trees are already naked.

You will find Minny much improved I think both in appearance, and in acquirements. She dances very cleverly, & is much more advanced in her music. The Claude you may either send [by the] Van, or bring it with you when you come; according to its size: but I conclude that the Van is the only proper conveyance.

Your friend Read got exalted the other day at a wine-party, & said that it would be hereafter remarked, "here Read walked & there he sketched." Report says in this place that you have founded "a school of painting".

Do not bring your boy with you at this time of year. It will do him no good—for he must pass his time in the house this rainy weather—and to us it will be inconvenient, as we are much crowded. Six children in the drawing room at one time, is more than my nerves will stand. Wait again for the summer.

We have been very sick here. But I concealed it from you, as I thought it might make you uneasy about Minny. My youngest boy had the Scar-letina very violently; and since then, Robert, that rosy servant-boy after

---

[1] Apparently the new picture, though the name would apply also to *The White Horse*.

. . . weeks illness, is dead! We took precautions, moved to the other side of the house, & whitewashed, but I do not beleive that there was any infection—The boy died of repletion.

Total failure of rents at Gillingham; in short I am in great difficulty & perplexity.—I know nothing that will give me more releif & pleasure than your company. So come soon.

Ever yours sincerely

John: Fisher.

Constable's last visit of all to Salisbury was made in November. It was probably a short one, undertaken for the purpose of bringing Minna home. A small pen and ink drawing of cows grazing is inscribed by him: '13 & 14 of Novr. 1829 done in the Evng—at Salisbury—from the sketch made at the bottom of the garden';[1] and a pencil drawing is dated the 23rd November.[2] These probably mark the limits of the stay.

Fisher's debts were now pressing upon him, and he had a difficult letter to write to Constable.

Osmington. Weymouth.
Decr. 15. 1829.

My dear Constable;

I have recovered in this climate, the use of my pen, and give you the first specimen of it; for what belongs to the tongue, goes often off by the pen. Long letter writers are great talkers.

But my letter at present goes to a matter of business. Will it disturb you much, if I ask you whether you can turn your two great pictures into money for me? And whether you will say what you think they will fetch. Or if you do not like my parting with them, whether you will advance me £200 on them, they remaining in pledge. If I repay the money, they remain mine. If I am hereafter unable the pictures are yours again. In that case they may continue to occupy my walls, and ornament my house: you having the loan of them whenever you wish. But the honestest and most satisfactory way will be for me to sell them.

A friend of mine has made me a present of a Souvenir or rather *the* Souvenir of this year: a most finished, magnificent, precious, meretricious, fulsome work. It is called the Keepsake. The writing is by the best Authors of the day, & the engravings after the best i.e. most fashionable, painters. But so morbid is the tendency of the compositions that I should not let Emma read them, if I can help it. Now what I think of the writing, just that you will say of the landscapes. There is Turner in all his glory: and Prout in imitation of Canaletti. Leslie and Stothard however almost redeem the book. What a farrago is Walter Scotts tragedy!

---

[1] Victoria and Albert Museum No. 316.
[2] Lot 102 in the Gregory sale of 1949.

I met Mrs Gen. Michell the other day, a connexion of Lord West-
morelands.[1] She talked of nothing else but the Sir: Josh: Reynolds and
the admirable manner in which it had been cleaned. She was very much
surprized when she found that I had the advantage of the acquaintance
of Mr Dunthorne who had the merit of the performance. Mrs F sends
her best regards to you and Minny.

Beleive me

my dear Constable

very faithfully yours

John: Fisher.

Of the two pictures which Fisher suggested that Constable should take back,
David Lucas definitely says that Constable bought back *The White Horse* for
100 guineas, and it seems to have returned to his studio soon afterwards to be
engraved by Lucas. The other appears to have been *Salisbury Cathedral from the
Bishop's Grounds* which Fisher had taken over.

Constable in a missing letter wrote back to say that he was prepared to take
back the pictures, though it would mean selling out from the Funds.

Osmington. Weymouth.
Dec. 29. 1829.

My dear Constable;

I am much gratified by your kind and friendly letter: I am delighted
to find that I once administered to your comfort and peace of mind, by
the purchase of the pictures; & assure you that you repay the obligation
by taking them off my hands at the present moment. I am greived to part
with them; but with six children I cannot afford to retain such valuable
luxuries.

Give me £200 for the paintings, & let the frames liquidate our present
account. If at some future time our circumstances change, I can again
assist you in my turn.

The sooner you sell out the better. Not a day should be lost; since the
funds are now higher than they will be again for a long time. Furthermore,
I am much in want of the money, being literally without any. I will write
to you again by tomorrows post telling you to what Banker you may pay it.

I am a great deal better in health & spirits. I suffered at Salisbury with
such an oppression on the chest, as to affect the organs of speech. I *could*
not talk. After being down here some days, I had palpitation of the heart.
But by perfect quiet, rational diet, & very little wine, I am better, & think
that I shall recover my health as well as I ever had it. But what an anomaly it

---

[1] Anne, daughter of the Hon. Henry Fane, M.P., was married in 1803 to Lt.-Gen.
John Michel of Dewlish and Kingston Russell in Dorset: she was a first cousin of the
10th Earl of Westmorland.

is, that when a man is ill, and consequently out of spirits, that the world upbraid him with being so: as if he would not gladly releive himself from such a state if it were in his power.

We shall be delighted to see you here whenever you like to come. But in the present hard weather we are positively prisoners in the house. The roads are so slippery, that we cannot move a horse. Thermometer at 20°. How stands it in London? I hope however that this severe winter promises a fine summer, such as of olden time. I congratulate you on the possession of your diploma. The *no* of the Music is 4, as Mrs. F. *believes*. Come hither as soon as the leaf returns. There is much of this country that is most grand, which you have never seen. Now I know it better, I can shew it to you. It is a country not known in a day. I cannot describe to you how much I enjoy myself in this entire seclusion. What to other men be dulness is to me luxury. Noise & bustle depress my spirits. I like however to *hear* of the world, so send me a little London gossip. In these parts we hear of nothing but "low prices" & "scarcity of money" & such melancholly subjects. My wife sends her kindest regards, and her thanks for your painting instruction, by which she profits. Beleive me, my dear Constable

most truly yours

John: Fisher.

Shew Evans his name, to prove that I have not forgotten his friendship.

1830

Osmington. Weymouth.
Janry. 26. 1830.

My dear Constable;

My banker had advised me of the receipt of £200 paid by you to my account at Williams's. I will pay the expences of sending up the Picture.—

We have passed here quite a Siberian winter. The snow drifted to ten & twelve feet deep between this place & Weymouth: and the road by the Sea-beach was completely blocked up. Our butcher with great difficulty could send us our provisions & I began to have a fear of a temporary famine. One day the Mail missed—and the Magnet Coach could not travel. I have not been out of the house for a week, and have imployed myself in reading Parry's North pole sojourn, & often imagined myself there.—

Your account of the the C——l of the R.A——y was most descriptive. But this evil reciprocally produces evil. They vote from interest & bad motives, and that again produces unreasonable expectations. Chantrey is the only man that unites knowledge of the world & legitimate art. How we think similarly at this distance.

I expect to be in London some ten days in April: but it will depend much upon the weather. I will not expose myself again to Wintry North Easters & streets saturated with wet. Emma requests room to add a few lines to Minny, which I will readily grant; for I have no news for you, but the history of old womens aches & catarrhs the result of this most ungenial season.

My dear Constable

faithfully yours

John: Fisher

This letter was enclosed in one written by Emma to Minna[1] and posted on the following day, from which we learn that Emma had been over to Southampton to have 'a most horrid gold machine' fitted for the regulation of her projecting lower teeth. It may be noted that Emma seems to have had a copy of the prohibited *Keepsake* safely under lock and key, and to have regarded the perusal of its romantic contents as the height of earthly bliss.

The following letter[2] bears the postmark of the 23rd March, though the final figure of the year is obscure.

Hatchetts Hotel, Dover St.

Tuesday evening.

My dear Mr Constable,

I enclose a note from Emma to Minnie and join in the hope expressed therein that we shall soon see the dear girl. We have just arrived and are at present at Hatchetts family Hotel having been frightened from going to the Charter House by a letter from my mother in law speaking of much sickness in Charter House Square. We intend to get into lodgings to-morrow or next day as I shall probably be obliged to stay some little time here for medical advice having been a sad invalid this winter.

I would have deferred writing to you till I had known where we *settle* only Emma was too impatient to send off notice of her arrival to her friend to brook any delay. I look forward with sincere pleasure to seeing you whom I always consider as one of my truest friends. I left Mr Fisher to take care of the nest as we were unwilling to leave the children to themselves. I will inform you where we set up our staff and I hope you will contrive soon to come to see us.

Your sincere and obliged friend

Mary Fisher

Charlotte St. May 24. 1830.

My dear Fisher

I have been so immured at the Royal Academy and at home since

---

[1] See S.R. V, pp. 123–4.
[2] In the Constable Collection.

X'mas, that I have been obliged to neglect almost every thing and every body. Most of all I have regretted the correspondence which we used to hold with each other. Time and events—and moral duties—and all the sad vicissitudes and concerns of life—have greivously usurped its place—and I feel bereaved of much which used to urge & cheer my anxieties & progress in the difficult mode of life which is my lot.

I saw your Mother and all your sisters on Saturday—when I heard for the first time of your illness—and I rejoice to say at the same time of your recovery. I have for long been anxious about you, & I have little doubt but all which you have suffered and which I trust is passed now, was coming at Salisbury. I am glad to find you remain at Osmington. Your Mother spoke with great pleasure of the comfort your last letter had afforded her—in which you mention your entire recovery, and which you write in so calm comfortable state of feeling.

I long to hear from you and if possible to see you. The world gets fast hold of me—my comforts are now much lessened—and I feel my situation not wholly a bed of roses—malignity, envy and such like are the price of being eminent. My duty as "Hangman",[1] has not been the most enviable —it may account for some of the scurrillities of the newspapers, the mouths of which who can escape who has others to please? Still I have got through pretty well—with regard to my publick duties I have acted conscientiously and my mind is at rest.

I could give you some amusement about the Academy but I will not molest you. My Wood[2] is liked but I suffer for want of that little completion which you always feel the regret of—and you are quite right. I have filled my head with certain notions of *freshness*—*sparkle*—brightness —till it has influenced my practice in no small degree, & is in fact taking the place of truth so invidious is manner, in all things—it is a species of self worship—which should always be combated—& we have nature (another word for moral feeling) always in our reach to do it with—if we will have the resolution to look at her.

My little book—entitled, "Various subjects of Landscape, characteristic of English Scenery"—is forth coming in Numbers—No. 1, next week—it will consist of 4 prints in each, & promises well. Should it pay I shall continue it. Write to me to know what I shall buy for Mrs Fisher—of flower peices &c at Colnaghis—or if any.

My pretty Minna has been ill—with cold & sore throat—and Mr Harris had to attend to her every morning—with a catheter for a week—but she is now well—& I dine with the seven[3] yesterday. Charley does not get on,

---

[1] Constable was on the Committee of Arrangement for the Royal Academy exhibition this year.

[2] *Helmingham Dell*, exhibited at the Academy this year, and now in the William Rockhill Gallery of Art at Kansas City.

[3] Constable's children.

it's now more than a year since he declined—Evans has not got him in
hand, and Dr Davis in our square has done him much harm by figging
him up with steel—a bad thing with fever.

John Dunthorne is much better—but so entirely busy I seldom see him
—he is much beloved by Lord Westmorland who has sent Lord Cadogan
to him & the Marquess of Aylesbury, whose collections he is to do.[1] The
latter in Wiltshire—Tottenham Park—where is that?[2]—John is much
esteemed, for his great integrity & skill—& what avails him more than
either, he is not feared by them—his mildness disarms them of dread.

Ever sincerely yours my dear Fisher

John Constable

Your sister will take Minni to see them at Kingston.

The above letter discloses another reason why Constable had been too busy to
write to Fisher before. During his visits to Salisbury in the previous year he may
have discussed his new project of having his works engraved in mezzotint by
David Lucas—more particularly since it was the Archdeacon who had once
suggested engraving as a form of publicity.

Close. Salisbury.
June 29. 1830.

My dear friend;

        You must not attribute to neglect, that your recollective letter has
remained so long unswered. But I have been ill, very ill: my malady shewed
itself when you were with us in October. In the winter, Gout, Asthma, and
fulness of blood in the head, appeared; and I suspect that both intellects
and life were in danger.

I left off meat and wine: but remained obstinate about medicine, until
May; when my better genius, in the shape of my wife, persuaded me to
try some; and by a course of mild purgatives I am, now, recovered; and
am in a most delicious state of health. My hand writing will tell you the
state of my nerves.

Times continue here as disheartening as ever. "Summer has set in with
its usual severity". The rains have swollen the rivers, and swamped all our
Dorsetshire meadows. The uncut hay is all muddled, the cows and sheep
are tainted with the coath: and every paddock is spoilt with what they call
technically, "cows-heels". This is the third consecutive year that this has
happened: and in consequence, all my Gillingham farmers are ruined, and
seven of them are now breaking stones on the road!

On the whole, I lost £400 in 1828; £500 in 1829;—and I suppose, must
expect as great a loss this year, now current. But I have been very prudent,

---

[1] That is, to restore.
[2] Near Marlborough.

and have weathered the storm thus far. You must allow me still to call the pictures mine, and next Spring to possess them again.

I am not without hopes some day of redeeming the "Mill and meadows",[1] from its imprisonment. It is at present like Ovid among the Scythians; poetry among savages. Poor Tinney has dropt into the mearest idiot: he calls himself Sir John Tinney and addresses his poor wife as Lady Tinney. I think the price of the picture would get it back.

I go next Monday the 4th on my Visitation. I return to *Osmington* in the last week of July. Pray come & pass August & September with me and astonish your brother Acads: with some marine scenery. I am quite myself again, so come.

J.F.

Pelican Inn. Newbury.
July 6. 1830.

My dear Constable;

You recollect a copy, hanging upon the staircase of this Inn, of Salvator Rosas Jacobs Ladder. And you always admired it. It is now newly varnished, which has discharged the dust & grime, & brought out the colours. It has such an appearance of "art", & appears so much a good memorandum of a picture, which I shall never see, certainly never possess; that I have half a mind to purchase it. The widow here leaves the price to my honour. Now shall I possess myself of it? Is it judicious? And if I do, what is it fairly worth.

I am at Abingdon on the 8th July. Windsor 10th & 11th July. Come & see me there: my wife is with me & is worth seeing. We shall be there likewise at the late Kings funeral.[2] At this place again on the 20th—

When I repossess your pictures again I must take them at their *now* value & not at the price at which an ignorant world then set them. At least you must have the interest of your money.

The critique of the Athenaeum, was true, characteristic, and highly clever.[3] The critic hit you off exactly. I have inserted it for next week in the Salisbury journal. Dinner on table.—

Hurry of Visitation.

J F.

35 Charlotte St.
July 7. 1830.

My dear Fisher

Your two most agreable letters make me entirely happy. I hasten to write now that you may receive it at Abingdon—and only wish I could be the bearer of it myself, for I well remember what a picturesque place it is.

---

[1] *Stratford Mill*
[2] George IV had died in June.
[3] A laudatory review of the first number of *English Landscape* written by Reynolds (probably S. W.) had appeared in the *Athenaeum* for June 25th, 1830.

With respect to the picture at Newbury I have an imperfect recollection of it, but only that *we* thought it respectable. Indeed the principle on which it is built is so unique & decided, that the most clumsy hand could not miss it. As to its value, if a picture is not worth 20£ it is not worth one £ and in such cases I always say "five guineas", as a sum that a gentleman can offer without disgrace to another party—perhaps you need not hesitate at 10, if you really think it administers (from a long and pleasant association) considerably to your pleasure. I hardly know how to say any thing more so singularly situated as we both are with respect to it—common dealing is out of the question.

I should like much to see you and dear Mrs Fisher at Windsor—only I fear it will be in the time of a bustle. Cannot you both come and take possession of Charlotte Street a few days—and see the great world and my little gallery?

I have just shown one of the proprietors of the Athenaeum your mention of his paper. In the next week last Saturday you may find an article of me headed, "Michael Angelo."[1]——I know nothing of that which you admire.

My "pretty Minna" is at Wimbledon with her foolish Aunt[2]—she has worked a basket for Mrs Fisher.

Nothing but moral impossibility shall make me not come to you at Osmington in the Autumn. I shall look forward to it.

Try and get Tinny's picture for me—I will give you what it cost—at once. Let them send it me, & will send a draft for 100£—directly or before if they choose.

Yours most truly and affectionately
John Constable

The King has sent to say he will see the Exhibition. We cannot therefore fix the time to dismantle.

You shall hear from me again at Windsor.

All my dear children are well. I have read of poor Haverfeilds[3] death.

The following undated and hastily scribbled note, left behind by Constable in Charlotte Street for his son John, was probably written by Constable on Saturday the 10th July.

Dear John

I am going to Windsor to see Mr Fisher and shall not come back to night, so do not wait dinner for me tomorrow.

---

[1] A note by Constable on the bas-relief presented by Sir George Beaumont to the Royal Academy, which appeared on the 3rd July.

[2] Mrs. Louisa Sanford.

[3] See above, p. 20.

I go at 3 this afternoon and Mr Fisher will I know take it very kind of me to meet him and pass a few hours as he has been so very ill—and has got well—& Mrs Fisher is with him.

It is not certain that I shall come to town on Sunday at all, but tell Roberts not to wait, dinner or any thing. I want to see Mr Fisher. Love to Charley and all and pray have what you like—and a little fruit if you please—

affecly yours

John Constable

The letter of the 6th July from Newbury is the last of Fisher's carefully composed epistles to survive. Possibly, however, he continued to write from time to time.

1831

Of 1831 there is little to record. A note on the back of a letter shows that Constable was to dine at the Charterhouse at the beginning of the year, and there no doubt he had news of the Archdeacon. A relapse into gloom seems indicated by the rough study for the painting on which he was now engaged, *Salisbury Cathedral from the Meadows*, the last and greatest of his Salisbury paintings. Here the tumultuous clouds, of which the Bishop would have so strongly disapproved, reflect little of the serenity brought about by Fisher's company when the drawing for it was made; but when he came to the finished version he was able to introduce the rainbow, the symbol of hope restored.[1]

On the 2nd June Constable wrote to Leslie: 'I have a good account of Fisher. He is preaching at Salisbury.'

If Fisher was well enough, it is difficult to believe that he would not have come up as usual to see *Salisbury Cathedral from the Meadows* when it appeared at Somerset House in the spring of 1831. He certainly came up later in the year, when another of Constable's old friends departed from this world. In the autumn Constable wrote to Leslie: 'Fisher has been in town—poor Mrs. Fisher the widow of the good bishop is dead.'

The following note is undated but must have been written about this time, and Constable adopted for the heading of his prospectus the first of the two mottos which had been suggested to him by Fisher.

A motto proposed for the Catalogue of the Exhibition, if not already had.

"Multa vident Pictores in eminentiâ et in umbris quae nos non videmus." Cicero.

Nizolius' Thesaurus will, probably give the reference.

"Ars pictoris est ars videndi." Cicero.

J. F.

---

[1] A small compositional study is in the National Gallery: a full-scale preliminary study is at the Guildhall: the finished version belongs to Lord Ashton of Hyde.

1832

Yet another link with the past was snapped at the beginning of 1832. Poor distracted Tinney died on the 24th January and was accorded the honour of an obituary notice in the *Gentleman's Magazine*. It may here be mentioned that this was not the end of the story of Tinney's picture. Two years later Constable wanted the picture back once again for Lucas to engrave and approached the widow through another Mr. Tinney—probably the brother he had met. The second Mr. Tinney begged Constable 'not to be over sanguine'; but Mrs. Tinney bore no malice. She explained that she was about to have her house full of company for a few days, but promised to forward the picture as soon as her guests were gone. Constable was careful to explain to Lucas that the removal of *Stratford Mill* would completely unfurnish Mrs. Tinney's drawing-room, of which it almost completely occupied one end; but now it was Constable's turn to be worried, for six months later Lucas still had the picture, and Constable was begging him to send it back to Mrs. Tinney.

Fisher's name occurs once or twice in Constable's letters written to Leslie during 1832, when *Waterloo Bridge*, so often discussed with Fisher, at last made its appearance at Somerset House. On the 3rd March we find: 'Archdeacon Fisher used to compare himself in some situations, to a lobster in the boiler— very agreeable at *first*, but as the water became hotter & hotter, he was grievously perplexed at the bottom'. On the 3rd July, when announcing the impending marriage of Dr. Evans, Constable wrote that Evans had every prospect of happiness—'but as Archdeacon Fisher's father would have told him—"it is all a mystery"—this said matrimony'.[1]

Fisher's health failed to improve in Dorset and in August he was taken over to France for a change of climate. His end came with dramatic suddenness about a week later, on the 25th of the month, in the forty-fifth year of his age.

The first news of his friend's death came to Constable in a black-edged letter from Fisher's sister Mary, which reached Well Walk on the 3rd September.

Close—Norwich.

My dear Sir

It has pleased God to visit me with a heavy affliction in the death of my dear Brother John—knowing the friendship which has so long subsisted between you, I should be sorry you should learn this most sad news first by the public papers.

Since you met my Sisters on the road, my poor dear Brother & Mary determined on both going into France for a time to try what change of Climate would do for his health, they had not been above a week at Boulogne (before Mrs Haverfield & Emma could join them), when poor dear fellow he was seized with violent spasms, which carried him off in a few hours. He had good medical advice & every assistance but it pleased

---

[1] Leslie, who had trouble in making out Constable's writing gives this as: 'as Archdeacon Fisher's father's coachman told him.'

God to take him from this world of pain & trouble—one of pain indeed for some years I fear it has been to him, & more perhaps than any of us have been aware of—

It is thought the spasms arose from Suppressed Gout—& Mary says of the same nature as those he has been suffering with of late—She was with him to the last—& thank God his sufferings ceased a few hours before he breathed his last—this melancholy Event took place on Saturday the 25th —My Father & Mother are as composed as we *can* expect under this heavy trial—I hope by this time Mr G. Cookson & Mrs Haverfield are with poor afflicted Mary—

Believe me, my dear Sir,

Yours very sincerely

Mary Harley Fisher

Norwich—August 31st.

The widow wrote next day to her friend Ann Haverfield, who was looking after the children at Osmington: 'My darling went off so peacefully that we could not tell the moment when he breathed his last. . . . He breathed his last at 11 at night & was taken ill at 4 in the morning, He was quite easy from 2 oclock & slept almost the whole time. His illness was decidedly not cholera.'[1] Fortunately she was surrounded by kind friends, including a Mr. Symons, at whose house she was staying.

Thus the friend in whose medical wisdom Constable had placed such implicit trust had not been able to heal himself. With him died these modest ambitions of making himself known in the world, to which we have listened as through the orifice of the confessional; and with him there lay buried the hopes which Constable had reposed in his powers. He could no longer polish up the rugged grandeur of Constable's own prose or act as his biographer, or use his worldly wisdom to look after those motherless children when the older man himself should be gone. The letter which Constable wrote on the 4th September to Fisher's successor in friendship may serve for his epitaph, truer than most.

My dear Leslie,

You will be grieved to hear that I have lost my dear friend Archdeacon Fisher. He went with Mrs Fisher to Boulogne, hoping to find some relief from a state of long and severe suffering both mental and bodily—he was benefited at first, began to take an interest in what was about him & poor dear Mrs Fisher was cheered with the prospect of his being speedily restored to health and spirits—when on Friday Agt 24— he was seized with violent spasms and dead in the afternoon of Saturday the 25.

I cannot say but this very sudden and awfull event has strongly affected me. The closest intimacy had subsisted for many years between us—we

---

[1] But see S.R. III, p. 95.

loved each other and confided in each other entirely—and his loss makes
a sad gap in my life & worldly prospects—he would have helped my
children, for he was a good adviser though impetuous, and a truly religious
man—God bless him till we meet again—I cannot tell how singularly his
death has affected me. I shall pass this week at Hampstead to copy the
Winter[1]—for which indeed my mind is in a fit state. . . .

John Constable.

Leslie tells us that he found in one of Constable's sketch-books a draft of the
dedication he had intended to prefix to his volume of engravings, in the form of
a letter to John Fisher: 'I know not if the landscapes I now offer to your notice
will add to the esteem in which you have always been so kind as to hold me as
a painter; I shall dedicate them to you, relying on that affection which you have
invariably extended to me under every circumstance.'

The dedication did not appear in print. Leslie says this was because Fisher
died before the work was published. That is not quite correct, for publication
was in fact completed in the spring of 1832; but Constable was continually
revising the letterpress to *English Landscape* and may have been thinking of
including the dedication to Fisher shortly before his friend died.

Perhaps in the end Constable preferred to dedicate the work in a different
way to two yet older friends than John Fisher, bringing us back full cycle to
where this work began. In the note on his own old home at East Bergholt, engraved as a frontispiece to the completed series, Constable wrote as follows:
'The late Dr. John Fisher, Bishop of Exeter, and afterwards Bishop of Salisbury,
and also the late Sir George Beaumont, Baronet, both well known as admirers
and patrons of Painting, often passed their summers at Dedham, the adjoining
village to Bergholt; to the latter of whom the Author was happily introduced
through the anxious and parental attention of his Mother; and for his truly
valuable acquaintance with Dr. Fisher, he was indebted to the kindness of his
early friends, the Hurlocks—of which circumstance he has a lively and grateful
remembrance. These events influenced his future life, and were the foundations
of a sincere and uninterrupted friendship, which terminated but with the lives
of these estimable men.'

Besides the memories evoked by the engravings of *Old Sarum* and *Stonehenge*,
Weymouth Bay and *Gillingham Mill*, all closely associated with John Fisher, and
The Glebe Farm, connected with the Bishop, another intimate memory was
called up in a note to Lucas, proposing that he should engrave 'Fisher's Garden',
where so many happy hours had been spent. This proposal, however, came to
nothing, probably because the sketch had never been carried far enough to make
it suitable for engraving.

At Salisbury the spoils were once more divided among the victorious living.
Seymour Street and Sarum Palace, Canons' Row and Salisbury Tower at
Windsor, Leydenhall and the Dorsetshire vicarages, houses where Constable
could once be certain of receiving a warm welcome, had passed into the hands

---

[1] A painting by Ruisdael in the collection of Sir Robert Peel. Constable used the copy
to illustrate one of his lectures, and it was among his pictures after his death.

of strangers. Only the Lodge at Charterhouse still remained, and it was here that young Mrs. Fisher brought herself and her children.

My dear Mr Constable,

It would be a great satisfaction to me to see you if you would have the kindness to call at the Charter House any day when you happen to be in Town. I am here now with my two poor girls and shall remain here some little time longer—a fortnight or more. I do not know where you may be at present but I direct this to Charlotte Street as if you are at Hampstead I dare say you will get it. Emma would be very glad to see Minnie if she is at home.

Ever very truly yours

Mary Fisher

Charter House. Sepr. 30th.

On the 7th October Constable wrote to Lucas: 'I did not come to London today, and it is now rather uncertain when I shall be in Charlotte Street. Perhaps to-morrow evening—as I bring to the Charterhouse my little girl on that day, to see poor Mrs. John Fisher, who is there with her children and wishes much to see me.'

It may be surmised that Fisher's affairs had been left in some disorder, for we presently find Constable requesting the assistance of Colnaghi 'respecting some engravings by Fisher to assist his widow'. In the meantime Osmond had been taken away from Eton, possibly to his relief; for his bent was towards mathematics, but under Dr. Keate he had been kept for most of the time to Latin elegiacs, and had never done a single sum. From now on he lived with his grandfather at the Charterhouse and went to school at King's College in the Strand.

Mary Fisher presently took her younger children to live with her in Southampton. Her settled income was now estimated at £254, to which Dr. Philip Fisher added another hundred pounds a year, while Ann Haverfield contributed to the house keeping.

It seems that Mrs. Fisher, however, was still in London when Constable wrote the next letter.[1]

My dear Mrs Fisher

I was much vexed to have missed the pleasure of seeing you when I called for the little girls I had so much to do that I could not avoid being too late.

I sent Roberts this morning to enquire with my kindest regards, how your self, & Mrs Haverfeild and the dear children are. I wish we could see you all here for a day. I was with "all seven" about me yesterday—all in great health and beauty—and it is delightfull to me to see how

---

[1] In the collection of Mr. John Fisher.

affectionate they all are to one another. John is as tall as I am, and they tell me he is not unhandsome—at all events he is clever and of a most mild and amiable character—quite like that of his gentle and affectionate Mother.

I called on Friday evening on Mr [Bradfeild][1]—I find he is at Salisbury & will remain there 'till Thursday—shall I write to him on the subject of which Mr G. Cookson made mention in his letter to me, about the pictures? I shall as you know be glad to be of any service—and if sending them to Charlotte Street will be an accommodation, I will clear a room for them. Some of them I am anxious about and will gladly take them at a valuation, rather than they should be dispersed—but as I know nothing of particulars I will not obtrude my observations or plans. I only beg with submission, to say what I have now done.

I do not think of bringing my family to London much on this side of X'mas, if possibly I can avoid it—for here I am retired & occupied, in quiet—and my dear children all enjoy this place in health—and here I seem still to live in the society of my departed Angel, here I can find the ministers to my own happiness & that of her dear children.

I beg my kindest regards to Mrs Haverfeild and to dear Emma—I hope your dear little girl is better [at Canbury].

I am, dear Mrs J. Fisher

always your obliged friend

John Constable

Well Walk—15th Octr. 1832.

Alfred is also the bearer of this note. Lionel begs hard to come. I want you to see his bright blue eyes—they are my Father's, who was very handsome—they are "smiling trophies, from the grave."

Fisher's death left Constable feeling very lonely. Of his older friends, Northcote had died in the previous year and Stothard was to go soon. Of the younger men, Johnny Dunthorne had died in the autumn. 'I am unfortunate in my friendships', Constable wrote to Leslie.

1833–1837

It does not seem to have been till six months after the event that the true cause of Fisher's death became known. On the 10th March 1833 Constable wrote to Leslie: 'Poor Fisher died of cholera in August at Boulogne when he went there'. On the 23rd March he wrote to one of the Colnaghis, whose shop he and Fisher had so often visited together: 'I heard from poor Fisher's family, of his death by cholera—but poor Mrs Fisher is not aware of that additional cause of greif.'

---

[1] Possibly Haverfield, who seems to have been Fisher's executor.

No more is heard of Fisher's family until some two years later when his widow wrote to Constable again, with reference to the collection of prints which he had played an active part in forming.

19 Portland Street, Southampton.
Feby. 7th 1835.

I feel that I need not apologize to you dear Mr Constable, for troubling you with a comission painful enough to me to give and which will I doubt not cost you some sad feelings in executing, I must not indulge myself any longer by retaining the prints which you assisted your dear friend to collect and am anxious to dispose of them to the best advantage. No one among my acquaintance can do this as well as yourself, and I am sure that none would be more ready to render me a service—

Mine must now be a life of continuous self denial as I have to provide for the education of my youngest boy who has till now been, since my bereavement, under the roof of a friend—This poor child has for some months past been in bad health, but thank God he is now getting well and as soon as he is strong enough I must send him to school which causes a drag upon my purse upon which I did not calculate when I took the house I am now in.

He has had the misfortune to lose a second father in the kind friend who had adopted him, and I must now accommodate myself to the additional burthen. I have given notice to quit this house in six months and am now looking out for another residence. The house rent in this place is so high and all articles of daily consumption so expensive that I think I must remove into some cheaper neighbourhood.

You will I dare say see Osmond who is now at the Charter House attending lectures at Kings College. He will I think be a great comfort to me, as he is peculiarly steady and well disposed. I think your dear girl would hardly know her friend Emma, who is taller than I am. When you answer this letter pray tell me a great deal about her as I must always feel a strong interest in her. I hoped to have seen her this spring as we looked forward to going to London, but this is now out of the question.—

You will I dare say have the kindness to tell me which prints it would be most advisable to send. There are some etchings of Rembrandt marked at £2 and £3 as price. Perhaps if I were to send a few of the most valuable now it would be wise to reserve the rest for some other pressing occasion—

I have in my possession a great many letters from you which are tied up in packets and which were preserved by my dear departed one with the most affectionate regard—Would you like that I should send them to you at the same time with the prints?

I hope that your brush has not been idle lately. Do pray tell me something of your nursery and—your own proceedings. Your name is coupled in my memory with such bright and happy days that I can scarcely believe in the reality of the tears which now dim my eyes. Adieu dear Mr Constable, believe me to remain

ever your sincere friend

Mary Fisher

Emma begs her kind love to dear Minnie and so do I.

The following letter is undated but was evidently written in reply to Constable's answer to the above.

A thousand thanks dear Mr Constable for your very interesting letter and for your friendly readiness to assist me in the disposal of the prints. With reluctant hands I have placed them in this box. Each one has a mine of recollections attached to it as I dare say you will feel when they again meet your eye. In parting with them I am fulfilling an injunction. He repeatedly told me I was to consider them as property and to apply to you respecting them.

Your account of your children is delightful. I have told Osmond that John has been to look for him and I doubt not if he has time he will try to see him but he is kept very close and complains that he has no time to follow his own inventions. I was much amused by your account of John's taste. Osmond is never so happy as when he is grubbing or crawling on his hands and knees in a coal pit with a candle stuck in his hat.—

Will you send the letter in the two penny post and allow the parcel to lie at your house till called for? I send you all the letters. They are as I found them. The strings have not been untied by me. I have sent all the prints with the prices marked upon them, the rest I keep till it is actually necessary to part with them—

With our united love to dear Maria & the rest of your party I am

Your sincerely obliged and affectionate friend

Mary Fisher

I wish I could be your tenant at Hampstead.

Constable did what he could to dispose of the prints and on the 25th February he wrote what has been described as 'a characteristic kind-hearted letter' to Dominic Colnaghi requesting his assistance for the benefit of Fisher's widow; but unfortunately Colnaghi was only prepared to give less than half of what had been paid for the engravings, and they were presently returned to Mrs. Fisher. Osmond was soon in touch with young John Constable again, and there is a letter from him to John dated the 28th May which will be given elsewhere.

Meanwhile Constable continued to enjoy friendly relations with the family of the Master of Charterhouse, who were now residing at Canbury Villa in Kingston-upon-Thames. In the summer of this year Constable arranged to pay a visit to his friend George Constable of Arundel, taking young John and Minna with him. The following letter from Dr. Philip Fisher's wife probably arrived after he had already left London, since he was due to reach Arundel on the 7th July.

Dear Mr Constable

My many engagements have not left me at liberty till now of claiming your promise of coming to see me at Kingston and bringing your daughter with you. I hope next Wednesday the 15, will find you disengaged and that you will come as early as you can and leave us as late as you can the next day. Maria you remember is to be left to make us the long promised visit and when she leaves me I will take care to have her safely returned to you again.

Dr Fisher and my daughters unite in best regards with my dear Sir

yours truly

M. Fisher

Kingston. Thursday, 9 July.

Constable wrote back from Arundel to request that the date of Maria's visit might be postponed till her return, and the next letter from Fisher's sister was addressed to him there.

Canbury Villa, Kingston.
13 of July.

My dear Mr Constable

Mama desires me to say we shall be equally glad to see Maria on Monday the 20th—We merely named Wednesday in this week because one of our neighbours had a little young party for the Bishop of London's children which we could have taken Maria to—but I dare say we shall be able to amuse her just as well the following—so that some time on Monday we shall expect to see her—I hope you will give us a day when you take her back—

Osmond I suppose found you out on Friday, when he called to say good bye—he is gone to his tutors till the 1st of October—We have been much pleased at his gaining a prize for Mathematics at K. Coll.—the Bishop of London presented him with a handsome set of Books—I hear they have noticed it in the Salisbury paper—Osmond is very modest & sensible about it—and never overrates himself—

His Mother moves into her new house 1 mile from Southampton to day —I am glad to find John is with you in fresh air—with kind regards

believe me, yours very sincerely

Mary Harley Fisher—

Minna was brought up from the country in time for the promised visit and two sketches by her father of the house and grounds of Canbury Villa at the end of his Sussex sketch-book[1] show that he was there himself on the 27th July, when he went to fetch her home.

In the last year of his life Constable gave utterance to some of the artistic views of which the warm ore had been hammered out in his letters to Fisher in the past. Memory of the time when they had planned together how to reduce those views to orderly form must have been constantly with him as he gave his lectures at the Royal Institution: but the voice of Fisher was indeed become as the voice of a ghost; he was not there to hear the lectures or to write them out, and only brief notes remain of what was said. It was the fourth of these lectures which Constable concluded with words taken from one of the Archdeacon's addresses to the clergy on a visitation of Berkshire.

Fisher's words were still ringing in his head when he sent his last dinner invitation to Leslie at the end of 1836, enforcing his summons with the words: ' "Prithie come—life is short—friendship is sweet," these were the last words of poor Fisher to me, in his last invitation.' Writing to Lucas on the 29th March next, he mentioned that he would be dining at the Charter House on Saturday. Saturday was the 1st April: but Constable was not able to keep the engagement with the last of his Fisher friends, the kindly old Master who could never remember his name, but always took an interest in his work, and could be relied upon to keep him amused. On the evening of the 31st March, 1837, Constable went out on one of his errands of mercy. On his return he retired to bed, with a book of Cowper's letters by his side. Before the night was over, the long struggle was over, and he had gone to join John Fisher.

He was buried in Hampstead, where he had once expressed to Fisher the hope that he might take his 'everlasting rest'. Wherever the two spirits may be now, we need not doubt that Claude and Ruisdael and Richard Wilson are of the company, with maybe Milton and Linnaeus as well.

1837–1838

The following letter from Fisher's widow was written to young John Constable soon after his father's death, from her house outside Southampton.

Freemantle Cottage. April 29th 1837.

My dear John,

I have received a letter this morning from my sister Mary[2] delivering your very kind message respecting the picture.[3]

When your dear father expressed a great wish to repossess that picture, as having a particularly strong attachment to it on account of its being one of his earliest productions and representing a favourite subject, he

---

[1] Victoria and Albert Museum No. 832.
[2] Miss Fisher.
[3] Probably the one given to Fisher by Constable in 1829.

offered to purchase it for twenty pounds, and at the same time said that he would seal up some prints, which I had asked him to dispose of and which were valued at that sum, and having written Osmond's name upon the envelope he would retain them in his own hands till Osmond wished to have them.

I was glad of an opportunity of obliging a friend for whom I felt such an esteem and I therefore declined *selling* him the picture but begged him to accept it. I also requested him to return the prints which Colnaghi had valued at less than half the money which had been given for them. They were accordingly sent back to me and I presented the picture to your father. Thus you see dear John it is as much your's as any other of his possessions—In defence of Colnaghi I ought to state that some of the prints had been injured, and their value diminished—

I have a letter ready written which I hoped to have forwarded to Minnie by a private hand before this time. I do not know her address at school but I shall send it to Charlotte Street some day next week and will thank you to let her have it. With regard to the packet of letters you have discovered I wish to have them forwarded to me by the first opportunity.[1] I transmitted to your father all his part of the correspondence which had been treasured up with equal care.

I am glad to hear you have commenced your Cambridge career. I feel sure that your health will improve by removal from London air. We heard from Osmond soon after his return to College. He was quite well but I dare say reading hard for his letter was a very short one. Emma desires to be very kindly remembered to you and believe me dear John with many thanks for your liberal kindness to remain

your sincere friend

Mary Fisher

It is pleasant to be able to record that the friendship was continued into the next generation. Osmond Fisher and John Charles Constable, nearly of the same age, had got to know each other as children. They both went up to Cambridge with a view to entering the Church, and both chose Jesus College. The following letters from Osmond to John[2] may be of interest to those who have followed the correspondence between their fathers. The first is addressed to East Bergholt, where John had evidently fallen ill.

My dear Constable   Jes Coll May 27 [1838]

The University requires you to keep half of each term but if you can make it appear that by reason of bad health you are unable to do this

---

[1] That is, the letters written by her husband to Constable. This would account for the fact that most of the letters written by Fisher are still with his family, while those written by Constable appear to have belonged at one time to his family.

[2] In the Plymouth Collection.

it will, if your case be a very strong one, allow you the term. The College has no power whatever to grant a term it only requires you to keep a part of it. Now since it is clear from what you say that you can come up before division you can *keep* this term: the university will not *grant* i.e. give it you without your keeping it. The College will allow you to keep the latter part of it if you choose. You must be here on the thirtieth & stay till the 6th of July. You can keep in College & will not have to go into the examination. Otherwise if you do not do this you will have to keep one term after you have passed the B A examination before you can take your degree. In either case you will have to go in for your little go with your own year. You have your choice, you must make up your mind directly. Write to me if you come & I will not change the draught. Also tell me whether or not you will want rooms at Mrs. Challis's. I am going down thro' Oxford.

> Yours truly,
> Osmond Fisher.

Bring your certificate of ill health with you. The form of the certificate is as follows

I hereby certify to the master & fellows of Jesus College Cambridge that Mr John Lookalive of Jesus Coll has been under my care (as to his legs) from the——day of——till the——day of——and that during that time he could not with safety on account of his (legs) health return to Cambridge.

Witness my hand this——day of——1831

> Bob Sawyer
> M D or Surgeon

It will be seen that young gentlemen at Cambridge were then reading *Pickwick Papers*. The next letter is undated: it appears to have been Osmond's turn to be absent through illness.

My dear Constable.

Walford & a smart Trinity man having been caught during a shooting expedition are coming here to dine while they Aclonizing. I take the opportunity of writing to you hoping that one or the other of the men will take it back. In all probability I shall stay here some time as I did much better when I first came but I am rather less well now. I slept at least 5 nights running, till the night before last. I am sorry to hear of poor Birketts head. I should have thought that a bad one was enough. Will you get me a box of pills from Orridges in the Market Place. Send them by the Linton Mail cart-man of whom you will hear tidings at the Post Office. I should say no more to any one else but [to] you I say do it directly for I know your dilatoriness. I should have like to see Webster. Lick Charley & Tap for me. I hope that the little dogs get enough food. I hope you see to this. I shall come over next week & sleep one night. I wish you could prevail on Farren to stay till Monday. I cannot come over any day this week. I have heard from William,[1] he does not like the climate of India much. The Charterhouse Chapmans are at Balsham. If you call on the Wilkins tell them where I am. Go on with the Magnet if you like it.

Yours truly

Osmond Fisher.

The last letter was written in 1840 and addressed to London, where it was first opened in error by another Mr. John Constable.

My dear John

As the rooms in the two Challis houses seem in great request for the vacation I wish you would let me know by return of post if you wish to have your old ones because Hughes will assuredly take them if you do not forestall him & I also want to take rooms for Frank.[2] I would take the two sets at Mrs Challis's for him & me if you do not want them but if you do I will take the lower ones there for him & at Mrs Challis's for me. Braithwait wants the upper ones for himself. I wish you would make haste up. Is it not grand my having got Frank up in the Long. He is to be a half pupil of Earnshaw's. The College is looking very nice & the men all want you up for the cricket.

Yours affly

Osmond Fisher

Write by return of post if it is in your nature.

The recipient of these letters died suddenly in the following spring. He had inherited that interest in natural phenomena which has been seen in his father's study of cloud formations, and had been reading medicine, which he thought might prove helpful to him as a clergyman, evidently influenced by Archdeacon Fisher's medical skill. Studying a case of scarlet fever in hospital, he caught the disease and died before taking his degree.

Osmond was able to help over sending John's books and pictures to his family and collected subscriptions among John's college friends for setting up a memorial tablet in the college chapel.

---

[1] The brother known as 'Belim'.
[2] Francis Fisher, who would now be eighteen.

After 1838

The Master of Charterhouse, doyen of the Fisher family, died five years after Constable, at the venerable age of ninety-two.

The Rev. Osmond Fisher, following the example of his grandfather and his grand-uncle, became a fellow and tutor of his college and eventually accepted a college living in order to get married. He lived into the present century, dying in 1914, when he enriched the Fitzwilliam Museum by leaving to it one of the pictures which Constable had painted for his father.

Of the younger children 'dear Belim', as mentioned in one of the above letters, had already gone out to India. He entered the 10th Regiment of Bengal Light Cavalry (one of his Cookson uncles had gone out to join the army in India), and became adjutant to the Governor-General's bodyguard. He fell at the battle of Moodkee on the 18th December, 1845, and a memorial cross was erected by his brother officers in the south transept of Salisbury Cathedral. 'Pretty Minna' was left in charge of the Constable family after her brother's death, and died unmarried in 1885.

T

INDEX

The Suffolk Records Society

DRAFT Report of the Council for 1966/67

At the 30th September 1967 membership stood at 397, including 4 Honorary and 5 Life members, a net increase of 17 on the previous year. Casual Sales totalled 710 volumes as against 508 the previous year as follows (the previous year's totals are given in brackets):

Volume I . . 18 (23)		Volume VII . . . 29 (221)	
Volume II . . 8 (14)		Volume VIII . . 178 (60)	
Volume III . . 28 (30)		Volume IX . . . 17	
Volume IV . . 64 (28)		Volume X . . . 182	
Volume V . . 15 (23)		Volume XI . . . 84	
Volume VI . . 87 (72)		Great Tooley of Ipswich 14 (37)	

The appearance of three volumes during the financial year, Volume IX *Poor Relief in Elizabethan Ipswich*, Volume X *John Constable's Correspondence IV* and Volume XI *John Constable's Correspondence V*, has greatly stimulated sales and membership also to some extent, in spite of the fact that Mr. Webb's volume appeared a year late.

The Society continues in the debt of the Mellon Foundation for their grants towards the publication of the Constable Correspondence, the final volume of which is due to appear as an extra volume early in 1968. The success of the series is now established, and the Mellon Foundation have kindly agreed to allow the Society to apply the income from the sale of earlier volumes towards the publication of a further volume of Constable material entitled *The Discourses*. It will be devoted to the painter's lectures and lecture notes. No date has been fixed for publication nor have the actual terms of distribution been settled. These will be announced in due course when sufficient funds are available. Besides the *Discourses* the Council has under consideration a number of other possible publications, including Dr. G. H. Martin's edition of the *Ipswich Recognizance Rolls*, Mr. Norman Scarfe's edition of the Candler Manuscripts, Mr. Derek Charman's edition of the *South Elmham Manuscripts*, and Mrs. M. P. Statham's volume of *17th Century Town Records of Bury St. Edmunds*, but the title of the regular annual volume for 1967/68 has not yet been finally selected.

The project for the publication of a *Suffolk Bibliography* continues under active consideration by the Council and a committee under the Chairmanship of Mr. J. Campbell is gathering the necessary bibliographical information. Miss Joan Corder who was a member of this committee has unfortunately had to give up owing to other commitments, but Mr. A. V. Steward has been co-opted to the Council since his retirement as Lowestoft Borough Librarian, and his assistance with the Bibliography will be greatly appreciated.

The year has been a successful one for the Society from the financial viewpoint despite the fact that the assets in the main account have decreased from £2,205 to £1,442. The former figure included a grant of £900 from the Pilgrim

Trust which was applied during the year in part payment of publication costs of Constable Volume III. The publication of Webb's *Poor Relief in Elizabethan Ipswich* and all other costs were, therefore, more than covered by income. This is especially satisfactory as the bulk of casual sales of volumes which rose from £527 to £827 was in respect of the Constable volumes and in fact £463 was transferred to the Paul Mellon Account.

The Mellon account itself covers the cost of, and income from, the Constable volumes subsequent to the initial grant from the Mellon Foundation and also shows a very satisfactory position.

It is with great regret that the Council has to report the resignation of the Hon. Treasurer, Mr. P. J. Sullivan, who has left Ipswich to take up a post elsewhere. The Council wish to record their appreciation of his services, not least in persuading his successor at Barclays Bank, Princes Street, Ipswich, Mr. K. R. Morbey, to take on the task. The Council are equally grateful to Mr. Morbey for consenting to do so.

The following Council members are due to retire at the Annual General Meeting in accordance with Rule 7, but are eligible for re-election:

Dr. R. Allen Brown	Mr. L. Dow
Mr. N. H. P. Turner	Dr. A. Hassell Smith

L. Dow
Chairman

SUFFOLK RECORDS SOCIETY

Statement of Income and Expenditure for the Year ended 30 September 1967

1965/66	INCOME	£ s. d.	£ s. d.
2,520	BALANCE Brought Forward		2,204 12 3
	GRANTS		
600	Marc Fitch Volume VII		
100	J. Corder Volume VII		
	British Academy—Constable IV		500 0 0
513	Subscriptions	510 17 9	
81	Arrears	19 0 0	
41	Advance	44 10 0	574 7 9
527	Sale of Volumes	826 18 4	
	Less transferred to Paul Mellon Account	463 5 0	
55	Tax Refund		363 13 4
49	Dividends on Investments		67 16 8
21	Premium 5% Defence Bonds		48 10 6
34	Interest on Deposit Account		44 8 6
1	Postage Refund		
1	Excess Subscription		
	Refund from Paul Mellon Account		492 0 0
	Charges re Constable III and IV		
£4,543			£4,295 9 0

1965/66	EXPENDITURE	£ s. d.
14	Annual General Meeting	23 3 1
1	Refund Subscription Overpaid	
1	Stamping Covenants	6 8
5	Gift to Mrs. Ager	
	Cheque Book	5 0
91	Petty Cash and Postages	202 0 7
18	Stationery	44 5 11
203	Prospectus	
151	H.M. Stationery Office Volume I	
117	Publication Costs	
219	Publication Constable II	
1,518	Publication Dictionary of Suffolk Arms	1,333 10 6
	Publication Constable III—Leslie	
	Publication Webb: Poor Relief in Elizabethan Ipswich—Volume IX	1,145 8 11
	Binding: Dictionary of Suffolk Arms	97 10 0
	Type Rent: Constable III	1 8 0
	Storage Charges	5 7 8
2,205	Balance Carried Forward	1,442 2 8
£4,543		£4,295 9 0

TOOLEY ACCOUNT

1965/66	INCOME	£ s. d.
51	Balance Brought Forward	59 13 6
36	Sales	12 13 2
£87		£72 6 8

1965/66	EXPENDITURE	£ s. d.
27	W. S. Cowell Limited	32 0 0
60	Balance Carried Forward	40 6 8
£87		£72 6 8

Records Account

1965/66			£	s.	d.		1965/66			£	s.	d.
253	Balance Brought Forward	.	239	12	11		2	British Records Association	.	2	10	0
24	East Suffolk County Council	.	11	1	8		46	Borough Treasurer	.	222	12	0
1	Payment for work done	.						E.M. Dance	.	31	19	10
1	Donation	.	6	7	3		240	Balance Carried Forward	.			
9	Interest on Deposit Account	.										
£288			£257	1	10		£288			£257	1	10

		£	s.	d.
Current Account	.	12	0	6
Deposit Account	.	19	19	4
		£31	19	10

Paul Mellon Account

Income		£	s.	d.		Expenditure		£	s.	d
Grant						Charges Constable III and IV refunded to				
Paul Mellon Foundation						main Account	.	492	0	0
Publication Constable III and IV	.	2,975	0	0		Publication Constable IV	.	3,091	8	0
Charges involved	.	492	0	0		Type Rent on Standing Type				
		3,467	0	0		Constable III	.	8	8	0
Sale of Volumes: VIII	.	246	0	0		Typing Copy of Index				
X	.	185	0	0		Constable V	.	1	2	6
XI	.	32	5	0		Postages Volume XI	.	38	8	8
		463	5	0		Balance Carried Down	.	306	14	9
Deposit Interest	.	7	16	11						
		£3,938	1	11				£3,938	1	11

Assets at 30th September 1967

Cash at Bank:	Current Account	.	.	£198	17	10
	Deposit Account	.	.	£107	16	11
				£306	14	9

carried forward

SUFFOLK RECORDS SOCIETY

ASSETS AT 30TH SEPTEMBER 1967

	£ s. d.	£ s. d.
Cash at Bank:		
Current Account	364 18 2	
Deposit Account	1,158 3 7	
		1,523 1 9
Cash in hand		14 9 10
Investments at Cost:		
£312 16 3 Jamaica 6%	300 0 0	
£750 5½% National		
Development Bonds	750 0 0	
		1,050 0 0
		2,587 11 7*
* Less Webb: Poor Relief owing but not paid at 30.9.67		1,145 8 11
		£1,442 2 8

I have examined the above Receipts and Expenditure Account, Paul Mellon Account, Records Account, and Tooley Account together with the books and vouchers relating thereto. I have confirmed the balances at Barclays Bank Limited and verified the investments. In my opinion the accounts and the statement of assets are correct according to the books and vouchers submitted.

F. WROE *Hon. Auditor*